Cyberbullying and the Critical Importance of Educational Resources for Prevention and Intervention

Gilberto Marzano
Rezekne Academy of Technologies, Latvia

Joanna Lizut
Janusz Korczak Pedagogical University in Warsaw, Poland

A volume in the Advances in Early Childhood and K-12 Education (AECKE) Book Series

IGI Global
DISSEMINATOR OF KNOWLEDGE

Published in the United States of America by
IGI Global
Information Science Reference (an imprint of IGI Global)
701 E. Chocolate Avenue
Hershey PA, USA 17033
Tel: 717-533-8845
Fax: 717-533-8661
E-mail: cust@igi-global.com
Web site: http://www.igi-global.com

Library of Congress Cataloging-in-Publication Data

Names: Marzano, Gilberto, author. | Lizut, Joanna, 1981- author.
Title: Cyberbullying and the critical importance of educational resources for prevention and intervention / by Gilberto Marzano and Joanna Lizut.
Description: Hershey : Information Science Reference, [2019]
Identifiers: LCCN 2018043591| ISBN 9781522580768 (hardcover) | ISBN 9781522580775 (ebook)
Subjects: LCSH: Cyberbullying. | Cyberbullying--Prevention.
Classification: LCC HV6773.15.C92 M3377 2019 | DDC 302.34/3--dc23 LC record available at https://lccn.loc.gov/2018043591

This book is published in the IGI Global book series Advances in Early Childhood and K-12 Education (AECKE) (ISSN: 2329-5929; eISSN: 2329-5937)

British Cataloguing in Publication Data
A Cataloguing in Publication record for this book is available from the British Library.

For electronic access to this publication, please contact: eresources@igi-global.com.

Advances in Early Childhood and K-12 Education (AECKE) Book Series

ISSN:2329-5929
EISSN:2329-5937

Editor-in-Chief: Jared Keengwe, University of North Dakota, USA

MISSION

Early childhood and K-12 education is always evolving as new methods and tools are developed through which to shape the minds of today's youth. Globally, educational approaches vary allowing for new discussions on the best methods to not only educate, but also measure and analyze the learning process as well as an individual's intellectual development. New research in these fields is necessary to improve the current state of education and ensure that future generations are presented with quality learning opportunities.

The **Advances in Early Childhood and K-12 Education (AECKE)** series aims to present the latest research on trends, pedagogies, tools, and methodologies regarding all facets of early childhood and K-12 education.

COVERAGE

- Bullying in the Classroom
- Literacy Development
- Standardized Testing
- Learning Outcomes
- K-12 Education
- Curriculum Development
- Reading and Writing
- Common Core State Standards
- Head Start and Pre-K Programs
- Early Childhood Education

The Advances in Early Childhood and K-12 Education (AECKE) Book Series (ISSN 2329-5929) is published by IGI Global, 701 E. Chocolate Avenue, Hershey, PA 17033-1240, USA, www.igi-global.com. This series is composed of titles available for purchase individually; each title is edited to be contextually exclusive from any other title within the series. For pricing and ordering information please visit http://www.igi-global.com/book-series/advances-early-childhood-education/76699. Postmaster: Send all address changes to above address.

Titles in this Series

For a list of additional titles in this series, please visit:
https://www.igi-global.com/book-series/advances-early-childhood-education/76699

Critical Essays on the New Moral Imperative for Supporting Marginalized Students ...
Rebecca J. Blankenship (Florida Agricultural and Mechanical University, USA)
Information Science Reference • ©2019 • 268pp • H/C (ISBN: 9781522577874) • US $175.00

K-12 STEM Education in Urban Learning Environments
Jillian L. Wendt (University of the District of Columbia, USA) and Danielle L. Apugo (University of the District of Columbia, USA)
Information Science Reference • ©2019 • 309pp • H/C (ISBN: 9781522578147) • US $190.00

Cases on Kyosei Practice in Music Education
Richard Keith Gordon (Seisa University, Japan & California State University, USA) and Taichi Akutsu (Shujitsu University, Japan & Seisa University, Japan)
Information Science Reference • ©2019 • 296pp • H/C (ISBN: 9781522580423) • US $175.00

Cultivating a Culture of Nonviolence in Early Childhood Development Centers and Schools
Simon George Taukeni (University of Namibia, Namibia)
Information Science Reference • ©2019 • 322pp • H/C (ISBN: 9781522574767) • US $185.00

Advanced Strategies and Models for Integrating RTI in Secondary Schools
Pam L. Epler (Grand Canyon University, USA)
Information Science Reference • ©2019 • 356pp • H/C (ISBN: 9781522583226) • US $185.00

Handbook of Research on Emerging Practices and Methods for K-12 Online and Blended ...
Tina Lane Heafner (University of North Carolina at Charlotte, USA) Richard Hartshorne (University of Central Florida, USA) and Richard Thripp (University of Central Florida, USA)
Information Science Reference • ©2019 • 608pp • H/C (ISBN: 9781522580096) • US $245.00

Cases on Service Delivery in Special Education Programs
Pam L. Epler (Grand Canyon University, USA)
Information Science Reference • ©2019 • 431pp • H/C (ISBN: 9781522580690) • US $185.00

For an entire list of titles in this series, please visit:
https://www.igi-global.com/book-series/advances-early-childhood-education/76699

IGI Global
DISSEMINATOR OF KNOWLEDGE

701 East Chocolate Avenue, Hershey, PA 17033, USA
Tel: 717-533-8845 x100 • Fax: 717-533-8661
E-Mail: cust@igi-global.com • www.igi-global.com

Table of Contents

Preface

Cyberbullying is directly connected with the spread of online technologies. Indeed, the greater availability of internet connections has resulted in a growth of cyberbullying cases. Over the last decade, the number of victims of cyberbullying has increased, whilst the wide distribution of mobile devices has generated new conditions that have contributed to the multifariousness of cyber aggression. It seems that, despite decreases in physical bullying in schools, cyberbullying is rising steadily, particularly amongst girls (Kessel Schneider, O'Donnell, & Smith, 2015).

In fact, although the internet has undoubtedly changed our lives, human nature has remained essentially the same. Accordingly, the spread of the new technologies has actually served to multiply the risks and threats faced by people when using the internet, since cyberspace is not forbidden to cheaters, perpetrators, and individuals who like to harm, harass, and victimize other people, especially those whom they perceive to be weak and vulnerable.

Cyberbullying is universally considered to be an alarming phenomenon (Hinduja & Patchin, 2014) that is closely tied to the relational changes that have been brought by digital technologies and online communication. Our opinion is that cyberbullying represents an attack on the socialization of an individual. Indeed, a large number of young people are continuously connected with their peers and use social networks to socialize with them, sharing all sorts of experiences, emotions, and secrets. For this reason, the majority of victims of cyberbullying are children and adolescents, and statistics reveal an extremely bleak situation (Lessne & Yanez, 2016). In 2014, according to the organization *No Bullying*, it has been reported that 52 percent of young people have been bullied online while 25 percent of teenagers have experienced repeated bullying through phone calls and text or on the internet. (Finley, 2016).

Recent global cyberbullying statistics (Table 1) show that this phenomenon is on the rise worldwide (Cook, 2018).

Table 1. Percentage of parents that report their child has been a victim of cyberbullying

Country	2018	2016	2011
India	37	32	32
Brazil	29	19	20
United States	26	34	15
Belgium	25	13	12
South Africa	26	25	10
Malaysia	23	–	–
Sweden	23	20	14
Canada	20	17	18
Turkey	20	14	5
Saudi Arabia	19	17	18
Australia	19	20	13
Mexico	18	20	8
Great Britain	18	15	11

Source: https://www.comparitech.com/internet-providers/cyberbullying-statistics/

How, then, can we confront this evil phenomenon of cyberbullying?

It is not simple. Although many forms of cyberbullying correspond to traditional harmful and aggressive behaviors (teasing, name calling, spreading rumors, threatening, and holding to ransom), the internet gives perpetrators new and powerful means with which to harass their victims. The appropriation of these new means by bullies is only one aspect of cyberbullying, since the technology has extended the opportunity to harm people without physical contact, thus increasing the range of stalkers and harassers. Furthermore, even who passively witness cyberbullying (bystanders) can be impacted since they will join bullies or develop a loss of their sense of security.

In the physical world, children, young people, and adults don't live separately, and so, consequently, the presence and supervision of adults is not easy to elude. Rather differently, in the virtual world, they can use mobile devices to interact and communicate with each other either when adults are not around, or even when they are. Teenagers are continuously online, and may use websites and messenger apps where they are free from adult supervision.

It has been noted that cyberbullying also differs from face-to-face bullying in that perpetrators can hide behind the anonymity that the internet provides. Furthermore, young people do not feel as responsible for their actions when they post messages online as they would in real life. They are not afraid of being punished for their actions. If anything, it is often the victims who are afraid or reluctant to report incidents, since they fear that adults will take away their mobile phone, computer, and/or internet access.

The objective of this book is to present cyberbullying from an essentially pedagogical perspective. It is the result of extended analysis and observations that were begun a few years ago, when the authors worked together on a joint European project, "Threats of Cyberspace: New skills of a social worker" (2012-2014).

We have organized this book into two parts. The first part, comprising Chapters 1 to 4, is devoted to a comprehensive presentation of cyberbullying in its various forms. The second part focuses on educational issues and preventive educational solutions.

Chapter 1 covers the definition of cyberbullying and provides an overview of the research issues.

Chapter 2 introduces the problems of establishing anti-cyberbullying legal policies. Attempting to discipline how to respond to incidents of cyberbullying is a crucial issue. This forms the necessary premise to present and discuss interventions aimed at cyberbullying prevention (in Chapter 6). Chapter 3 explores the phenomenon of social networking sites. In this chapter, the use of social media is analyzed, as well as some more specific aspects, such as online hate speech and online rudeness. Chapter 4 illustrates and discusses the technological solutions that can be adopted to prevent and reduce cyberbullying.

Chapter 5 analyzes the dynamics underlying the behavior of cyberbullies, victims, and bystanders, and introduces the prevention strategies that will be illustrated and discussed in Chapter 7, following the presentation of the most popular anti-cyberbullying approaches (in Chapter 6). Chapter 8 discusses the role of parents and educators whilst Chapter 9 focuses on cyberbullying prevention in schools. Finally, in Chapter 10, the authors argue their idea of entrusting cyberbullying prevention to a new specialized figure, represented by a specifically trained social educator.

The sequence of the chapters follows the development of an ideal educational program on cyberbullying prevention. The first chapters are devoted to presenting the multiple facets of this phenomenon, then the educational approaches are introduced and discussed, and finally the roles and contributions of the actors involved in a cyberbullying prevention program are analyzed and discussed. The last chapter presents our idea for combatting cyberbullying. This takes two factors into account. The first is that we are experimenting a social transformation that is without precedent. The second is that cyber safety should be seen as part of the more general problem of school safety and societal safety.

The disruptive impact of technology has vastly changed the effect of our actions, and it is therefore necessary to elaborate educational solutions to respond to the issues that technology can produce when inexperienced and/ or malicious individuals appropriate it.

Owing to its multifarious nature, it is difficult to prevent or combat cyberbullying head-on. Schools are vulnerable to the effects of cyberbullying since they represent theatres of socialization, and cyberbullying, ultimately, represents a social problem of harassment, intimidation, bullying, and unjustified aggression (Ortega-Ruiz & Núñez Pérez, 2012). In order to prevent cyberbullying in schools, the involvement of teachers is crucial (Del Rey, Ortega-Ruiz, & Casas, 2019; Guarini, Menin, Menabò, & Brighi, 2019), but teachers cannot be expected to fulfill all of the tasks and shoulder all of the responsibilities. It is necessary, instead, to have the continuous involvement of professionalized figures. Specialized cyber school social workers should be available to intervene and be responsible for enacting the appropriate measures in order to ensure the cyber safety of all students.

Furthermore, the spread of digital technologies pushes for the creation of synergies between different disciplines. An example of this is the renewed interest in mechatronics, the multidisciplinary branch of engineering that encompasses a combination of mechanical, electrical, electronic, computer, telecommunications, and systems engineering.

The rise of cyberbullying calls for the synergetic contribution of various disciplines such as psychology, social anthropology, social pedagogy, jurisprudence, and computer science. The specialists of these disciplines often remain prisoners of their specificity. Experts in digital technologies, for example, tend to overestimate the use of filters as a means of preventing cyberbullying. Often, during conferences and meetings, we have witnessed software companies claiming to have significantly reduced cyberbullying through their automatic detection of online harassment. On the other hand, it is undeniable that different design features of information technology artifacts can influence factors such as deindividuation and accountability, and so affect imbalances of control (Lowry, Moody, & Chatterjee, 2017).

Another aspect that deserves attention is the cultural context. The research into cyberbullying has spread globally, but despite the use of unified terminology and similar approaches, it is rather unlikely that the phenomenon of cyberbullying is identical everywhere in the world.

A study carried out a few years ago, for example, showed that the way cyberbullying is perceived in Russia is rather different from how it is perceived in most European countries (Boronenko, Menshikov, & Marzano, 2013). In Russia, bullying and cyberbullying are often interpreted as a social means of mitigating divergent behavior among young people and of persuading them to develop attitudes that will be more successful for their further life. Recently, it has been observed that in Turkey and France the relation between traditional bullying and cyberbullying is weaker, and in some contexts (as in Thailand), cyberbullying is actually becoming more common than traditional bullying (Livingstone, Stoilova, & Kelly, 2016).

In fact, the cultural context can affect preventative actions, but this aspect has often been undervalued.

We have endeavored to cover as wide a geographical area as possible in our study in order to highlight the ongoing global transformation of society due to the digital revolution. However, we are aware of the limitations of our efforts.

Finally, we conclude this prelude with an important observation. In this book, we have introduced a few references to newspaper articles alongside reported episodes from our own direct experience. Indeed, newspapers can be an interesting source for understanding people's feelings and attitudes towards complex social phenomena. Often, newspapers interpret people's opinions and present facts in a simplified way. Therefore, although newspaper articles cannot be taken as evidence, they can serve to illuminate the impact of events on the social community. Furthermore, reporting and discussing single episodes can be useful for synthesizing pieces of evidence, for introducing an issue, or for underlining a question.

REFERENCES

Boronenko, V., Menshikov, V., & Marzano, G. (2013). Topicality of cyberbullying among teenagers in Russia and Latvia. *Social Sciences Bulletin*, *1*(16), 84–104.

Cook, S. (2018). Cyberbullying facts and statistics for 2016-2018. *Comparitech*. Available at: https://www.comparitech.com/internet-providers/cyberbullying-statistics/

Del Rey, R., Ortega-Ruiz, R., & Casas, J. A. (2019). Asegúrate: An Intervention Program against Cyberbullying Based on Teachers' Commitment and on Design of its Instructional Materials. *International Journal of Environmental Research and Public Health, 16*(3), 434. Available at: https://www.mdpi.com/1660-4601/16/3/434

Finley, L. L. (Ed.). (2016). *Crime and Punishment in America: An Encyclopedia of Trends and Controversies in the Justice System* (2 vols.). ABC-CLIO.

Guarini, A., Menin, D., Menabò, L., & Brighi, A. (2019). RPC Teacher-Based Program for Improving Coping Strategies to Deal with Cyberbullying. *International Journal of Environmental Research and Public Health, 16*(6), 948. doi:10.3390/ijerph16060948 PMID:30884790

Hinduja, S., & Patchin, J. W. (2014). *Bullying beyond the schoolyard: Preventing and responding to cyberbullying*. Corwin Press.

Kessel Schneider, S., O'Donnell, L., & Smith, E. (2015). Trends in cyberbullying and school bullying victimization in a regional census of high school students, 2006-2012. *The Journal of School Health, 85*(9), 611–620. doi:10.1111/josh.12290 PMID:26201758

Lessne, D., & Yanez, C. (2016). Student Reports of Bullying: Results from the 2015 School Crime Supplement to the National Crime Victimization Survey. Web Tables. NCES 2017-015. *National Center for Education Statistics*. Available at: https://files.eric.ed.gov/fulltext/ED572035.pdf

Lowry, P. B., Moody, G. D., & Chatterjee, S. (2017). Using IT design to prevent cyberbullying. *Journal of Management Information Systems, 34*(3), 863–901. doi:10.1080/07421222.2017.1373012

Ortega-Ruiz, R., & Núñez Pérez, J. C. (2012). Bullying and cyberbullying: Research and intervention at school and social contexts. *Psicothema, 24*(4), 603–607. PMID:23079358

Acknowledgment

The authors wish to acknowledge the contributions of the numerous teaching staff and parents of students who have shared their experiences in order to promote the greater understanding of cyberbullying issues. A particular acknowledgment is due to Irēna Žogla for her precious suggestions in the pedagogical scope, and to Stephen Soane for his linguistic support. Finally, the authors would like to thank the Janusz Korczak Pedagogical University in Warsaw and the Rezekne Academy of Technologies for the materials related to the project, *Threats of cyberspace - new competences of a social worker*.

Chapter 1
Cyberbullying:
A Research Overview

Gilberto Marzano
Rezekne Academy of Technologies, Latvia

ABSTRACT

Cyberbullying represents a topical risk, especially for the online generation that is continuously connected and socializes through the internet. This chapter presents an overview of the research on cyberbullying, from the earliest studies to the most recent. It discusses the broad variety of definitions of cyberbullying that exist and highlights its essential differences from traditional bullying. The authors then go on to illustrate and discuss the multifarious facets of cyberbullying, including the (relative) anonymity of perpetrators and the repetition of bullying acts. Further research developments are explored in the light of criticisms of Olweus, who argued that inconsistent findings and exaggerated claims plague much of the research on cyberbullying. Finally, new emerging forms of harassment, such as revenge porn and virtual rape, are also introduced.

THE INTERNET IS A LIVING THING

Over the last two decades, Information and Communication Technologies (ICTs) have grown exponentially, spreading through all sectors of life. Today, the internet represents the technological channel through which the digital revolution is taking place. It has radically changed the way data is collected, information is exchanged, and interactive communications occur, ultimately

DOI: 10.4018/978-1-5225-8076-8.ch001

not only between people, but also intelligent programs and smart objects (Curran, Fenton, & Freedman, 2016).

The internet is essentially a massive network of networks that encompasses hundreds of thousands of individual networks worldwide. It originated in the 1960s with ARPANET, a project funded by the Defense Advanced Research Projects Agency, an arm of the US Department of Defense. ARPANET was created in cold war times to safeguard the operability of the US military communications network in the case that the enemy destroyed one or more of its nodes.

In the 1970s, the internet protocol suite (TCP/IP) became the standard networking protocol on the ARPANET and, for the first time, the term "internet" appeared in a conference paper (Cerf & Kahn, 1974), although, initially, the term was used as an adjective to distinguish inter-networking communications. Only in the 1990s, was 'internet' used as a noun to designate the network of computers adopting the TCP/IP technology to communicate.

The internet network infrastructure ceased to be public in 1991 when the USA government authorized private individuals to improve and use it for commercial purposes. In the same period (1990-1991), Berners-Lee defined the HTTP (*Hypertext Transfer Protocol*), that allowed the creation on the Internet of content pages and their non-sequential accessing by means of references, called *hyperlinks,* contained in the other pages.

Berners-Lee also created the World Wide Web (WWW), a user-friendly interface based on the Hyper Text Markup *Language (HTML)* through which the structure of internet pages was described. Using HTML, pages containing files, text, images, sound, video, and hyperlinks were created and accessed on the internet by programs, called *web browsers* or, simply, *browsers*. In 1993 the first browser, *Mosaic*, was launched, whose characteristics were similar to current browsers. Nowadays, the terms Internet and Web are essentially synonymous and are used interchangeably.

Over the years, the distinctive characteristics of the Web have changed. In fact, until now, the Web has evolved through four main stages of development (Choudhury, 2014), namely the Web of documents (Web 1.0), the Web of people (Web 2.0), the Web of data (Web 3.0), and the Web of things (Web 4.0). Table 1 synthesizes the main stages of the Web evolution to date.

Following an initial characterized by the ability to access contents recorded in fixed pages linked together by hyperlinks, the Web quickly transitioned towards dynamic pages that assembled data from different page sources and/or resulted from database searches. These web pages were also dynamically created and customized in order to maximize their usability.

Table 1. The main stages of the Web evolution

Web 1.0	Web 2.0	Web 3.0	Web 4.0
1991-2001	2002+	2006+	2014+
Read Only	Read and Write Web	Executable Web	Interoperating Web
Links	People participation and interaction	Understanding contents	Full connections
Websites	Social networks	Semantic web	Internet of things
One Directional	Bi-Directional	Multi-user Virtual environment	Multi-layer real-virtual environment
Static content	Dynamic content	Intelligent analysis	Intelligent actions

Source: author's own elaboration

The Web revolution, however, truly began with the launch of a new generation of interactive services, such as blogs, online forums, chat rooms, wikis, and social networks, that reinvented and redefined our mode of communication. Thanks to these, people ceased to be passive consumers of contents and instead became content producers, able to express opinions and interact online. For example, blogging software allows inexpert users to publish their opinions on any given topic on the Web and receive comments from those who read them. A paradigmatic example of this revolution is Wikipedia, the web encyclopedia, that is completely dependent on users to create, update, and provide quality control of its content. In the space of just a few years, social networking sites and messenger platforms such as Yahoo Messenger, Facebook Messenger, WhatsApp, LINE, SnatchApp, and many others, have proliferated, becoming by far the most popular means of communicating on the web, especially amongst young people.

Social networking sites started to be used from the early 1990s, but they were not the virtual meeting places where people share personal information, as they are today. Rather, they were initially conceived to support professional communities, as in the case of *Theglobe.com* created in 1994, *Geocities* unveiled in 1994, and *Cyworld,* launched in 1999 by students of the *Korea Advanced Institute of Science and Technology* essentially as a discussion board for topics relating to their research projects.

The turning point of social networking sites really came in the early 2000s, with the success of the Facebook and Myspace platforms at meeting the new attitudes and expectations of users for communicating and sharing information. However, in the beginning of the 2000s, already existing web networking sites changed their basic features to better accord with their users' preferences. For example, in 2002, Cyworld changed its format in order to offer functions by which users could express themselves, with features such as a main picture, history, user profile, photo story, story room, background music, photo album, diary, bulletin board, video clips, and the ability to decorate their own virtual space.

The primary aim of social networking sites become socialization. Through them, an individual externalize their feelings and opinions, often without distinction between home and work, and bring together aspects that belong to different spheres of their lives into a single virtual place.

As a consequence, in only a few years, the internet has been overwhelmed by a deluge of personal content, including photos and videos.

The ever-increasing growth of online social activities would seem to contradict Putnam's view that technology, through the internet and virtual reality, will bring people to individualize their leisure time, isolating them in the process (Putnam, 2001). In fact, social networking platforms have, on the contrary, actually facilitated people to establish and cultivate social relationships, and thus helped to overcome the trend towards individualism and fragmentation of modern society. Unfortunately, there are also negative consequences that correspond to this positive effect. Cyberbullying is one of them.

Continuing our introductory excursion into the internet, the mid 2000s saw the advent of a new stage, Web 3.0, whose development was less striking than Web 2.0 but no less broadly impacting. Artificial Intelligence solutions were implemented to overcome the limitations of traditional web-based applications. New ways were developed to provide users with functions of intelligent information retrieval. Semantic Web technology was developed to format data in machine-readable form in order to enable inferences to be drawn over that data, laying the foundations for interacting social machines. In a note published in 1999 on the site of the World Wide Web Consortium (W3C), Berners-Lee, Connolly, and Swick argued that the Web could be designed more intelligently in order to be more intuitive to meet user's needs. They argued that the Web was maturing into a Semantic Web. Indeed, traditional search engines continuously indexed massive volumes of content, but they had little ability to select the information that a user really wanted to find. To achieve this goal, new types of descriptors and techniques of data classification would be necessary. Berners-Lee and Hendler explained the concept of the Semantic Web as follows:

The Semantic Web will bring structure to the meaningful content of Web pages, creating an environment where software agents roaming from page to page can readily carry out sophisticated tasks for users.

[…] The Semantic Web is not a separate Web but an extension of the current one, in which information is given well-defined meaning, better enabling computers and people to work in cooperation. The first steps in weaving the Semantic Web into the structure of the existing Web are already under way. In the near future, these developments will usher in significant new functionality as machines become much better able to process and "understand" the data that they merely display at present. (Berners-Lee, Hendler, & Lassila, 2001, p. 29)

However, the Semantic Web was not the only novelty of Web 3.0. The so-called *intelligent data analysis*, an interdisciplinary field that encompasses *Data mining* and *Big Data* was also introduced. It was quickly evident that the huge volume of data resulting from peoples' activities on the internet would require new powerful analytic models, algorithms, and tools. Data mining is "the extraction of implicit, previously unknown, and potentially useful information from data" (Witten, Frank, Hall, & Pal, 2016, xxiii), whilst Big Data is usually defined in terms of four elements, namely the four V's that are: volume, variety, velocity, and veracity (Marz & Warren, 2015). Big Data analytics concerns the use of techniques and tools that optimize the statistical analysis of large data sets. Nowadays, data available on the Web is collected and analyzed to define effective marketing strategies, as well as to provide companies with business intelligence by identifying critical issues and favorable opportunities.

The latest stage of the internet is Web 4.0. This is the new frontier of interconnectivity, known as the *Internet of Things* (IoT), or the *Internet of Everything*, that enables interaction among programs, objects, namely intelligent devices, and people (Lee, 2017). A growing number of smart objects can auto-regulate themselves and exchange data with human beings, virtual agents, and other smart objects. The IoT enables applications whereby people can interact with real-world objects, as well as programs based on network-assisted machine-to-machine interchanges. The IoT is set to change the way we work and interact with the world in every possible manner. Many applications based on the integration of data gathered via smart sensors and deployed in the domestic environment are already operative.

Nevertheless, the advances of the internet continue. At the moment, we are heading towards a new stage of the Web, that of Web 5.0. This has yet to be precisely defined, but it is expected to bring about a *Sensory Emotive Web* that is able to take into account the feelings of users. It should be able to make use of technologies that already operate in the field of neuro-technology to measure feelings and their effects. Web 5.0 aims at developing a *Symbionet Web*, making machines able to read conscious thoughts, emotions, facial expressions, and head motions (Algosaibi, Albahli, & Melton, 2015).

The great improvements in the internet over a period of less than 20 years cements the image we have of it as a living thing (Nigam & Collier, 2010). In fact, it is endlessly evolving, bringing repercussions through all aspects of social life, since the internet provides users with a degree of independence and interactivity that are not possible with traditional media. This is evident in regard to both the modality of use and the way of creating and handling online content.

Regrettably, there have also been collateral effects. People can express and spread opinions and feelings, but also defamatory gossip, offensive comments, malicious denigration, and harmful allusions as well. This, however, is something that seems to be intrinsic to non-face-to-face interactions. In fact, since the diffusion of email from the 1990s, hostile and aggressive messages have proliferated, even reaching the in-boxes of academics (Wang & Hong, 1995). *Flaming*, that refers to the use of insults, swearing, and hateful, intense language, has been singled out as being a distinctive characteristic of email:

Disagreements are fine, but attacking someone personally for their posting is not good form (although common). This is known in the trade as flaming. (Krol & Ferguson, 1995, p. 199)

In the early days of the internet, flaming messages posted on computer bulletin boards were already at the center of legal considerations that, in many aspects, anticipated the current debate regarding cyberbullying. A computer bulletin board was a computer program that simulated the functions of the bulletin boards to be found in any supermarket, university, and other public gathering place (Gilbert, 1985). It allowed individuals to post new messages, read existing ones, and add comments. In a report that analyzed, from a legal point of view, the defamatory statements made by users of computer bulletin boards, it is claimed that:

Defamation that occurs over computer bulletin board systems is best categorized as libel rather than its sibling tort, slander. While both torts allow recovery for defamation, libel generally covers written or printed defamation, while slander traditionally covers oral defamation. (Weber, 1995)

Indeed, the author of this report observed that the messages on a computer bulletin board could easily become a printed message and, therefore, gain a greater permanence and reach a broader audience than a spoken message could. Ultimately, he argued, postings on bulletin boards more closely resembled written rather than spoken communications.

In 2001, the *New Yorker* denounced the alarming spread of the practice of online harassment in an article entitled "The New Bathroom Wall" (Paumgarten, 2001), and the themes it raised were swiftly taken up by the media at large. Patchin and Hinduja mentioned one "particularly horrendous anecdotal account" of an incident that occurred at the same time:

In May of 2001, viciously offensive messages denigrating and humiliating a high school sophomore girl who suffered from obesity and multiple sclerosis were posted anonymously to an online message board associated with a local high school in Dallas, Texas (Benfer, 2001). In time, the bullying crossed over to the physical world as the victim's car was vandalized, profanities were written on the sidewalk in front of her home, and a bottle filled with acid was thrown at her front door — which incidentally burned her mother. (Hinduja & Patchin, 2014, p. 41)

The debate around the legal implications of messages posted on social networking sites that immediately arose continues to this day, but although the problem of audience and permanence remain the same, the issue is aggravated by the fact that the materials posted on the Web can now also be photos and videos, as well as just texts.

Social media have never been immune to the negative attitudes of rabid and rude people. This is evident from the number of terms that have been coined to denote harmful interactions in cyberspace: cyberbullying, cyber-mobbing, cyber-intimidation, cyber-stalking, cyber-rape, revenge porn, cyber-humiliation, and so on. They encompass a large variety of acts aimed at discrediting and hurting a physical person in the virtual world. Unfortunately, it would seem, despite the changes brought about by technology, human nature has remained essentially the same, and the internet hasn't changed people's inherent capacity for evil behavior. Paradoxically, thanks to the internet, people have even more ways to cheat at their disposal, and perpetrators can make use of new, ever more powerful, means through which to harm and harass their victims (Marzano, 2018).

All too often, due to the increasing novelty of the forms of cyber violence, victims remain helpless, and the legal system is impotent to persecute their perpetrators.

How, then, can we combat the evil phenomena affecting the Web, and cope with its continual evolution?

The first step is to understand the context in which these phenomena take place. The metaphor that the internet is a living thing should warn us that we require instruments that are adequate to contextualize its multifarious and variable nature.

The focus of this book is cyberbullying and, accordingly, it is useful to start by shining a light on the context in which cyberbullying occurs, presenting an overview of the scope of study on this topic.

FIRST STUDIES ON CYBERBULLYING

With the increasing access of youngsters to digital technology in the first decades of the 21st century, the new emergent phenomenon referred to as *online harassment* started to be studied. Although the early systematic studies were conducted by Ybarra & Mitchell (2004a, 2004b), according to Smith et al., awareness of *online bullying* in the UK appears to have originated in around 2001:

The DfES pack 'Don't suffer in silence' (2000) does not mention cyberbullying; but a revision published in 2002 mentions 'sending malicious emails or text messages on mobile phones' (p. 9). Press reports have since become frequent. (Smith, Mahdavi, Caravalho, Fisher, Russell, & Tippett, 2008, p. 377)

It is noteworthy that, in 2003, the *Cristian Science Monitor* reported that at the Calabasas High School in California there was a website - schoolscandals.com - on which vicious gossip and racist and threatening remarks had grown so rampant that most of the school was affected:

The actions themselves - rumors, threats, gossip, humiliation - are nothing new. But among today's adolescents - a generation of instant messengers, always connected, always wired - bullies are starting to move beyond slam books and whisper campaigns to e-mail, websites, chat rooms, and text messaging. While in some ways it's no worse than old-fashioned bullying, cyberbullying has a few idiosyncrasies. Websites and screen names give bullies a mask of anonymity if they wish it, making them difficult to trace. (Paulson, 2003)

Studies on cyberbullying increased exponentially from 2006, the year in which the suicide of 13-year-old Megan Meir, victim of harassment on MySpace, brought the subject of cyberbullying very much to the fore (Ruedy, 2007). Scholars made efforts to identify, assess, organize, and interpret the growing body of research and data on this topic. In the beginning, the principal lines of investigation were the definition and categorization of cyberbullying and its legal implications, whilst the first scholarly perspectives were:

- The psychological perspective (e.g., counseling of victims);
- The legal perspective (e.g., policing and regulating of cybercrimes, the prosecution of cybercriminals);
- The technological perspectives (e.g., prevention and detection software);
- The educational perspective e.g., practical guidance, individual or multiple case studies, anecdotal observations, etc.).

Hanewald reports that many of the early studies on cyberbullying originated from the USA, with investigations conducted between 2000 and 2007 by the *Internet Report, the National Centre for Missing and Exploited Children, I-Safe America*, and the *National Crime Prevention Council* (Hanewald, 2009).

In these early studies, various terms were used to address the cyberbullying phenomenon. For example, Herring (2002) used the term *cyber violence* to encompass online harassment, online degradation, cyber stalking, and a hybrid form that he labelled *online contact/offline harm*.

Willard (2005) identified the following forms of online harassment:

- Repeated sending of offensive messages to a person;
- Intimidating a person through threats;
- Denigrating somebody by means of false or cruel information;
- Pretending to be somebody and sending inappropriate material in their name;
- Spreading sensitive or embarrassing information about a person;
- Intentionally excluding somebody from an online group.

Focusing on the aspect of sexual harassment in cyberspace through inappropriate sexual messages, pornographic materials, offensive nicknames, and other outrageous acts, Barak (2005) introduced the sub-categories of *gender harassment*, *unwanted sexual attention*, and *sexual coercion*.

Meanwhile, Kowalski and Limber used the term *electronic bullying* to underline the analogy with traditional bullying. The authors argued that electronic bullying is "a new means of bullying" that includes bullying through e-mail, instant messaging, in a chat room, on a website, or through digital messages or images sent to a cell phone (Kowalski & Limber, 2007). Ybarra and Mitchel (2004a) used the term *online harassment* in their first study to distinguish between two distinct behaviors:

- Making rude or nasty comments to someone through the internet;
- Using the internet to harass or embarrass someone with whom there was a relationship.

The authors carried out one of the first surveys into cyberbullying, conducting telephone interviews with 1,498 regular internet users between the ages of 10 and 17 (2004b). From their survey, it emerged that 19% of youth respondents had been on either the giving or receiving end of online aggression during the previous year. The vast majority of perpetrators (84%) knew their victim in person, whereas only 31% of victims knew their harasser in person. The ability of perpetrators to keep their identities unknown was interpreted as a form of power and dominance over victims. Note, here, the analogy with the *power imbalance* of traditional bullying.

Although the majority of early investigations into cyberbullying were conducted in the USA and UK, studies have rapidly sprung up in all corners of the world: Australia, Japan, Finland, Korea, Italy, China, Belgium, Taiwan, Germany, Greece, Singapore, Serbia, Sweden, the Czech Republic, Poland, and the Baltic countries (Li, 2006; Zych, Ortega-Ruiz, & Del Rey, 2015; Foody, Samara, & Carlbring, 2015), as well as Russia (Polishchuk, Vorobyov, Orlova, & Abovyan, 2017), Turkey (Yilmaz, 2011), Pakistan (Musharraf & Anis-ul-Haque, 2018), and Iran (Shahghasemi, Karami, & Rabiei, 2017).

Over the last few years, numerous literature reviews have sprung up, with varying methodological orientations, temporal frameworks, and thematic scopes (Aldridge & McChesney, 2018; Kiriakidis & Kavoura, 2010; Reed, Cooper, Nugent, & Russell, 2016; Zych, Ortega-Ruiz, & Del Rey, 2015).

CYBERBULLYING AND INTERNET USE

There is broad consensus that heavy internet use significantly increases the likelihood of cyberbullying.

The relationship between internet use and cyberbullying was immediately evident:

The potential for cyberbullying has grown with the increasing penetration of networked computers and mobile phones among young people. The Mobile Life Report (2006) found that 51% of 10-yearolds and 91% of 12-year-olds in the UK have a mobile phone. (Smith, Mahdavi, Carvalho, Fisher, Russell, & Tippett, 2008, p. 376)

The positive and negative effects of the internet on children and adolescents have been variously analyzed. The self-disclosure of experiences on the internet is not negative *per sé,* but the disclosure of personal information on social networks can increase the risk of cyberbullying (Navarro, Serna, Martínez, & Ruiz-Oliva, 2013). In this regard, Livingstone and Brake observed that the internet offers new opportunities for self-expression and communication:

Identities are constituted through interaction with others. Increasingly, the sites in which young people perform and experiment with identify include the online domain. As both technology and its uses evolve, this reconfigures the possibilities for social identity construction in ways that are not yet fully understood.

[...] Teenagers have long decorated their bedroom walls with images expressive of their identity, also keeping a diary or photo album, sending notes and chatting to friends. So, does online social networking make a difference? (Livingstone & Brake, 2010, pp. 76-77)

However, compared to non-victims, cybervictims do seem to report higher rates of chatting, e-mailing, web surfing, blogging, gaming, and instant messaging (Walrave & Heirman, 2011).

In a survey some years ago, Vandebosch and Van Cleemput (2009) noted that youngsters who are more dependent on the internet have a higher likelihood of becoming victims of cyberbullying. They also observed that respondents whose parents were less involved with their use of the internet had a higher chance of becoming cyberbullies. In this light, the parental context, including the parent's internet literacy, as well as the school context should be investigated in order to verify their impact on cyberbullying prevention strategies.

A few year ago, Casas, Del Rey, and Ortega-Ruiz (2013) formulated the hypothesis that exercising little control over personal information on the internet and internet addiction are both predictor factors for cyberbullying. The results of their study confirmed the supposition that cognitive distortion produced by excessive, impulsive, or addictive use of the internet tends to increase episodes of violence.

Furthermore, many researchers investigated the relationship between online behavior and cyberbullying, especially focusing on the negative relationship between aggressive behavior and empathy (Steffgen, König, Pfetsch, & Melzer, 2011).

Park, Na, and Kim investigated the relationship between online activities, netiquette, and cyberbullying (2014). Arguing that little is known about the way that online activities influence online misbehavior, they conducted a literature review to find answers to three essential questions;

Q1: Are the amount and type of online activities associated with cyberbullying behavior?
Q2: Are moral values and moral disengagement related to cyberbullying behavior?
Q3: Does netiquette have a moderating impact on cyberbullying behavior?

From their analysis, it emerges that the amount of time spent online, the activities conducted on social networking sites, as well as the amount of free time available were positively associated with the likelihood of becoming cyberbullies, cybervictims, and cyberbystanders. Netiquette appears negatively correlated with the use of social networking sites and online activities, since spending more time online does not automatically imply greater netiquette. On the contrary, those who frequently use the internet and social networking sites often exhibit poorer netiquette. The authors underlined an interesting element:

[…] netiquette and daily communication with parents both were negatively related to cyberbullying, confirming the moderating effect of netiquette. Age had a negative correlation with online bullying and victimization but was not significantly associated with the witnessing online bullying. (Park, Na, & Kim, 2014, p. 77)

THE VARIOUS FACETS OF CYBERBULLYING

At the moment, there is no universally accepted definition of cyberbullying. This is due to the fact that cyberbullying is a relatively recent phenomenon, closely tied to the progress of technology. In many ways, it can be considered a collateral effect of the behavioral changes that digital technologies are producing in the spheres of communication and social interaction, namely the sphere of socialization.

As a consequence, cyberbullying represents a multifaceted phenomenon, since the more the internet and social networks spread, the more socialization assumes new forms and, accordingly, the more new forms of harassment and violence emerge on the web.

Before the term cyberbullying became popular, other expressions, such as online harassment, online bullying, and cyberstalking (Benfer, 2001; Bocij, 2004; Ellison, 2003; Wolak, Mitchell, & Finkelhor, 2007), were used to describe the harmful and malicious acts enacted through electronic means.

The harmful consequences of the spread of electronic communications began to appear very early on as people started using the internet for communication. In the 1980s, one unpleasant phenomenon was particularly widespread, namely the heated exchange of messages expressing hostility or acrimony toward others, commonly known as *flaming* (Baron, 1984). Respondents of a survey conducted in two divisions of a large US firm declared that they had experienced flaming in electronic mail messages an average of 33 times a month (Sproull & Kiesler, 1986).

By the 1990s, online harassment, especially against women, was a serious problem, and many female teachers stopped giving out their e-mail addresses as a result:

[…] many women are discouraged from speaking up online for fear of being targeted for some sort of sexual advance or another. I wonder how many women have stopped posting their words because they were sick of constantly being attacked for their opinions. (Brail, 1996, p. 152)

Note that, for the most part, harassment involves forms of discrimination but bullying could not involve discrimination.

Furthermore, at the end of the 1990s, many cases came to light of children being solicited by adults for illegal sexual activities over the internet. The risks related to unwanted or illegal exposure of children and adolescents to sexual solicitation, harassment, and pornography on the internet was reviewed and analyzed at different levels (Finkelhor, Mitchell, & Wolak, 2000).

The term cyberbullying first appeared in the early 2000s. It quickly became popular, and was preferred to the expressions 'online harassment' or 'online bullying' (Ybarra & Mitchell, 2004a; 2004b). Nevertheless, researchers often made distinctions between the different terms. The expression cyberbullying sometimes appeared too allusive of traditional bullying and not properly expressive of the specific phenomenon observed. However, according to Wolak, Mitchell, and Finkelhor (2007), there has never been a standard definition of *online harassment*.

Designing the questionnaire for a survey, Hinduja and Patching felt the need to inform respondents that:

[...] online bullying can include bothering someone online, teasing in a mean way, calling someone hurtful names, intentionally leaving persons out of things, threatening someone and saying unwanted, sexually related things to someone. (Hinduja & Patchin, 2008, p. 138)

Currently, the debate continues about what constitutes cyberbullying and how this phenomenon is similar or different to traditional forms of bullying (Menesini *et al.*, 2012; Thomas, Connor, & Scott, 2015), usually referred to as *conventional bullying*, *physical bullying*, *face-to-face bullying*, *offline bullying*, or simply *bullying*.

Olweus argues that the phenomenon of bullying is:

[...] characterized by the following three criteria: (a) It is aggressive behavior or intentional "harmdoing" (b) which is carried out "repeatedly and over time" (c) in an interpersonal relationship characterized by an imbalance of power. One might add that the bullying behavior often occurs without apparent provocation. This definition makes it clear that bullying can be considered a form of abuse, and I sometimes use the term peer abuse as a label for the phenomenon. (Olweus, 1994, 1173)

Many definitions of cyberbullying refer to Olweus's definition that describes the bullying phenomenon in its essential characteristics. It is notable that Olweus emphasizes the peer condition of bullying, but this condition can be difficult to verify in cyberspace, due to the relative anonymity of communications.

Literature offers a broad variety of definitions of cyberbullying (Alipan, Skues, Theiler, & Wise, 2016; Dooley, Pyżalski, & Cross, 2009; Franco, Bellerín, Borrego, Díaz, & Molleda, 2012; Heirman & Walrave, 2012; Hinduja & Patchin, 2006, 2007, 2008; Kowalski, Giumetti, Schroeder, & Lattanner, 2014; Lenhart, 2010; Ortega-Ruiz & Nunez, 2012; Palladino, Nocentini, & Menesini, 2012; Paul, Smith, & Blumberg, 2012; Thomas, Connor, & Scott, 2015; Vandebosch & Van Cleemput, 2008; Vandebosch, Beirens, D'Haese, Wegge, & Pabian, 2012; Ybarra, Mitchell, Wolak, & Finkelhor, 2006; Ybarra & Mitchell, 2007; Wachs, Wolf, & Pan, 2012).

Some of the most often cited definitions of cyberbullying are:

An aggressive, intentional act carried out by a group or individual, using electronic forms of contact, repeatedly and over time against a victim who cannot easily defend him or herself. (Smith et al., 2008, p. 376)

[…] any behavior performed through electronic or digital media by individuals or groups that repeatedly communicate hostile or aggressive messages intended to inflict harm or discomfort on others. (Tokunaga, 2010, p. 278)

Cyberbullying involves the use of information and communication technologies to support deliberate, repeated, and hostile behavior by an individual or group, that is intended to harm others. (Belsey, 2013)

[…] cyberbullying is when someone repeatedly makes fun of another person online or repeatedly picks on another person through email or text message or when someone posts something online about another person that they don't like. (Hinduja & Patchin, 2014, p. 3)

Bullying is a type of aggressive (purposefully harmful) behavior that is intentional, repeated, and based on a power imbalance between the aggressor and the target. Cyberbullying, then, is bullying perpetrated with digital technology. (Bauman, 2013)

Like traditional bullying, cyberbullying is an act of aggression intended to cause harm or distress, it has a repetitive quality (e.g. a single e-mail may be sent to hundreds of different individuals), and it occurs among individuals whose relationship is characterized by a power imbalance [...]. Importantly, whereas with traditional bullying this power imbalance might reflect differences in physical strength or social status, with cyberbullying it might also reflect differences in technological expertise. (Whittaker & Kowalski, 2015, p. 12)

A 2007 version of the *Oxford English Dictionary* contained the term "cyberharassment", but this term all but disappeared from use in 2009 when the term "cyberbullying" took hold (Felt, 2015).

A comprehensive synthesis of cyberbullying definitions is contained in an article by Del Rey et al., (2015, p. 142), referencing the authors who identified and discussed the main characteristics of this phenomenon, such as the clearly intentional or hostile behavior repeatedly carried out through an electronic device, and the establishing of a power imbalance between the aggressor and the victim.

In 2009, the European Commission launching a campaign against cyberbullying, proposing the following definition of cyberbullying:

[... any] repeated verbal or psychological harassment carried out by an individual or a group against others through online services and mobile phones. It can take many forms: mockery, insults, threats, rumors, gossip, "happy slapping", disagreeable comments or slander. Interactive online services (e-mail, chat rooms, instant messaging) and mobile phones have given bullies new opportunities and ways in which they can abuse their victims. (European Commission, 2009)

In the majority of recent literature, it is generally accepted that cyberbullying is the use of electronic communication technologies to bully others (Låftman, Östberg, & Modin, 2017; Zhao & Mao, 2017). More specifically, cyberbullying includes direct abuse, social exclusion, impersonation, and sharing offensive materials by means of an electronic communication medium.

BULLYING AND CYBERBULLYING

Bullying is a phenomenon characterized by negative repeated actions towards a peer, with the intention to hurt (Olweus, 1991, 1993). Table 2 details the three general categories of bullying.

According to Olweus, a student is being bullied when another student, or several other students:

- Say mean and hurtful things or make fun of him or her or call him or her mean and hurtful names;
- Completely ignore or exclude him or her from their group of friends or leave him or her out of things on purpose;
- Hit, kick, push, shove around, or lock him or her inside a room;
- Tell lies or spread false rumors about him or her, or send mean notes and try to make other students dislike him/her;
- Engage in other similar hurtful acts.

Similarly, Kowalski and Limber (2007) suggest that many insiders consider cyberbullying to be a particular form of bullying, and describe it as bullying that occurs through media and communication devices such as mobile phones, email, and the internet (e.g., social networking sites, web pages, chat rooms,

Table 2. The three categories of bullying

Bullying category	Actions
Verbal Bullying: Saying and/or writing mean things	• Teasing • Name-calling • Inappropriate sexual comments • Taunting • Threatening harm
Social Bullying: Hurting someone's reputation or relationships	• Intentionally excluding someone • Telling others not to be friends with someone • Spreading rumors about someone • Embarrassing or offending someone in public
Physical Bullying: Hurting a person's body or possessions	• Hitting/kicking/pinching • Spitting • Tripping/pushing • Taking or breaking someone's things • Making mean or rude hand gestures or facial expressions

Source: author's own elaboration

and blogs). In this regard, the expression "old wine in new bottles" used by Li (2007) seems particularly apt when speaking about cyberbullying.

Interpreting online harassment as a form of bullying was an attempt to set this new alarming phenomenon into a well-known and well-structured framework. Indeed, the analogy between bullying and cyberbullying leapt out, since, as in bullying, there are persecutors and cruelly humiliated and mocked victims.

However, some differences immediately appeared (Dooley, Pyżalski, & Cross, 2009; Smith et al., 2008), the first of which being the relative anonymity of persecutors. Anonymity afforded by online interaction introduces new elements in the bullying framework. On one hand, anonymity extends the capability to bully others to a physically weak individual, on the other, it prevents the victim from knowing the identity of their persecutor who can be anyone, even a friend, as, in fact, is very often the case. In cyberspace, persecutors can disguise their real identity and, as a consequence, another point that characterizes bullying may be missing, namely the fact that bullying normally takes place between peers.

Nevertheless, anonymity on the web is relative (Palme & Berglund, 2002). Although there are many who believe that one can hide their identity behind a nickname, it is not so easy to remain anonymous on the web. As will be illustrated in Chapter 3, when a device connects to the internet it receives a unique identifier, called an Internet Protocol, or simply IP, address. This is required to send and receive information to/from servers hosting data and is assigned by an Internet Service Provider (ISP). A temporary IP number can be used for a single internet session but even then, that number is logged by the ISP, and it is possible to go back to the identity of its user. Moreover, other methods exist for breaking anonymity which will be highlighted hereafter.

It has been observed that relative anonymity makes the internet user free of inhibitions. Research shows that people communicate more freely when they are online than they do in real life: many people tend to self-disclose if they are talking with an unknown person or when are not in a real face-to-face conversation (Lapidot-Lefler & Barak, 2015). According to Suler, there are six factors that contribute to create online disinhibition: dissociative anonymity, invisibility, asynchrony, solipsistic introjection, dissociative imagination, and reduction of authority (Suler, 2004). Disinhibition leads people to share very personal things, giving them a propensity to disclose their innermost secret emotions, fears, and desires.

Another relevant difference between bullying and cyberbullying is closely related to the nature of the internet itself, and concerns the range of audience:

the usual audience of traditional bullying is confined to small groups, whilst cyberbullies can reach very large audiences.

Moreover, compared to traditional forms of bullying, a cyberbully may be less aware or even completely unaware of the consequences of his or her actions.

In Table 3, the most common effects of acts of cyberbullying on their victims are synthesized, referring them to the emotional, behavioral, and cognitive spheres.

Cyberbullies take advantage of the specific features of online communication (anonymity, asynchronicity, and accessibility) to torment their targets (Valkenburg & Peter, 2011), and cyberbullying differs from face-to-face bullying in that:

- Perpetrators of cyberbullying can hide behind their anonymity.
- Perpetrators can pretend to be someone else.
- Cyberbullies can penetrate the home environment: there are no spatial or time limitations.
- Private pictures can be uploaded to the internet without consent.
- Messages posted on the internet can reach a very broad audience.
- Messages are instantaneous, meaning that they arrive immediately to the victim and propagate rapidly.
- Depending on the policy of the owner of the platform used, once sent, messages are irreparably sent, and the sender is not able to erase them.

Table 3. Consequences of cyberbullying

Type of consequence	Appearance
Emotional	• Anxiety symptoms • Depressive states • Sense of shame • Sense of abandonment, despair • Various somatizations
Behavioral	• Exclusion, marginalization • Sleeping and eating disorders • Postural problems • Aggressive responses • Self-harm • Substance Abuse
Cognitive	• Attention disturbance • Learning and speech difficulties • Confusion • Poor academic results

Source: author's own elaboration

Table 4 shows the main differences between bullying and cyberbullying.

Moreover, empirical reports have identified highly connected youngsters as being the group most vulnerable to cyberbullying (Baldry, Farrington, & Sorrentino, 2016), and, finally, although, traditional bullying and cyberbullying overlap in many respects, cyberbullying is essentially an aggression against the socialization sphere of the victim. It can assume the form of a large-scale attack against their social image and intimate reputation. This aspect assumes a relevant importance to designing and building effective prevention and coping strategies.

THREE DISTINCTIVE ASPECTS

From analysis of the literature, three aspects emerge which raise discussions among researchers and practitioners.

The first specific aspect is related to the lack of complete control of digital technology by users. For example, malicious digital content (message, text, picture, or video), once sent out or uploaded to the internet, can be downloaded, forwarded, and disseminated by anyone else, not only by the initial perpetrator, and the harmful flux cannot be stopped. In this way, the

Table 4. Bullying vs. Cyberbullying

Bullying	Cyberbullying
Face-to-face	Any time, everywhere; no geographical limitation
Bullying acts occurring on school premises	Bullying acts occurring both on and off school premises
Bullies can be identified	Cyberbullies can be (relatively) anonymous
Repetition of bullying acts	Web dissemination
Limited audience	Wide audience and viral spreading on the web
Victims can find a safe space or escape	It's hard for victims to escape
Bullies can see facial and body reactions of victims	It is difficult for bullies to empathize with victims
Bullies and targets are distinct	A target can easily become a bully themselves
Harassment: physical, verbal, non-verbal	Harassment: verbal
Emotional reactions: easily determined	Emotional reactions: cannot be easily determined
Physical power imbalance	Technological or psychological power imbalance
Bullying decrease through middle and high school	Age is not a distinctive factor

Source: author's own elaboration

victim can also experience the same aggression many times over, with the same toxic digital item being accessed and run repeatedly. Internet memory is out of the control of both perpetrator and victim.

The second aspect is related to the notion of power imbalance, which can involve different spheres of domination and weakness (Law, Shapka, Hymel, Olson, & Waterhouse, 2012). Cyberbullies may be less technologically skilled than their victims, using digital technologies only as an extension of their face-to-face aggression or as a means to document it. Conversely, it has been observed that the hidden nature of electronic communication can offer victims, or self-presumed victims, of traditional bullying the opportunity to retaliate online or to attack their real-world perpetrators (Kowalski, Limber, & Agatston, 2008). Surveys conducted on students revealed that revenge and retaliation can become a motive for cyberbullying (Farkas, 2016), and victims of traditional bullying sometimes cyberbully their persecutors in turn (König, Gollwitzer, & Steffgen, 2010; Wong, Chan, & Cheng, 2014).

The third distinctive concerns repetition.

Following the classic definition of bullying, the majority of researchers and practitioners include repetition amongst the basic characteristics of cyberbullying. Repeated verbal or psychological harassment coming from an individual or a group, such as mockery, insults, threats, rumors, or gossip, are classified as acts of cyberbullying, and email, instant messaging, and social networks provide ample opportunities for this.

Nevertheless, if one adopts an extensive definition of cyberbullying, repetition becomes a problematic issue (Dooley, Pyżalski, & Cross, 2009). It has been observed that repetition within cyberbullying is not so straightforward (Slonje, Smith, & Frisén, 2013). On the internet, a single toxic act can cause reverberating and widespread mockery and humiliation of the victim without any continued involvement from the original perpetrator themselves (Smith, 2012). A bully can create a defaming webpage, upload an embarrassing video on YouTube, or post a derogatory message on a social network. Malicious content can reach not only the victim but also a multitude of people that may reiterate it. In this respect, Langos differentiated between direct and indirect cyberbullying (Langos, 2012). 'Direct cyberbullying' occurs in communications between the perpetrator and the victim, whilst 'indirect cyberbullying' occurs in a public cyberspace and, in fact, in the absence of repetition, could be more appropriately spoken of as cyber-joking or playful cyber-teasing.

However, we prefer to distinguish between repetition of harmful acts and web dissemination of harmful content. Although, from the perspective of the victim, the same harmful content may be experienced as an original harmful act being repeated, the act itself may be an isolated event. Moreover, in the case of web dissemination of harmful content, much depends on the medium and the author.

It has been observed that pictures/video clips and phone calls are perceived to have more impact on the victim than traditional forms of bullying, whilst website and txt messages are rated as being about equal in impact to traditional bullying (Smith, Mahdavi, Carvalho, & Tippett, 2008).

From this perspective, it is important to evaluate the seriousness of an offense and the context in which it occurs.

Jones, Mitchell, and Finkelhor (2013), in analyzing online harassment, namely threats or other offensive behavior targeted directly at a young person through new technology channels (e.g., the internet, text messaging) or messages posted online about them for others to see, noted that many incidents of online harassment involve single events that are not particularly distressing for youngsters (Wolak, Mitchell, & Finkelhor, 2007) and that do not, actually, meet the criteria for bullying often used in the field of peer victimization, viz, repeated incidents perpetrated by more powerful youth with the intention to hurt the victim physically or emotionally.

A SIMPLIFIED PHENOMENOLOGY OF CYBERBULLYING

Cyberbullying can take two main forms, depending on the different use to which the communication technology is put: it can be used only as a means to enhance or extend traditional harassment, or it can be used *per se,* namely for its own intrinsic and specific qualities.

There is no doubt that online bullying can be a simple, albeit very serious, extension of face-to-face bullying: a case of "new wine in old bottles". Victims know their perpetrators, and the dynamics existing between them are essentially the same as in traditional bullying. In many cases, technology merely represents another means by which to extend persecution. This is the case when posting a video on the web that shows the humiliation of or aggression against a victim. In this instance, the question of repetition loses its importance: the act of posting the video is just part of the bullying behavior.

However, there is another face of cyberbullying that takes place totally in cyberspace. It depends completely on communication technology, and on the nature of virtual relationships. The victim does not know the perpetrator who attacks their virtual sphere. Perpetrators, using a nickname, anonymously torment and threaten their victims, posting hateful comments on social networking sites or uploading disparaging pictures and videos to the internet. This form of cyberbullying is sneaky and actually dangerous since it involves the intimacy of victims and their relational sphere. Indeed, the internet has expanded the relational sphere of an individual, creating a new widespread communicative dimension. The result is that, on the internet, the image of an individual, namely their virtual profile, is disclosed to a vast audience. This exposure can feed narcissism (Chen & Marcus, 2012; Eftekhar, Fullwood, & Morris, 2014), but to receive disapproval or scorn can have profound consequences on self-esteem. Today, a virtual profile is an extension of a person's character, expanding their identity to the virtual domain. As a consequence, harassment that occurs in cyberspace has a heavy impact on the real life of victims since digital technology is often the dominant medium for communicating and socializing, especially among young people.

Four main categories of cyberbullying have been identified: text messages, emails, phone calls, and picture/video clips (Slonje & Smith, 2008). However, different forms of cyberbullying can occur contemporaneously. For example, a victim can receive malicious text messages and calls at the same time, or the cyberbullying can also be indirect, if public forums and social media are used (Langos, 2012). This means that, in cyberbullying, much depends on the context and on the type of harassment.

Simply put, the principal characteristic of cyberbullying are:

- Worldwide audience, posts can become viral;
- Anonymity, many sites allow users to remain anonymous;
- Permanence, even when picture and videos are removed, the chances of them being found on the internet are high;
- Inescapable, cyberbullies are omnipresent.

We must also note, here, a new serious phenomenon, so-called revenge pornography or revenge porn, that has recently been spreading. This involves a perpetrator – typically an ex-partner from a previous romantic relationship – uploading nude, semi-nude, or sexual images/videos of a person to the internet without their consent. Revenge porn represents an extremely serious violation of a person's privacy and is recognized as a criminal injury, as a Californian court ruled in a recent judgment.

In developing an effective educational anti-cyberbullying program, we cannot ignore the fact that cyberbullying involves various implicated actors (perpetrators, victims, bystanders, educators, and parents) and, consequently, multiple socio-cultural factors. In our modern multicultural society, culture and historical heritage can also have an influence on the phenomenon or at least on its perception:

[An] …important consideration to keep in mind when comparing studies are cultural similarities and differences in both the prevalence of research on the topic of cyberbullying and the prevalence of cyberbullying itself within a particular culture. (Kowalski, Limber, & Agatston, 2012, p. 89)

Finally, our opinion is that, in developing policies against cyberbullying, one should also make a distinction between bullying on one hand, and the playful exchange of ridiculing remarks among friends on the other. Sometimes, it is difficult to determine when a certain behavior crosses the line and turns into bullying. In this regard, one should consider the following story cited by Walker (2013):

Jess didn't think anything of it when she texted David, her friend Laura's crush, about the math homework. But when Jess went on Facebook later, her heart dropped. Laura and their friend Allie had created a "We Hate Jess" page, where they accused Jess of moving in on David. Jess's eyes filled with tears. How could her friends post such hateful comments?

For Walker, this story concerns both bullying and drama. It is drama since "Laura and Allie feel they've been wronged, so they're not just targeting Jess for no reason". However, the internet changes the drama into bullying when Laura and Allie create the web page and make their feelings against Jess public.

RECENT RESEARCH DEVELOPMENTS

In a recent article, Olweus and Limber argued that the existing research on cyberbullying is plagued by inconsistent findings and exaggerated claims (Olweus & Limber, 2018). In the same article, they underlined that:

- To build a coherent body of knowledge, a consensual definition is essential;

- Cyberbullying overlaps a lot with traditional bullying;
- It is important to measure cyberbullying in a bullying context;
- Cyberbullying should be regarded as a subcategory of bullying.

These points represent relevant hints for the direction of further research into cyberbullying.

One should bear in mind that Olweus's severe criticism of the current state of research on cyberbullying is not a novelty. Some years ago, claiming that his arguments were based on empirical analyses of several large-scale studies, he sustained that cyberbullying was a phenomenon that was greatly exaggerated by the media and had very little scientific support (Olweus, 2012a). On the basis of this assumption, he argued that effective measures to prevent cyberbullying should include investment in technical competence, the identification of real cases of cyberbullying, and the involvement of students in their discussion (Olweus, 2012b).

However, although the data coming from the numerous studies on cyberbullying is often non-homogeneous, many survey results seem to contradict Olweus's view. For example, data collected by the *Cyberbullying Research Center* from more than 20,000 middle and high school students from across the United States in twelve unique projects revealed that, on average, around 28% of participants of the 10 most recent studies admitted to having been a victim of cyberbullying at some point in their lives (Figure 1).

Figure 1. Lifetime cyberbullying victimization rates – Ten different studies 2007-2016
Source: Patchin, 2016

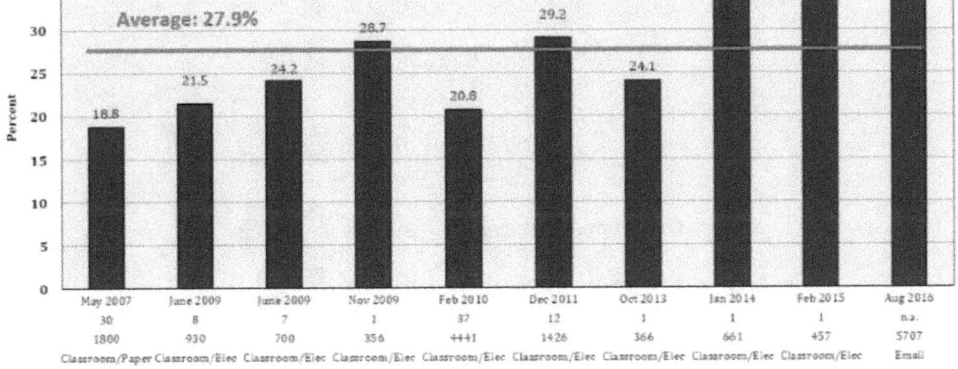

Furthermore, a recent research by the *Pew Research Center* (Duggan, 2017) reveals that roughly four-in-ten Americans have experienced some form of online harassment (Figures 2 and 3).

In this regard, some could object that the definition of online harassment doesn't meet the criteria of Olweus definition of cyberbullying, nevertheless the data presented above clearly indicates the increase in online harassment, which is considered a form of cyberbullying.

Indeed, it is difficult to delineate the borders of cyberbullying and, as illustrated in the paragraph regarding the multifarious facets of cyberbullying, the current definitions of this phenomenon differ in many specific aspects.

In any event, the comparison of the data from two surveys conducted by *UK Kids Online* in 2010 and 2014 that used the same methodology suggests that cyberbullying is growing more widespread in European countries, especially among girls and the youngest age groups (Figure 4). The data is not recent, but does demonstrate a relative trend.

Figure 2. % of U.S. adults who have experienced online harassment
Source: Survey conducted Jan. 9-23, 2017 by the Pew Research Center

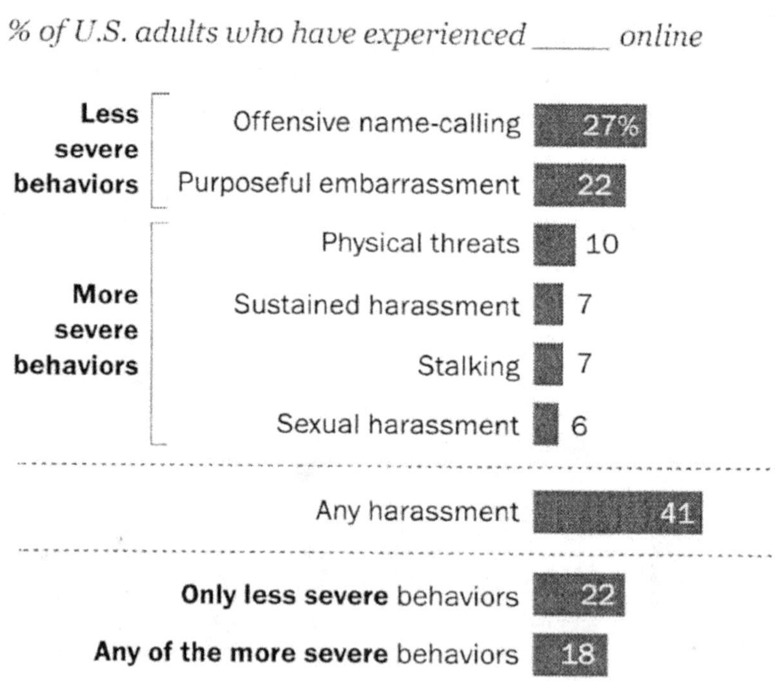

Figure 3. % of U.S. adults who say they have experienced each type of online harassment in 2014 vs. 2017
Source: Survey conducted Jan. 9-23, 2017 by the Pew Research Center

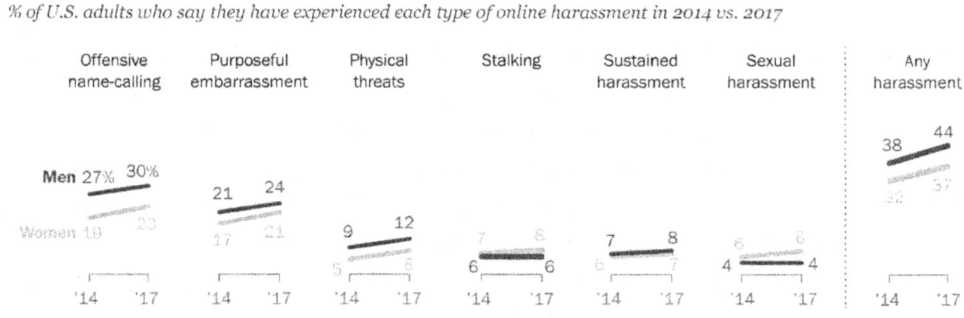

Figure 4. % of cyberbullying and bullying experiences
Source: Livingstone, Mascheroni, Ólafsson, & Haddon, November 2014

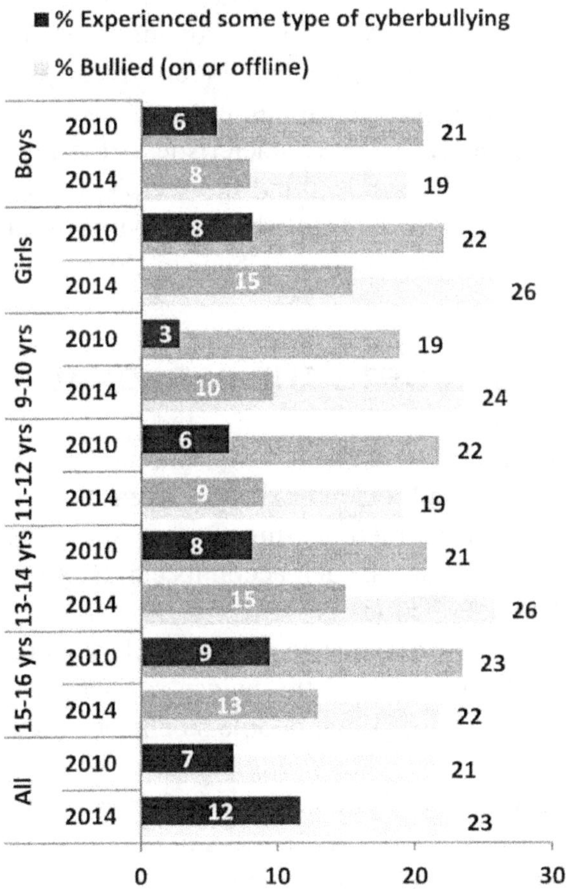

Further developments on cyberbullying investigations include new forms of online harassment such as revenge porn, virtual rape or cyber rape, and cyber gender harassment.

Revenge porn involves a perpetrator – typically an ex-partner from a previous romantic relationship – uploading sexually explicit content (nude, semi-nude, or sexy images/videos) of a person to the internet without their consent out of spite or to seek revenge (Citron & Franks, 2014).

Virtual rape is a non-consensual sexual act committed in the virtual world. It was common in Second Life and also occurred in other virtual worlds, such as in the case of virtual rape described by Dibbell (1994).

In Chapter 3, issues relating to the digital world and its direct interaction with the physical world will be addressed. Accordingly, revenge porn, virtual rape, and other forms of harassment that relate closely to an individual's physical sphere will be explored.

Further developments in the sphere of cyberbullying also comprise advances in technologies that can support its prevention and detection. In this regard, over the last few years, there has been a growing interest of researchers in new software applications based on techniques typically used for document classification, topic detection, and sentiment analysis. Their aim is to detect electronic bullying by analyzing the characteristics of the messages themselves, and of the behavior of the senders and the recipients. It should be noted, however, that detecting patterns of cyberbullying is intrinsically more difficult than merely detecting abusive content (Salawu, He, & Lumsden, 2017).

JOURNALISTS' REPORTS AND PERSONAL EXPERIENCE

Although not deriving from controlled experiments or systematic research, some journalists' reports and personal experiences can be significant, and spark new lines of investigation. Sometimes, in contrast to many socio-philosophical and socio-psychological thesis, such accounts can help in reaching a better understanding of social phenomena.

Moreover, under certain circumstances, personal contacts with students and teachers, as well as the non-systematic analysis of social network content can help to illuminate aspects of young people's behavior that would otherwise remain in the dark, such as: what young people think about cyberbullying; whether their perception of what constitutes cyber harassment is the same as that of adults; if the point of view of lawyers or police officers is the same as that of teachers; and what teenagers' inclination is to transgression?

Often, journalists merely offer representations of mainstream opinions, but sometimes they arrive at insightful discoveries of what happens under the surface of the dominant beliefs. Accordingly, some newspaper articles, despite lacking academic relevance, are valuable for depicting the social context. What did it mean, for instance, to hear teenagers talk about the relevant number of Yik Yak posts they exchanged about sex?

In the introduction to *American Girls: Social media and the Secret Life of Teenagers*, the author, journalist Nancy Jo Sales, reports her experience about an obscure, limited, but exemplary episode, known as the Syracusesnap story. One Saturday night in October 2015, when a freshman at Cornell University was taking a break from studying to check her phone, she opened a snapchat featuring Syracuse University and began watching. "Oh my gosh, Syracuse is so much crazier than us," she said to her friends. Soon, everybody was talking about it, and the Syracuse snapchat story quickly went viral. Within hours of its creation, Syracusesnap was being followed by college students and teenagers across the country.

The Syracusesnap story was a stream of pictures and videos running 24 hours a day that depicted an almost constant torrent of sex, drugs, and money:

[…] Syracusesnap featured pictures of kids in college dorm room drinking and doing drugs, but what was getting it all this attention were its many images of naked girls. Girls having sex. Sex with boys, sex with girls. The sex with boys was almost always in a standing, bent-over position, the girls' heads pointing toward the ground. Some of these shots were adorned with cartoon pictures of footballs and references to Syracuse's annual "Orange Central" homecoming and reunion week. (Sales, 2016, p. 5)

Sales says that as she watched the Syracusesnap story playing on her phone, she was struck with how analogous it was with the report she was writing at the time about girls and social media. She commented on the episode as follows:

It's clear that what had made Syracusesnap a hit were its many pictures of naked girls – girls having sex, a girl being threatened with assault, and girls assaulting each other. There's no proof of where any of these images come from, from this side of the screen. But they were. And they got people talking, and watching, and clicking, and wanting more. (Sales, 2016, p. 9)

Sales's reporting about young girls and social media is not an academic work, however it does contain many elements and observations that are useful and which stimulate a more thorough exploration.

Equally interesting in this respect is an experience reported by Fisk. The author noted that young people don't discuss issues of internet safety in the same way that adults do, and don't speak about internet safety with the same frequency that adults do:

Toward the end of my research in schools, I held several focus groups with students, and although they discussed harassment and other forms of violence, they failed to use the term cyberbullying *without first being prompted by an adult. In one middle school session, students were asked if cyberbullying was a term they used in conversations with each other and if they did not use it, then who did? When I asked the first question to a group of high schoolers, they answered, "No". When asked who did use the word, they responded loudly, and in unison: "Techers, adults". Similarly, students in a middle school focus group said, "Nobody uses it". One middle school girl sitting next to me rolled her eyes and said under her breath, "It's an old lady word". Various other participants commented by stating that "It just sounds, like, weird" and "We don't really talk about it." (Fisk, 2016, pp. 166-167)*

Indeed, often, adults and young people involved in discussions about issues relating to cyber security confuse episodes of drama with actual cyberbullying events.

There are also many anecdotes about bad taste jokes made by students using digital technologies. Here is a university story which occurred in 2016:

A Pitt student claimed there were mealworms in the cafeteria food. He took a video of the bugs squirming in the food - and sent it to the Pitt News; the paper's website linked to the video. Instead of just privately communicating with the student - the dining service kept issuing statements. Finally, Campus Police picked up the student for an interview! With each new response by administration - the paper and its website once again showed the footage of the squirming bugs. Perhaps I am perverse - but it was (repeatedly) both disgusting and hilarious. Inept crisis management.

I received the above story by email from a professor commenting on an article of mine concerning cyberbullying. Of course, the professor was aware that the episode they recounted was not an act of cyberbullying, but nevertheless it is interesting for the analogous connection that they drew.

Furthermore, during the writing of the present book, I received many links to newspaper articles from colleagues all around the world. It is remarkable that most of these articles reported cyberbullying episodes that ended with the victim's suicide. This fact is indicative of the current climate surrounding cyberbullying. Newspapers highlight cyberbullying tragedies since these extreme cases upset and shock, and the victim's suicide is widely accepted as being firmly collocated to the image cyberbullying has.

Investigating how different classes of adults perceive cyberbullying could be strategic to enhancing the current prevention practices. Collecting and analyzing all the various narratives on cyberbullying could help in contextualizing the interventions, as well as in finding new ways to increase awareness of the phenomenon and limit biases on how to address it.

CONCLUSION

Cyberbullying as a form of online harassment is an evil phenomenon that represents a serious form of misbehavior amongst young people, and its spread among young adolescents is alarming. However, according to Rogers (2010), whilst cyberbullying is a deliberate act, some cyberbullying episodes start off as a joke. Sometimes, derogatory remarks passed between friends that circulate outside the intended group can lead to embarrassment and hurt.

This chapter illustrated that there isn't a complete and universally shared definition of cyberbullying, and that this legitimates the criticism of Olweus and his doubts about its spread. Reviewing the literature as it is, however, the most shared definitions of cyberbullying have been presented, starting from the early studies when the phenomenon first came to attention.

From our overview, it emerges that there a few pieces of evidence regarding cyberbullying that should be carefully considered. One is that the dramatic expansion of social media technologies has brought many young people aged 11-16 to have profiles on social networking sites. As a consequence, the sharing of information is more and more widespread among young people today, and their risk of being an object of online harassment has significantly increased.

Another is that among new forms of online harassment, revenge porn is particularly malicious, and in developing an effective anti-cyberbullying educational program, the spread of this evil phenomenon cannot be downplayed.

REFERENCES

Aldridge, J. M., & McChesney, K. (2018). The relationships between school climate and adolescent mental health and wellbeing: A systematic literature review. *International Journal of Educational Research, 88*, 121–145. doi:10.1016/j.ijer.2018.01.012

Algosaibi, A. A., Albahli, S., & Melton, A. (2015). World Wide Web: A Survey of its Development and Possible Future Trends. *The 16th International Conference on Internet Computing and Big Data-ICOMP'15*, 79-84.

Alipan, A., Skues, J., Theiler, S., & Wise, L. (2015). Defining cyberbullying: A multiple perspectives approach. Annual review of cybertherapy and telemedicine 2015: Virtual reality in Healthcare: Medical simulation and experiential interface, 219, 9-13.

Barack, A. (2005). Sexual harassment on the Internet. *Social Science Computer Review, 23*(1), 77–92. doi:10.1177/0894439304271540

Baron, N. S. (1984). Computer mediated communication as a force in language change. *Visible Language, 18*(2), 118.

Bauman, S. (2013). Cyberbullying: What does research tell us? *Theory into Practice, 52*(4), 249–256. doi:10.1080/00405841.2013.829727

Belsey, B. (2005). *Cyberbullying: An emerging threat to the 'always on' generation*. Available from: http://www.billbelsey.com/?p=1827

Benfer, A. (2001, July 3). *Cyber slammed*. Salon Media Group. Available at: https://www.salon.com/2001/07/03/cyber_bullies/

Berners-Lee, T., Connolly, D., & Swick, R. R. (1999). Web architecture: Describing and exchanging data. *W3C Note*. Available at: https://www.w3.org/1999/04/WebData

Berners-Lee, T., Hendler, J., & Lassila, O. (2001). The semantic web. *Scientific American, 284*(5), 28–37. doi:10.1038cientificamerican0501-34 PMID:11341160

Bocij, P. (2004). *Cyberstalking: Harassment in the Internet age and how to protect your family*. Greenwood Publishing Group.

Brail, S. (1996). The price of admission: Harassment and free speech in the wild, wild west. In L. Cherny (Ed.), *Wired women: Gender and new realities in cyberspace* (pp. 141–157). Avalon Publishing Group.

Casas, J. A., Del Rey, R., & Ortega-Ruiz, R. (2013). Bullying and cyberbullying: Convergent and divergent predictor variables. *Computers in Human Behavior*, *29*(3), 580–587. doi:10.1016/j.chb.2012.11.015

Cerf, V.G. & Kahn, R.E. (1974). A protocol for packet network interconnection, *IEEE Trans. Comm. Tech.*, *22*(5), 627-641.

Chen, B., & Marcus, J. (2012). Students' self-presentation on Facebook: An examination of personality and self-construal factors. *Computers in Human Behavior*, *28*(6), 2091–2099. doi:10.1016/j.chb.2012.06.013

Choudhury, N. (2014). World wide web and its journey from web 1.0 to web 4.0. *International Journal of Computer Science and Information Technologies*, *5*(6), 8096–8100.

Citron, D. K., & Franks, M. A. (2014). Criminalizing revenge porn. *Wake Forest Law Review*, *49*, 345–391.

Curran, J., Fenton, N., & Freedman, D. (2016). *Misunderstanding the internet*. Routledge. doi:10.4324/9781315695624

Dalla Pozza, V., Di Pietro, A., Morel, S., & Psaila, E. (2016). *Cyberbullying among young people*. Directorate General for Internal Policies Policy Department C: Citizens' Rights and Constitutional Affairs. Available at: http://www.europarl.europa.eu/RegData/etudes/STUD/2016/571367/IPOL_STU(2016)571367_EN.pdf

Del Rey, R., Casas, J. A., Ortega-Ruiz, R., Schultze-Krumbholz, A., Scheithauer, H., Smith, P., ... Guarini, A. (2015). Structural validation and cross-cultural robustness of the European Cyberbullying Intervention Project Questionnaire. *Computers in Human Behavior*, *50*, 141–147. doi:10.1016/j.chb.2015.03.065

DfES. (2002). *Bullying: Don't suffer in silence. An anti-bullying pack for schools*. London: HMSO. Available at: http://webarchive.nationalarchives.gov.uk/20040722082817/http://www.dfes.gov.uk/bullying/pack/02.pdf

Dibbell, J. (1994). A rape in cyberspace or how an evil clown, a Haitian trickster spirit, two wizards, and a cast of dozens turned a database into a society. *Ann. Surv. Am.*, *L*, 471.

Dooley, J. J., Pyżalski, J., & Cross, D. (2009). Cyberbullying versus face-to-face bullying: A theoretical and conceptual review. *The Journal of Psychology*, *217*(4), 182–188.

Duggan, M. (2017). *Online harassment in focus: Most recent experience*. Pew research Center. Available at: https://www.pewinternet.org/2017/07/11/online-harassment-in-focus-most-recent-experience/

Eftekhar, A., Fullwood, C., & Morris, N. (2014). Capturing personality from Facebook photos and photo-related activities: How much exposure do you need? *Computers in Human Behavior*, *37*, 162–170. doi:10.1016/j.chb.2014.04.048

Ellison, L. (2003). Cyberstalking: Tackling harassment on the Internet. In Crime and the Internet (pp. 153-163). Routledge.

Farkas, D. (2016). *A Phenomenological Study to Examine the Motives of Tenth Grade Students Perpetrating Cyberbullying*. A Dissertation Presented in Partial Fulfillment Of the Requirements for the Degree Doctor of Education at Liberty University. Available at: https://digitalcommons.liberty.edu/cgi/viewcontent.cgi?referer=https://scholar.google.it/&httpsredir=1&article=2357&context=doctoral

Felt, M. (2015). The incessant image: How dominant news coverage shaped Canadian cyberbullying law. *UNBLJ*, *66*, 137–160.

Finkelhor, D., Mitchell, K. J., & Wolak, J. (2000). *Online Victimization: A Report on the Nation's Youth*. Available at: https://files.eric.ed.gov/fulltext/ED442039.pdf

Fisk, N. W. (2016). *Framing internet safety: The governance of youth online*. MIT Press. doi:10.7551/mitpress/10311.001.0001

Foody, M., Samara, M., & Carlbring, P. (2015). A review of cyberbullying and suggestions for online psychological therapy. *Internet Interventions*, *2*(3), 235–242. doi:10.1016/j.invent.2015.05.002

Franco, L. R., Bellerín, M., Borrego, J., Díaz, F., & Molleda, C. (2012). Tolerance Towards Dating Violence in Adolescents. *Psicothema*, *24*(2), 236–242. PMID:22420351

Gilbert, J. (1985). Computer bulletin board operator liability for user misuse. *Fordham Law Review*, *54*, 439.

Hanewald, R. (2009). Cyberbullying research: The current state. *Australian Educational Computing: Journal of the Australian Council for Computers in Education, 24*(1), 10-15.

Heirman, W., & Walrave, M. (2012). Predicting adolescent perpetration in cyberbullying: An application of the theory of planned behavior. *Psicothema, 24*(4), 614–620. PMID:23079360

Herring, S. C. (2002). Computer-mediated communication on the Internet. *Annual Review of Information Science & Technology, 36*(1), 109–168. doi:10.1002/aris.1440360104

Hinduja, S., & Patchin, J. (2006). Bullies move beyond the schoolyard: A preliminary look at cyberbullying. *Youth Violence and Juvenile Justice, 4*(2), 148–169. doi:10.1177/1541204006286288

Hinduja, S., & Patchin, J. (2007). Offline consequences of online victimization: School violence and delinquency. *Journal of School Violence, 6*(3), 89–112. doi:10.1300/J202v06n03_06

Hinduja, S., & Patchin, J. (2008). Cyberbullying: An exploratory analysis of factors related to offending and victimization. *Deviant Behavior, 29*(2), 129–156. doi:10.1080/01639620701457816

Hinduja, S., & Patchin, J. W. (2014). *Cyberbullying: Identification Prevention and Response*. Cyberbullying Research Center. Available at: https://cyberbullying.org/Cyberbullying-Identification-Prevention-Response-2018.pdf

Jones, L. M., Mitchell, K. J., & Finkelhor, D. (2013). Online harassment in context: Trends from three youth internet safety surveys (2000, 2005, 2010). *Psychology of Violence, 3*(1), 53–69. doi:10.1037/a0030309

Kiriakidis, S. P., & Kavoura, A. (2010). Cyberbullying: A review of the literature on harassment through the internet and other electronic means. *Family & Community Health, 33*(2), 82–93. doi:10.1097/FCH.0b013e3181d593e4 PMID:20216351

Kowalski, R. M., Giumetti, G. W., Schroeder, A. N., & Lattanner, M. R. (2014). Bullying in the digital age: A critical review and meta-analysis of cyberbullying research among youth. *Psychological Bulletin, 140*(4), 1073–1137. doi:10.1037/a0035618 PMID:24512111

Kowalski, R. M., & Limber, S. P. (2007). Electronic bullying among middle school students. *The Journal of Adolescent Health, 41*(6), S22–S30. doi:10.1016/j.jadohealth.2007.08.017 PMID:18047942

Kowalski, R. M., Limber, S. P., & Agatston, P. W. (2008). *Cyber Bullying: The new moral frontier*. Blackwell Publishing. doi:10.1002/9780470694176

Kowalski, R. M., Limber, S. P., Limber, S., & Agatston, P. W. (2012). *Cyberbullying: Bullying in the digital age*. John Wiley & Sons.

Krol, E., & Ferguson, P. (1995). *The whole Internet for Windows 95: user's guide & catalog*. O'Reilly & Associates Inc.

Langos, C. (2012). Cyberbullying: The challenge to define. *Cyberpsychology, Behavior, and Social Networking, 15*(6), 285–289. doi:10.1089/cyber.2011.0588 PMID:22703033

Law, D. M., Shapka, J. D., Hymel, S., Olson, B. F., & Waterhouse, T. (2012). The changing face of bullying: An empirical comparison between traditional and internet bullying and victimization. *Computers in Human Behavior, 28*(1), 226–232. doi:10.1016/j.chb.2011.09.004

Lee, I. (Ed.). (2017). *The Internet of Things in the Modern Business Environment*. IGI-Global. doi:10.4018/978-1-5225-2104-4

Lenhart, A. (2010). Cyberbullying 2010: what the research tells us. *Youth Online Safety Working Group*. Available at: http://www.pewinternet.org/2010/05/06/cyberbullying-2010-what-the-research-tells-us/

Li, Q. (2006). Cyberbullying in schools: A research of gender differences. *School Psychology International, 27*(2), 157–170. doi:10.1177/0143034306064547

Li, Q. (2007). New bottle but old wine: A research of cyberbullying in schools. *Computers in Human Behavior, 23*(4), 1777–1791. doi:10.1016/j.chb.2005.10.005

Livingstone, S., & Brake, D. R. (2010). On the rapid rise of social networking sites: New findings and policy implications. *Children & Society, 24*(1), 75–83. doi:10.1111/j.1099-0860.2009.00243.x

Livingstone, S., Mascheroni, G., Ólafsson, K., & Haddon, L. (2014, November). *Children's online risks and opportunities: Comparative findings*. EU Kids Online and Net Children Go Mobile. Available at: http://netchildrengomobile.eu/reports/

Marz, N., & Warren, J. (2015). *Big Data: Principles and best practices of scalable realtime data systems*. Manning Publications Co.

Marzano, G. (2018). Cyberbullying. In *Encyclopedia of Information Science and Technology* (4th ed.; pp. 4157–4167). IGI Global. doi:10.4018/978-1-5225-2255-3.ch360

Menesini, E., Nocentini, A., Palladino, B. E., Frisén, A., Berne, S., Ortega-Ruiz, R., . . . Naruskov, K. (2012). Cyberbullying definition among adolescents: A comparison across six European countries. *Cyberpsychology, Behavior, and Social Networking, 15*(9), 455-463. Available at: https://www.ncbi.nlm.nih.gov/pmc/articles/PMC3443335/

Musharraf, S., & Anis-ul-Haque, M. (2018). Cyberbullying in different participant roles: Exploring differences in psychopathology and well-being in university students. *Pakistan Journal of Medical Research, 57*(1), 33–39.

Navarro, R., Serna, C., Martínez, V., & Ruiz-Oliva, R. (2013). The role of Internet use and parental mediation on cyberbullying victimization among Spanish children from rural public schools. *European Journal of Psychology of Education, 28*(3), 725–745. doi:10.100710212-012-0137-2

Nigam, H., & Collier, A. (2010). *Youth safety on a living internet: Report of the online safety and technology working group*. Academic Press.

Olweus, D. (1994). Bullying at school: Basic facts and effects of a school based intervention program. *Journal of Child Psychology and Psychiatry, and Allied Disciplines, 35*(7), 1171–1190. doi:10.1111/j.1469-7610.1994.tb01229.x PMID:7806605

Olweus, D. (2012a). Cyberbullying: An overrated phenomenon? *European Journal of Developmental Psychology, 9*(5), 520–538. doi:10.1080/17405629.2012.682358

Olweus, D. (2012b). Comments on cyberbullying article: A rejoinder. *European Journal of Developmental Psychology, 9*, 559–568.

Olweus, D., & Limber, S.P. (2018). Some problems with cyberbullying research. *Current Opinion in Psychology, 19*, 139-143.

Ortega-Ruiz, R., & Nunez, J. C. (2012). Bullying and cyberbullying: Research and intervention at school and social contexts. *Psicothema, 24*(4), 603–607. PMID:23079358

Palladino, B. E., Nocentini, A., & Menesini, E. (2012). Online and Offline peer led models against bullying and cyberbullying. *Psicothema*, *24*(4), 634–639. PMID:23079363

Palme, J., & Berglund, M. (2002). *Anonymity on the Internet*. Available at: https://people.dsv.su.se/~jpalme/society/anonymity.pdf

Park, S., Na, E. Y., & Kim, E. M. (2014). The relationship between online activities, netiquette and cyberbullying. *Children and Youth Services Review*, *42*, 74–81. doi:10.1016/j.childyouth.2014.04.002

Patchin, J. W. (2016). *Summary of Our Cyberbullying Research (2004-2016)*. Cyberbullying Research Center. Available at: https://cyberbullying.org/summary-of-our-cyberbullying-research

Patchin, J. W., & Hinduja, S. (2006). Bullies move beyond the schoolyard: A preliminary look at cyberbullying. *Youth Violence and Juvenile Justice*, *4*(2), 148–169. doi:10.1177/1541204006286288

Paul, S., Smith, P. K., & Blumberg, H. H. (2010). Addressing cyberbullying in school using the quality circle approach. *Australian Journal of Guidance & Counselling*, *20*(02), 157–168. doi:10.1375/ajgc.20.2.157

Paulson, A. (2003). Internet bullying. *The Christian Science Monitor*. Available at: https://www.csmonitor.com/2003/1230/p11s01-legn.html

Paumgarten, N. (2001, June 4). The New Bathroom Wall. *New Yorker*. Available at: https://www.newyorker.com/magazine/2001/06/04/the-new-bathroom-wall

Polishchuk, N. I., Vorobyov, S. M., Orlova, A. A., & Abovyan, E. P. (2017). On the Question of the Concept and Forms of Cyberbullying in Russia. *Journal of Advanced Research in Law and Economics*, *8*(3), 987–993.

Putnam, R. D. (2001). *Bowling alone: The collapse and revival of American community*. Simon and Schuster.

Reed, K. P., Cooper, R. L., Nugent, W. R., & Russell, K. (2016). Cyberbullying: A literature review of its relationship to adolescent depression and current intervention strategies. *Journal of Human Behavior in the Social Environment*, *26*(1), 37–45. doi:10.1080/10911359.2015.1059165

Rogers, V. (2010). *Cyberbullying: Activities to help children and teens to stay safe in a texting, twittering, social networking world*. Jessica Kingsley Publishers.

Ruedy, M. C. (2007). Repercussions of a Myspace teen suicide: Should anti-cyberbullying laws be created. *NCJL & Tech.*, *9*, 323–346.

Salawu, S., He, Y., & Lumsden, J. (2017). Approaches to Automated Detection of Cyberbullying: A Survey. *IEEE Transactions on Affective Computing*. Available at: https://research.aston.ac.uk/portal/files/23259407/Approaches_to_Automated_Detection_of_Cyberbullying.pdf

Sales, N. J. (2016). *American girls: Social media and the secret lives of teenagers*. Vintage.

Shahghasemi, E., Karami, Z., & Rabiei, A. (2017). *Cyberbullying: A Study on Iranian News Coverage*. Sociology & Anthropology.

Slonje, R., Smith, P. K., & Frisén, A. (2013). The nature of cyberbullying, and strategies for prevention. *Computers in Human Behavior*, *29*(1), 26–32. doi:10.1016/j.chb.2012.05.024

Smith, P. K. (2012). Cyberbullying: Challenges and opportunities for a research program—A response to Olweus (2012). *European Journal of Developmental Psychology*, *9*(5), 553–558. doi:10.1080/17405629.2012.689821

Smith, P. K., Mahdavi, J., Carvalho, M., Fisher, S., Russell, S., & Tippett, N. (2008). Cyberbullying: Its nature and impact in secondary school pupils. *Journal of Child Psychology and Psychiatry, and Allied Disciplines*, *49*(4), 376–385. doi:10.1111/j.1469-7610.2007.01846.x PMID:18363945

Sproull, L., & Kiesler, S. (1986). Reducing social context cues: Electronic mail in organizational communication. *Management Science*, *32*(11), 1492–1512. doi:10.1287/mnsc.32.11.1492

Steffgen, G., König, A., Pfetsch, J., & Melzer, A. (2011). Are cyberbullies less empathic? Adolescents' cyberbullying behavior and empathic responsiveness. *Cyberpsychology, Behavior, and Social Networking*, *14*(11), 643–648. doi:10.1089/cyber.2010.0445 PMID:21554126

Suler, J. (2004). The online disinhibition effect. *Cyberpsychology & Behavior*, *7*(3), 321–326. doi:10.1089/1094931041291295 PMID:15257832

Thomas, H. J., Connor, J. P., & Scott, J. G. (2015). Integrating traditional bullying and cyberbullying: Challenges of definition and measurement in adolescents–a review. *Educational Psychology Review*, *27*(1), 135–152. doi:10.100710648-014-9261-7

Tokunaga, R. S. (2010). Following you home from school: A critical review and synthesis of research on cyberbullying victimization. *Computers in Human Behavior*, *26*(3), 277–287. doi:10.1016/j.chb.2009.11.014

Valkenburg, P. M., & Peter, J. (2011). Online communication among adolescents: An integrated model of its attraction, opportunities, and risks. *The Journal of Adolescent Health*, *48*(2), 121–127. doi:10.1016/j.jadohealth.2010.08.020 PMID:21257109

Vandebosch, H., Beirens, L., D'Haese, W., Wegge, D., & Pabian, S. (2012). Police actions with regard to cyberbullying: The Belgian case. *Psicothema*, *24*(4), 646–652. PMID:23079365

Vandebosch, H., & Van Cleemput, K. (2008). Defining cyberbullying: A qualitative research into the perceptions of youngsters. *Cyberpsychology & Behavior*, *11*(4), 499–503. doi:10.1089/cpb.2007.0042 PMID:18721100

Wachs, S., & Wolf, K.D., & Pan, C-C. (2012). Cybergrooming: Risk factors, coping strategies and associations with cyberbullying. *Psicothema*, *24*(4), 628–633. PMID:23079362

Walker, M. (2013). Is it bullying or drama. *Huffpost*. Available at: https://www.huffpost.com/entry/bullying-or-drama_n_4268218

Walrave, M., & Heirman, W. (2011). Cyberbullying: Predicting victimisation and perpetration. *Children & Society*, *25*(1), 59–72. doi:10.1111/j.1099-0860.2009.00260.x

Wang, H., & Hong, Y. (1995). *Flaming: More Than a Necessary Evil for Academic Mailing Lists*. Technical Report. Available at: https://files.eric.ed.gov/fulltext/ED385261.pdf

Weber, J. S. (1995). Defining Cyberlibel: A First Amendment Limit for Libel Suits Against Individuals Arising from Computer Bulletin Board Speech. *Case W. Res. L. Rev.*, *46*, 235.

Whittaker, E., & Kowalski, R. M. (2015). Cyberbullying via social media. *Journal of School Violence*, *14*(1), 11–29. doi:10.1080/15388220.2014.949377

Willard, N. (2005). *An educator's guide to cyberbullying and cyberthreats*. Center for Safe and Responsible Internet Use. Available at: https://www.wcs.k12.va.us/users/honaker/cyberbullying-for-teachers.pdf

Witten, I. H., Frank, E., Hall, M. A., & Pal, C. J. (2016). *Data Mining: Practical machine learning tools and techniques*. Morgan Kaufmann.

Wolak, J., Mitchell, K. J., & Finkelhor, D. (2007). Does online harassment constitute bullying? An exploration of online harassment by known peers and online-only contacts. *The Journal of Adolescent Health*, *41*(6), S51–S58. doi:10.1016/j.jadohealth.2007.08.019 PMID:18047945

Wong, D. S., Chan, H. C. O., & Cheng, C. H. (2014). Cyberbullying perpetration and victimization among adolescents in Hong Kong. *Children and Youth Services Review*, *36*, 133–140. doi:10.1016/j.childyouth.2013.11.006

Ybarra, M., & Mitchell, K. (2007). Prevalence and frequency of Internet harassment instigation: Implications for adolescent health. *Adolesc Health*, *41*(2), 89–95. doi:10.1016/j.jadohealth.2007.03.005 PMID:17659224

Ybarra, M., Mitchell, K., Wolak, J., & Finkelhor, D. (2006). Examining characteristics and associated distress related to Internet harassment: Findings from the Second Youth Internet Safety Survey. *Pediatrics*, *118*(4), 69–77. doi:10.1542/peds.2006-0815 PMID:17015505

Ybarra, M. L., & Mitchell, K. J. (2004a). Youth engaging in online harassment: Associations with caregiver–child relationships, Internet use, and personal characteristics. *Journal of Adolescence*, *27*(3), 319–336. doi:10.1016/j.adolescence.2004.03.007 PMID:15159091

Ybarra, M. L., & Mitchell, K. J. (2004b). Online aggressor/targets, aggressors, and targets: A comparison of associated youth characteristics. *Journal of Child Psychology and Psychiatry, and Allied Disciplines*, *45*(7), 1308–1316. doi:10.1111/j.1469-7610.2004.00328.x PMID:15335350

Zych, I., Ortega-Ruiz, R., & Del Rey, R. (2015). Systematic review of theoretical studies on bullying and cyberbullying: Facts, knowledge, prevention, and intervention. *Aggression and Violent Behavior*, *23*, 1–21. doi:10.1016/j.avb.2015.10.001

KEY TERMS AND DEFINITIONS

Bullying: The repeated use of force, threat, or coercion to abuse, intimidate, or aggressively dominate others.

Critical Media Literacy: An educational response aimed at expanding the notion of literacy to include different forms of mass communication, popular culture, and new technologies.

Cyberbullying: Repeated aggressive, intentional acts carried out by a group or individual using electronic media.

Empathy: The capacity to feel and share another person's emotions.

Flaming: Refers to the use of insults, swearing, and hateful, intense language.

Information Exposure: The intentional or unintentional disclosure of information to someone who is not explicitly authorized to have access to that information.

Machine Learning: A subfield of artificial intelligence that focuses on the development of computer programs that can teach themselves without being explicitly programmed.

Olweus Bullying Prevention Program: The most researched and best-known bullying prevention program available today, designed to improve peer relations and make schools safer.

Online Denigration: The spreading of rumors via electronic communication devices.

Power Imbalance: A situation of inequality between parties that leaves one side relatively unable to defend its own interests.

Social Networking Site: An online place where a user can create a profile and build a personal network that connects him or her to other users.

Chapter 2
Setting Anti-Cyberbullying Legal Policies

Gilberto Marzano
Rezekne Academy of Technologies, Latvia

ABSTRACT

It is a broadly shared opinion that establishing the illegitimacy of cyberbullying is a primary action in combating it. In this regard, schools should openly declare that cyberbullying is not an acceptable or admissible behavior, and firm rules regarding this phenomenon should be implemented by them. In this chapter, the problem of setting anti-cyberbullying legal policies will be addressed. Two cases are illustrated and discussed, the famous case of Lori Drew related to the suicide of Megan Meier that occurred in 2006, and the Italian case of Tiziana Cantone whose suicide occurred 10 years later. In fact, the latter was not a cyberbullying case, but it is remarkable since it generated a huge emotional reaction among Italian people that ultimately led to the implementation of the Italian law against cyberbullying in 2017 and, in 2019, brought about the law against the unsolicited sharing of compromising erotic pictures or video, known as revenge porn. Both cases illustrate the issues that may arise in drawing effective anti-cyberbullying laws. The absence of a univocal definition of cyberbullying and the pressure of public opinion negatively affects the establishment of appropriate legal policies. Indeed, the formulation of a law implies unequivocally identifying an infraction and having clear rules to punish it. The current legal situation of cyberbullying in different countries is highlighted, focusing on the USA and Europe, and the general questions regarding the criminalization and punishment of cyberbullying are also analyzed. Finally, the use and positive influence of anti-cyberbullying regulations at schools are reviewed and discussed.

DOI: 10.4018/978-1-5225-8076-8.ch002

INTRODUCTION

One of the key principles of the *Olweus Bullying Prevention Program* is setting "firm limits on unacceptable behavior" (Olweus, 2003, 15). Indeed, a few years ago, Hinduja and Patchin also suggested a similar principle, arguing that it is crucial to "teach students that all forms of bullying are unacceptable and that cyberbullying behaviors are potentially subject to discipline" (Hinduja & Patchin, 2018).

However, defining anti-cyberbullying policies is a challenging issue. According to modern law sociologists, laws and legal systems are social constructions and are not matters of nature but of artifice (Hart, Hart & Green, 2012). A law formalizes in a rule or a set of rules what society considers important to regulate, reflecting the moral beliefs and values of a particular time. As a consequence, legal systems don't remain static.

Nowadays, new technologies are disrupting social attitudes, and making adequate legal policies is a necessity. Indeed, a great effort is being made at a global level to establish common policies to harmonize and manage the impact of ICT, for example to regulate the legal value of digital documents, electronic signatures, and e-commerce transactions. In the last decade, endeavors have been made to enforce privacy protection as well as to introduce anti-cyber crime policies.

In this scenario, cyberbullying is attracting social, political, and academic interest (Martinez-Pecino & Durán, 2016). In this regard, it has been observed that while there aren't many calls for changing laws to prevent and punish students who engage in face-to-face bullying, there are many calls for laws against anti-cyberbullying (Campbel & Zavrsnik, 2013).

There could be two main reasons for this. The first is that in the last three decades it was common to find school staff and parents who believed that bullying was not a concern (Rigby, 2008). They not only underestimated its frequency but also considered the experience of bullying as a normal part of growing up for children ("Kid will be kids"; "Kids need to learn to deal with bullying on their own"; "Don't let it get to you"; "You're too sensitive ... toughen up"). Even though the observed consequences of bullying are depression, anxiety, and serious psychosomatic effects including suicide, there are still those even now who view it as an inevitable part of growing up (Copeland, Wolke, Angold, & Costello, 2013).

The second reason is a consequence of the increasing attention of the media on cyberbullying. Extreme cases that end with the suicide of the victim are extensively reported and commented on by experts, especially psychologists and lawyers. People tend to adapt their responses to the worst and most shocking cases. Researchers in the area of social control have long posited a relationship between media, popular culture, and perceptions of punishment, including punitive attitudes (Callanan & Rosenberger, 2011; Demker, Towns, Duus-Otterstrom, & Sebring, 2008; Dowler, 2003) and support for capital punishment (Britto & Noga-Styron, 2014).

Moreover, cyberbullying is the label used by media to encompass a broad range of online misbehavior. The situation is similar in other contexts. In fact, it has been observed that the "myth of homogeneity" regarding the sex offender population has permeated the domains of media and public policy (Galeste, Fradella, & Vogel, 2012).

In the following paragraphs, the question of criminalization of cyberbullying will be tackled and two notorious cases will be illustrated and analyzed. The first is the case of Dori Drew, the mother that helped her daughter to create the false account used to cheat and hurt the thirteen-year-old Megan Meier. The victim committed suicide, but all attempts to incriminate Dori Drew failed. Although no charge was made against Lori Drew relating to the suicide of Megan, this case continues to be presented as a classic example of cyberbullying,

The second case is that of Tiziana Cantone, 31-year-old Italian women who committed suicide following the online circulation of clips of her sex video. This was neither a cyberbullying case nor a revenge porn episode but her suicide, widely reported by the press and online media, was used to compel the introduction of an anti-cyberbullying law in Italy.

LEGAL ISSUES

It is common opinion that the exceptional increase in online interaction should lead to changes in the current legal policies. Accordingly, various attempts have been made to combat cyberbullying through enacting specific laws or modifying existing legislation.

The first US act relating to the prevention of cyberbullying was introduced in April 2009, but, to date, relatively few states have enacted specific anti-bullying sanctions in their criminal legislation.

Despite the general awareness of the serious potential consequences of cyberbullying, there is no matching clarity in regards to its legal status, and cyberbullying remains an area of legal limbo (El Asam & Samara, 2016). In fact, it is difficult to extricate and distinguish what really constitutes online harassment, defamation, and hate speech at a legal level. Although this behavior represents a significant problem, there are few legal remedies for victims (Marwick & Miller, 2014). Accordingly, when considering this issue, one should keep in mind an observation made by Linda Sanchez, cited by Meredith:

I want the law to be able to distinguish between an annoying chain email, a righteously angry political blog post, or a miffed text to an ex-boyfriend, all of which are and should remain legal; and serious, repeated, and hostile communications made with the intent to harm. (Meredith, 2010, 330)

The main difficulty with cyberbullying is deciding which offense has to be charged as cyberbullying. As a general principle, presumed online offenses should be assessed in order to decide which represent criminal acts. In common law, an offense is committed if there is a credible threat to a person/property or a communication is made that contains offensive, indecent, false or obscene content. This means that the prosecution ought to prove beyond any reasonable doubt that the accused made a threat by words or conduct intended to exert force on the victim or that the content really was offensive, indecent, false, or obscene.

Nevertheless, a cyberbullying law should include offences that don't typically involve the making of a threat to apply force, such as 'happy slapping', 'denigration' (by any means), 'harassment', 'exclusion', 'masquerading' or 'impersonation', and 'outing and trickery'. Table 1 shows the common types of harassment practiced by cyberbullies.

A crucial issue is how to draft a law that doesn't infringe upon the freedom of expression that is fundamental to every democratic state and is enshrined in the Universal Convention of Human Rights of 1948.

On a general level, the concept of freedom of speech is different in the US and in Europe.

In the USA, cyberbullying legislation must not infringe on the First Amendment rights that guarantees freedom of speech and protects citizens from arbitrary governmental intrusion.

In Europe, the Constitutional Court of the EU member states and the European Court of Human Rights have provided for a much greater limitation to freedom of speech:

Table 1. Common forms of cyberbullying harassment

Types of harassment	Description
Name-calling	The use of language intended to defame, demean, or degrade individuals or groups.
Flaming	Posting hostile and insulting messages to intentionally harass somebody
Exposure	Posting or forwarding of personal communication, images, or video which contain sensitive personal information or are detrimental to an individual
Exclusion	Cruelly excluding someone from an online group
Denigration	Sending, posting, or publishing cruel rumors, gossip, and untrue statements about an individual to intentionally damage their reputation or friendships.
Impersonation	Impersonating somebody to make unpopular online comments or creating fake profiles to post defaming information
Image and video dissemination	Disseminating images and video to humiliate and disparage an individual
Happy slapping	A victim is physically attacked or embarrassed in person, and video or pictures of the incident are recorded and diffused
Tagging	Inappropriate images and texts are tagged so that hurtful information appears on the victim's timeline
Cyberstalking	Cyberstalking includes threats of harm, intimidation, and/or offensive comments sent through Information and Communications Technology channels.
Threats	Threatening a victim via cell calls or messages
Blackmail	The threat of revealing personal information in order to obtain ransom payments

Source: author's own elaboration

Everyone has the right to freedom of expression. This right shall include freedom to hold opinions and to receive and impart information and ideas without interference by public authority and regardless of frontiers. This Article shall not prevent States from requiring the licensing of broadcasting, television, or cinema enterprises.

The exercise of these freedoms, since it carries with it duties and responsibilities, may be subject to such formalities, conditions, restrictions, or penalties as are prescribed by law and are necessary in a democratic society, in the interests of national security, territorial integrity, or public safety, for the prevention of disorder or crime, for the protection of health or morals, for the protection of the reputation or rights of others, for preventing the disclosure of information received in confidence, or for maintaining the authority and impartiality of the judiciary (Article 10 of the European Convention on Human Rights)[1]

The European regulation of free speech gives the power to states of deciding by law what is or is not acceptable speech for citizens to hear, or say.

As a consequence, in Europe, free speech is conceived as a right that can be limited when other constitutional freedoms must be safeguarded (for example, public order or national security), whilst in the US, freedom of speech is protected by the First Amendment and is limited only in a few exceptional cases.

The divergent legal point of view doesn't help the drafting of common legal policies against cyberbullying in the US and Europe.

It has been observed that the United States Supreme Court, although has declined to address how First Amendment protections apply to cyberbullying prohibitions (Briggs, 2018), in many case denied writ of presumed cyberbullying, e. g., when a student created an online chat room to ridicule a fellow student (Kowalski v. Berkeley City Schs., 565 U.S. 1173, 2012) as well as when another student created a false online profile of her principal (Blue Mt. Sch. Dist. v. J.S. ex rel. Snyder, 565 U.S. 1156, 2012. However, in the latter case, the Court rejected the appeal presented by the student sustaining the violation of the First Amendment free speech rights:

This appeal presents a challenge to J.S.'s suspension from Blue Mountain Middle School after she created from her home computer a MySpace.com Internet profile featuring her principal, James McGonigle. The profile did not state McGonigle's name, but included his photograph from the website of Blue Mountain School District (the "School District"), as well as profanity-laced statements insinuating that he was a sex addict and pedophile. On appeal, J.S. and her parents assert that the District Court erred in granting summary judgment in favor of the School District, arguing that the School District violated J.S.'s First Amendment free speech rights by punishing her for creating the profile; the School District violated J.S.'s parent's fundamental right to direct the upbringing of their child by regulating her out-of-school conduct […] Because we believe school authorities could reasonably have forecasted a substantial disruption of or material interference with the school as a result of the MySpace profile, as defined by Tinker v. Des Moines Independent Community School District, 393 U.S. 503 (1969), we conclude that the School District did not violate J.S.'s First Amendment free speech rights by disciplining her for creating the profile. (FindLaw, 2010)

EXCEPTIONS TO THE FIRST AMENDMENT

The First Amendment does not protect some well-defined and narrowly limited classes of speech. Indeed, the Supreme Court decided that *fighting words*, *obscenity*, *incitement*, and *true threats* can be restricted without violating the Constitution.

In *Chaplinsky v. State of New Hampshire*, the Supreme Court defined fighting words as words that, by their very utterance, inflict injury or tend to incite an immediate breach of the peace.[2]

The Supreme Court has also upheld restrictions on speech that contains *obscene material*, that is material dealing with sex in a manner appealing to prurient interest and "offend[s] the common conscience of the community by present-day standards".[3]

Moreover, the First Amendment does not protect speech that is "directed to inciting or producing imminent lawless action and is likely to incite or produce such action." [4] In this regard, Briggs observes:

[…] organizing, equipping, and urging people to participate in "virtual sit-ins" that caused website servers to slow down was incitement because virtual sit-ins are unlawful and the lawless conduct actually occurred. But religious protestors making vulgar and disparaging comments towards another religion was not inciting speech because the protestors did not advocate for imminent lawlessness. (Briggs, 2018, 1074-1075)

Finally, true threats are the fourth notable exception to First Amendment guarantees. A true threat is the serious expression of intent to perform an illegal violent act that is directed toward a particular person or group.

A recent article by Rory Little (2018) about the drafting of a hate speech statute shows why, for federal states, it is not easy to design cyberbullying legislation that passes the judicial review of constitutionality by the Supreme Court.

CRIMINALIZATION OF CYBERBULLYING

Punishment and retribution are essential elements of a justice system. They are invoked as a deterrent to wrong-doing so as to encourage a right social behavior.

However, is punishment and retribution a deterrent in preventing cyberbullying?

If it is, what kind of punishment and retribution actions would be the most effective to manage and prevent cyberbullying incidents?

Is the fear of punishment really a deterrent for young people?

In the case of cyberbullying, children and adolescents are often unaware of the law, and may not be able to foresee the consequences of their behavior. Young people's legal literacy is a complex issue that involves the socialization dimension (Fagan & Tyler, 2005). Terms such as harassing and annoying can be confusing to youth, and they may not even be aware that their behavior is illegal (Coburn, Connolly, & Roesch, 2015).

Furthermore, young perpetrators believe that they are protected by anonymity. Finally, they seem to perceive the virtual world in a different way to adults; they can also possess invaluable knowledge about the use and abuse of interactive technology (Paul, Smith, & Blumberg, 2012).

As Shariff explained to the Standing Committee on Justice and Human Rights of the House of Commons, Canada, one must take into account that:

Children receive confusing messages on the legal boundaries and rape culture, for example. Children confront difficult challenges at both ends. On the one hand, they must prove their strength in a digital and online social network where even friends can demean them publicly and excuse themselves by saying, "Just joking" when under peer pressure they might impulsively react or post comments and photographs they would ignore in different circumstances. Teenage girls are especially vulnerable when they decide to assert their sexuality like female celebrity idols, but end up being publicly humiliated through slut shaming when images sent in trust are distributed without consent. This is not going to be the panacea to addressing some of these issues because it's complex. (Shariff, 2014).

THE CASE OF LORI DREW

The famous US v. Lori Drew case in 2009 is instructive and illuminating on the difficulties that arise when one dials with cyberbullying legislation. It shows how the absence of a univocal definition of cyberbullying can lead to ineffective legal disputes.

This lawsuit was originated by a tragic case that took place in 2006 and was widely reported in the international media at the time, becoming a landmark in the scope of cyberbullying.

Lori Drew, a woman in her late 40s, together with her thirteen-year daughter, Sarah, and her 18-year-old employee, Ashley Grills, created a false account on MySpace.com in September 2006, in order to contact a classmate, the thirteen-year-old Megan Meier, who was a neighbor. The account falsely claimed to belong to an attractive sixteen-year-old boy named Josh Evans. Lori Drew declared that the purpose of the fake profile was to obtain confidential information on what Megan was saying about her daughter.

The Megan Meier story, that ended with her suicide, is recounted in detail in the website of the Megan Meier Foundation (Figure 1) that was created in December 2007 by Tina Meier, Megan's mother, with the aim of supporting and inspiring actions to end bullying, cyberbullying, and suicide.

The facts are as follows. Megan had just started eighth grade at a new school, *Immaculate Conception*, in Dardenne Prairie. In the past, she had suffered from depression and had a lifelong struggle with weight and self-esteem, but in that moment, she was feeling exceptionally well. She had shed 20 pounds, getting down to 175. With the help of her mother, Megan opened an account on MySpace and soon after she received a message from

Figure 1. The site of the Megan Maier Foundation (https://www.meganmeierfoundation.org/)

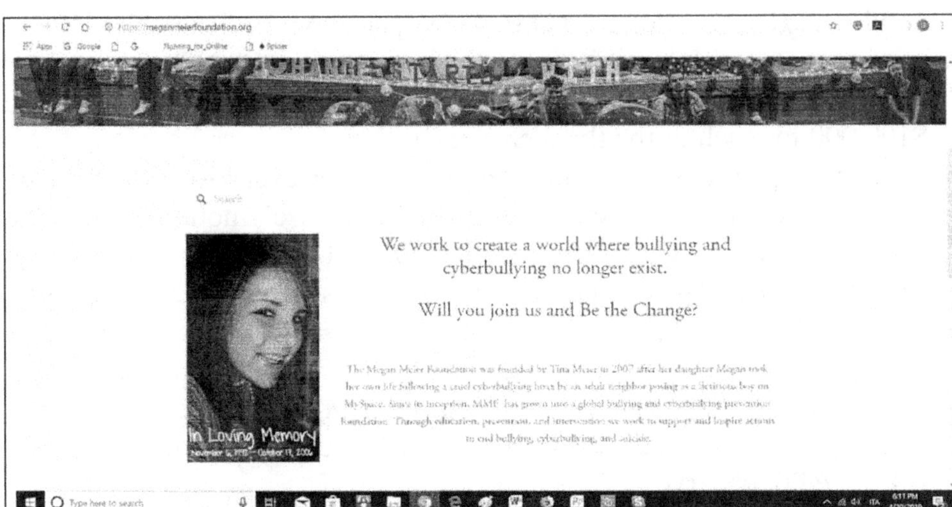

Josh and became online friends. Megan was very happy to have a flirtatious relationship with Josh since she had finally found a boy who, she believed, really thought she was pretty. But, on October 15, 2006, Megan received a puzzling and disturbing message from Josh. This message said: "I don't know if I want to be friends with you anymore because I've heard that you are not very nice to your friends". On October 16, Megan received many more similar messages, and bulletins were posted reporting "Megan Meier is a slut" and "Megan Meier is fat". Finally, Megan received an instant message from Josh saying that he no longer liked her and that "the world would be a better place without you". That same day, Meier committed suicide, hanging herself with a belt in her bedroom closet and dying the next day. This was three weeks before her 14th birthday.

A parent, who learned of the MySpace account from her own daughter who had access to the Josh profile, told Megan's parents about the hoax in a counselor's office about six weeks after Megan died.

Drew and her accomplices were accused of using MySpace to intentionally perpetrate a cruel internet hoax on a vulnerable teenage girl.

On December 1, 2007, the federal jury ruled to acquit Lori Drew of felony charges. Indeed, as the St. Charles County Prosecutor, Jack Banas, announced at a conference, there wasn't enough evidence to press criminal charges in connection with the death of Megan Meier.

Instead, the jury in Los Angeles convicted Lori Drew of three misdemeanor computer crimes for her role in setting up the MySpace false account. The jury decided that the creation of the "Josh Evans" profile had violated the Terms of Service and Privacy Policy (TOS) of MySpace.com, and that this violation rendered access to MySpace's computers to be "without authorization" and "in excess of authorized use". Drew faced up to one year in prison and a fine of $100,000 for each of the three charges.

A year later, an ensuing guilty verdict was, however, overturned by the federal judge handling the case, who granted the defense's motion for acquittal. As a matter of statutory construction, the TOS did not govern authorization: in fact, MySpace had given authorization to access its computers by creating the Josh Evans account and allowing the group to send and receive messages using it (Kerr, 2009). At trial, the Vice President of Customer Care at MySpace testified that the sheer volume of 400 million MySpace accounts made it almost impossible to determine which accounts were in violation of its TOS.

As Meredith observes:

Practically speaking, the repercussions for violating the MySpace TOS involve MySpace contacting law enforcement directly only in rare circumstances. More likely, MySpace would simply warn the violative users that their actions might warrant involvement of law enforcement or the removal of the offensive profile from the MySpace site. (Meredith, 2010, p. 321)

The popular reaction against the Drews was like a storm, fostered by an article by Steve Pokin in the St. Charles Journal on November 11, 2007 (Pokin, 2007).

Although in the first newspaper articles, the names of the adults involved in the Megan case had not been issued so as to protect the minor child from the Drew family, the identity of Lori Drew was revealed by Sarah Wells on her blog in November 2007. She identified Lori Drew when she learned that the woman had filed a police report against Megan's father who had destroyed her foosball table in anger and grief (Zetter, 2007).

Immediately, Lori Drew's name and picture spread on the Web. The Drews had their home and work addresses, phone and cell phone numbers, and aerial photos of their home posted on the Internet. The Drew's property was also vandalized.

As a reaction to Megan's case, a few anti-cyberbullying laws have already been created.

There was also a federal proposal for what was called the Megan Meier Act, but this proposal was not approved by the Supreme Court in 2009. This was, however, the first push for a national response to cyberbullying. Missouri passed Megan's Law in 2008, criminalizing electronic harassment of juveniles by adult perpetrators. Another example is the Dardenne Prairie city ordinance outlawing cyberstalking and cyberharassment with punishments of a maximum fine of $500 and up to ninety days in jail. The Ordinance states:

A person commits the offense of cyber-harassment if he/she, with intent to harass, alarm, annoy, abuse, threaten, intimidate, torment or embarrass any other person, [. . . transmits or causes the transmission of an electronic communication, or knowingly permits an electronic communication to be transmitted from an electronic communication device under the person's control to such other person or a third party:

a. using any lewd, lascivious, indecent or obscene words, images or language, or suggesting the commission of any lewd or lascivious act;

b. anonymously or repeatedly whether or not conversation occurs; or

c. threatening to inflict injury on the person or property of the person communicated with or any member of his or her family or household. (Dardenne Prairie, Mo., Municipal Code § 201.030, 2007).

THE CASE OF TIZIANA CANTONE

In 2019, the Italian parliament unanimously approved a new law criminalizing the unsolicited sharing of compromising erotic pictures or video, known as revenge porn.

Revenge porn was at the centre of the case of Tiziana Cantone that gripped Italy in 2017.

Although there are many cases of cyberbullying, we decide to focus on the case of Tiziana Cantone since it is an example of the power of media and shows how emotional reactions of people can influence legislation.

Tiziana Cantone was a 31-year-old Italian woman who committed suicide after some of her amateur porn videos were posted on WhatsApp and Facebook. Although this incident involved neither cyberbullying nor revenge porn, but was rather a case of violation of privacy, the Italian parliament exploited it to start a campaign against cyberbullying, proposing a special law to censure internet content.

The facts of the case, according to an article on BuzzFeed, are as follows:

In spring 2015, Tiziana Cantone from Naples, Italy, sent a video to her ex-boyfriend of her performing a sex act on another man.

This video was then shared to WhatsApp and various social media websites. After it was uploaded, it became a meme, with people sharing stills and quotes from it.

A quote from the video, "Mi stai facendo il video? Bravo" (which translates to "You're making the video? Good") was used for comedic purposes not only by members of the public, but also by Italian companies.

Cantone had filed legal requests with Google, Facebook Ireland, Yahoo Italy, and YouTube to have videos and references to her removed.

[…]

According to [the Italian newspaper] il Fatto Quotidianao, she had won the Facebook case and the other three had already removed relevant content. She had also had her right to be forgotten rejected and was asked to pay legal fees. She was in the process of changing her name. (Krishna, 2016)

The case of Tiziana (BBC News, 2016) was presented as a case of revenge porn by media, e.g., <nm (International Business Times, September 16, 2016); "Tiziana Cantone: Sex tape suicide fuels revenge porn debate" (The Week, September 16, 2016).

Revenge porn involves a perpetrator uploading nude, semi-nude, or sexual images/videos of a person to the internet without their consent, but Tiziana is said to have sent six different videos, including one of her performing a sex act on a man, to a handful of acquaintances whom she trusted. Nevertheless, her video clips spread across social media. When Tiziana found out that her videos had gone viral she quit her job, moved to another region, and tried to change her name. Tiziana also engaged in a long court battle and won a "right to be forgotten" ruling ordering the video to be removed from various sites and search engines, including Facebook. However, she was also ordered to pay 20,000 euros ($ 22,500) in legal costs. According to several Italian newspapers, this was a final "insult" which may have driven her to take her own life.

On September 20, a few days after the suicide of Tiziana, the Italian Chamber of Deputies approved an anti-cyberbullying law.

The promoter of the anti-cyberbullying law, Donata Lenzi, a member of the Italian parliament for the Democratic Party, when commenting on the law, established a relationship between the case of Carolina Picchio, a fourteen-year-old, who committed suicide after a video was circulated in which she appeared drunk and disorientated at a party, and the case of Tiziana:

"The draft law was created in memory of Carolina, but we would now like to dedicate it to [Tiziana Cantone] as well," she told ANSA. "We are faced with illegal acts that can no longer be passed off as childish pranks" (Forster, 2016).

The Telegraph also reported that:

"As a government, there's not a lot that we can do," said Prime Minister Matteo Renzi. "It's mainly a cultural battle – also a social and political battle. Our commitment is to try to do everything we can... Violence against women is not an ineradicable phenomenon" (The Telegraph, 2016).

The Italian law introduced an all-embracing definition of cyberbullying that includes any form of pressure, aggression, harassment, blackmail, insult, denigration, defamation, as well as any form of identity theft, alteration, illicit acquisition, manipulation, or illicit processing of personal data. In addition, all websites, newspapers, and social networks were required to censor contents deemed violating "the personal and social conditions of victims" (Senato della Repubblica, 2016). As a consequence, a cyberbullying content might have been dependent on what an individual considers injurious and harmful. Cory Doctorow, the famous Canadian-British blogger, journalist, and science fiction author, heavily criticized this proposed law in a blog entitled "Italy on the verge of the stupidest censorship law in European history" (https://boingboing.net/2016/09/18/italy-on-the-verge-of-the-stup.html).

The Italian law is not an isolated case in Europe. Recently, in October 2017, Germany passed a law against hate speech, known locally as NetzDG. This law commits social media giants to promptly remove potentially illegal material within 24 hours of being notified or face paying fines of up to €50 million.[5]

SOME CONSIDERATIONS

The difference between common law systems and civil systems are evident in the case of the Italian law against cyberbullying. Civil law systems are based on legislation (by parliament or other legislative bodies) whilst common law systems are based on judicial decisions.

The Italian law demonstrates the importance of the definition of cyberbullying. In the previous paragraph, it has been illustrated how researchers have different opinions above repetition and power imbalance. These elements are not considered essential to characterize an episode as cyberbullying by some researchers (Dooley, Pyżalski, & Cross, 2009; Menesini & Nocentini, 2009; Smith, 2012). Indeed, they argue that, in the virtual context, a single aggressive act can lead to an indefinite number of repetitions without the contribution of the original perpetrators. In social networking sites, messages, pictures, and video can be shared with countless users all of whom can express their opinion with likes and comments and further disseminate them on the internet. In this light, "looking from the victim's perspective, the cyberbully does not need to repeat an act several times to perpetrate a bullying act" (Menesini et al., 2013, 31), even though, doubtless, it may seem as such from the victim's perspective, so is an aspect to consider in defining coping and rehabilitation strategies. Nevertheless, in a law, the aspect of repetition is important. The perpetrator's perspective should also be considered, since it is different to harass the victim once or continuously over a period of time. And what about the haters who attacked Lori Drew? How is one to consider the conduct of Sarah Wells who revealed the identity of Lori Drew and exposed her personal data?

The question of internet haters will be faced in the next chapter, but it is important, here, to underline that the majority of cyberbullying episodes include group cyber-aggressions.

Furthermore, the case of Tayler Clementi confirms that, in the US, the criminal persecution of cyberbullying is unjustified in the absence of an anti-cyberbullying statute that had passed strict scrutiny. Tayler Clementi, eighteen-years-old, committed suicide after being spied on, unknowingly, by his roommate Dharun Ravi via computer webcam. Tayler was filmed in his room kissing another guy. Ravi tweeted about this and invited other friends to join in the show. A few days later, on September 22, 2010, Tayler jumped to his death from the George Washington Bridge (Foderaro, 2010). On March 16, 2012, Ravi was convicted on all 15 counts for his role in the webcam spying incidents. On May 21, 2012, Ravi was sentenced to 30 days in jail, 3 years' probation, 300 hours of community service, a $10,000 fine, and counseling on cyberbullying and alternative lifestyles. Both the prosecution and the defense filed separate appeals. On October 27, 2016, Ravi accepted a plea deal and pleaded guilty to one count of attempted invasion of privacy, a third-degree felony. He was sentenced to time already served and fines paid, and the remaining charges against him were dropped (Schweber & Foderaro, 2016).

Creating anti-cyberbullying legal policies is a delicate matter. In the legal field, causal relationships that tie events must be demonstrated and proved. Moreover, if a cyberbullying act is unpremeditated, it is impossible to imagine how any punishment can be a deterrent.

Our opinion is that academics should carefully evaluate the social impact of their opinions and collaborate with legal experts in order to disclose disputable issues and the risk of biases.

The definition of anti-cyberbullying policies should involve conversations with students about what cyberbullying means for them. This is the essential premise in order to create comprehensive formal clauses that identify cyberbullying as an example of inappropriate behavior.

Finally, one should consider that the emphasis given by the media to cases of students with mental health problems who committed suicide can enhance criminalization attitudes:

[...] sensationalistic tragedy attracts media attention, and officials solemnly pledge to "do something" to prevent similar events in the future. All too often, this "something" consists in the enactment of a new offense: a crime du jour, Additions to codes are welcome and necessary when statutes proscribe harmful and culpable conduct that was previously noncriminal (Husak, 2008, 36).

NO-CYBERBULLYING EDUCATIONAL POLICIES

The idea of an anti-bullying policy is shared by many schools in the USA that have adopted a zero-tolerance solution against bullying and cyberbullying.

Another crucial aspect for a no-cyberbullying educational program at schools is the participation of students, educators, and families in the development of the program itself. Many researchers and experts suggest using peer mentoring to promote positive online interactions, e.g., organizing lessons by older students who informally teach and share learning experiences with younger students. Another important point is to cultivate a positive school climate. It is crucial to establish and maintain a climate of respect and integrity in schools, in which violations result in informal or formal sanctions. In this regard, it can be useful to utilize specially-created cyberbullying curricula, or general information sessions such as assemblies and in-class discussions, for raising awareness among young people.

Finally, specialists should be invited to talk to staff and students, send information out to parents, and organize educational events involving parents, relatives, and other relevant adults. Such efforts should emphasize the positive advantages offered by the use of new technologies.

It should be remembered that social networking and virtual relationships are useful for people who experience difficulties in forming and maintaining social relationships, and online anonymity may lower the barriers in making new friends. Social networking sites help people to reach large audiences to talk about what is going on in their lives and how they feel (Heirman &

Walrave, 2008). Social networking can also help people to find others who share mainstream but specific interests or who share aspects of identity that are culturally devalued, which could otherwise be quite difficult to do in their everyday social world (McKenna & Green, 2002).

Also, following from Meredith (2010), we would add a consideration to the above suggestions regarding the overcriminalization of cyberbullying. We broadly agree with her observations that one ought to avoid overcriminalization, and are careful to criminalize only criminal acts. In this regard, Meredith reports a general failure to distinguish between the cyberbullying perpetrated by minors from that perpetrated by adults, and underlines the difficulty of regulating unpleasant speech that doesn't actually reach the level of being a true threat. She cites some cases (p. 328) in which the legal establishment considered cyberbullying to be a juvenile issue and thus ruled that schools create policy to deal with it. This is a sort of shifting of the blame which charges schools with extra responsibility.

From this perspective, greater efforts should be concentrated on increasing the level of education about internet safety. Educators ought to be empowered with the proper tools to inform students and parents about how to use technology in a prudent manner. It is crucial to provide information that raises awareness about the risks of cyberspace. In the first place, children should be taught to utilize the positive aspects of the internet without becoming victims of the hidden dangers that lurk inside.

Sanchez alludes to a legislative effort, but her focus could also be extended to software producers who have the possibility of helping to prevent cyberbullying through the introduction of new and sophisticated software tools for the safe use of their products. Moreover, the role of the media should also not be ignored.

USA LEGISLATIVE CONCERNS REGARDING CHILD SAFETY ONLINE

Since the early 1980s, the USA has made considerable legislative efforts to protect children when they play and communicate on line. In 1998, the *Child Online Protection Act* (COPA) was approved. This was a law whose purpose was to restrict online access to "material that is harmful to minors" or that depicted actual or simulated sexually explicit content "in a manner patently offensive with respect to minors" (Child Online Protection Act, 1998).[6]

The motivation of this act was the spread of internet use among children:

In 1998, sixteen million children under age eighteen were reported to be using the Internet, nearly doubling the number of children reported to be online in 1997. Over six million of these children were age twelve and under, up from the 3.5 million reported to be online the previous year. One of the perils for children of surfing the Internet, particularly the World Wide Web, is the proliferation of "adult" sites on the Web that promote and sell pornographic materials. There are currently estimated to be over 30,000 such sites, which generate nearly $1 billion in annual revenues (Zick, 1998, 1147).

In 2000, the Children's Internet Protection Act (CIPA) was enacted by Congress. This act addressed concerns about children's access to obscene or harmful content over the Internet. CIPA imposes certain requirements on schools or libraries that receive discounts for Internet access or internal connections through the E-rate program – a program that makes certain communications services and products more affordable for eligible schools and libraries.

The protection measures must block or filter Internet access to pictures that are: (a) obscene; (b) child pornography; or (c) harmful to minors (for computers that are accessed by minors).

In early 2001, the Federal Communication Commission issued rules implementing CIPA and provided updates to those rules in 2011.

In 2007, the Broadband Data Services Improvement,[7] also known as the Protecting Children in the Twenty-first Century Act, added a provision to CIPA requiring that schools receiving e-rate and other technology funds must provide instruction in internet safety. It established that all schools receiving e-rate discounts must teach students "about appropriate online behavior, including interacting with other individuals on social networking sites and chat rooms and cyberbullying awareness and response" (Public Law 110-385).

In December 2012, the Federal Trade Commission amended the COPPA rule. This revision, effective from the first of July 2013, introduced additional parental notice and consent requirements, amended definitions, and added other obligations for organizations that:

- Operate a website or online service that is "directed to children" under 13 and that collects "personal information" from users;

- Knowingly collects personal information from persons under 13 through a website or online service.

On November 19, 2015, the Federal Trade Commission approved a new method for companies to get parental consent for their children to access online services covered by the COPPA Rule.

Based on an application submitted by Riyo Verified Ltd., the Commission approved the use of "face match to verified photo identification" (FMVPI) as a method to verify that the person providing consent for a child to use an online service is in fact the child's parent. FMVPI consists in a two-step process:

In the first step, a parent provides an image of their photo identification, such as a passport or driver's license. The authenticity and legitimacy of the document is then verified using various technologies that analyze the image to ensure that it is an authentic government-issued identification. In a second step, the parent is then prompted to provide a picture of themselves taken with a phone or web camera, which is analyzed to confirm that the photo is of a live person and not a photo of a still photo. The image is then compared to the identification photo using facial recognition technology to confirm whether the person submitting the photo is in fact the one in the identification. (FTC, 2015).

Ultimately, cyberbullying replaced the legislative concerns about online sexual predators. It is now the topical internet safety issue:

Despite the sentiments of the attorneys general responding to the report of Internet safety Technical Task Force, cyberbullying eventually gained the attention of policymakers. Although at the federal level there has been little movement beyond a provision of the Broadband Data Improvement Act of 2008 that linked cyberbullying education to continued e-rate funding, forty-eight states have passed cyberbullying statutes that cover forms of "electronic harassment" (Hinduja and Patchin 2015). But state laws were widely criticized because they frequently included unfunded mandates and were seen as ineffective in preventing cyberbullying behavior among students in everyday practice (Clark, 2013). At the same time, the rise of cyberbullying led adults to feel that bullying had become epidemic, and it is increasingly being framed as a public health issue rather than a crime. (Fisk, 2016, 67-68)

CONCLUSION

The definition of anti-cyberbullying statutes is a hugely complex issue.

Nevertheless, it is important to combat cyberbullying in a legal scope. This requires an exploration of the various aspects of cyberbullying in order to acquire a greater awareness of its multifarious facets. It is impossible to design an effective prevention program without an extended knowledge of the legal implications of acts of cyberbullying.

Moreover, teachers and educators must keep in mind that current regulations have a low impact in combatting and punishing cyberbullying. Investments are needed in developing and running effective education programs.

Social networking sites such as Instagram, Twitter, Facebook, and Snapchat allow anyone older than fourteen to become members once they register. Registration requires users to submit personal information, choose a password, and agree to the Terms of Service and Privacy Policy (TOS) by checking a box or completing other operations for accepting the service. However, despite the age limits, many under age kids have social media profiles (BBC News, 2017).

The majority of them are unaware of the threats that can exist in cyberspace, since they don't know how the internet works and are not experienced about the consequence of their online behavior.

The acquisition of knowledge about the world of social networks is therefore essential, as is knowledge about the legal implications of online behavior.

The next chapter will focus on technical and societal aspects of social networks that contribute to improving the cyberbullying mosaic.

REFERENCES

BBC News. (2017). *Under-age social media use 'on the rise', says Ofcom*. Available at: https://www.bbc.com/news/technology-42153694

Briggs, R. M. (2018). Criminalization of Cyberbullying: The Constitutionality of Creating an Online Neverland for Children Under a Tinker-Bell Analysis. *Louisiana Law Review*, *78*(3), 1059–1100.

Britto, S., & Noga-Styron, K. E. (2014). Media consumption and support for capital punishment. *Criminal Justice Review*, *39*(1), 81–100. doi:10.1177/0734016814522645

Callanan, V. J., & Rosenberger, J. S. (2011). Media and public perceptions of the police: Examining the impact of race and personal experience. *Policing and Society*, *21*(2), 167–189. doi:10.1080/10439463.2010.540655

Campbel, M., & Zavrsnik, A. (2013). Should cyberbullying be criminalized? In P. K. Smith & G. Steffgen (Eds.), *Cyberbullying through new media* (pp. 65–82). Psychology Press.

Clark, M. (2013). *49 states now have anti-bullying laws. How that working out?* Available at: http://www.governing.com/news/headlines/49-States-Now-Have-Anti-Bullying-Laws-Hows-that-Working-Out.html

Coburn, P. I., Connolly, D. A., & Roesch, R. (2015). Cyberbullying: Is federal criminal legislation the solution? *Canadian Journal of Criminology and Criminal Justice*, *57*(4), 566–579. doi:10.3138/cjccj.2014.E43

Copeland, W. E., Wolke, D., Angold, A., & Costello, E. J. (2013). Adult psychiatric outcomes of bullying and being bullied by peers in childhood and adolescence. *JAMA Psychiatry*, *70*(4), 419–426. doi:10.1001/jamapsychiatry.2013.504 PMID:23426798

Demker, M., Towns, A., Duus-Otterström, G., & Sebring, J. (2008). Fear and punishment in Sweden: Exploring penal attitudes. *Punishment & Society*, *10*(3), 319–332. doi:10.1177/1462474508090228

Dooley, J. J., Pyżalski, J., & Cross, D. (2009). Cyberbullying versus face-to-face bullying: A theoretical and conceptual review. *The Journal of Psychology*, *217*(4), 182–188.

Dowler, K. (2003). Media consumption and public attitudes toward crime and justice: The relationship between fear of crime, punitive attitudes, and perceived police effectiveness. *The Journal of Criminal Justice and Popular Culture*, *10*(2), 109–126.

El Asam, A., & Samara, M. (2016). Cyberbullying and the law: A review of psychological and legal challenges. *Computers in Human Behavior*, *65*, 127–141. doi:10.1016/j.chb.2016.08.012

Fagan, J., & Tyler, T. R. (2005). Legal socialization of children and adolescents. *Social Justice Research*, *18*(3), 217–241. doi:10.100711211-005-6823-3

FindLaw. (2010). *Snyder V. Blue Mountain School District*. Available at: https://caselaw.findlaw.com/us-3rd-circuit/1506476.html

Fisk, N. W. (2016). *Framing internet safety: The governance of youth online*. MIT Press. doi:10.7551/mitpress/10311.001.0001

Foderaro, L. W. (2010). Private moment made public, then a fatal jump. *The New York Times*. Available at: https://www.nytimes.com/2010/09/30/nyregion/30suicide.html

Forster, K. (2016). Tiziana Cantone: Woman's suicide after sex tape went viral prompts calls for stronger online privacy laws. *The Independent*. Available at: https://www.independent.co.uk/news/world/europe/tiziana-cantone-sex-tape-revenge-porn-suicide-death-italy-online-privacy-laws-campaign-overhaul-a7310956.html

FTC. (2015). *Grants Approval for New COPPA Verifiable Parental Consent Method*. Available at: https://www.ftc.gov/news-events/press-releases/2015/11/ftc-grants-approval-new-coppa-verifiable-parental-consent-method

Galeste, M. A., Fradella, H. F., & Vogel, B. (2012). Sex offender myths in print media: Separating fact from fiction in US newspapers. *Western Criminology Review*, *13*, 4–24.

Hart, H. L. A., Hart, H. L. A., & Green, L. (2012). *The concept of law*. Oxford University Press. doi:10.1093/he/9780199644704.001.0001

Heirman, W., & Walrave, M. (2008). Assessing Concerns and Issues about the Mediation of Technology in Cyberbullying. *Cyberpsychology: Journal of Psychosocial Research on Cyberspace, 2*(2), article 1. Available at: http://cyberpsychology.eu/view.php?cisloclanku=2008111401&article=1

Hinduja, S., & Patchin, J. (2015). *State cyberbullying laws: A brief review of state cyberbullying laws and policies*. Cyberbullying Research Center. Available at: https://cyberbullying.org/Bullying-and-Cyberbullying-Laws.pdf

Hinduja, S., & Patchin, J. W. (2018). *Preventing cyberbullying: Top ten tips for educators*. Available at: https://cyberbullying.org/preventing-cyberbullying-top-ten-tips-for-educators

Husak, D. (2008). *Overcriminalization: The limits of the criminal law*. Oxford University Press.

International Business Times. (2016). *Italian revenge porn victim Tiziana Cantone commits suicide*. Available at: https://www.ibtimes.co.uk/italian-revenge-porn-victim-tiziana-cantone-commits-suicide-1581555?utm_medium=Social&utm_campaign=Echobox&utm_source=Twitter&utm_term=Autofeed#link_time=1473980735

Kerr, O. (2009). *Lori Drew Opinion Handed Down – Judge Grants Motion to Dismiss on Vagueness Grounds*. Available at: http://volokh.com/posts/1251601962.shtml

Krishna, R. (n.d.). This Woman Killed Herself After Her Leaked Sex Tape Became A Meme. *BuzzFeed*. Available at: https://www.buzzfeednews.com/article/krishrach/this-woman-reportedly-killed-herself-after-an-explicit-video#.bqyGwOx8y0

Little, R. K. (2017). Hating Hate Speech: Why Current First Amendment Doctrine Does Not Condemn a Careful Ban. *Hastings Constitutional Law Quarterly*, *45*, 577.

Martinez-Pecino, R., & Durán, M. (2016). I love you but I cyberbully you: The role of hostile sexism. *Journal of Interpersonal Violence*. doi:10.1177/0886260516645817 PMID:27118344

Marwick, A. E., & Miller, R. (2014). Online harassment, defamation, and hateful speech: A primer of the legal landscape. *Fordham Center on Law and Information Policy Report*, (2).

McKenna, K. Y., & Green, A. S. (2002). Virtual group dynamics. *Group Dynamics*, *6*(1), 116–127. doi:10.1037/1089-2699.6.1.116

Menesini, E., & Nocentini, A. (2009). Cyberbullying definition and measurement: Some critical considerations. *The Journal of Psychology*, *217*(4), 230–232.

Menesini, E., Nocentini, A., Palladino, B. E., Sheithauer, H., Schultze-Krumbholz, A., Frisén, A., ... Blaya, C. (2013). Definitions of cyberbullying. In *Cyberbullying through the New Media* (pp. 23–36). Psychology Press.

Meredith, J. P. (2010). Combating cyberbullying: Emphasizing education over criminalization. *Federal Communications Law Journal*, *63*(1), 311–340.

Olweus, D. (2003). A profile of bullying at school. *Educational Leadership*, *60*(6), 12–17.

Paul, S., Smith, P. K., & Blumberg, H. H. (2012). Investigating legal aspects of cyberbullying. *Psicothema*, *24*(4), 640–645. PMID:23079364

Pokin, S. (2007, November 11). *MySpace Hoax Ends with Suicide* of Dardenne Prairie Teen. *Suburban Journals.*

Rigby, K. (2008). *Children and bullying: How parents and educators can reduce bullying at school.* Blackwell Publishing.

Schweber, N., & Foderaro, L. W. (2016). Roommate in Tyler Clementi Case Pleads Guilty to Attempted Invasion of Privacy. *The New York Times*. Available at: https://www.nytimes.com/2016/10/28/nyregion/dharun-ravi-tyler-clementi-case-guilty-plea.html

Shariff, S. (2014). *Evidence given to the Standing Committee on Justice and Human Right at the House of Commons, Canada*. Available at: http://www.ourcommons.ca/DocumentViewer/en/41-2/JUST/meeting-28/evidence

Smith, P. K. (2012). Cyberbullying and cyber aggression. In S. Jimerson, A. Nickerson, M. J. Mayer, & M. J. Furlong (Eds.), *Handbook of school violence and school safety* (pp. 111–121). Routledge.

The Telegraph. (2016). *Four questioned in Italy after woman abused online over viral sex video commits suicide*. Available at: https://www.telegraph.co.uk/news/2016/09/15/four-questioned-in-italy-after-woman-abused-online-over-viral-se/

The Week. (2016). *Tiziana Cantone: Sex tape suicide fuels revenge porn debate*. Available at: https://www.theweek.co.uk/76654/tiziana-cantone-sex-tape-suicide-fuels-revenge-porn-debate

Zetter, K. (2007). Cyberbullying Suicide Stokes the Internet Fury Machine. *Wired*. Available at: https://www.wired.com/2007/11/cyberbullying-suicide-stokes-the-internet-fury-machine/

Zick, T. (1998). Congress, the Internet, and the intractable pornography problem: The Child Online Protection Act of 1998. *Creighton Law Review*, *32*, 1147–1204.

KEY TERMS AND DEFINITIONS

Child Online Protection Act (COPA): A law approved in the US in 1998 whose purpose was restricting minors from access to online harmful and offensive material.

Civil Law: Also called the *continental* or *Romano-Germanic* legal system, is based on concepts, categories, and rules derived from Roman law.

Common Law: The ancient law of England based upon societal customs and recognized and enforced by the judgments and decrees of the courts.

First Amendment: The US principle that prevents Congress from making any law respecting an establishment of religion, prohibiting the free exercise of religion, or abridging the freedom of speech, the freedom of the press, the right to peaceably assemble, or the right to petition for a governmental redress of grievances.

Law Sources in the USA: There are five sources: constitutional law, statutory law, treaties, administrative regulations, and the common law (which includes case law).

Outing and Trickery: Is when someone hacks an account and starts posting embarrassing photos, texts, conversations, and more.

Revenge Porn: The publication of sexually explicit material portraying someone who has not consented to the image or video being shared.

Strict Scrutiny: A form of judicial review that courts use to determine the constitutionality of certain laws.

Supreme Court: The highest federal court of justice of the US and the final interpreter of federal laws including the Constitution; it may act only within the context of a case in which it has jurisdiction.

True Threat: The serious expression of intent to perform an illegal violent act that is directed toward a particular person or group.

ENDNOTES

1. The European Convention on Human Rights was drafted in 1950 and has been in force since 1953.
2. *Chaplinsky*, 315 U.S. at 572, (1942).
3. *Roth*, 354 U.S. at 487, (1957).
4. 22 Ill.357 U.S. 458 U.S. 886, 102 S. Ct. 3409, 73 L. Ed. 2d 1215 (1982).

5 Federal Ministry of Justice and Consumer Protection: https://www.gesetze-im-internet.de/netzdg/BJNR335210017.html; last accessed on 24.07.2018.

6 https://www.congress.gov/bill/105th-congress/house-bill/3783; last accessed 04.22.2019.

7 https://www.fcc.gov/general/broadband-data-improvement-act; last accessed 04.22.2019.

Chapter 3
Cyberbullying and Social Networking Sites

Gilberto Marzano
Rezekne Academy of Technologies, Latvia

ABSTRACT

Media pay considerable attention to episodes that involve children and adolescents and the internet. Usually, the excessive time spent on social networking sites is highlighted as the principal source of risk for cyberbullying as well as for the various types of cyber addictions that can develop. Anonymity is reported to be one of the principal factors that favor cyberbullying, whilst sexting and homophobia are indicated as being among the principal circumstances that bring victims to commit suicide. In this chapter, some relevant aspects of the use of social networking sites will be illustrated and some notions regarding how the internet works will be introduced. Other questions, such as the spread of cyber hate and online incivility will be discussed, and a case of the incautious use of Facebook by a higher public education institution will be reported. Many concepts highlighted here will be useful in the following chapters in which strategies for the prevention of cyberbullying will be considered.

INTRODUCTION

Over the last two decades, the growth of the internet in every field of contemporary society has been spectacular. The impact of digital media has been without precedent. Internet users can, at the same time, be both content consumers and content producers, directly addressing a large number of other

DOI: 10.4018/978-1-5225-8076-8.ch003

potential users. To all effects, they are *prosumers* (producers *and* consumers), to use the term coined many years ago by Toffler (1980).

Young people are often portrayed as being ever connected and spending their time exchanging messages with virtual mates, and various negative effects of social media have been broadly underlined (Smith, Morgan, & Monks, 2017; Turner & Lefevre, 2017; Vossen & Valkenburg, 2016). On the other hand, many educators exalt the positive contribution of social media to learning, since it offers exceptional opportunities for the lifelong learning process and for building personalized educational paths. Digital Social Learning has been attracting the interest of many researchers, who share the notion that "learning is a social activity" where individuals achieve their learning goals by interacting with each other (Hamid, Waycott, Kurnia, & Chang, 2015; Liao, Huang, Chen, & Huang, 2015).

A large segment of the total users of the internet are children, adolescents, and university students, and they tend to view the internet as their primary means of socialization.

The *Pew Research Center* indicates that a full 95% of the USA teens have access to a smartphone, and 45% say they are online almost invariably (Anderson & Jiang, 2018). Eurostat (2016) has observed the situation to be similar in Europe (Figure 1).

Figure 2 shows that roughly half (51%) of the USA teens, aged 13 to 17, claim they use Facebook, notably fewer than use YouTube, Instagram, or Snapchat.

Figure 1. The proportion of people making daily use of the internet in 2016, by age and by formal educational attainment
Source: Eurostat, online data code: isoc_ciegi_ac and isoc_ci_ac_i

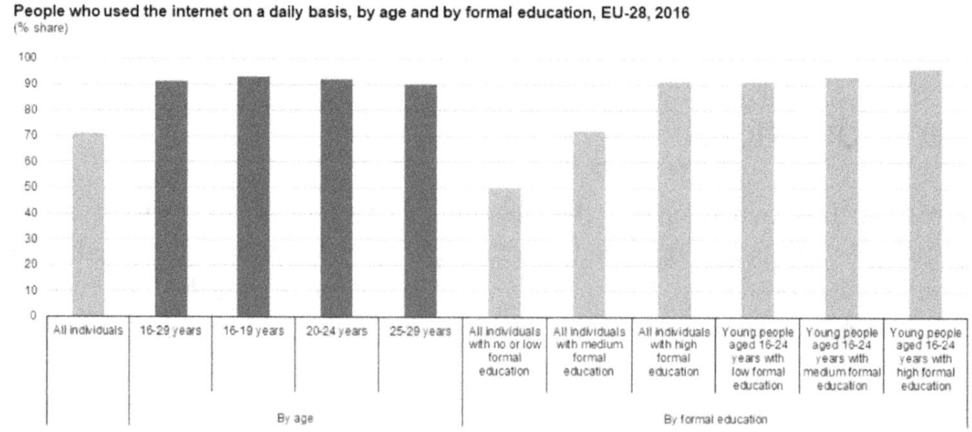

Figure 2. The most popular online platforms among teens
Source: Pew Research Center, survey conducted March 7-April 10 2018

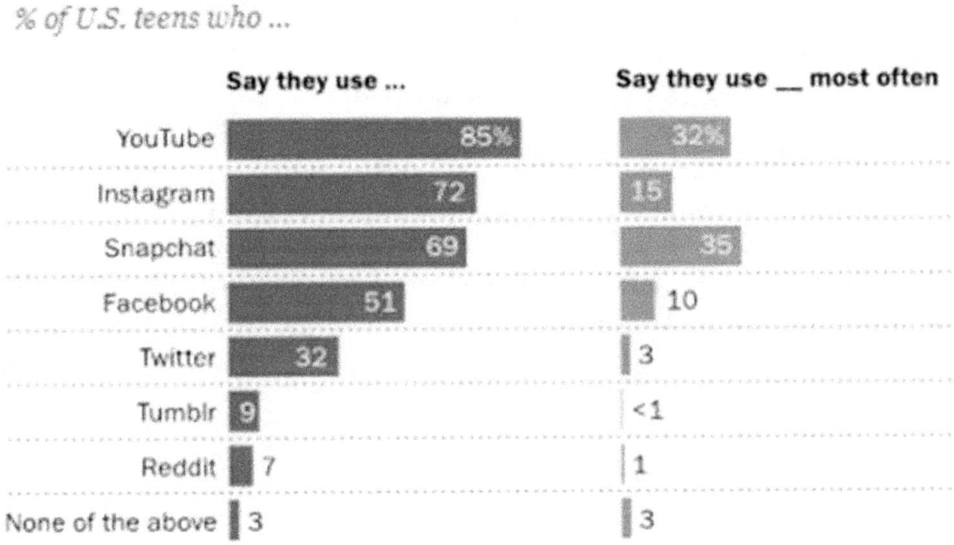

In the last few years, the nature of the internet has passed from stationary connection to always-on connections, and young people represent the leading edge of mobile connectivity. Their way of using technology often signals future social changes (Madden et al., 2013; Agosto, Abba, & Naughton, 2012). Nowadays, youngsters are more likely to use smartphones than laptops, and this is influencing their social relationships. Moreover, the massive use of smartphones often has the effect of decreasing their attention to the contents exchanged. Emails and online messages are read and answered hastily, reacting quickly, and sometimes without fully understanding the meaning.

One element to consider is the overvaluation of social networks as a source of information, especially in respect to Facebook. A popular belief is that Facebook is a very good way to access information, and many people are persuaded that it is a valid and compelling source of news (Ellison, Vitak, Gray & Lampe, 2014). In this regard, some researchers suggested that Facebook could positively impact on education (Muñoz & Towner, 2009). Students could use Facebook to contact peers in order to exchange information on course assignments, and teachers could send students useful links. However, no empirical findings have been observed that support these suggestions (Hew, 2011). Indeed, Facebook is not a learning tool but, rather, an application designed to allow users to share photographs and personal information, and join groups of friends (Buckman, 2005).

Facebook is considered the leading social networking site, although other sites such as Snapchat have been designed with the same aim to connect people. In the USA, surveys report that Facebook is ubiquitous among students, with over 90% participation amongst undergraduates (Ellison, Steinfield, & Lampe, 2007; Patterson, 2012; Stutzman, 2006).

The following paragraphs focus on how young people use social networking sites and construct their virtual identity. Understanding their perspective of social media is essential to figure out their vulnerability to cyberbullying.

However, before moving on to address social networking sites, it would be useful to introduce the definition given by Boyd and Ellison, even reporting the distinction the authors made between *social network sites* and *social networking sites*:

We define social network sites as web-based services that allow individuals to (1) construct a public or semi-public profile within a bounded system, (2) articulate a list of other users with whom they share a connection, and (3) view and traverse their list of connections and those made by others within the system. The nature and nomenclature of these connections may vary from site to site.

While we use the term "social network site" to describe this phenomenon, the term "social networking sites" also appears in public discourse, and the two terms are often used interchangeably. We chose not to employ the term "networking" for two reasons: emphasis and scope. "Networking" emphasizes relationship initiation, often between strangers. While networking is possible on these sites, it is not the primary practice on many of them, nor is it what differentiates them from other forms of computer-mediated communication or CMC. (Boyd & Ellison, 2007, p. 211)

In this book, the terms *social networking sites* and *social networks* are preferred to *social network site*s since, currently, they are the most used, as a search on Google can confirm.

WHY YOUNG PEOPLE USE SOCIAL NETWORKING SITES

The explosion of social networking sites has been put in relation with the desire of people, especially youngsters, to express their social identity to others (Tsay-Vogel, 2016). In them, a user can easily reconfigure their social identity, modifying their profile as they wish (Cheng & Guo, 2015). Moreover, the same user can create multiple, different profiles corresponding to the different roles they have in real life or offering different images of themselves. At the heart of the explosion in online communication is people's desire to construct a cherished representation of themselves that is appreciated by peers (Livingstone & Brake, 2010). Table 1 reports some important dates along the timeline in social media history.

Contrary to the popular belief that young people are isolated and are loners, virtual communication is now also a daily habit for sociable young people with active face-to-face social lives.

Online communications, including social networks, are primarily used to sustain local friendships already established offline, rather than to make new

Table 1. The most pivotal moments in social media's history

Date	Event
1998	Google was funded
2003	MySpace opened
2003	Mark Zuckerberg launched Facemash
2004	Facebook started
2004	Gmail was born
2005	YouTube opened
2006	YouTube was purchased by Google
2006	Twitter started tweeting
2007	Tumblr come on the scene
2009	WhatsApp started
2010	Instagram was launched
2010	Pinterest started
2010	Snapchat opened
2012	Facebook celebrates one billion
2014	Twitter proclaimed 2014 as the "Year of the Selfie"
2015	Periscope became the favorite app for streaming and watching live events
2016	Facebook live was launched
2016	The U.S. election and social media's fake news crisis
2017	Twitter doubles the character limit
2018	Cambridge Analytica scandal
2018	Instagram launches IGTV app for long-form video

Source: Author's own elaboration

contacts with distant strangers (Boneva, Quinn, Kraut, Kiesler & Shklovski, 2006; Ellison, Steinfield & Lampe, 2007; Gross, 2004; Mesch & Talmud, 2007; Steijn, 2014; Valkenburg & Peter, 2007, 2009).

Young people are connected with their peers anywhere and anytime to stay in touch, express themselves, and share daily experiences. Research shows there isn't any discontinuity between online and offline, or virtual and face-to-face, interactions, a fact that Lenhart had already recognized many years ago:

However, these new tools seem to ignore a fundamental disconnect between our online and offline identities. In the offline world, we don't present ourselves in the same way to all people in our lives - we show different sides of ourselves to our mothers, our friends, our employers. And even in the age of fine-grained privacy tools, those tools do not eliminate the complexity of figuring out how to best present oneself in a multi-use public space, particularly for those who have personal, professional and family contacts on these sites. (Lenhart, 2008)

It is astonishing that, even now, young people don't realize that their messages and personal information can not only be read by their mates but also spread around on the web, and that they will endure almost permanently. Furthermore, they would be surprised to know that colleges and potential employers actively investigate the social networking profiles of applicants before granting acceptance or interviews.

In 2010, Eric Schmidt, the CEO of Google, claimed that young people should be entitled to change their identity to escape their misspent youth, which is now recorded in excruciating detail on social networking sites such as Facebook (Wardrop, 2010).

Most students don't evaluate the content they are publishing online, and that could bring about negative consequences even months or years down the road.

The internet and social networks have changed the way we think about privacy and share personal information outside our friendship group. Researchers indicate an *online disinhibition effect* as being responsible for the loosening of the normal social inhibitions present in face-to-face interactions. People are more likely to share personal information or display more emotional behavior when they are online, including anti-social behavior such as rude language and harsh criticisms.

The spread of smartphones has increased the opportunity for young people to livestream and post photos at times when they are vulnerable, for example when they have been drinking or are very emotional. Accordingly, the risk of 'sharing too much' hugely increases. Regulatory frameworks on issues such as data protection and privacy have not kept pace with technological changes, and this hinders young people's ability to control their online presence.

Currently, concerns have been raised about the sending of nude images online, although the evidence indicates that this is not a widespread problem. Only a small minority of young people are likely to send naked pictures of themselves via social media. A 2016 study by Middlesex University for the National Society for the Prevention of Cruelty to Children (NSPCC) found that only 2.9 per cent of children aged 11 to 16 had taken a fully naked picture of themselves (Martellozzo et al., 2016).

MOBILE MESSENGER APPS

Social networking sites are not the only means young people use to socialize. Mobile messenger apps such as WhatsApp, Facebook Messenger, Instagram, and Twitter are their most common way of communicating. These apps enable messages, photos, and video to be sent online to selected contacts over the internet. WhatsApp is the most widely used, while others such as GroupMe and Kik Messenger are also popular. They allow users to be connected and to communicate without fees or limits.

Microblogging sites such as Twitter and Tumblr are also widely used.

Snapchat is one of the most appreciated messenger apps since it was the first to support the function of deleting messages after viewing them.

Recently, WhatsApp and Gmail added the possibility to delete and revoke messages after sending them. It is possible to remove a message up to a few minutes after it has been posted, making it disappear entirely from conversations or group chats. This feature was conceived as a means of remedying unintentional mistakes, but it can also offer cyberbullies a means to harass their victims. They can post offensive messages that vanish after a while, eliminating any proof. In this way, a function aimed at solving the issue of sending wrong or incomplete messages can be used to bewilder victims without leaving any trace of the harassment. However, the receiver can store or forward the message if they are quick before it is deleted. WhatsApp warns users about this possibility.

To better understand internet dynamics and to further consider the concept of relative anonymity associated with cyberbullying, some basic notions on how the internet works will be developed in the next paragraphs.

HOW THE INTERNET WORKS

Nowadays, there are more than 3 billion internet users across the globe, representing some 40 per cent of the world's population (Figure 3).

In chapter 1, it was emphasized that the internet is not one single network but a massive network of networks.

Figure 4 shows the difference between centralized systems, decentralized systems, and networking systems.

When dealing with the internet, one has to take into account that the World Wide Web (WWW, or simply Web) is not a synonym of the internet. The WWW is merely the combination of all the resources and users that, on the internet, are using the Hypertext Transfer Protocol (HTTP).

Tim Berners-Lee was the inventor of the WWW, namely a communications model that, through HTTP, enables the exchange of information over the internet. In fact, the Web is just one of the ways that information can be disseminated over the internet, and the HTTP protocol is only one of the languages spoken over the internet to transmit data. For example, most e-mail systems use SMTP (Simple Message Transfer Protocol) to send emails from one server to another.

Browsers, such as Google Chrome, Internet Explorer, or Mozilla Firefox, allow users to access Web documents, called web pages, that are linked to each other via hyperlinks. Web pages can contain graphics, sounds, text, and video.

Figure 3. Internet access by the world's population
Source: World Bank, 2016, p. 8

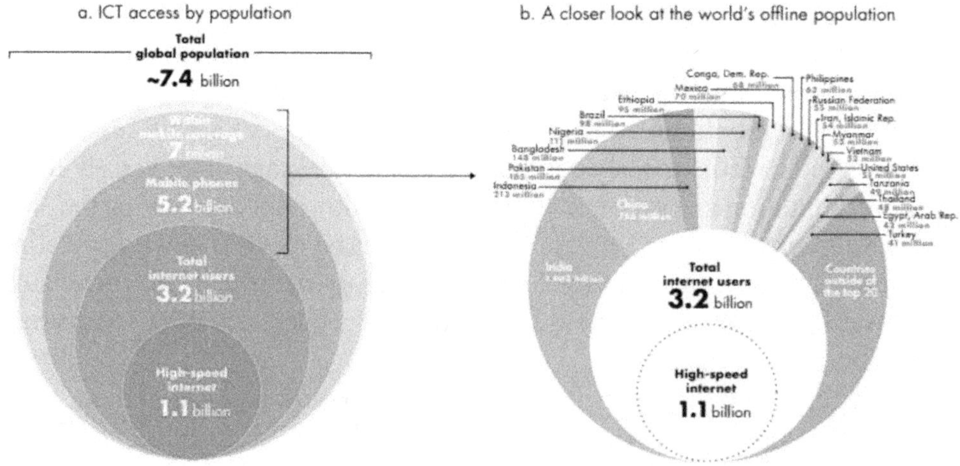

Figure 4. The three basic computing architectures
Source: author's own elaboration

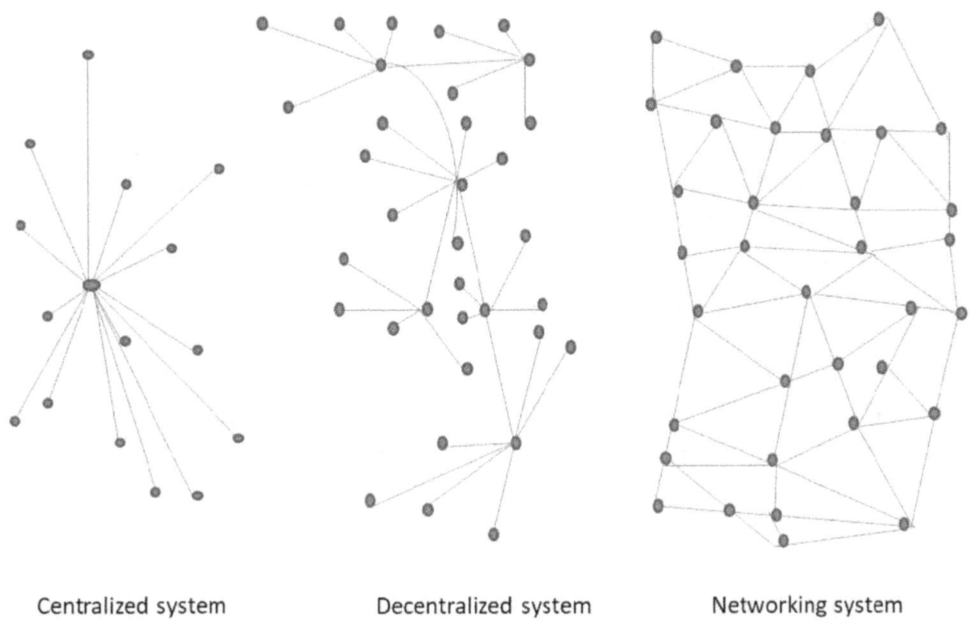

The Web, also referred to as the *surface web*, represents just a part of the internet, albeit a large one. The complement of the surface web is the *deep web* that is enormous in comparison to the surface web. The deep web, also called *hidden web* or *invisible web*, encompasses all of the information stored online that isn't indexed by standard search engines, such as Google or Bing. It includes email systems, bank account activity, private, government, and other organizational networks, and so on. The deep web is not a single, centralized place. Just like the surface web, it is scattered through servers across the world.

The deep web is often confused with the *darknet*, also called the *dark web*, *black web*, or *black net*. The dark web forms a small part of the deep web. Darknet websites are accessible only through browsers such as Tor ("The Onion Routing" project) and I2P ("Invisible Internet Project"). The darknet is also used for illegal activity, such as illegal trade, forums, and as a media of exchange for pedophiles and terrorists.

From a technical point of view, however, to reach information on the surface web or deep web, as well as the dark web, one merely needs to know the address of the server containing the desired information.

How is it possible, though, to find the servers that host the information one is looking for?

To do that, an Internet Protocol (IP) address is necessary. An IP address is a uniquely assigned string of characters that functions as the address for endpoints on the internet. Every electronic device (computer, tablet, smartphone, etc.) needs an IP address assigned by an authorized Internet Service Provider. To reach the server that hosts the site (domain) containing the desired information, one needs to know its corresponding IP address. This is possible since each domain is registered in the Domain Name System (DNS) that serves as an index in which IP addresses are associated with univocal human-friendly computer hostnames.

The DNS is global and decentralized. Its architecture can be thought of as a tree. Entry into the top-level domains is controlled internationally through the Internet Corporation for Assigned Names and Numbers (ICANN), a private, non-profit organization created in 1998 to run the various internet administration and operation tasks that had previously been performed by US government organizations.

When a web page is requested, the request is broken down into packets and sent across the internet through the so-called transport and network layers that are responsible for making sure that all the chunks arrive free of errors at their destination and are reassembled in the correct order. The response from a server to the client asking for the information follows the same process.

But how do these packets know how to get across the internet to their destination? The internet is a network of networks. These networks, in turn, form nodes called Autonomous Systems (AS). Traffic is routed locally through the AS and controlled by the policies of that organization. Each AS has a set of contiguous blocks of IP addresses and forms the "home" of these destinations. All have at least one connection to another AS, while large ISPs might have many. As such, routing to a particular IP address is simply a matter of finding its AS.

This can present problems, since the internet is really big and AS interconnections change and shift over time. Because of the impossibility of creating a global address index, a fairly simple principle of routing has been adopted. At each point of the network, a router examines the address of the incoming packet. If the destination is inside the network, it keeps the packet and sends it to the relevant computer. Otherwise, it consults a routing table to determine the best next step to send the packet closer to its destination. Each router constructs its own internal, temporary model of how best to route the traffic passing through. This model, in turn, is shared so that a router's neighbor knows how it will pass along new traffic.

In synthesis, all devices connected to the internet are associated with a unique identifier, namely the IP. It consists of a numeric or alphanumeric string assigned by an Internet Service Provider (ISP), and is required to send and receive information to/from servers hosting data. Even in the case in which an internet connection is made using a temporary IP number assigned for a single session, that number is logged by the ISP, and it is possible to go back to the identity of its user.

From this brief illustration of how the internet works, two important elements emerge. The first is that the entire internet system functions without any top-down coordination. This requires that internet users and gatekeepers behave properly. Simply put, the internet is based on trust. It is a system that works efficiently, but it can be broken, either by accident or by maliciously feeding the system bad data. The second is that true anonymity on the internet is not easy to obtain. Indeed, the internet was originally developed as a means of linking military networks, and with the aim of providing them with disruption tolerance and at low cost. Accountability and identity were not among the highest priorities for the developers. When one accesses the internet, an IP address is assigned that can be unique or randomly changing, depending on the nature of the connection. Thus, a traceable IP is left embedded in emails or in whatever one does online. A cell phone IP can similarly be traced, and even located exactly on the map, if someone has advanced technologies and suitable network algorithms. Dynamic IP's can be traced too, using Reverse-DNS where the network or ISP allows for it. Being truly anonymous on the internet is. therefore, not easy, and the anonymity offered should really be defined as a *relative anonymity*.

For a deeper background knowledge, although a little out of date now, *How the Internet works* by Gralla (2006) explains, in plain language and pictures, all that it is essential to know about the internet.

THE RELATIVE ANONYMITY OF THE INTERNET

It is a commonly held belief that the internet is anonymous, yet the recent case of Cambridge Analitica (Guzdial & Landau, 2018; Kak, 2018) clearly demonstrates that internet users are, actually, monitored continuously. Their data is gathered, recorded, and processed without their knowledge. Sophisticated computer programs track and analyze what a user is doing on the Web. Their preferences are classified, and profiles are built analyzing their online behavior. Indeed, the trading of personal data by the dominant social network and search engine providers has long been reported, denounced, and investigated (Schwartz, 2003; Acquisti, Taylor, & Wagman, 2016). User data is not only used for direct marketing and sales promotions, but also in efforts to capture votes in political elections.

When users go online to search for information, e.g., for travels, books, or goods, they risk that data brokers are collecting their preferences and personal data. Internet activities are logged, and the sites and pages visited are recorded. The incognito browsing mode only prevents any chronology from being created. The tracks of the navigating are not hidden, and data-mining companies can easily create detailed profiles of internet users, even when they post information anonymously or pseudonymously. Despite the various tricks one can use to try to hide their identity, real anonymity is not granted on the internet. To communicate on the internet, every device must use an IP, even if temporary, and avoiding being tracked is therefore impossible. However, risks to privacy can be reduced. On the web, one can find tips, tricks, and shortcuts to help preserve privacy and stay anonymous online (Friesland, 2018; Irvine, 2018; Tufnell, 2015).

One of the most popular software for protecting user navigation is the *Tor browser*, that has been improved and maintained by a non-profit organization. Tor is the acronym of *The Onion Router*, and is derived from the name of a project initially developed in the mid 1990s by the U.S. Navy as a way to protect government communications. The Tor coding was released under a free license in 2004 by the Naval Research Laboratory. In 2006, The Tor Project, a research-education nonprofit organization, was founded to improve and maintain the Tor software. As reported on its website (https://www.torproject.org/), Tor is a free software that provides an open network aimed at defending against traffic analysis. The Tor network connects a group of volunteer-operated servers that create virtual tunnels which allow people and groups to improve their privacy and security on the internet. The Tor browser can be downloaded for free and, when it is used, websites or individuals have great difficulty in tracking online activity and location.

In general, to be anonymous online, people mask their identity by using nicknames, pseudonyms, and similar tricks. Nevertheless, the person's legal name and location are the easiest elements that can be identified. Many pseudonyms are derived from the person's legal name or can provide clues to identify it. Some years ago, a list of seven dimensions of identity knowledge was drawn up (Marx, 2001, 312). It still remains valid to this day:

1. Identification may involve a person's legal name; the use of first names only can offer partial anonymity.
2. Identification can refer to a person's address. This involves location and "reachability", whether in the real world or in cyberspace (telephone number, mail or e-mail address, an account number).
3. Identification may involve unique alphabetic, numeric, or other symbols such as a social security number, biometric patterns, or pseudonyms, which can be linked back to a person or an address under restricted conditions.
4. Identification may involve symbols, names, or pseudonyms which can be linked back to a person or an address.
5. Identification may be made by reference to the distinctive appearance or behavior patterns of a person.
6. Identification may involve social categorization. Sources of identity may be gender, ethnicity, religion, age, class, education, region, sexual orientation, linguistic patterns, organizational memberships and classifications, health status, employment, leisure activities, and friendship patterns.
7. Identification may involve certification in which the possession of knowledge (secret passwords, codes) or artifacts (tickets, badges, tattoos, uniforms) or skills (performances such as the ability to swim) labels one as a particular kind of person to be treated in a given away.

However, there is a profound difference between *being* anonymous and *feeling* anonymous online. Many people who navigates on the web feel themselves to be anonymous, simply because they are using a nickname.

It is well known that anonymity lifts inhibitions, and this applies to online relationships as well. It seems that people are more likely to act out online than in real life: while online, several people self-disclose or act out more frequently than they would in person (Lapidot-Lefler & Barak, 2015).

Six interacting factors have been identified as contributing to the creation of the online disinhibition effect: dissociative anonymity, invisibility, asynchronicity, solipsistic introjection, dissociative imagination, and the minimization of authority (Suler, 2004). Disinhibition can bring people to share extremely personal things about themselves and reveal secret emotions, fears, and wishes that they would never think to share in person.

Sometimes the loss of inhibitions has negative effects leading to online misbehavior, such as posting harsh or rude messages or committing illegal and harmful acts. However, anonymity can also have positive effects, since it can reduce the social risks when discussing taboo topics or arguing an unpopular point of view, or when expressing political opinions in non-democratic countries where regimes don't respect human rights. Suler distinguishes two types of online disinhibitions, *benign disinhibition* and *toxic disinhibition* (Suler, 2002). Benign disinhibition represents a person's attempt to understand themselves better and to resolve interpersonal and intrapsychic problems, as well as explore new emotional and experiential dimensions. Instead, toxic disinhibition produces rude language, harsh criticisms, anger, hatred, and threats.

The literature shows that many web users are convinced that anonymity helps them to manage social relationships online (Correa, Hinsley, & De Zuniga, 2010; Ganley & Lampe, 2009; McKenna & Bargh, 2000; Turkle, 2011; Wallace, 2015).

Above all, anonymity can offer the opportunity to the same subject to create various different virtual identities. These are all part of an individual personality. Their choices of the virtual identities they create, even if contrasting with the 'real' identity exhibited in the physical world, are an expression of the subject's personality. The phenomenon of having multiple virtual identities has been referred to as *dissociative anonymity*. It identifies an online compartmentalized behavior that can also include hostilities or deviant attitudes (Hollenbaugh & Everett, 2013; Orchard & Fullwood, 2010). However, usually, online behavior is less dramatic and pathological. Often, people maintain different virtual identities as well as multiple social media accounts merely in order to follow their different interests. Sometimes distinct profiles are necessary to separate different spheres of life and establish a separation between private life and work.

Research shows that people interacting in social networks seek to boost their reputation and are very sensitive to the opinions of others. In this light, they need to preserve the same identity over time and not continuously change it.

Often, in social networks, it is a case of the few interacting with the many. The mass of social network members are bystanders, and limit their activity to posting likes and dislikes. When someone submits a new question to the attention of an online community, only a few regular members engage in a discussion. It is an easily verifiable fact that, often, the people posting messages on social networks are always the same. On TripAdvisor, for example, there are some 7,525 posts dating from 2001 that correspond to the username Chrisj alone (Marzano & Ochoa, 2016).

However, who can prove that it was the same person who posted all of the messages ascribed to Chrisj?

ANONYMOUS SOCIAL NETWORKING SITES

In 2014, anonymous social networking sites recorded a real boom (Balingit, 2015). Apps that allow users to send messages without disclosing their real names have multiplied. Some of the most used apps make the content of messages visible to all, or only to a restricted number of users, e.g., by establishing geographical limitations. Indeed, many newer apps support anonymity but are hyperlocal, and in this way the authors of messages can be recognized even if their names are not explicitly mentioned in the posts (Singh, Radford, Huang, & Furrer, 2017).

Recently, an app, After School (Figure 5), has been exiting the enthusiasm of teenagers. After School allows someone to send a message entirely anonymously. It masks the sender from the risk of incurring unpleasant consequences. Despite the clamor raised in the media as to the dangers of this app, in that its anonymity allows the worst side of people to emerge, students continue to use it.

Sarahah is another controversial anonymous app (Sommer, 2018). It was initially created for users to send feedback to their coworkers, but has recently become popular amongst teenagers.

Drawing upon the contact list on your phone, it lets you connect with friends and send anonymous comments to them. Anybody who has your link can send you an anonymous message, they don't even need to have an

Figure 5. The After School home page (https://afterschoolapp.com/)

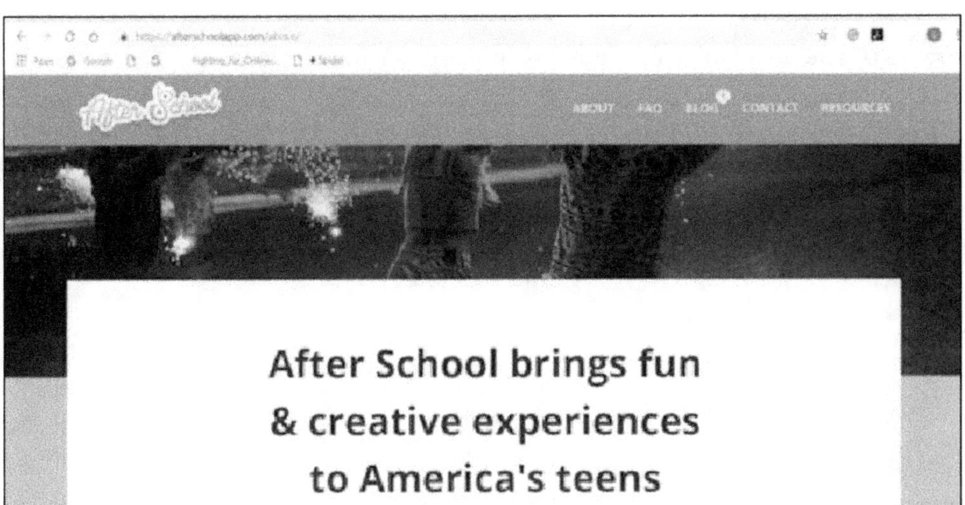

account on the app, they can just type and send. With a way to connect the app to Snapchat, teens are the most users of Sarahah that has risen to the top of the App Store in several countries.

Another app, *xcusy*, is a free and anonymous random chat room (Figure 6). According to the site's home page, it allows users to "get connected with boys and girls from around the world and send text messages, pictures and videos or start a video chat". It presents itself as an anonymous alternative to Chatroulette, a social networking site that was very popular in the late 2000s. As Chatroulette, xcusy provides the casual connection of unknown couples from all over the world, allowing them to chat online through the use of webcams.

Chatroulette has been described as a site where it is not difficult to meet someone who shows offensive and obscene material, or who uses the webcam to expose their genital organs. This should not be surprising, since voyeurism and exhibitionism are quite common on the Web (Hopkins, Green, Carnes, & Campling, 2016). Of course, this is a serious problem since many users of sites like Chatroulette are underage kids (Xing, Liang, Cheng, & Dang, 2011). Unfortunately, it is almost impossible to apply age restrictions for access to these sites, precisely because of the nature of the service offered, which is based on the anonymity of users.

Wizters (http://www.wizters.com), Postsecret (http://postsecret.com/), and Insider (app) (http://www.theinsider.cc) do not ask their members to create user profiles, claiming that anonymity is useful for preventing online bullying and for offering users the opportunity to confess, without suffering

Figure 6. The home page of the xcusy website (www.xscusy.com)

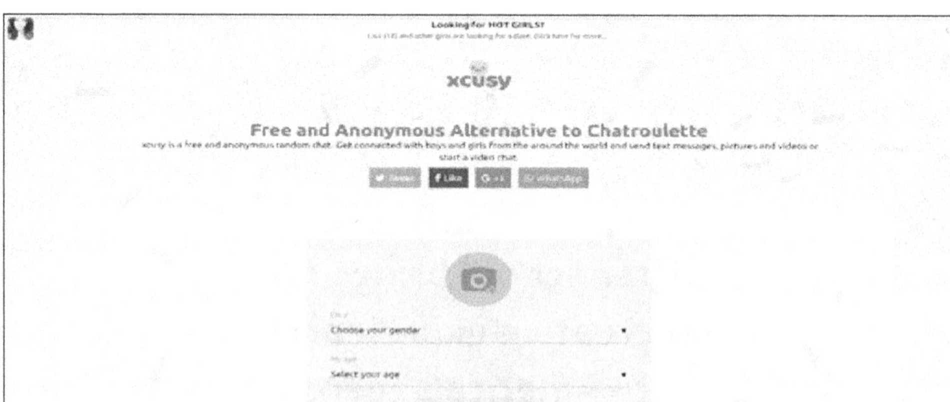

any consequences, facts that could ruin marriages or friendships, or that could cause them to lose their job. Figure 7 shows the Wizters home page.

VIRTUAL IDENTITY

Identity theft is one of the boom frauds on the internet, and forms part of the internet safety programs, often untested, that police officers and lawyers hold in schools.

Although virtual identity theft represents a serious problem, it is only one of many threats to the virtual identity of internet users. There are more sinister risks related to virtual identity, since it is not something separate to the physical identity of an individual, but is the self-image that they offer to the web (Gonzales & Hancock, 2011; Wang, 2017).

Self-presentation and the construction of identity on the internet have been broadly investigated. Initially, research was focused on the construction of identity in anonymous environments such as chat rooms and bulletin boards. The authors of a study based on the content analysis of 63 Facebook accounts argue that:

[...] identity is not an individual characteristic; it is not an expression of something innate in a person, it is rather a social product, the outcome of a

Figure 7. The Wizters home page (http://www.wizters.com)

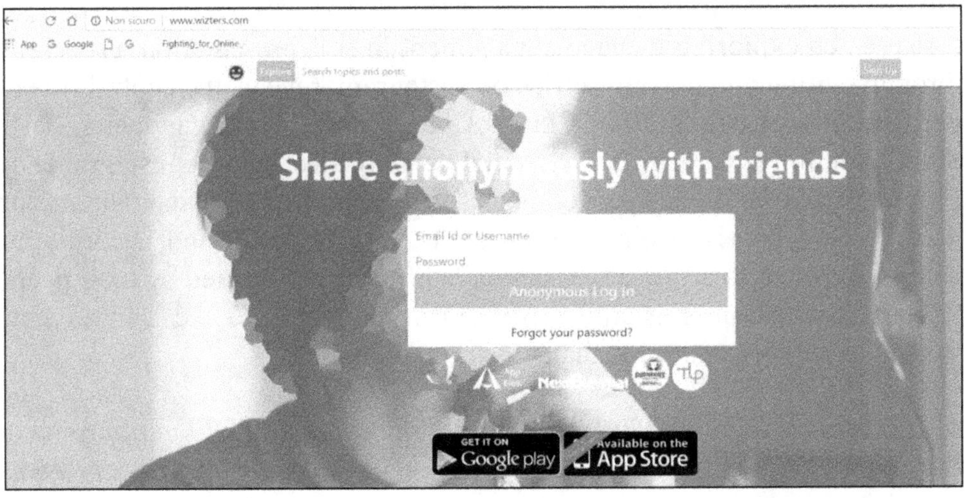

given social environment and hence performed differently in varying contexts. Depending on the characteristics of the environment in which they find themselves, individuals will choose to claim identities that can help them better situate within the given social environment. ''True selves,'' ''real selves,'' and ''hoped-for possible selves'' are products of different situations rather than characteristics of different individuals. (Zhao, Grasmuck, & Martin, 2008)

The observation that the construction of individual identity is socially sensitive warns of the risk coming from attacks against the virtual profile of an individual, especially if they are teenagers and adolescents. To destroy or even only undermine the "hoped-for possible selves" virtual dimension of a vulnerable person can have severely detrimental effects.

Studies have been carried out analyzing the efforts people make to present a precise, often idealized, version of themselves on their online profile. Recent results present many analogies with those of a study that Dove, the popular personal care brand owned by Unilever, commissioned in 2005 that was aimed at providing an authoritative foundation for changes in the ways in which girls and women think and talk about beauty and body image (Etcoff, Orbach, Scott, & D'Agostino, 2006). From this research, it emerges that beauty ideals can create *appearance anxiety* for women globally, girls aged 15-17 being the most vulnerable. Another relevant aspect is that, in terms of their body satisfaction, teenage girls' greatest influences are their peers and their mothers (Figure 8), albeit with a contrasting effect. Whilst maternal influence is more related to more positive appearance satisfaction and self-esteem, peer and media influence is more related to negative appearance satisfaction and self-esteem.

Research exploring teenage engagement in self-presentation, especially through editing and posting selfies on Instagram, reveals the central role of peer comparison (Chae, 2017; Chua & Chang, 2016; Fox & Vendemia, 2016; Shin, Kim, Im, & Chong, 2017). Social network sites such as Instagram and Facebook have facilitated peer comparison regarding looks and image among teenagers. Comparison reinforces the media ideal of beauty and, accordingly, people endeavor to achieve the standards of beauty projected by their peers. Social appreciation is usually expressed in the form of 'likes'. In a recent study, the authors underline that:

[..] some girls explicitly link their social acceptance with the approval of their online self-presentation, thus reconfiguring the number of likes received

Figure 8. The impact of the most powerful influencers on appearance satisfaction for girls 15-17
Source: Etcoff, Orbach, Scott, & D'Agostino, 2006

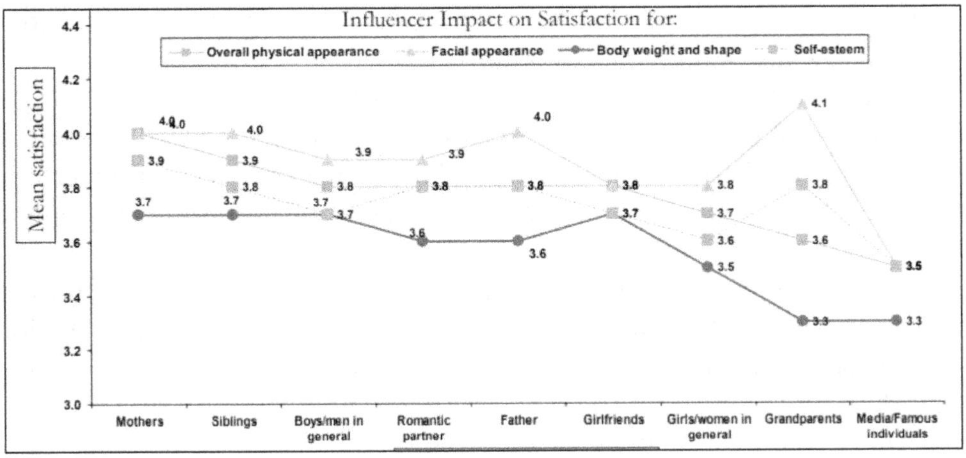

to the pictures they share online as symbolic tokens of social inclusion. (Mascheroni, Vincent, & Jimenez, 2015)

In a study concerning photos posted to Facebook, it emerged that most of those sharing photos commented with messages along the lines of: "Look how sociable I am!", "How beautiful/handsome I am!", "How attractive I am!", and "How happy I am!" (Şener & Özkoçak, 2014).

In the last few years, there have been a growing number of research works that have examined the expression of personality on the internet using the *five-factor model* (Back et al., 2010). The Big Five framework refers to a model of personality that was refined and improved in the 1990s by the American personality psychologist Goldberg (1990). It consists of five factors (Figure 9) representing personality traits:

1. Extraversion, typically characterized by being sociable, gregarious, assertive, talkative, and active;
2. Neuroticism, includes being anxious, depressed, angry, embarrassed, emotional, insecure, and worried;
3. Openness to experiences, related to characteristics such as imagination and insight;
4. Agreeableness, associated with being courteous, flexible, trusting, good-natured, cooperative, forgiving, and tolerant.

5. Conscientiousness, includes high levels of thoughtfulness, with good impulse control and goal-directed behaviors (Barrick & Mount, 1991).

This framework is used to classify individual differences in personalities (Gosling, Rentfrow, & Swann, 2003).

The application of the Big five framework to the content generated by users in social media has been considered a more accurate method for measuring personality than the questionnaire method based on self-presentation reporting, since people tend to better disclose their real personality traits to their online friends (Lin, Fang, & Jin, 2017).

Research on virtual identity is important to understand the dynamics of cyberbullying among children and adolescents. The role of online reputation and peer opinion is enormous and should not be underestimated. In fact, children and adolescents are extremely vulnerable to negative and derisive comments, especially regarding their physical appearance. Negative comparisons that circulate online can drastically affect their self-esteem, causing stress and depression.

Figure 9. The Big five personality traits
Source: author's own elaboration

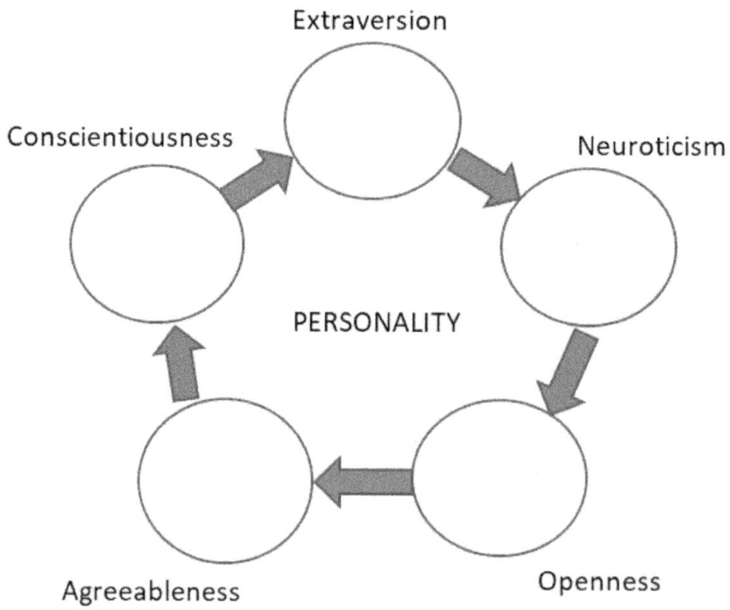

What occurs in social media is a sort of *individualist conformism* that is different from the oxymoron of *conformist individualism* used by Riesman and Slater (Ogilvy, 1992a). They both pointed to the fact that individualism can be remarkably conformist. This was the case, in the 1960s, of youth mass rebellion:

The youth movement of the sixties was non-conformist – but remarkably collectivist. Solidarity among members of the counterculture was manifest in mass demonstrations and in communal lifestyles. Even in their non-conformity to mainstream styles, the blue denim on political activists and the tie-dyed costumes of hippies were as instantly recognizable as military uniforms. (Ogilvy, 1992b, p. 225)

Nevertheless, individualist conformism makes an individual feel special since they fit the globally recognized ideal standards: "I am a special person because I am popular and I am popular since I meet the ideal of the most".

In the 1960s, young people affirmed their individuality by adopting a uniform that made them feel immediately different to society. Many of them aspired to community models of life and, in Europe, also looked sympathetically on collectivist ideals.

Today, the word *crowd* recurs increasing often in various contexts, and solutions that can be carried out through collaborative efforts are emphasized. But any collectivist intention has been swept away. On the web, it is clear that young people try to satisfy their narcissistic individualism by gaining popularity among their peers. Since young people try to gain their individuality from the appreciation of others, it follows that they must conform to others' preferences. One could say that the young people of the sixties were conformist for *idealism* whereas, today, young people appear to be conformist for *convenience*, namely to gain popularity. Because of technology, they are continuously under evaluation and, as a consequence, the opinion of their peers can be a source of anxiety. Indeed, being the subject of online rumors or mockery focusing on the body image can produce low levels of self-esteem in the victims that, in certain cases, can develop into severe forms of depression. Moreover, young people, particularly those who are more vulnerable, could be absorbed by the web and develop addictive behaviors.

CYBER ADDICTIONS AND SOCIAL MEDIA

It has been observed that for some people, especially youngsters, the internet has become the central focal point of their daily lives (Durkee et al., 2016).

Statistics show that the hours per week people spend online has risen exponentially over the last two decades. Some individuals spend between 20 and 80 hours per week on the internet, with single sessions lasting up to 15 hours. Researchers agree that the overuse of the internet can contribute to the onset of negative effects on people's mental health and well-being (Carli & Durkee, 2015, p. 273), although they haven't agreed on a unique term to describe the concept of internet overuse or abuse. Many different terms and definitions are used to address this phenomenon: Internet Addiction, Internet Addiction Disorder, Pathological Internet Use, Problematic Internet Use, Excessive Internet Use, Compulsive Internet Use, Cyberspace Addiction, Online Addiction, Net Addiction, Internet Addicted Disorder, High Internet Dependency, Screen addiction, and so on (Davis, Flett, & Besser, 2002; Griffiths & Pontes, 2014; Hur, 2006; Widyanto & Griffiths, 2006). Internet Addiction Disorder (IAD) is the most widely used term.

IAD is increasingly being recognized as a mental disorder by many scholars (Block, 2008; Griffiths, Billieux, & Pontes, 2016; Kuss, Griffiths, & Binder, 2013). In 2013, the Diagnostic and Statistical Manual of Mental Disorder (DSM-5) included IAD as an entry in Section 3 ("Emerging Measures and Models"), although not as an officially recognized disorder. However, while many researchers were disappointed by this decision, there are evident reasons for not recognizing IAD as a form of mental disorder, chiefly the difficulty of developing effective treatment protocols specifically designed for patients presenting IAD. As a consequence, therapeutic fees for IAD are not covered by medical insurance. Indeed, the excessive use of the internet can actually be to fuel other types of addictions (Griffiths, 2000).

IAD computer use or pathological computer use usually indicates the inability of an individual to control their use of the internet. However, this compulsive-impulsive behavior can encompass both online and offline computer overuse. Often, it masks other problems, but can also represent a wrong way of coping with stress.

Although individuals affected by IAD present common clearly definable traits in real life connected to their excessive online behavior, little is known about the pathophysiological and cognitive mechanisms responsible for IAD (Weinstein & Lejoyeux, 2010). Accordingly, due to the lack of methodologically adequate research, it is impossible to recommend evidence-based treatments. Prevention programs appear the best way to address these problematic behaviors. An effort should be made to understand their nature and underlying dynamics.

Not every excessive use of the internet automatically corresponds to IAD. In this vein, too, the differences between Social User, Abuser, and Addict are worth noting:

- A Social User is a person who uses something (e.g. alcohol, drugs, etc.) simply to enhance the pleasure of normally pleasurable situations;
- An Abuser is a person who uses something to enhance pleasure and/or compensate for something negative, such as physical or emotional pain, insecurity, fear, anger, etc.;
- An Addict is a person who compulsively or obsessively uses something to celebrate, to compensate, or for another reason, legitimate or otherwise.

From the first research on the pathological use of the internet, five specific sub-types of IAD emerged (Young, Pistner, O'Mara, & Buchanan, 1999):

1. **Cybersexual Addiction:** Compulsive use of adult web sites for cybersex and cyberporn.
2. **Cyber-Relationship Addiction:** Over-involvement in online relationships.
3. **Net Compulsions:** Obsessive online gambling, shopping, or online trading.
4. **Information Overload:** Compulsive web surfing or database searches.
5. **Computer Addiction:** Obsessive computer game playing (e.g., Doom, Myst, or Solitaire).

Thereafter, three principal subtypes of IAD have been defined (Block, 2007):

1. Internet gaming addiction;
2. Sexual preoccupations;
3. Email/text messaging.

PROBLEMATIC USES OF THE INTERNET

Recently, new problematic uses of the internet have been spreading:

- **Sexting:** The sending and receiving of sexually explicit messages, especially using mobile phones. The number of teens who send sexually suggestive pictures or videos of themselves to someone via email, cell phone, or by another mode is alarming. Research shows that, among geographically located samples of youths, sexting estimates tend to fall anywhere in the range of 7 to 27 per cent (Cooper, Quayle, Jonsson, & Svedin, 2016).
- **Internet Infidelity and Online Affairs:** Individuals who suffer from an addiction to chat rooms, social networking, or texting become over-involved in online relationships or may engage in virtual adultery. Screen addiction results in online friends who quickly become more important to the individual at the expense of real life relationships with family and friends, often leading to divorce, separation, or family instability.
- **Video Games and Gaming Addiction:** As anyone who has experienced it knows all too well, video game addiction is real. Although gaming addiction is not yet officially recognized as a diagnosable disorder by the American Medical Association, there is increasing evidence that people of all ages, especially teens and pre-teens, are facing very real, sometimes severe consequences associated with compulsive use of video and computer games. Video games are becoming increasingly complex, detailed, and compelling to a growing international audience of players. With better graphics, more realistic characters, and greater strategic challenges, it's not surprising that some teens would rather play the latest video game than hang out with friends, play sports, or even watch television. Of course, all gamers are not screen addicts – many teens can play video games for a few hours a week, successfully balancing school activities, grades, friends, and family obligations. But for some, gaming becomes an uncontrollable compulsion. Studies estimate that 10 to 15 per cent of gamers exhibit signs that meet the World Health Organization's criteria for addiction. Just as with gambling and other compulsive behaviors, teens can become so enthralled in the fantasy world of gaming that they neglect their family, friends, work, and school.

- **Net Compulsions and Screen Addiction:** Can be generalized compulsive behavior to Internet gambling, online shopping, or eBay. These focus, in different ways, on aspects of winning and the emotional boost that follows, and often cause financial problems, relationship problems, and work-related problems among addicts. Gamblers will be mesmerized as they play slot machines, craps, blackjack, and roulette on tablets and phones. Millions of Americans play various gambling games on the internet, even though the businesses are typically illegal, unregulated, and offer no consumer protection. An estimated 1,700 offshore sites accept bets, with the annual market in the U.S.A. alone estimated to be some $4 to $6 billion. Beyond the regulatory issues, gambling addiction is often called the "hidden illness" because there are no obvious physical signs or symptoms as there are in drug or alcohol addiction. Problem gamblers typically deny or minimize the problem. They also go to great lengths to hide their gambling. For example, problem gamblers often withdraw from their loved ones, sneak around, and lie about where they've been and what they've been up to.
- **Information Overload:** The wealth of data available nowadays has created a new type of compulsive behavior regarding excessive internet and database searching. Screen addiction in this case results in spending greater amounts of time searching and collecting data from the web and organizing information. Obsessive compulsive tendencies and reduced work productivity are associated with this behavior.

In the following paragraph, sexting and revenge porn will be illustrated since both are usually included in the scope of cyberbullying. Indeed, sexual and gender harassment is widespread within the online context, and women are particularly vulnerable to this (CCSO Cybercrime Working Group, 2013; Faucher, Jackson, & Cassidy, 2014; Jane, 2017). In fact, according to Halder and Karuppannan, 2009), women are the second most vulnerable group online, after children.

SEXTING AND REVENGE PORN

Sexting refers to the sending and receiving of sexually suggestive images, videos, or texts via the internet, principally by mobile phone. The term itself is taken from the words sex and text, but also encompasses the sending of pictures and videos with a sexual theme.

Researchers have analyzed the sexting phenomenon, especially amongst adolescents and young adults, from different perspectives, in terms of legal aspects, risk factors, and sexual behavior (Temple et al., 2012), and also in relation to romantic attachment, as a means for initiating or maintaining a love relationship (Weisskirch & Delevi, 2011).

Despite newspaper and media warnings about the dangers of sexting (Amta, 2015; Bastians, Courier, 2017; Weale, 2015), the phenomenon is on the rise. What is the reason for this popularity?

Data shows that sexting mostly concerns women, usually young women, but also the very young and the not so young. It seems to be the modern version of the erotic letters that lovers have exchanged throughout the ages.

The fact that sexting is so prevalent among young people may be due to some environmental factors, such as young people's skills in using mobile technologies, their difficulty in having spaces for intimacy, and to their curiosity about sex. The desire to seduce and excite the partner, and not just themselves, may be an additional element. Young people often seek to prove their capability to attract sexually. Being seen as sexy reinforces their identity, decreases their uncertainties, and, not least, increases their reputation and standing within peer groups. The sexual competition factor may be present in many forms, including the number of likes. Moreover, when it comes to social behavior, emulation and transgression are not to be underestimated.

Finally, for women, there is the old cultural heritage of sex seen as being a gift to a partner and a proof of love. Consequently, given the cultural importance of sex, the empowerment of women cannot be realized without there being a new way to design and manage amorous and sexual relationships. Accordingly, the role that women have in transmitting cultural values doesn't make it easy to proceed towards gender equality. The cultural constraints affect males and females equally and, therefore, the affirmation of gender equality is not possible without a profound cultural change taking place on both sides.

However, some changes that are underway in Western society may have been elicited by the new technologies. Samimi and Alderson (2014) found in a survey of undergraduate students that males and females are equally likely

Figure 10. Sexting among middle and higher school students
Source: Patchin, 2017

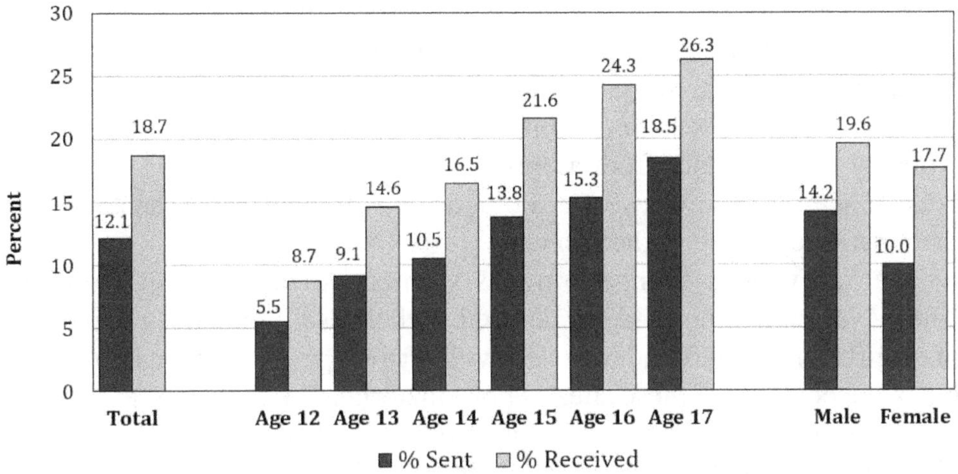

to engage in sexting. Sexting has become a regular part of relationships, and as a new means for teenagers (and others) to explore their sexuality.

Patchin reports that together with Hinduja, data was collected from over 5,500 middle and high school students from across the United States (Patchin, 2017). They asked the sample of 12 to 17 year olds to refer to the problems they had experienced online, including sexting (Figure 10). Overall, 12% of students admitted to having sent an explicit image of themselves to another person at some point in their lifetime. About 4% said they had done so within the prior month. Similarly, about 19% said they had received a sexually explicit image from someone else at some point in their lifetime (about 6% within the last month).

Patchin notes that these values are much lower than those of some media reports (which tend to sensationalize the issue), but are in line with other more rigorous national research studies. The author goes on to observe that it doesn't appear that sexting has increased dramatically over the last few years.

Unfortunately, in certain cases, sexting can cause negative, sometimes tragic, consequences, especially among young people. One case, that occurred in June 2009, is emblematic of this. Thirteen-year-old Hope Witsell (Hunter, 2010) took a topless photo of herself with her cell phone camera, and sent the photo via text message to a boy she liked. The boy sent the photo to his friends, who went on to send it to their friends at Witsell's middle school and at a nearby high school. Students at Witsell's school bullied her about the photo, both in person and over the internet. Witsell began self-harming, and blogged about the harassment, until, in September 2009, she committed suicide. The case of Hope Witsell is classified as cyberbullying.

However, literature and statistics show that a new phenomenon, often related with sexting, which is so-called revenge pornography or revenge porn, has recently been spreading. Revenge porn involves a perpetrator – typically an ex-partner from a previous romantic relationship – uploading nude or semi-nude images/videos of a person online without the consent of the person appearing in the content.

There are various revenge porn sites, such as IsAnyoneUp.com, gfrevenge.com, Myex.com, Iknowthatgirl.com, etc., where users upload X-rated photos of ex-girlfriends/boyfriends or lovers without their permission. Search engines index the contents of these sites as porn materials. In 2015, Google enabled users to remove revenge porn images from Google's search index. As Amit Singhal, the head of Google Search, admitted, this doesn't solve the problem but it will help.

Several revenge porn websites encourage users to submit nude photos of their ex-partner(s) for revenge. The purpose of revenge porn is to shame and humiliate, and to destroy the lives and reputations of people, who are very often young women.

Revenge porn is legally defined as the sharing of private, often sexual or explicit, photos or videos, of another person with the purpose of causing embarrassment or distress.

Two-thirds of revenge porn incidents involve women under 30, and there are eight female complainants to every one male. In a twist on this phenomenon, in 2014 a hacker using the name Tristan posted the photographs of mainly female celebrities, including those of singer Rihanna and actress Jennifer Lawrence (Topping, 2014).

Certainly, the advent of the web has led to changes in the sphere of sex crimes, and the stereotype of the sex offender as a man in a grubby raincoat lurking around street corners belongs to the past, however our current virtual world is no less dangerous than the dark and isolated streets of yester-year.

Looking at images of naked bodies and sexually explicit materials is a long standing human tradition at all latitudes and in all cultures. The internet has only made it easier to produce and access porn materials. However, revenge porn is something very different from pornography, and the effects that it can have on victims is devastating.

It has been observed that, despite recent media attention on revenge porn, relatively few academic studies have focused on this issue, and those that do largely concentrate on the legal aspects and legal theories related to revenge porn cases (Bates, 2015).

Although some feminists have tried to shift the debate to a positive one focusing on female sexuality (Valenti, 2009), sex-positivity is not yet a mainstream belief. In reality, women lose their jobs because of revenge-porn, and have to face a plethora of unpleasant behavior once there are naked photos of them online (Rocha & Perry, 2019).

CYBER HATERS

Online hate is a devastating phenomenon. Indeed, the cyber world is inundated with legions of haters who post angry and/or uninformed comments about a topic with the intent of harming someone, usually the author of a post or another person who posted a comment (Delaney & Madigan, 2016).

It has been observed that the term *hater* likely began with the expression "Haters gonna hate" from hip-hop culture (Reagle, 2015).

Maggie Haberman, a famous American journalist, explained why she decided to leave Twitter, as follows:

I woke up last Sunday morning feeling anxiety in my chest as I checked the Twitter app on my phone, scrolling down to refresh, refresh, refresh. There was a comment I started to engage with — I opened a new post, tapped out some words, then thought better of it and deleted the tweet. The same thing happened repeatedly for the next two hours.

The evening before, I had complained to a close friend that I hated being on Twitter. It was distorting discourse, I said. I couldn't turn off the noise. She asked what was the worst that could happen if I stepped away from it.

There was nothing I could think of. And so just after 6 p.m. last Sunday, I did.

After nearly nine years and 187,000 tweets, I have used Twitter enough to know that it no longer works well for me. I will re-engage eventually, but in a different way. (The New York Times, July 20, 2018)

Flaming comments are often top-rated on the internet. They are derogatory messages that don't contain any constructive feedback or any improving ideas, but a swearing, hateful, and harmful diatribe. People who post this type of messages are called haters. A hater can be defined as someone who posts a negative comment that doesn't offer any helpful information but only contains offenses and insults.

Flaming is indeed a severe issue that is currently happening throughout the online world, but it has actually been present since the advent of the first online applications that provided people with the opportunity to express their comments and opinions.

In efforts to combat online hate speech, in 2013 the *Sentinel Project for Genocide Prevention and Mobiocracy* launched the *Hatebase project* based on a crowdsourcing approach (Mondal, Silva & Benevenuto, 2017; Silva, Mondal, Correa, Benevenuto & Weber, 2016). It aims to collect all the hate terms and expressions from around the world in one online repository. Users can add terms and contribute to increasing the database content. At this time, Hatebase is the world's largest online repository of structured multilingual, usage-based hate speech. Core components of the Hatebase application are *HateBot*, a robot which interacts with external APIs to retrieve potential sightings, and *HateBrain*, a linguistic parser which automates some of the tasks of identifying hate speech acquired by HateBot. Figure 11 shows the most common types of hate speech.

Angry comments can also be posted by infiltrated *scammers* and *trolls*. Comments can be used to manipulate others users through scams and fakery,

Figure 11. The most common types of hate speech
Source: https://www.hatebase.org/popular, October 2018

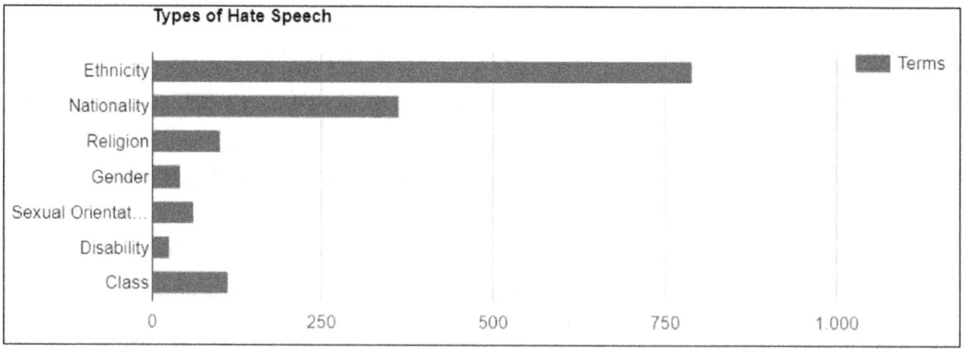

or to alienate an individual or more often a group of people. Haters hit on not only politicians, celebrities, journalists, bloggers, and public figures but also ordinary internet users. Nowadays, receiving insults is the price people pay for being visible online, especially if they are women.

ONLINE INCIVILITY

Incivility is a term that is difficult to define, since what one person considers to be uncivil behavior might be perfectly acceptable to another. However, the term is usually used more narrowly to connote any rude or disruptive social behavior that results in physical and/or psychological distress for the person involved. Incivility encompasses exhibiting rude manners and disrespect, as well as any form of abusive and even violent or harmful behavior. Uncivil behavior ranges from low risk to high risk, from disruptive to threatening, and from distracting or annoying behaviors to aggressive and potentially violent behaviors (Clark, 2017).

Scholars have devoted considerable attention to incivility in the domains of interpersonal relationships in the workplace, and recently to incivility in the context of the online environment too (Miner, Diaz, Wooderson, McDonald, Smittick & Lomeli, 2018). Health care institutions are one of the workplaces where incivility is widespread as a consequence of their particular stressful environment (Marshall, 2010). In the workplace, incivility can take many forms, from demeaning reproaches and mockery in front of an audience to the refusal to accept or acknowledge a co-worker's assistance, as well as spreading rumors, giving angry responses, and hiding information in order to damage a colleague.

There is a broad consensus that online incivility is an extremely critical issue that is spreading through social networks. Incivility is a common feature of many news blogs and affects political discourse (Coe, Kenski & Rains, 2014). Many politicians post uncivil messages on social networks, generally Twitter and Facebook, in order to attract attention and increase their exposure to potential voters. Their attitude is emulated by common citizens who are encouraged to post uncivil comments to online news articles, repeating the politicians' offensive behavior. Digital technology is changing the concept of public opinion, in that followers' consensus simplifies debate to a question of likes or dislikes, a dichotomous division *pro* or *contra*. Instead of being a forum for interpersonal discussions, social networks have become an arena where opinions are affirmed and preexisting values are nurtured and reinforced. Those reading uncivil comments in a blog may judge a message to be hostile only if it contravenes their own opinions, rather than for the content of the message itself (Smith, John, Sturgis, & Nomura, 2009).

It has been observed that online incivility is an online behavior that would certainly include cyberbullying (Kowalski, Limber, Limber, & Agatston, 2012).

Nowadays, a general trend is evident of a declining level of politeness and a broad acceptance of exhibitions of impolite attitudes or behavior, such as the extensive use of vulgarity and obscenity in television programs as well as in the theater, movies, music, and literature (Barkin, 2016; Crane, Kawashima, & Kawasaki, 2016).

It has been noted that vulgar words appear with a frequency estimated at between 0.5% and 0.7% in everyday conversation, whilst it is 1.15% in Twitter (Cachola, Holgate, Preoţiuc-Pietro, & Li, 2018).

The diffusion of incivility online can facilitate cyberbullying since the exposure to incivility on social media can make people more likely to be aggressive in turn. What starts off as the posting of hostile messages can easily turn into an episode of cyberbullying.

However, beyond the individual personality of perpetrators, there may be contextual factors that, in certain cases, encourage and perpetuate online incivility. For instance, the advent of email has provided university students with online contact with their professors, as well as decreased the formality of exchanges between professors and students. It has been observed that the informal nature of online discourse has contributed to uncivil online exchanges and cyberbullying at higher education institutions (Wildermuth & Davis, 2012). Contextual factors can also influence the possibility of contrasting incivility and cyberbullying. This is common in certain types of organizations such as higher education institutions:

Much of the cyberbullying is taking place under the radar of administrators since faculty are unlikely to communicate their experiences to those in charge, unless they can be assured that appropriate actions will be taken to help the victim and deal effectively with the perpetrator. (Cassidy, Faucher, & Jackson, 2014, p. 295)

The threshold that separates online incivility from cyberbullying can be very easy to cross. From rudeness to harassment there is a great distance, but an escalation in uncivil behaviors can bring violent reactions. Accordingly, preventing online forms of uncivility should be included in any anti-bullying program. At the same time, civility should be promoted, underlining the advantages of a positive, collaborative, and supportive behavior.

In the following paragraph, a case of online incivility is reported. It didn't result in cyberbullying, but did create serious emotional stress for the victim, and also shows the indifference of top-managers towards the victims of workplace incivility.

THE CASE OF THE DIONYSUS EAR

The inappropriate use of online technology can cause problems.

Wallace (2015) reported on the case of a university administrator who sent out an email to 40,000 students encouraging them to opt-in to the paperless delivery of tuition form 1098-T. A big problem arose when:

The students quickly discovered they could reply to all, and what became known as replyallcollapse ensued. A suddenly empowered student body shared jokes, friendly comments, cries for help, and complaints, along with many calls to stop replying to all as their inboxes flooded, the employee who made the mistake apologized but the floodgate was already open. (Wallace, 2015, pp. 25-26)

The following case is exemplary of the problematic consequences of the offhand use of social networks in an organization. It also shows how easy it is to underestimate the risks of privacy infringement when using social networks.

Some years ago, an Italian public university created the Facebook-based "HelpX" service. It was aimed at giving students a virtual place where they could interact among themselves, posting their questions, tips, complaints, compliments, and comments:

If you have any question about academic life, if you have any advice to give to your University, if you want to vent your grievance or if you want to make a compliment ... you're in the right place! This group is promoted and managed from the External Relations of the University in order to convey information quickly and provide 'documented' answers which will be the result of collaboration between the staff of the University and the relationships that the University has with external parties.[1]

In 2014, the HelpX service generated a huge problem when a student posted a message wrongly accusing and offending a University employee. To give a brief overview of the functioning of HelpX Facebook group, to be part of the HelpX Facebook group, registration is required. The registration request is verified by the HelpX university staff, enabling access to trusted users only. If a registration is accepted, a new member receives a temporary password, that, at the first login, must be changed with a personal permanent password, following which they are permitted to read and post messages without restriction.

A University staff group, which doesn't include professors, interacts with students, posting messages, commenting, answering questions, giving advice, and publicizing events. This staff group struggles to demonstrate the maximum understanding and empathy regarding the student issues. It is important to note that the University also has an official help desk where students can ask for and receive information (by phone and by email).

The HelpX case can be summarized as follows. A student posted a message in which they complained about "scandalous answers" (in Italian "risposte scandalose") received from an employee of the service. The supervisor of the university HelpX staff group asked the student to indicate the name of the author of the "scandalous answers" and provide more details. The student immediately replied, giving the name of the employee, and added that it was not the first time that this employee had caused vexation. The student went on to request help enforcing their personal rights. At that stage, the head of the HelpX staff group intervened, asking the student to forward the emails sent by the employee. The student did so, apologizing for the trouble the matter was causing. The head of the HelpX staff group replied: "You don't have to apologize: we should".

At this point, there was an escalation in tone: the student heavily inveighed against the employee, and threatened to write to the rector to officially report the employee's behavior. The student didn't receive a reply, and after some days wrote to the rector. Throughout this time, the libeled employee had been completely unaware of what was happening, not having being warned by colleagues among the HelpX university staff. Finally, the head of the student affairs administration summoned the employee to answer to the student's allegations. From the time of the student posting the first message, some 20 days had passed, and in that time the messages posted by the student had been racking up numerous "likes", and were obviously harmful to the employee's professional position. The employee consulted a lawyer, but a lawsuit was avoided since the employee, after proving themselves to be free of fault, decided to defer action.

The following reflections and findings derive from the preliminary analysis of one year of messages exchanged within the Facebook HelpX group. The analysis integrated informal interviews and conversations with some key persons (professors, researchers, and staff).

The damage to social reputation and social relationships can ensue in different ways, for example in the spreading of rumors and gossiping, the breaking of confidences, and in ridiculing and calling professionalism and competence into question. The literature on misbehavior has grown, and new terms have been added to the academic lexicon (Tepper & Henle, 2011).

Backstabbing and treachery are very common in the workplace, and can take multifarious forms: intentionally passing misinformation, withholding useful information, or spreading damaging rumors (Beehr, 2014; Mackey, Frieder, Brees, & Martinko, 2017). The following are the best tips for combating a coworkers' treachery:

- Avoid the gossip machine;
- Keep your ears open, all the same;
- Talk to the backstabber directly;
- Remain humble;
- Know your enemies;
- Know your allies.

However, while the above tips may be good for a classic workplace, they are not so effective if you are attacked in a virtual place, and even less so if the one attacking you is not one of your co-workers or your boss, but a third party, who is viewed as a customer by the management, as students are in the HelpX case.

Another factor which characterizes the HelpX case is the helplessness of the victim, who didn't receive any support from their colleagues ("You don't have to apologize: we should") and could not resolve the situation, since they were completely unaware they were being libeled.

This circumstance shows the power imbalance between the individual victim and the Facebook group as a functioning entity.

In fact, despite their obviously different roles, the students and the HelpX university staff are mutually supportive, since they share the same objective: to help the students. This is evident in the name of the service itself, which is formed by the word *help* and the acronym of the university, which we replaced with "X".

An interesting aspect concerns the HelpX university staff's language and behavior. An accurate analysis, conducted after the above-mentioned case, shows that the HelpX university staff employs the same conversation stereotypes that young people regularly use on social networks, struggling to emulate their expressions, and their chatting behavior. The HelpX university staff make great efforts to establish a peer relationship with the students, which is remarkable, given that the generation gap between the students and the head of the team is about 40 years.

Analysis of the messages reveals that students feel themselves at ease with the HelpX university staff, and do not disclose any problems when dealing with it. They forget that the HelpX service is an institutional service, and behave as if they were on their own Facebook page, chatting with mates. But ultimately, this is not the case.

One might ask, finally, that if the HelpX service only provides a soft friendly communicative support to students, what its utility is? How its cost can be justified? A conversation with some university professors provides the answer. It is simple: the HelpX service is the *Ear of Dionysus*[2] of the university top management. On one hand, it allows the monitoring of the student's mood on campus, on the other hand, the student's comments offer the opportunity to monitor the university staff. For this reason, the HelpX service is still very much in operation.

The principal findings that emerge from analysis of the Facebook HelpX group messaging are as follows:

- In contrast to other students' social networks, HelpX doesn't show inflammatory or harmful messages against peers or the HelpX university staff.
- There are a high number of requests for information about the exam timetable and the university fees.
- Complaints against professors are not numerous, and are related to formal issues (e.g. the exam timetable).
- Complaints against administrative staff generally refer to the fact that their responses are not clear, and often concern presumed errors of the informative system.
- Most of the requests for help are occasioned by the lack of knowledge regarding the university structure, the information system, and the internal regulations and procedures.

CONCLUSION

In this chapter, many problematic aspects of social networks have been illustrated. This doesn't mean that they are an evil thing, *per se*. Social networks are part of contemporary life, representing a powerful means of communication and socialization. Their usefulness is indisputable since they can vastly improve people's livability. What we can do then, is to draw two important aspects to attention.

The most important is that social networks exponentially amplify the circulation of materials irrespective of their content. Often, they are used by individuals as a means of sharing the minutiae of their daily lives with the wider world. Social networking sites are essentially open diaries where people report all sorts of information: their desires, preferences, and dislikes, as well as what time they wake up, what they eat for breakfast (even adding pictures), and what the weather is like. Social networks can be an incredible source of information about human behavior and attitudes. The systematic analysis of the content of social networks could inaugurate a new age of research in the human sciences. It is for sure that they have already initiated a new marketing era and a new way for political competition.

The second aspect to take into account is the social networks interactivity. This is a disruptive element. Interactivity offers opportunities for discussion and collaboration, but also provides possibilities for expressing hate and inciting virtual lynching mobs online.

REFERENCES

Acquisti, A., Taylor, C., & Wagman, L. (2016). The economics of privacy. *Journal of Economic Literature*, *54*(2), 442–492. doi:10.1257/jel.54.2.442

Agosto, D. E., Abbas, J., & Naughton, R. (2012). Relationships and social rules: Teens' social network and other ICT selection practices. *Journal of the American Society for Information Science and Technology*, *63*(6), 1108–1124. doi:10.1002/asi.22612

Amta. (2015). *Warning on the dangers of "Sexting"*. Available at: http://www.amta.org.au/articles/amta/Warning.on.the.dangers.of.Sexting

Anderson, A., & Jiang, J. (2018). *Tees, Social media & Technology 2018*. Pew Research Center. Available at: http://www.pewinternet.org/2018/05/31/teens-social-media-technology-2018/

Back, M. D., Stopfer, J. M., Vazire, S., Gaddis, S., Schmukle, S. C., Egloff, B., & Gosling, S. D. (2010). Facebook profiles reflect actual personality, not self-idealization. *Psychological Science*, *21*(3), 372–374. doi:10.1177/0956797609360756 PMID:20424071

Balingit, M. (2015, December 8). Millions of teens are using a new app to post anonymous thoughts, and most parents have no idea. *Washington Post*. Available at: https://www.washingtonpost.com/local/education/millions-of-teens-are-using-a-new-app-to-post-anonymous-thoughts-and-most-parents-have-no-idea/2015/12/08/1532a98c-9907-11e5-8917-653b65c809eb_story.html?noredirect=on&utm_term=.adf63c7b24cb

Barkin, S. M. (2016). *American Television News: The Media Marketplace and the Public Interest: The Media Marketplace and the Public Interest*. Routledge. doi:10.4324/9781315290935

Barrick, M. R., & Mount, M. K. (1991). The big five personality dimensions and job performance: A meta-analysis. *Personnel Psychology*, *44*(1), 1–26. doi:10.1111/j.1744-6570.1991.tb00688.x

Bastians, K., & Courier, W. (2017, May 17). Students warned about the legal consequences of sexting in wake of filmed teen sex assault. *Daily Telegraph*. Available at: https://www.dailytelegraph.com.au/newslocal/wentworth-courier/students-warned-about-the-legal-consequences-of-sexting-in-wake-of-filmed-teen-sex-assault/news-story/53c007bfc39c333ee7443ee20c7244a1

Bates, S. L. (2015). *"Stripped": an analysis of revenge porn victims' lives after victimization* (Doctoral dissertation). Arts & Social Sciences: School of Criminology.

Beehr, T. A. (2014). *Psychological stress in the workplace (Psychology revivals)*. Routledge. doi:10.4324/9781315795560

Block, J. J. (2007). Prevalence underestimated in problematic Internet use study. *CNS Spectrums*, *12*(1), 14–15. doi:10.1017/S1092852900020459 PMID:17387811

Block, J. J. (2008). Issues for DSM-V: Internet Addiction (2008). *The American Journal of Psychiatry*, *165*(3), 306–307. doi:10.1176/appi.ajp.2007.07101556 PMID:18316427

Boneva, B. S., Quinn, A., Kraut, R., Kiesler, S., & Shklovski, I. (2006). Teenage communication in the instant messaging era. *Computers, phones, and the Internet: Domesticating information technology*, 201-218.

Boyd, D. M., & Ellison, N. B. (2007). Social network sites: Definition, history, and scholarship. *Journal of Computer-Mediated Communication*, *13*(1), 210–230. doi:10.1111/j.1083-6101.2007.00393.x

Buckman, R. (2005, December 8). Too much information? Colleges fear student postings on popular Facebook site could pose security risks. *The Wall Street Journal*. Available at: https://www.wsj.com/articles/SB113400519172816925

Cachola, I., Holgate, E., Preoţiuc-Pietro, D., & Li, J. J. (2018). Expressively vulgar: The socio-dynamics of vulgarity and its effects on sentiment analysis in social media. *Proceedings of the 27th International Conference on Computational Linguistics*, 2927-2938.

Carli, V., & Durkee, T. (2015). Pathological use of the Internet. In e-Mental health. Springer.

Cassidy, W., Faucher, C., & Jackson, M. (2014). The dark side of the ivory tower: Cyberbullying of university faculty and teaching personnel. *The Alberta Journal of Educational Research*, *60*(2), 279–299.

CCSO Cybercrime Working Group. (2013). *Cyberbullying and the non-consensual distribution of intimate images* (Report to the Federal/Provincial/Territorial Ministers Responsible for Justice and Public Safety). Ottawa, Canada: Department of Justice, Canada. Available at: http://www.justice.gc.ca/eng/rp-pr/other-autre/cndii-cdncii/pdf/cndii-cdncii-eng.pdf

Chae, J. (2017). Virtual makeover: Selfie-taking and social media use increase selfie-editing frequency through social comparison. *Computers in Human Behavior*, *66*, 370–376. doi:10.1016/j.chb.2016.10.007

Cheng, Z. C., & Guo, T. C. (2015). The formation of social identity and self-identity based on knowledge contribution in virtual communities: An inductive route model. *Computers in Human Behavior*, *43*, 229–241. doi:10.1016/j.chb.2014.10.056

Chua, T. H. H., & Chang, L. (2016). Follow me and like my beautiful selfies: Singapore teenage girls' engagement in self-presentation and peer comparison on social media. *Computers in Human Behavior, 55*, 190–197. doi:10.1016/j.chb.2015.09.011

Clark, C. (2017). *Creating & sustaining civility in nursing education*. Sigma Theta Tau.

Coe, K., Kenski, K., & Rains, S. A. (2014). Online and uncivil? Patterns and determinants of incivility in newspaper website comments. *Journal of Communication, 64*(4), 658–679. doi:10.1111/jcom.12104

Cooper, K., Quayle, E., Jonsson, L., & Svedin, C. G. (2016). Adolescents and self-taken sexual images: A review of the literature. *Computers in Human Behavior, 55*, 706–716. doi:10.1016/j.chb.2015.10.003

Correa, T., Hinsley, A. W., & De Zuniga, H. G. (2010). Who interacts on the Web? The intersection of users' personality and social media use. *Computers in Human Behavior, 26*(2), 247–253. doi:10.1016/j.chb.2009.09.003

Crane, D., Kawashima, N., & Kawasaki, K. I. (Eds.). (2016). *Global culture: Media, arts, policy, and globalization*. Routledge. doi:10.4324/9781315538792

Davis, R. A., Flett, G. L., & Besser, A. (2002). Validation of a new scale for measuring problematic Internet use: Implications for pre-employment screening. *Cyberpsychology & Behavior, 5*(4), 331–345. doi:10.1089/109493102760275581 PMID:12216698

Delaney, T., & Madigan, T. (2016). *Lessons learned from popular culture*. SUNY Press.

Durkee, T., Carli, V., Floderus, B., Wasserman, C., Sarchiapone, M., Apter, A., . . . Cosman, D. (2016). Pathological internet use and risk-behaviors among European adolescents. *International Journal of Environmental Research and Public Health, 13*(3), 294. Available at: http://www.mdpi.com/1660-4601/13/3/294

Ellison, N. B., Steinfield, C., & Lampe, C. (2007). The benefits of Facebook "friends:" Social capital and college students' use of online social network sites. *Journal of Computer-Mediated Communication, 12*(4), 1143–1168. doi:10.1111/j.1083-6101.2007.00367.x

Ellison, N. B., Vitak, J., Gray, R., & Lampe, C. (2014). Cultivating social resources on social network sites: Facebook relationship maintenance behaviors and their role in social capital processes. *Journal of Computer-Mediated Communication, 19*(4), 855–870. doi:10.1111/jcc4.12078

Etcoff, N., Orbach, S., Scott, J., & D'Agostino, H. (2006). *Beyond stereotypes: Rebuilding the foundation of beauty beliefs: Findings of the 2005 Dove Global Study*. Available at: http://www.beperkthoudbaar.info/upload/documents/dove/DoveBeyondStereotypesWhitePaper.pdf

Eurostat. (2016). *Being young in Europe today - digital world.* Available at: http://ec.europa.eu/eurostat/statistics-explained/index.php?title=File:People_who_used_the_internet_for_civic_activities,_EU-28,_2016_(%25_share)_BYIE18.png

Faucher, C., Jackson, M., & Cassidy, W. (2014). Cyberbullying among university students: Gendered experiences, impacts, and perspectives. *Education Research International, 2014*. Available at: https://www.hindawi.com/journals/edri/2014/698545/abs/

Fox, J., & Vendemia, M. A. (2016). Selective self-presentation and social comparison through photographs on social networking sites. *Cyberpsychology, Behavior, and Social Networking, 19*(10), 593–600. doi:10.1089/cyber.2016.0248 PMID:27732079

Friesland, K. (2018, July 9). How to Stay Anonymous Online – 15 Steps To Your Complete Digital Freedom! *TecNadu*. Available at: https://www.technadu.com/how-to-stay-anonymous-online/6898/

Ganley, D., & Lampe, C. (2009). The ties that bind: Social network principles in online communities. *Decision Support Systems, 47*(3), 266–274. doi:10.1016/j.dss.2009.02.013

Goldberg, L. R. (1990). An alternative "description of personality": The big-five factor structure. *Journal of Personality and Social Psychology, 59*(6), 1216–1229. doi:10.1037/0022-3514.59.6.1216 PMID:2283588

Gonzales, A. L., & Hancock, J. T. (2011). Mirror, mirror on my Facebook wall: Effects of exposure to Facebook on self-esteem. *Cyberpsychology, Behavior, and Social Networking, 14*(1-2), 79–83. doi:10.1089/cyber.2009.0411 PMID:21329447

Gosling, S. D., Rentfrow, P. J., & Swann, W. B. Jr. (2003). A very brief measure of the Big-Five personality domains. *Journal of Research in Personality, 37*(6), 504–528. doi:10.1016/S0092-6566(03)00046-1

Gralla, P. (2006). How the Internet Works (8th ed.). Indianapolis, IN: Que.

Griffiths, M. (2000). Does Internet and computer "addiction" exist? Some case study evidence. *Cyberpsychology & Behavior, 3*(2), 211–218. doi:10.1089/109493100316067

Griffiths, M. D., Kuss, D. J., Billieux, J., & Pontes, H. M. (2016). The evolution of Internet addiction: A global perspective. *Addictive Behaviors, 53*, 193–195. doi:10.1016/j.addbeh.2015.11.001 PMID:26562678

Griffiths, M. D., & Pontes, H. M. (2014). Internet addiction disorder and internet gaming disorder are not the same. *Journal of Addiction Research & Therapy, 5*(4). doi:10.4172/2155-6105.1000e124

Gross, E. F. (2004). Adolescent internet use: What we expect, what teens report. *Journal of Applied Developmental Psychology, 25*(6), 633–649. doi:10.1016/j.appdev.2004.09.005

Guzdial, M., & Landau, S. (2018). Programming programming languages, and analyzing Facebook's failure. *Communications of the ACM, 61*(6), 8–9. doi:10.1145/3204443

Halder, D., & Karuppannan, J. (2009). Cyber socializing and victimization of women. *The Journal on Victimization, 12*(3), 5-26. Available at: https://papers.ssrn.com/sol3/papers.cfm?abstract_id=1561774

Hamid, S., Waycott, J., Kurnia, S., & Chang, S. (2015). Understanding students' perceptions of the benefits of online social networking use for teaching and learning. *The Internet and Higher Education, 26*, 1-9. Available at: https://umexpert.um.edu.my/file/publication/00007217_106152.pdf

Hew, K. F. (2011). Students' and teachers' use of Facebook. *Computers in Human Behavior, 27*(2), 662–676. doi:10.1016/j.chb.2010.11.020

Hollenbaugh, E. E., & Everett, M. K. (2013). The effects of anonymity on self-disclosure in blogs: An application of the online disinhibition effect. *Journal of Computer-Mediated Communication, 18*(3), 283–302. doi:10.1111/jcc4.12008

Hopkins, T. A., Green, B. A., Carnes, P. J., & Campling, S. (2016). Varieties of intrusion: Exhibitionism and voyeurism. *Sexual Addiction & Compulsivity, 23*(1), 4–33. doi:10.1080/10720162.2015.1095138

Hunter, A. (2010). Hope Witsell Cyberbully Suicide: Did She Have a Chance? *CBS News*. Available at: https://www.cbsnews.com/news/hope-witsell-cyberbully-suicide-did-she-have-a-chance-pictures/

Hur, M. H. (2006). Demographic, habitual, and socioeconomic determinants of Internet addiction disorder: An empirical study of Korean teenagers. *Cyberpsychology & Behavior, 9*(5), 514–525. doi:10.1089/cpb.2006.9.514 PMID:17034317

Irvine, R. (2018, May 15). Create a convincing pseudonym, mask your location and keep your phone number private with these tips. *ITPRO*. Available at: http://www.itpro.co.uk/privacy/30584/how-to-stay-anonymous-online/page/0/2

Jane, E. A. (2017). Gendered cyberhate, victim-blaming, and why the internet is more like driving a car on a road than being naked in the snow. In E. Martellozzo & E. A. Jane (Eds.), *Cybercrime and its victims* (pp. 61–78). Routledge. doi:10.4324/9781315637198-4

Kak, A. U. (2018). Cambridge Analytica and the Political Economy of Persuasion. *Economic & Political Weekly, 53*(20). Available at: https://www.epw.in/engage/article/cambridge-analytica-and-political-economy-persuasion

Kowalski, R. M., Limber, S. P., Limber, S., & Agatston, P. W. (2012). *Cyberbullying: Bullying in the digital age*. John Wiley & Sons.

Kuss, D. J., Griffiths, M. D., & Binder, J. F. (2013). Internet addiction in students: Prevalence and risk factors. *Computers in Human Behavior, 29*(3), 959–966. doi:10.1016/j.chb.2012.12.024

Lapidot-Lefler, N., & Barak, A. (2015). The benign online disinhibition effect: Could situational factors induce self-disclosure and prosocial behaviors? *Cyberpsychology: Journal of Psychosocial Research on Cyberspace, 9*(2). Available at: https://cyberpsychology.eu/article/viewFile/4335/3401

Lenhart, A. (2008). *Facebook Connect and a failure to understand online identity management*. Pew Research Center. Available at: http://www.pewinternet.org/2008/12/02/facebook-connect-and-a-failure-to-understand-online-identity-management/

Liao, Y. W., Huang, Y. M., Chen, H. C., & Huang, S. H. (2015). Exploring the antecedents of collaborative learning performance over social networking sites in a ubiquitous learning context. *Computers in Human Behavior*, *43*, 313–323. doi:10.1016/j.chb.2014.10.028

Lin, C., Fang, W., & Jin, J. (2017). You are what you post in "circle of friends" of WeChat: Self-presentation and identity production from a personality perspective. *Global Media and China*, *2*(2), 138–152. doi:10.1177/2059436417728855

Mackey, J. D., Frieder, R. E., Brees, J. R., & Martinko, M. J. (2017). Abusive supervision: A meta-analysis and empirical review. *Journal of Management*, *43*(6), 1940–1965. doi:10.1177/0149206315573997

Madden, M., Lenhart, A., Cortesi, S., Gasser, U., Duggan, M., Smith, A., & Beaton, M. (2013). Teens, social media, and privacy. *Pew Research Center*, *21*, 2–86.

Marshall, E. S. (2010). *Transformational leadership in nursing: From expert clinician to influential leader*. Springer Publishing Company.

Martellozzo, E., Monaghan, A., Adler, J. R., Davidson, J., Leyva, R., & Horvath, M. A. (2017). *"I wasn't sure it was normal to watch it..." A quantitative and qualitative examination of the impact of online pornography on the values, attitudes, beliefs and behaviours of children and young people*. NSPCC & Children's' Commissioner & Middlesex University. Available at: https://learning.nspcc.org.uk/media/1187/mdx-nspcc-occ-pornography-report.pdf

Marx, G. (2001). *Identity and anonymity: Some conceptual distinctions and issues for research*. Princeton University Press.

Marzano, G., & Ochoa Siguencia, L. (2016). A Preliminary Exploratory Research on The Turning Point of Place Branding Management. *International Journal on Global Business Management & Research*, *5*(2), 31–45.

Mascheroni, G., Vincent, J., & Jimenez, E. (2015). "Girls are addicted to likes so they post semi-naked selfies": Peer mediation, normativity and the construction of identity online. *Cyberpsychology: Journal of Psychosocial Research on Cyberspace, 9*(1), 5. Available at: http://eprints.lse.ac.uk/62933/1/__lse.ac.uk_storage_LIBRARY_Secondary_libfile_shared_repository_Content_Vincent,%20J_Girls%20addicted_Vincent_2015_Girls%20addicted_2015.pdf

McKenna, K. Y., & Bargh, J. A. (2000). Plan 9 from cyberspace: The implications of the Internet for personality and social psychology. *Personality and Social Psychology Review*, *4*(1), 57–75. doi:10.1207/S15327957PSPR0401_6

Mesch, G. S., & Talmud, I. (2007). Similarity and the quality of online and offline social relationships among adolescents in Israel. *Journal of Research on Adolescence*, *17*(2), 455–465. doi:10.1111/j.1532-7795.2007.00529.x

Miner, K. N., Diaz, I., Wooderson, R. L., McDonald, J. N., Smittick, A. L., & Lomeli, L. C. (2018). A workplace incivility roadmap: Identifying theoretical speedbumps and alternative routes for future research. *Journal of Occupational Health Psychology*, *23*(3), 320–337. doi:10.1037/ocp0000093 PMID:28749162

Mondal, M., Silva, L. A., & Benevenuto, F. (2017, July). A measurement study of hate speech in social media. *Proceedings of the 28th ACM Conference on Hypertext and Social Media*, 85-94. 10.1145/3078714.3078723

Muñoz, C., & Towner, T. (2009, March). Opening Facebook: How to use Facebook in the college classroom. In Society for information technology & teacher education international conference. Association for the Advancement of Computing in Education (AACE).

Ogilvy, J. (Ed.). (1992a). *Revisioning philosophy*. SUNY Press.

Ogilvy, J. (1992b). Beyond individualism and collectivism. InJ. Ogilvy (Ed.), *Revisioning philosophy* (pp. 217–233). SUNY Press.

Orchard, L. J., & Fullwood, C. (2010). Current perspectives on personality and Internet use. *Social Science Computer Review*, *28*(2), 155–169. doi:10.1177/0894439309335115

Patchin, J. W. (2017). *New teen sexting data*. Cyberbullying Research Center. Available at: https://cyberbullying.org/new-teen-sexting-data

Patterson, A. (2012). Social-networkers of the world, unite and take over: A meta-introspective perspective on the Facebook brand. *Journal of Business Research*, *65*(4), 527–534. doi:10.1016/j.jbusres.2011.02.032

Reagle, J. M. Jr. (2015). *Reading the comments: Likers, haters, and manipulators at the bottom of the web*. MIT Press. doi:10.7551/mitpress/10116.001.0001

Rocha, V., & Perry, T. (2015, February 3). Kamala Harris: Lives ruined, women terrified in 'revenge porn' case. *The Guardian*. Available at: https://www.theguardian.com/world/2014/sep/01/jennifer-lawrence-rihanna-star-victims-hacked-nude-pictures

Samimi, P., & Alderson, K. G. (2014). Sexting among undergraduate students. *Computers in Human Behavior, 31*, 230–241. doi:10.1016/j.chb.2013.10.027

Schwartz, P. M. (2003). Property, privacy, and personal data. *Harvard Law Review, 117*(7), 2056–2128. doi:10.2307/4093335

Şener, G., & Özkoçak, Y. (2014). Going Visible in Social Networks: Strategies of Self-Presentation in Facebook Photos. *Journal of Media Critiques, 2*(2), 91–114. doi:10.17349/jmc114205

Shin, Y., Kim, M., Im, C., & Chong, S. C. (2017). Selfie and self: The effect of selfies on self-esteem and social sensitivity. *Personality and Individual Differences, 111*, 139–145. doi:10.1016/j.paid.2017.02.004

Silva, L. A., Mondal, M., Correa, D., Benevenuto, F., & Weber, I. (2016, March). Analyzing the Targets of Hate in Online Social Media. *Proceedings of the Tenth International AAAI Conference on Web and Social Media ICWSM*, 687-690.

Singh, V. K., Radford, M. L., Huang, Q., & Furrer, S. (2017). "They basically, like, destroyed the school one day": On Newer App Features and Cyberbullying in Schools. *CSCW, 17*, 1210–1216.

Smith, G., John, P., Sturgis, P., & Nomura, H. (2009, September). Deliberation and internet engagement: initial findings from a randomised controlled trial evaluating the impact of facilitated internet forums. *ECPR General Conference*. Available at: https://www.researchgate.net/profile/Peter_John4/publication/228123544_Deliberation_and_Internet_Engagement_Initial_Findings_from_a_Randomised_Controlled_Trial_Evaluating_the_Impact_of_Facilitated_Internet_Forums/links/02e7e517aac29685a1000000.pdf

Smith, R., Morgan, J., & Monks, C. (2017). Students' perceptions of the effect of social media ostracism on wellbeing. *Computers in Human Behavior, 68*, 276–285. doi:10.1016/j.chb.2016.11.041

Sommer, L. (2018, August 10). Sarahah and other anonymous messaging apps guide. *Stayhipp*. Available at: https://stayhipp.com/news/how-to-prevent-cyberbullying-on-anonymous-messaging-apps-like-sarahah/

Steijn, W. M. (2014). A developmental perspective regarding the behaviour of adolescents, young adults, and adults on social network sites. *Cyberpsychology: Journal of Psychosocial Research on Cyberspace, 8*(2). Available at: https://cyberpsychology.eu/article/view/4306/0

Stutzman, F. (2006). An evaluation of identity-sharing behavior in social network communities. *Journal of the International Digital Media and Arts Association, 3*(1), 10–18.

Suler, J. (2004). The online disinhibition effect. *Cyberpsychology & Behavior, 7*(3), 321–326. doi:10.1089/1094931041291295 PMID:15257832

Suler, J. R. (2002). Identity management in cyberspace. *Journal of Applied Psychoanalytic Studies, 4*(4), 455–460. doi:10.1023/A:1020392231924

Temple, J. R., Paul, J. A., Van den Berg, P., Le, V. D., McElhany, A., & Temple, B. W. (2012). Teen sexting and its association with sexual behaviors. *Archives of Pediatrics & Adolescent Medicine, 166*(9), 828–833. doi:10.1001/archpediatrics.2012.835 PMID:22751805

Tepper, B. J., & Henle, C. A. (2011). A case for recognizing distinctions among constructs that capture interpersonal mistreatment in work organizations. *Journal of Organizational Behavior, 32*(3), 487–498. doi:10.1002/job.688

The New York Times. (2018). *Maggie Haberman: Why I Needed to Pull Back from Twitter*. Available at: https://www.nytimes.com/2018/07/20/sunday-review/maggie-haberman-twitter-donald-trump.html

Toffler, A. (1980). *The Third Wave*. New York: Morrow.

Topping, A. (2014). Jennifer Lawrence and Rihanna among celebrity victims of hacked nude photos. *The Guardian*. Available at: https://www.theguardian.com/world/2014/sep/01/jennifer-lawrence-rihanna-star-victims-hacked-nude-pictures

Tsay-Vogel, M. (2016). Me versus them: Third-person effects among Facebook users. *New Media & Society, 18*(9), 1956-1972.

Tufnell, N. (2015, March 6). 21 tips, tricks, and shortcuts to help you stay anonymous online. *The Guardian*. Available at: https://www.theguardian.com/technology/2015/mar/06/tips-tricks-anonymous-privacy

Turkle, S. (2011). *Life on the Screen*. Simon and Schuster.

Turner, P. G., & Lefevre, C. E. (2017). Instagram use is linked to increased symptoms of orthorexia nervosa. *Eating and Weight Disorders-Studies on Anorexia, Bulimia and Obesity*, *22*(2), 277–284.

Valkenburg, P. M., & Peter, J. (2007). Online communication and adolescent well-being: Testing the stimulation versus the displacement hypothesis. *Journal of Computer-Mediated Communication*, *12*(4), 1169–1182. doi:10.1111/j.1083-6101.2007.00368.x

Valkenburg, P. M., & Peter, J. (2009). Social consequences of the Internet for adolescents: A decade of research. *Current Directions in Psychological Science, 18*(1), 1-5. Available at: https://s3.amazonaws.com/academia.edu.documents/46743837/Social_Consequences_of_the_Internet_for_20160623-12266-aq0re3.pdf?AWSAccessKeyId=AKIAIWOWYYGZ2Y53UL3A&Expires=1555784185&Signature=%2Fr6YT%2F5or%2BIZeJGoWGCDhr87Q6g%3D&response-content-disposition=inline%3B%20filename%3DSocial_consequences_of_the_internet_for.pdf

Vossen, H. G., & Valkenburg, P. M. (2016). Do social media foster or curtail adolescents' empathy? A longitudinal study. *Computers in Human Behavior*, *63*, 118–124. doi:10.1016/j.chb.2016.05.040

Wallace, P. (2015). *The psychology of the Internet*. Cambridge University Press. doi:10.1017/CBO9781139940962

Wang, D. (2017). A study of the relationship between narcissism, extraversion, drive for entertainment, and narcissistic behavior on social networking sites. *Computers in Human Behavior*, *66*, 138–148. doi:10.1016/j.chb.2016.09.036

Wardrop, M. (2010, August 18). Young will have to change names to escape 'cyber past' warns Google's Eric Schmidt. *The Telegraph*. Available at: https://www.telegraph.co.uk/technology/google/7951269/Young-will-have-to-change-names-to-escape-cyber-past-warns-Googles-Eric-Schmidt.html

Weale, S. (2015, November 10). Sexting-becoming-the-norm-for-teens-warn-child-protection expert. *The Guardian*. Available at: https://www.theguardian.com/society/2015/nov/10/sexting-becoming-the-norm-for-teens-warn-child-protection-experts

Weinstein, A. & Lejoyeux, M. (2010). Internet Addiction or Excessive Internet Use. *The American Journal of Drug and Alcohol Abuse, 36*(5), 277-283.

Weisskirch, R. S., & Delevi, R. (2011). "Sexting" and adult romantic attachment. *Computers in Human Behavior*, *27*(5), 1697–1701. doi:10.1016/j.chb.2011.02.008

Widyanto, L., & Griffiths, M. (2006). 'Internet addiction': A critical review. *International Journal of Mental Health and Addiction*, *4*(1), 31–51. doi:10.100711469-006-9009-9

Wildermuth, S., & Davis, C. B. (2012). Flaming the faculty: Exploring root causes, consequences, and potential remedies to the problem of instructor-focused uncivil online student discourse in higher education. In L. A. Wankel & C. Wankel (Eds.), *Misbehavior online in higher education: Cutting-edge technologies in higher education* (pp. 379–404). Emerald Group Publishing Bingley. doi:10.1108/S2044-9968(2012)0000005020

World Bank. (2016). *Digital Dividends. World Development Report 2016*. The World bank.

Xing, X., Liang, Y. L., Cheng, H., Dang, J., Huang, S., Han, R., ... Mishra, S. (2011, March). Safevchat: Detecting obscene content and misbehaving users in online video chat services. In *Proceedings of the 20th International Conference on the World Wide Web*, (pp. 685-694). ACM. 10.1145/1963405.1963501

Young, K., Pistner, M., O'Mara, J., & Buchanan, J. (1999). Cyber disorders: The mental health concern for the new millennium. *Cyberpsychology & Behavior*, *2*(5), 475–479. doi:10.1089/cpb.1999.2.475 PMID:19178220

Zhao, S., Grasmuck, S., & Martin, J. (2008). Identity construction on Facebook: Digital empowerment in anchored relationships. *Computers in Human Behavior*, *24*(5), 1816–1836. doi:10.1016/j.chb.2008.02.012

KEY TERMS AND DEFINITIONS

Dark Web: Also called *darknet*, *black web*, or *black net*, is a part of the internet that is accessible only through specific software such as the Tor ("The Onion Routing" project) or I2P ("Invisible Internet Project") browsers and which often doesn't use standard communication protocols and ports.

Deep Web: Also called *invisible web* or *hidden web*, is the huge (90%) un-indexed part of the World Wide Web containing contents that are inaccessible to conventional search engines such as Google, Yahoo, Bing, etc. Bank accounts and emails are examples of deep web contents. The dark web and the deep web aren't synonyms.

Internet: A massive network of networks.

Internet Incivility: Behavior that can include being rude, discourteous, impolite, and lacking in respect, as well as violating workplace norms of behavior.

Internet Protocol (IP): The set of rules that defines how a digital device sends and receives data on the internet.

Internet Relative Anonymity: Since anonymity is not granted on the internet, the expression relative anonymity should be preferred.

Sexting: The sending and receiving of sexually explicit messages, especially using mobile phones.

Social Networking Sites: Web-based services that allow individuals to (1) construct a public or semi-public profile within a bounded system, (2) articulate a list of other users with whom they share a connection, and (3) view and traverse their list of connections and those made by others within the system.

Trolls, Trolling: Terms used to refer to those who deliberately try to cause distress to others online through disruption, often anonymously.

WWW: The acronym for World Wide Web. It was the name of the first internet browser created by Tim Berners-Lee in 1990, namely a communications model that, through the Hypertext Transfer Protocol (HTTP), enables the exchange of information over the internet. WWW is not a synonym of the internet, but only the combination of all the resources and users that, on the internet, are using the HTTP.

ENDNOTES

1 For obvious reasons, the Facebook group address is not provided.

2 The *Ear of Dionysius* is the name given to a cave in Syracuse, Sicily (Italy), by the painter Caravaggio. The cave possesses amazing acoustical properties that let a person inside the ear whisper to someone at the other end. Caravaggio created the legend that the cave was used as a prison which let Dionysius eavesdrop on the conversations inside.

Chapter 4
Technological Help to Prevent and Reduce Cyberbullying

Gilberto Marzano
Rezekne Academy of Technologies, Latvia

ABSTRACT

This chapter intends to present the most common technological solutions that can be implemented to prevent and reduce cyberbullying. Three main questions will be addressed: How can children stay safe online? What can the information technology (IT) industry do to combat cyberbullying? How effective is automatic cyberbullying detection? The chapter will illustrate the progress that has been made to reduce cyberbullying through technological means and discuss the notion of industry self-regulation. Indeed, the IT industry has a responsibility to respect societal obligations towards users, especially when users are children. While many companies in the industry are working responsibly on solutions for the safer use of technology, some global internet service providers are involved in the illicit use of users' personal data. As a consequence, problems of online safety cannot be solved locally, but through concerted actions undertaken at an international level.

INTRODUCTION

Home is no longer a private space. It is penetrated by social networks, rooms for online chatting, and virtual spaces for shopping, entertainment, and socialization.

Children and youngsters perceive the internet, smartphones, and related technologies as essential tools for their social life. Until a few years ago, many

DOI: 10.4018/978-1-5225-8076-8.ch004

parents had difficulties in using the new technologies themselves, and didn't understand the risk hidden in them. In fact, plenty of parents candidly admit that it was their children who taught them how to use the internet.

Today, the situation is completely different. Parents know how to manage digital technologies, and are able to protect their children by activating parental control tools.

In this regard, applications have been implemented to fight cyberbullying by using blocking and filtering options on a computer. Parents can prevent access to dangerous websites using commercial as well as open source and freeware programs that provide functions of parental control. Most of these functions enable parents to check the internet activities of their children, prevent their access to certain websites, and limit the time they spend online. However, whilst such preventive measures are useful, they are not infallible since parental controls can be bypassed. In the same vein, a child can use a computer or a smartphone where no filters are configured. Moreover, the proliferation of mobile technologies offers ever more new opportunities for accessing the internet.

Trying to avoid the problem of cyberbullying by preventing children from using the internet altogether is, however, not the answer. In fact, it has been observed that banning a child's access to the internet is not only impossible but can, paradoxically, actually damage their educational and social development (Coyne & Gountsidou, 2013).

Taking the drastic step of completely banning children from using the internet and smartphones, may not, in any case, solve the actual cyberbullying itself, as the following case illustrates.

To avoid acts of online bullying, the parents of a young girl, whom we will refer to as E., prevented her from surfing on the internet in their absence, and only allowed her to use an old mobile phone that was not equipped with multimedia functions and an internet connection. When E. was thirteen, however, she became a victim of cyberbullying. How could this happen? Some of her classmates showed her that there were messages on Facebook denigrating and ridiculing her. These messages were posted by other classmates who, in front of her, behaved in a kind and friendly manner. The consequence was that E. was doubly upset: she could not understand why her friends were denigrating her and, at the same time, she was unable to respond. Indeed, she could not connect to the internet herself and, consequently, was reliant on friends to see the hurtful messages concerning her. This created serious stress problems for E., and eventually her parents were forced to move her to a different school.

In this light, it is remarkable that, in 2010, a law was approved in France that banned the use of smartphones during any teaching activity (Shaban, 2018; Smith, 2018). Going further, in fact, the French parliament have recently (July 30, 2018) banned smartphones along with other kinds of internet-connected devices such as tablets from schools entirely. This prohibition has been imposed on schoolchildren between 3 and 15 years of age. French secondary schools are left to decide whether to adopt the phone ban for their students.

In the regard, Shariff observed a few years ago that:

The 'weapons' being used in attempts to control cyber-bullying consist of lobbying by teachers' unions, parents and school administrators who want their governments to implement laws and policies that censor social communication tools such as Facebook and YouTube from being accessed at schools. Some call for bans on cellular and mobile phones that have photographic and text-messaging capabilities. Others want to restrict computer use while children are at school; impose school board monitored firewalls; and enforce zero-tolerance policies that include suspensions and, in some cases expulsion (Education Act, R.S.O., 1990), as deterrents to bullying. (Shariff, 2008, p. 3)

Many psychologists share the conviction that cyberbullying is essentially a relational and personality problem. Accordingly, in order to prevent it, they suggest intervening in the relational behavior and attitudes of young people (Goodboy & Martin, 2015; Kowalski, Giumetti, Schroeder, & Lattanner, 2014; van Geel, Goemans, Toprak, & Vedder, 2017).

Nevertheless, the positive contribution that technological interventions has in reducing cyberbullying and mitigating its effects should not be left unevaluated. Strategies of cyberbullying prevention should focus either on the study of aspects of socialization, or on researching solutions for the automatic detection of cyberbullying.

Applications for the automatic detection of cyberbullying are still at an experimental stage, but advances being made in relation to cybersecurity, for example algorithms developed for detecting invalid information (Kumar, Jiang, Jung, Luo, & Leskovec, 2018), could be applied to cyberbullying.

All this said, of course, any technical remedy remains useless without an adequate educational endeavor on the part of children, parents, and teachers.

In this chapter, the contribution of technology to the prevention and reduction of cyberbullying will be discussed, and the issue of the IT industry's societal obligations will be explored.

Stay Safe Online

In 2007, the UK government commissioned a review on the risks that children face from the internet and video games. It was aimed at protecting children from these risks, enabling them to play video games and surf the internet in a safe and informed way. The review was known as the *Byron Review*, after its author Dr. Tanya Byron, a clinical psychologist specialized in child and adolescent mental health.

The results of the Byron Review were published on April 27, 2008 in a report entitled *Safer Children in a Digital world.* In the report, the author argued for the involvement of the IT industry in restricting access to harmful and dangerous content online:

[…] industry should ensure that computers sold for use in the home in the UK should have Kite marked parental control software which takes parents through clear prompts and explanations to help set it up and that ISPs offer and advertise this prominently when users set up their connection.

[…] search providers should agree to make it obvious to users what level of search is on (e.g. safe or moderate) and give users the option to 'lock it' on and that every search engine have a clear link to child safety information and safe search settings on the front page of their website – this is particularly important as most parents are comfortable using search functions. (Byron, 2008)

Byron was persuaded that the safety of children on the internet should involve representatives from the industry, third sectors, child sectors, parents, and government institutions. Moreover, in her opinion, firms should have to implement a voluntary code of practice defining the minimum standards to which the industry must subscribe. An independent monitoring system, based on self-assessment, should also be created. The Byron strategy is synthetized in the following points of the report's executive summary:

- In relation to the internet, we need a shared culture of responsibility with families, industry, government, and others in the public and third sectors all playing their part to reduce the availability of potentially harmful material, restrict access to it by children, and increase children's resilience.

- I propose that we seek to achieve gains in these three areas by having a national strategy for child internet safety which involves better self-regulation and better provision of information and education for children and families" (Byron, 2008).

At the time that Byron was conducting her study, the IT industry was just starting to concern itself with users' safety, however, remarkable progress has been made in the decade since then.

In 2008, in concomitance with the Byron Review, the European Commission created ESNTF (the European Social Networking Task Force) involving a broad group of stakeholders, such as social networks providers, scientists, and organizations dealing with child care. The ESNTF worked to develop guidelines for minimizing online potential harm to children and young people. The result was the *Seven Safer Social Networking Principles* (ESNTF, 2009):

Principle 1: Raise awareness of safety education messages and acceptable use policies among users, parents, teachers, and carers in a prominent, clear and age-appropriate manner.

Principle 2: Work towards ensuring that services are age-appropriate for the intended audience.

Principle 3: Empower users through tools and technology.

Principle 4: Provide easy-to-use mechanisms to report conduct or content that violates the terms of service.

Principle 5: Respond to notifications of illegal content or conduct.

Principle 6: Enable and encourage users to employ a safe approach to personal information and privacy.

Principle 7: Assess the means for reviewing illegal or prohibited content/ conduct.

In 2010, The *Child Exploitation and Online Protection* command (CEOP) of the UK National Crime Agency introduced the *Click CEOP*, a safety or panic button, to provide children, young people, parents, and professionals with trusted online safety advice, help, and support. It also included access to an online mechanism for reporting known or suspected child sexual exploitation or child sexual abuse directly to CEOP (Figure 1).

Facebook agreed on the suggestion of allowing users to report offensive content but disliked the graphic of the CEOP button, since they believed it would intimidate and confuse people. Facebook preferred a different "report

Figure 1. The CEOP safety button

button" to provide users with the option to report to CEOP as well as to other moderators (Barnet, 2010).

At the end of the 2010s, many software providers such as Google and Microsoft started to focus on developing tips and advice for staying safe on the Web.

In 2010, Google launched the Google Family Safety Center intended to help children to safely use the internet and handle cyberbullies (Google, 2010).

The introduction to *Get off to a safe start* has remained the same:

There are so many fascinating things to do and explore online, but there are also times when the Internet can be a little bit scary. Just like in the offline world, it's important to keep yourself safe and secure. Whether you're a new Internet user or an old hand, it's good to stay updated on the best practices when it comes to sharing your data online and browsing safely.

The list of advice for staying more secure on the web cover the following areas:

- Secure your passwords
- Sign in and out
- Manage multiple accounts
- Check your Gmail settings
- Use secure networks
- Lock your screen or device
- Keep your device clean
- Online shopping safety
- Is Google Calling or is it a Scam?

One of first of the big software providers to engage in online safety was Microsoft, starting to develop programs to protect children on the internet at an early time. In fact, in the middle of the 2000s, together with other partners, Microsoft created the *Web Watchers*, a program to support online safety.

The *Web Watchers* was launched in 2005. It was an internet security and safety program aimed at providing teachers in the U.S. with age-appropriate and curriculum-valid lessons to help students better understand the opportunities and risks of the internet (Microsoft, 2005).

Nowadays, Microsoft offers many free applications for parental control which allow them to manage their children's computer activity: which websites were visited, the programs used, and the length of time spent on the computer. In particular, Microsoft parental controls provide:

- Web restrictions. It is possible to restrict the websites that children can visit, make sure children only visit age-appropriate websites, prevent or allow file downloads, and set up filters to block or allow particular content.
- Time limits. It is possible to set time limits to control when children are allowed to log on to the computer. Time limits prevent children from logging on during the specified hours and, if they are already logged on, they will be automatically logged off.
- Games. It is possible to control access to games, choose an age rating level, choose the types of content you want to block, and decide whether you want to allow or block unrated or specific games.
- Allow or block specific programs. This function prevents children from running specific programs.

However, in the last few years, an increasing number of software solutions have been developed in order to supervise the online activity of children. These are necessary as parents cannot control what kids are doing online alone, since kids are continuously connected and use a wide range of devices to communicate.

Usually, parental control software runs both on computers and mobile devices, and allows parents to block unwanted web content, limit screen time, restrict the use of risky applications, and more. Most products available on the market support Windows and Android and many of them are also compatible with mac OS and iOS.

Content filtering functions allow access to be blocked to websites that match particular categories such as hate, violence, and porn. However, these functions work with secure (HTTPS) sites and a smart teen could bypass the filter by using a secure anonymizing proxy website or an anonymizing browser. Nevertheless, many products can now keep a detailed log of the web activity of the user, and can help parents to control the online activity of their kids to some degree.

Recent advances in products provide functions to track the viewing history of kids on YouTube and video streaming channels, check their location, or even remotely lock down a device to force them to stop them using it entirely, perhaps while they are at school.

Geofencing is a new feature. Geofencing is a location-based service which uses GPS, RFID, Wi-Fi, or cellular data to trigger a pre-programmed action when a mobile device or RFID tag enters or exits a virtual boundary set up around a geographical location, which could be a museum, monument, park, or specific building (Wong, Sang, & Peng, 2017). Depending on the application, a geofence service could prompt mobile push notifications, trigger text messages or alerts, or even disable certain technology.

Geofencing applications are currently being experimented in many sectors, such as marketing, audience engagement, and security. Specific solutions have also been implemented for online child safety (Day, Wise, Sigler & Roarke, 2016).

Table 1 shows the main functions of parental control products.

In this regard, the *Australian Government's Cybersafety Help B*utton initiative introduced in 2010 also merits a mention. It was designed in order to provide internet users, particularly children and young people, with easy online access to cybersafety information and advice. Recently, the *eSafety*

Table 1. The main functions of parental control products

Function	Type
Time scheduler	Basic
Content filtering	Basic
Filter HTTPS sites	Basic
Access scheduling	Basic
Social Network monitoring	Basic
Remote management	Recommended
Geofencing	Advanced
Location tracking	Advanced

Source: author's own elaboration

Commission substituted the button with a form for *cyberbullying complaints* contained in a set of extended cybersafety information and resources. Figure 2 shows a section of the form available for reporting cyberbullying episodes.

Recently, Topcu-Uzer and Tanrikulu have analyzed 16 apps specifically related to cyberbullying (2018). Most of these (11) aim to enhance cyberbullying prevention measures by providing practical information, whilst the others focus on intervention (4) or on both prevention and intervention (1).

What the IT Industry Can Do

Firms operating within the IT industry are involved with cyberbullying safety to varying degrees, since the IT industry encompasses a variety of subjects, from Internet Service Providers (ISPs), mobile phone producers, social networking site developers and providers, developers of computer games, providers of chat and messenger apps, and so on. Additionally, the same organization might provide users with a number of services that could require different types of safety actions.

Age control is a crucial aspect for the protection of children. The most popular instant messaging apps state in their policies that users must be a minimum of 13 years of age. In their community guidelines, social network providers declare that threats and violence, harassment and bullying, hate speech, and impersonation are banned.

Figure 2. A section of the form provided by the Australian government to report a cyberbullying event
Source: Office of the eSafety Commissioner, https://esafety.gov.au/complaints-and-reporting/cyberbullying-complaints/i-want-to-report-cyberbullying

Section 4 – What is happening?

Tell us as much as possible about the cyberbullying.

What has been happening? **Have you told friends, family or anyone else?** **Do you have support?** **How are you feeling about the cyberbullying?** **Is there anything else we should know?**	*Enter text here*
How long has this been going on for?	☐ Just today ☐ Up to one week ☐ Up to one month ☐ Longer than one month

Some apps provide a function to report cyberbullying incidents, for example SnapChat advises its users:

If you ever experience any harassment, bullying, or any other safety concern, you can always report it right to us! Every report we receive is reviewed by someone at Snapchat, usually within 24 hours.

Together we can make Snapchat a safer place and a stronger community.

To report a Story on Snapchat, just press and hold on the offending Snap until a button appears in the bottom-left corner. Tap it to report the Story and let us know what's going on. (Snapchat Support, 2018)

Social media companies such as Facebook, Twitter, Instagram, Snapchat, LinkedIn, Pinterest, Tumblr, Reddit, and YouTube all have policies against bullying and cyberbullying that are published in their websites, and often collect and present tips that could help their users. However, although these companies emphasize that their user's safety is paramount to them, it has been observed that

[...] specific criteria of effectiveness, evidence of effectiveness, or the details behind how the effectiveness of this effort is measured remain difficult to determine in the case of established and new companies alike. (Milosevic, 2018, p. 121)

Internet Service Providers also offer parental control and network-level filters.

Google with Gmail, and Microsoft with Outlook, have implemented filters to block messages containing harassing, offensive, and threatening content, and provide users with a service to report abuse. Microsoft users, for example, are advised as follows:

* *Customers who wish to report* **abuse** *about harassment, impersonation, child exploitation, child pornography etc., received* **from a outlook.com account** *should send their complaint to abuse@outlook.com with all the relevant information (abuse@hotmail, or abuse@outlook.com)*

* **If you are being threatened please call your local law enforcement.**

* *If you wish to report abuse against a non-Microsoft account, please send the complaint to abuse@xxxxxx.com, where xxxxxx.com is the text that appears after the "@" symbol in the sender's e-mail address. For example, if the unwanted email came from someone@mymail.com then report the email message to abuse@mymail.com. You can also use the site http://abuse.net to identify the correct abuse reporting address. (Microsoft, 2018)*

Chatroulette, a social chat website launched in 2009 that has been the source of many controversies over the years with problems of nudity, harassment, and stalking, provides users with clear rules and regulations for using their chat service, two of its restrictions being:

1. Deceptive behavior is a restriction here on **chatroulette**:
    - Troubling others with vulgar, intimidating comments;
    - Teasing other **chatroulette users** in concerns of their color, birth, race etc.;
    - Degrading others' dignity through text, image, or video chat.
2. It is not allowed to behave disgracefully with other chat partners:
    - Chatting and showing bare chest without a face;
    - Maltreat your chat companion with sexual abuse;
    - Asking to get involved in sex or intercourse virtually;
    - Displaying the body parts that are not socially acceptable;
    - Exhibiting the genital body organs;
    - Touching, scratching, rubbing, or putting your hands on private parts;
    - Directing camera angle lower than your chest;
    - Doing any sexually or physically intimate activity.

Currently, the IT industry is both implementing technical features and empowering users in their efforts towards keeping kids safe online (Nocentini, Zambuto, & Menesini, 2015).

Table 2 synthetizes the main types of solutions currently being developed.

In the last few years, mobile operators have been multiplying their investments in staying safe online. In 2015, GSMA, an organization that represents the interests of mobile operators worldwide, established a partnership with Child Helpline International (CHI) aimed at helping young people deal with issues such as cyberbullying, sexual extortion, and online privacy. Mats Granryd, director general, reported that in 2018, GSMA started an initiative called Mobile Alliance Against Child Sexual Abuse Content

Table 2. Information and Communication engagement for keeping kids safe online

Implementing technical features	Empowering users
• Blocking messages • Providing filtering • Monitoring internet usage • Activating instant alerts • Setting time limits • Defining community guidance • Providing services for reporting abuse	• Providing education and guidance on safe internet use • Offering tips to stop cyberbullying

with the involvement of more than 100 mobile operators from 65 different countries around the world. Under this initiative, members sign up to deliver on three objectives (Granryd, 2018):

- To notify law enforcement of abusive content and aim to have it removed at source.
- To support the implementation of a reporting-mechanism, such as a hotline, in all countries where they operate.
- To work towards restricting access, where allowed, to URLs or websites which feature child sexual abuse content, and to do this by using INTERPOL or other international organizations' lists of known sites.

Wide-ranging efforts are being made, both at a public and private level, to improve the performance of automatic detection of unbecoming, harmful, and threatening content. Indeed, the fight against terrorism has made automatic content detection a very important task for state security. Numerous algorithms are being experimented for military purposes (cyberwar) as well as for the detection of fake news (Shu, Sliva, Wang, Tang, & Liu, 2017). One can expect that within a relatively short time, this research will lead to commercial and low-cost apps that are useful for combatting cyberbullying.

Automatic Detection of Cyberbullying

On May 15 2018, Facebook published its first report detailing the activities it has instigated to enforce its community standards (Facebook, 2018). Media consider this report to be the company's response to the increased scrutiny it has been under following the Cambridge Analytica scandal and other revelations that have emerged relating to the US presidential election in 2016 (Magid, 2015).

The report covers the period from October 2017 to March 2018. However, Facebook said it could not estimate the prevalence of posts containing violating content. For example, the company stated that it is still developing measurement methods for detecting hate speech and, accordingly, is unable to provide reliable data for the reported period.

In fact, Figure 3 reveals that the Facebook algorithms flagged only 38% of identified hate speech posts over the period, meaning that 62% were only addressed because users had reported them.

It is clear, then, that the development of the Facebook platform for the automatic detection of problematic posts is a work in progress and still at an experimental stage, as one particular episode illustrates. In July 2018, the algorithm developed to remove advertisements with sexually oriented content (but which also routinely flag artistic or educational nudes) censored a series of promotions for the Belgian region of Flanders because they featured works by Flemish artists mostly known for their detailed depictions of lush, curvaceous women and cherubs (BBC News, 2018).

This said, the reliance on automatic monitoring of social networks and the automatic detection of dangerous and harmful content is, absolutely, an essential route, given the immense volume of posts that people make on a daily basis.

Figure 3. Facebook statistics on identification of hate speech posts
Source: Facebook, 2018

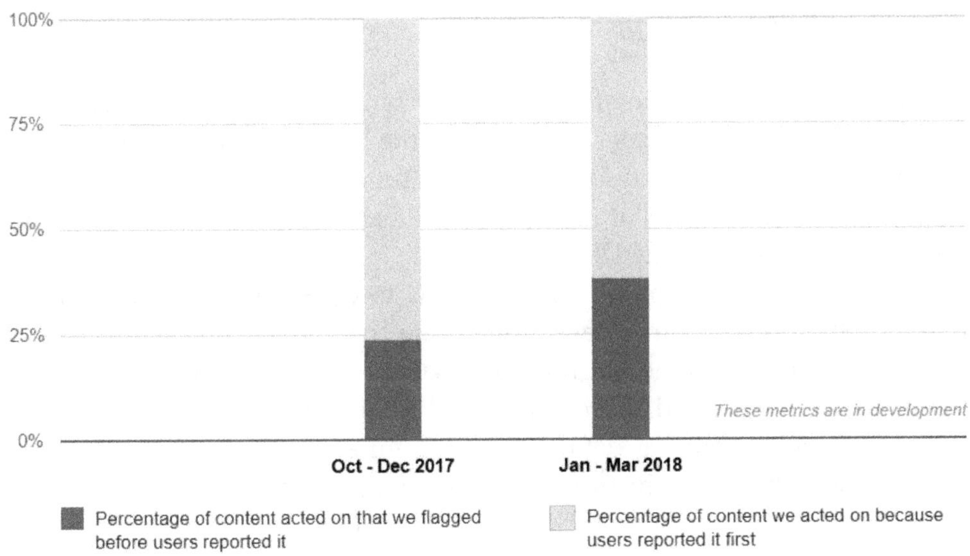

Furthermore, although parental control tools might block undesirable content, and many social networks make use of keyword lists to intercept harmful posts, these capabilities are not enough to combat cyberbullying. Often, cyberbullies send subtle and implicitly harassing messages in which no offensive word actually appears.

Intelligent applications are being experimented in the field of the content analysis of social networks that might be able to find a solution to this problem. Since the 1960s, automatic content analysis has been a scope of investigation for researchers interested in information retrieval and natural language processing. The difficulties related to natural language analysis emerged early on. At the end of the 1960s, Salton, one of the most eminent researchers in the field of information retrieval observed:

If the information items to be dealt with are written documents or books, the basic elements are words in the natural language, and the larger units are sentences, paragraphs, or chapters. Unhappily, although it is relatively easy to isolate the individual word in a text, an interpretation of the meaning of the words is much more difficult. Furthermore, there is no-well-defined set of rules by which the individual words in the language are combined into meaningful word groups or sentences. Specifically, the correct identification of the meaning of word groups depends at least in part on the proper recognition of syntactic and semantic ambiguities, on the correct interpretation of homographs, on the recognition of semantic equivalences, on the detection of words relations, and on general awareness of the background and environment of a given utterance. (Salton, 1969, pp. 152-153)

Despite these difficulties, however, important advances have been made in the field of automatic content analysis over the last decades, and the research is moving so fast these days that it is sometimes hard to keep up (Appavu, Rajaram, Muthupandian, Athiappan, & Kashmeera, 2009; Schwartz & Ungar, 2015; Willig & Rogers, 2017).

Currently, the most promising solutions to cyberbullying detection are based on hybrid (Dadvar, Trieschnigg, & de Jong, 2014) and supervised or semi-supervised machine learning approaches (Nahar, Al-Maskari, Li, & Pang, 2014). Supervised approaches involve the construction of a classifier based on labeled training data, whereas semi-supervised approaches rely on classifiers that are built from a training corpus containing a small set of labeled and a large set of un-labelled instances (Van Hee et al., 2018).

Building effective applications for automatic cyberbullying detection is, though, far from easy. For example, online conversations lack the signals of a face-to-face interaction such as intonation, facial expressions, and gestures, which makes them more ambiguous than real-life conversations (Duarte, Llanso, & Loup, 2018; Vandebosch & Van Cleemput, 2009). As such, the receiver may sometimes get the wrong impression that they are being offended or ridiculed when that was not the intent. In this regard, we can wonder how a machine can be expected to detect the sarcastic expression that frequently occurs in forums, blogs, and microposts if it is difficult for even a human to recognize it. Nevertheless, in 2013, the news spread that the French company Spotter had indeed managed to develop an analytics tool that was able to identify sarcastic comments posted online (BBC News, 2013). Nowadays, the researchers who are working on sarcasm detection follow different approaches (Maynard & Greenwood, 2014; Tsur, Davidov, & Rappoport, 2010).

Community Moderation

In her book regarding the cyberbullying policies of social media companies (2018), Tijana Milosevic analyzed the state of the art for how companies deal with cyberbullying. She is persuaded that social media companies play an important role in addressing cyberbullying, and the aim of her book was to analyze how these companies address cyber risks, what policies have been developed, and what the real remedies are. The author denounces that there is an overall lack of transparency within social media companies:

While the more established companies appear to succeed in projecting an image of decisive and effective handling of bullying, they nonetheless provide extremely limited information about their operational policies. A widespread use of non-disclosure agreements (NDAs) in the industry prevents much insight into concrete evidence for the effectiveness of anti-bullying enforcement mechanisms, in both the less established and more established companies alike. (Milosevic, 2018, p. 6)

The author observes that, nowadays, social media platforms have begun to introduce flagging or reporting options for users. In this way, part of the responsibility for moderation is transferred to users. Flagging is a mechanism for reporting offensive content to a social media platform that is present in many social media platforms, including Facebook, Twitter, Vine, Flickr,

YouTube, Instagram, etc. By using flagging or reporting options, users can express their concerns and feedback regarding particular content.

Social media companies point to user flagging to legitimize their own content management decisions as a measurable expression of "community standards".

However, although flags have becoming a ubiquitous mechanism of social media governance, they cannot be assumed to be a means to directly represent community sentiments. In fact, the algorithms that are behind the processing of flags are not transparent and stable (Crawford & Gillespie, 2016). Furthermore, flagging could offer a legitimation to remove undesired content on behalf of the user community at large. Flags on social media could be used to legitimize the content management by social media companies under the pretense of upholding community decisions, since their algorithms would be the measure of the community expression.

Milosevic argues that a debate is necessary regarding the critical consequences of the privatization of the digital public sphere, and to address the challenges presented by cyber threats, especially by cyberbullying. Indeed, she urges that this debate should also encompass the risks related to community moderation by private entities which pursue commercial interests.

Facebook is currently testing a feature that allows users to "downvote" comments (Figure 4). The downvote function should allow users to signal

Figure 4. An example of a downvote
Source: Constine, 2018

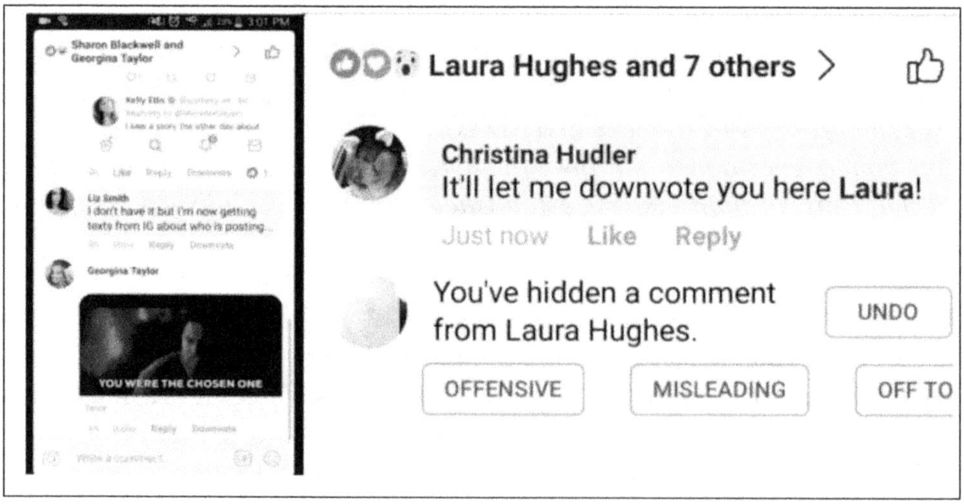

that a comment is "inappropriate, uncivil, or misleading." Facebook has pointed out that this is not a "dislike" button per se, but is simply a measure for collecting responses and feedback for comments (Constine, 2018). But then again, who trusts Facebook these days?

Look for Signs of Cyberbullying

Adults, especially parents, should actively search for signs of cyberbullying in their children.

They need to integrate automatic parental controls with their own analysis of the behavior of their children, looking for anything that appears odd.

There are certain recognizable signs that may indicate the existence of problems of cyberbullying. Parents should be alert to these signs and explore whether any cyberbullying problem has arisen. Ignoring the following signs can lead to serious consequences:

- Unexplainable injuries, since teens may physically injure themselves by cutting, burning, or enacting other forms of self-harm as a way of coping with emotional pain;
- Depressive state, frequent headaches or stomachaches;
- Fake illnesses;
- Lost or destroyed personal items;
- Changes in eating behavior, such as skipping meals or eating too much;
- Difficulty in sleeping and frequent nightmares;
- Loss of interest in schoolwork;
- Not wanting to go to school;
- Avoidance of social situations;
- Decreased self-esteem.

However, parents should also be able to recognize signs that correspond to a cyberbully's behavior. These are:

- Having relationships with bullies;
- Getting involved in verbal or physical fights;
- Having unexplained extra money or new items such as pens, smartphones, watches, etc.;
- Blaming others for their problems;
- Being aggressive and violent.

Above all, parents should never forget that most children won't report that they have experienced cyberbullying to an adult. As such, they must immediately intervene if they suspect that their child is involved in an incidence of cyberbullying. They should seek the help of an educator or another professional, and preserve the evidence of the cyberbullying by printing screenshots and emails as well as saving the URL of the location where the cyberbullying took place.

At the same time, they should also consider that some adolescents are actually engaging in a new form of self-aggression, so-called digital self-harm. Some adolescents post, anonymously, mean and derogatory comments about themselves on social media. Teens bully themselves online as a way to manage feelings of sadness and self-hatred, and to gain attention from their friends (Patchin & Hinduja, 2017).

Finally, in seeking to protect their children, parents need to understand the language they use to communicate among themselves. Some of the more essential internet acronyms that parents need to know are shown in Table 3.

Table 3.

Acronym	Meaning
1174	Party meeting place –nude club
143, 459, ILU	I love you
182	I hate you
420	Marijuana
53X	Sex
8	Oral sex
9	Parent watching
99	Parent gone
Broken	Hungover from alcohol
CID	Acid (the drug)
GNOC	Get naked on camera
IPN	I am posting naked
LH6	Let's have sex
NIFOC	Naked in front of a computer
PRON	Porn
SUGARPIC	Suggestive or erotic photo

CONCLUSION

In his introduction to *In Real life*, Doctorow observes:

This is the golden age of organizing. If there's one thing the Internet's changed forever, it's the relative difficulty and cost of getting a bunch of people in the same place, working for the same goal. That's not always good (thugs, bullies, racists, and loonies never had it so good), but it is fundamentally game-changing. (Doctorow & Wang, 2014, p. viii)

A brief examination of the technological tools available for preventing and intervening in cases of cyberbullying confirms Doctorow's claims. Cyberbullying is a complex phenomenon since technology is disrupting the dynamics of socialization. However, the same technology can also help to prevent and reduce cyberbullying by providing automatic filtering and monitoring programs. Nevertheless, relying only on technology is not sufficient to eradicate cyberbullying. Combatting cyberbullying requires an orchestrated action that includes, of course, technology, but also encompasses other forms of interventions such as regulatory statements by internet service providers and social network providers, and effective and continuous educational program for children, parents, and teachers. Moreover, although the efficacy of anti-cyberbullying measures introduced by technological tools have been proclaimed in many experimental studies (Garaigordobil & Martínez-Valderrey, 2015; Menesini & Salmivalli, 2017), these benefits have yet to be demonstrated on a large scale. To evaluate the effects of such tools, larger investigations are required, and appropriate standards and procedures for evaluation need to be defined.

In this regard, a study by the European Commission that benchmarked a number of parental control tools available on the market between 2012 and 2017 suggested that most parental control tools fail to sufficiently address the needs of the parents to protect children against online risk (Vulcano, Angeletti, Chancen, & Croll, 2017). The study found that some tools are good at filtering adult content, but they also over-block non-harmful content. In general, the tools are not able to block violence or self-harm:

The overall effectiveness of tools, in general, is low for both PC and mobile tools. Those with a high rate of over-blocking consequently have a low under-blocking rate and vice versa. [...] Content-filtering tools are less effective when dealing with user-generated content, which is difficult to categorize.

In fact, tools present lower effectiveness with user-generated and Web 2.0 content. In all qualitative tests conducted on web 2.0, all the tools failed. (Vulcano, Angeletti, Chancen, & Croll, 2017, p. 32)

The study underlines that the effectiveness of parental controls, however, varies according to the particular social and specific familial context. It seems that highly educated parents are more successful in using available parental control tools, while children of lower educated classes are more exposed to unsafe internet use.

Finally, regarding the use of technological tools, there are other problematic elements that should be considered. In many aspects, internet technology appears to be market sensitive, and recent revelations about the selling of personal data has provided a timely warning about the risk that social networks can be used in a discriminatory and/or manipulative way, even invading the sphere of individual liberty, for example, by invoking community moderation or applying other non-transparent forms of e-democracy.

Paradoxically, policy makers should, at the same time, focus on the safe use of the tools that have been developed for the safe use of the internet by children and adolescents.

REFERENCES

Appavu, S., Rajaram, R., Muthupandian, M., Athiappan, G., & Kashmeera, K. S. (2009). Data mining based intelligent analysis of threatening e-mail. *Knowledge-Based Systems*, *22*(5), 392–393. doi:10.1016/j.knosys.2009.02.002

Barnet, E. (2010). Facebook refuses to add safety buttons saying they 'confuse' and 'intimidate' users. *The Daily Telegraph*. Available at: https://www.telegraph.co.uk/technology/facebook/7585688/Facebook-refuses-to-add-safety-buttons-saying-they-confuse-and-intimidate-users.html

BBC News. (2018, July 24). *Facebook angers Flanders with Rubens ban*. Available at: https://www.bbc.co.uk/news/technology-44936601

BBC News. (2013, July 3). *Authorities use analytics tool that recognizes sarcasm*. Available at: https://www.bbc.co.uk/news/technology-23160583

Byron, T. (2008). *Safer children in a digital world: The report of the Byron Review: Be safe, be aware, have fun*. Available at: http://dera.ioe.ac.uk/7332/7/Final%20Report%20Bookmarked_Redacted.pdf

Constine, J. (2018). Facebook confirms test of a downvote button for flagging comments. *Techcrunch.com*. Available at: https://techcrunch.com/2018/02/08/facebook-downvote-button/

Coyne, L., & Gountsidou, V. (2013). The role of industry in reducing cyberbullying. In P. K. Smith & G. Steffgen (Eds.), *Cyberbullying through new media* (pp. 83–98). Psychology Press.

Crawford, K., & Gillespie, T. (2016). What is a flag for? Social media reporting tools and the vocabulary of complaint. *New Media & Society*, *18*(3), 410–428. doi:10.1177/1461444814543163

Dadvar, M., Trieschnigg, D., & de Jong, F. (2014, May). Experts and machines against bullies: A hybrid approach to detect cyberbullies. In *Canadian Conference on Artificial Intelligence*, (pp. 275-281). Springer. 10.1007/978-3-319-06483-3_25

Davidov, D., Tsur, O., & Rappoport, A. (2010, August). Enhanced sentiment learning using twitter hashtags and smileys. In *Proceedings of the 23rd international conference on computational linguistics: posters*, (pp. 241-249). Academic Press.

Day, I. R. W., Wise, E., Sigler, S., & Roarke, J. P. (2016). *U.S. Patent No. 9,485,206*. Washington, DC: U.S. Patent and Trademark Office.

Doctorow, C., & Wang, J. (2014). *In real life*. Macmillan.

Duarte, N., Llanso, E., & Loup, A. (2018, January). Mixed Messages? The Limits of Automated Social Media Content Analysis. *FAT Conference*. Available at: https://cdt.org/files/2017/12/FAT-conference-draft-2018.pdf

ESNTF. (2009). *Safer Social Networking Principles for the EU*. Available at: https://www.sbs.ox.ac.uk/cybersecurity-capacity/system/files/European%20Commission%20-%20Safer%20Social%20Networking%20Principles.pdf

Facebook. (2018). *Community Standard Enforcement Preliminary Report*. Available at: https://transparency.facebook.com/community-standards-enforcement#hate-speech

Garaigordobil, M., & Martínez-Valderrey, V. (2015). The effectiveness of Cyberprogram 2.0 on conflict resolution strategies and self-esteem. *The Journal of Adolescent Health*, *57*(2), 229–234. doi:10.1016/j.jadohealth.2015.04.007 PMID:26206445

Goodboy, A. K., & Martin, M. M. (2015). The personality profile of a cyberbully: Examining the Dark Triad. *Computers in Human Behavior*, *49*, 1–4. doi:10.1016/j.chb.2015.02.052

Google. (2010). *Announcing our new Family Safety Center*. Available at: https://googleblog.blogspot.com/2010/09/announcing-our-new-family-safety-center.html

Granryd, M. (2018, March 28). Blocking child sexual abuse content is common sense. *NetClean*. Available at: https://www.netclean.com/2018/03/28/mats-granryd-gsma-blocking-child-sexual-abuse-content-is-common-sense/

Kowalski, R. M., Giumetti, G. W., Schroeder, A. N., & Lattanner, M. R. (2014). Bullying in the digital age: A critical review and meta-analysis of cyberbullying research among youth. *Psychological Bulletin*, *140*(4), 1073–1137. doi:10.1037/a0035618 PMID:24512111

Kumar, S., Jiang, M., Jung, T., Luo, R. J., & Leskovec, J. (2018, February). MIS2: Misinformation and Misbehavior Mining on the Web. *Proceedings of the Eleventh ACM International Conference on Web Search and Data*. Available at: https://www.researchgate.net/publication/322971747_MIS2_Misinformation_and_Misbehavior_Mining_on_the_Web

Magid, L. (2015, May 15). Facebook reports numbers on nudity, sex, violence, hate speech and other banned contents. *Forbes*. Available at: https://www.forbes.com/sites/larrymagid/2018/05/15/facebook-reports-numbers-on-nudity-sex-violence-hate-speech-and-other-banned-content/#55fb38772968

Maynard, D. G., & Greenwood, M. A. (2014, March). Who cares about sarcastic tweets? investigating the impact of sarcasm on sentiment analysis. In LREC 2014 Proceedings. ELRA.

Menesini, E., & Salmivalli, C. (2017). Bullying in schools: The state of knowledge and effective interventions. *Psychology Health and Medicine*, *22*(sup1), 240–253. doi:10.1080/13548506.2017.1279740 PMID:28114811

Microsoft. (2018). *To report abuse*. Available at: https://answers.microsoft.com/en-us/outlook_com/forum/osecurity-oother/fraudulent-hotmail-account/713d7303-6054-47ac-9e20-4795d2f0bb18

Microsoft. (2005, March 23). *Web Watchers: Teaching Kids to Stay Safe Online*. Available at: https://news.microsoft.com/2005/03/23/web-watchers-teaching-kids-to-stay-safe-online/

Milosevic, T. (2018). *Protecting Children Online? Cyberbullying Policies of Social Media Companies*. The MIT Press. doi:10.7551/mitpress/11008.001.0001

Nahar, V., Al-Maskari, S., Li, X., & Pang, C. (2014, July). Semi-supervised learning for cyberbullying detection in social networks. *Australasian Database Conference*, 160-171. 10.1007/978-3-319-08608-8_14

Nocentini, A., Zambuto, V., & Menesini, E. (2015). Anti-bullying programs and Information and Communication Technologies (ICTs): A systematic review. *Aggression and Violent Behavior*, *23*, 52–60. doi:10.1016/j.avb.2015.05.012

Patchin, J. W., & Hinduja, S. (2017). Digital self-harm among adolescents. *The Journal of Adolescent Health*, *61*(6), 761–766. doi:10.1016/j.jadohealth.2017.06.012 PMID:28935385

Rowland, W. D. I., Wise, E., Sigler, S., & Roarke, J. P. (2016). *U.S. Patent No. 9,485,206*. Washington, DC: U.S. Patent and Trademark Office.

Salton, G. (1968). *Automatic information organization and retrieval*. McGraw-Hill.

Schwartz, H. A., & Ungar, L. H. (2015). Data-driven content analysis of social media: A systematic overview of automated methods. *The Annals of the American Academy of Political and Social Science*, *659*(1), 78–94. doi:10.1177/0002716215569197

Shaban, H. (2018, July 31). France bans smartphones in schools. *The Washington Post*. Available at: https://www.washingtonpost.com/technology/2018/07/31/france-bans-smartphones-school/?noredirect=on&utm_term=.bdce77a99648

Shariff, S. (2008). *Cyber-bullying: Issues and solutions for the school, the classroom and the home*. Routledge. doi:10.4324/9780203928837

Shu, K., Sliva, A., Wang, S., Tang, J., & Liu, H. (2017). Fake news detection on social media: A data mining perspective. *ACM SIGKDD Explorations Newsletter*, *19*(1), 22–36. doi:10.1145/3137597.3137600

Smith, R. (2018, July 31). France bans smartphones from schools. *CNN*. Available at: https://edition.cnn.com/2018/07/31/europe/france-smartphones-school-ban-intl/index.html

Snapchat Support. (2019). *Report Abuse on Snapchat*. Available at: https://support.snapchat.com/en-US/a/report-abuse-in-app

Topcu-Uzer, C., & Tanrikulu, I. (2018). Technological solution for cyberbullying. In M. Campbell & S. Bauman (Eds.), *Reducing cyberbullying in schools: international evidence-based best practices* (pp. 33–47). Academic Press. doi:10.1016/B978-0-12-811423-0.00003-1

van Geel, M., Goemans, A., Toprak, F., & Vedder, P. (2017). Which personality traits are related to traditional bullying and cyberbullying? A study with the Big Five, Dark Triad and sadism. *Personality and Individual Differences*, *106*, 231–235. doi:10.1016/j.paid.2016.10.063

Van Hee, C., Jacobs, G., Emmery, C., Desmet, B., Lefever, E., Verhoeven, B., . . . Hoste, V. (2018). *Automatic Detection of Cyberbullying in Social Media Text*. Available at: https://arxiv.org/abs/1801.05617

Vandebosch, H., & Van Cleemput, K. (2009). Cyberbullying among youngsters: Profiles of bullies and victims. *New Media & Society*, *11*(8), 1349–1371. doi:10.1177/1461444809341263

Vulcano, M. A., Angeletti, M. R., Chancen, S. D., & Croll, C. (2017). Benchmarking of parental control tools for the online protection of children. *European Union*. Available at: https://ec.europa.eu/digital-single-market/en/news/benchmarking-parental-control-tools-online-protection-children

Willig, C., & Rogers, W. S. (Eds.). (2017). *The SAGE handbook of qualitative research in psychology*. Sage. doi:10.4135/9781526405555

Wong, J., Sang, D., & Peng, C. S. (2017). An Android Geofencing App for Autonomous Remote Switch Control. World Academy of Science, Engineering and Technology. *International Journal of Computer and Information Engineering*, *4*(3), 288–296.

KEY TERMS AND DEFINITIONS

Automatic Cyberbullying Detection: The implementation of methods to automatically analyze the content of messages to detect harming, harassing, and abusive sentences as well as insulting words.

Byron Review: A study commissioned in 2007 by the UK government and conducted by Tanya Byron on the risks children face from the internet and video games.

Information Retrieval: A sector of the computer sciences that focuses on implementing solutions for searching information in large collections of resources, both structured and unstructured, such as natural language texts, images, and videos.

Machine Learning: A field of artificial intelligence (AI) that aims to provide systems with the ability to automatically learn and improve from experience without being explicitly programmed.

Parental Control Tools: Various blocking capabilities serving mainly for controlling young users when they are online.

Chapter 5
Cyberbullying Victims, Perpetrators, and Bystanders

Joanna Lizut
Janusz Korczak Pedagogical University in Warsaw, Poland

ABSTRACT

The documented effects of cyberbullying take a burden on all those involved, but also impact the wider social environment as well. Victims experience difficult emotions: feelings of humiliation and worthlessness, shame, fear, despair, and sadness. In the long run, they may suffer reduced self-esteem and interpersonal problems: difficulties in establishing contacts and a tendency to withdrawal and isolation. The consequences for perpetrators include the consolidation of aggressive patterns of behavior, the lowering of the sense of responsibility for their own actions, the tendency to antisocial behavior, and the easy slide into conflicts with the law. Witnesses of violence, who are not able to effectively oppose it, or who do not try, often keep their feelings of guilt, dissatisfaction, and self-recrimination for years. For some, it will internalize patterns of passivity, helplessness, and unresponsiveness in difficult situations. This being the case, deepening our knowledge about all of the participants involved in cyberbullying and their mutual relations is of crucial importance.

DOI: 10.4018/978-1-5225-8076-8.ch005

INTRODUCTION

The phenomenon of cyberbullying has its own specificity but, at the same time, is based on many of the same mechanisms recognizable in "traditional" bullying, including the essential triad - the victim, the perpetrator, and the act itself. This triad, comprising the basic components of cyberbullying, is extended by a fourth element - bystanders.

The analogy of online activities to those of 'real life' is significant. For example, just as in the "real world", most victims of cyberbullying know their perpetrators, and 4 out of 5 people are harassed by a person that he/she knows. Also, as in real life, girls and women are still more often the victims of online violence (Breiding et al., 2014). In particular, stalking (harassment), most often occurs in the context of an intimate relationship, namely, by a former partner. The essential differences between cyberbullying and traditional forms of bullying regard the higher level of anonymity of the perpetrator (related to the specificity of the virtual environment), and the use of specific technological tools such as email, chat, instant messengers, websites, blogs, social networks, discussion groups, SMS services, and MMS. There are a number of different types of harassing behaviors enacted on the internet, for which various terms have been coined, such as electronic aggression, online harassment, internet harassment, cyberbullying, and internet bullying.

An online survey of more than 50,000 young people ages 13 to 18 conducted from December 19, 2016, to January 10, 2017, found that student reports of incidents of bullying and harassment had increased. Seventy percent of the survey respondents reported having witnessed incidents of bullying, hate messages, or harassment in the months since the 2016 presidential election. Of these respondents, 70% said they witnessed incidents involving race and ethnicity; 63%, incidents involving sexual orientation; 59%, immigration status; and 55%, gender. (Turner, 2017, as cited in Policy White Paper, Bullying Prevention in the Technology Age)

Cyberbullying is usually expressed through such behavior as: verbal aggression (threatening, offensive wording), recording, creating, and presenting compromising videos, and posting negative and/or otherwise untrue information. As a concept, it connects with the notion of mobbing, constituting a particular form (Kowalski & Limber, 2007) that is expressed through media and communication devices, such as mobile phones, email, and the internet (e.g. social networks, websites, and blogs).

It needs to be highlighted that in the context of other, similar, terms, cyberbullying is distinguishable by four key elements: repeatability (even if not fully exploited); the intention to hurt the other person (although this element will be discussed later); power imbalance (although this refers to the features of communication mediated by the technology and the features of the material itself published in the subject's social network, rather than to the perpetrator per se); and the fact that the aggression is well-known about within the social group, particularly in younger age groups (Pyrzalski, 2008, p. 5).

Other researchers emphasize that in order to recognize a behavior as bullying (regardless of whether it is enacted in the real or virtual world), it must demonstrate two additional aspects (Badura & Dobrzyńska-Mesterhazy, 2000, p. 14.), namely that the behavior:

- Violates the rights of the victim - the perpetrator using the advantage of strength violates their basic personal rights (e.g. the right to dignity, respect, etc.);
- Causes suffering and harm to the victim - the perpetrator exposes the victim's lifestyle and wellbeing to serious harm. Experiencing pain and suffering makes the victim less capable of self-defense.

The Norwegian researcher Dan Olweus distinguished three key elements of bullying, being aggression, repetition, and power (Olweus, 1993).

Although there are strong correlations and analogies between cyberbullying and traditional bullying, our study pays particular attention to those aspects that distinguish it, in the context of the behavior of perpetrators, victims, and bystanders (Smith, 2012, pp.95-96):

- It depends on the perpetrator's degree of technological expertise;
- It is more anonymous, mostly indirect rather than face-to-face;
- The perpetrator does not usually see the victim's reaction, at least in the immediate term;
- The variety of bystander roles in cyberbullying is more complex than in most scenarios of traditional bullying;
- One motive for traditional bullying is thought to be the status gained by showing (abusive) power over others in front of witnesses, but the perpetrator will often lack this in cyberbullying;

- The breadth of the potential audience is increased, as cyberbullying can reach particularly large audiences in a peer group compared to the generally small groups that are witness to traditional bullying;
- For victims, it is difficult to escape from the cyberbullying. The harassment will be present wherever the victim is.

In the context of cyberbullying, it is likely that non-victims of cyberbullying perceive cyberbullying as situation that can be changed, and thus would expect to apply problem-solving coping strategies, such as seeking social support. Victims, however, are probably more likely to evaluate a situation of cyberbullying as less changeable. They may feel that they have no choice but to accept the situation, which would result in the application of more emotion-focused coping responses such as avoidance, escape, anger, feeling helpless, or feeling depressed (Vollink et. al, 2013, p. 8).

Cyberbullying can take a variety of forms (Table 1).

The form of cyberbullying, its severity, and its frequency are mainly related to the age and sex of the perpetrator, the frequency with which they use the internet, their level of technological skills (Lubkina & Marzano, 2014), to certain cultural factors, and to the victim's knowledge of security strategies (Li, 2007).

On this point, the research is not consistent, and there is some variation in the results. Some studies show clear gender differences in terms of the engagement in various forms of cyberbullying, with boys typically applying psychological harassment and girls verbal violence, and the probabilities of

Table 1. Types of cyberbullying

TRADITIONALBULLYING	CYBERBULLYING
Direct bullying Physical (e.g. hitting): Property (e.g. damaging someone's personal belongings) Verbal (e.g. calling someone names) Non-verbal (e.g. making obscene gestures) Social (e.g. excluding someone from a Group **Indirect bullying (e.g. spreading false rumors)**	**Direct bullying** Physical: Property (e.g. purposely sending a virus-infected file) Verbal (e.g. using the internet or mobile phone to insult or threaten) Non-verbal (e.g. sending threatening or obscene pictures or illustrations) Social (e.g. excluding someone from an online group) **Indirect bullying** 'Outing' of email entrusted information Masquerading, e.g. deceiving someone by pretending to be someone else Spreading gossip by mobile phone, email or chat Taking part in voting on a defamatory polling website

Source: H. Vandebosch, K. van Cleemput (2010). Cyberbullying among youngsters: profiles of bullies and victims. New Media & Society 11(8). http://nms.sagepub.com, p. 1352.

Figure 1. Cyberbullying by gender
Source: Patchin & Hinduja (2015), Cyberbullying Research Center, www.cyberbullying.org

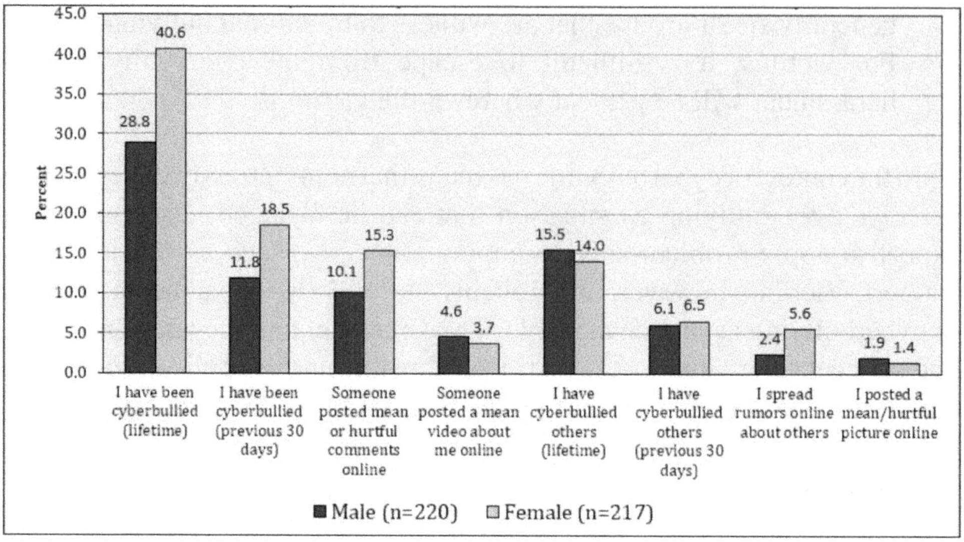

involvement as the offender - boys - or as the victim - girls, (Wang et. al, 2009), whilst other research results reveal no statistically significant differentiation (Smith et al., 2008).

Perpetrators

Perpetrators adopt different forms of cyberbullying depending on their age and gender, although these differences become less pronounced with increasing age (Pepler et al., 2008). School children generally use telephone conversations and teasing by text message. In older age groups, intimidation by mobile phone accompanies the posting of video clips (Nansel et al., 2001), and older teenagers and adults are most often involved in stalking.

In most studies, attention is drawn to the fact that cyberbullying is associated with functioning within the school community and peer group (which does not mean that all acts of violence take place inside the school), and the relative positions taken in the online social network very often reflect the realities and status of traditional contacts. Especially for younger age groups, social relations at school, as well as the characteristics of the educational and upbringing environment, including school norms and safety rules (Ostaszewski, 2012), affect both the proclivity to cyberbullying on the part of perpetrators, and the type of response from the victim, also in terms of their likelihood to ask for an adult's help (Lizut & Wrońska, 2015).

The National Research Council's report cites four characteristics of schools that may contribute to violence: (a) relatively high numbers of students occupy a limited amount of space; (b) the capacity to avoid confrontations is somewhat reduced; (c) the imposition of behavioral routines and conformity may contribute to feelings of anger, resentment, and rejection; and (d) poor building design features may facilitate the commission of violent acts. (Violence & Youth, p. 21)

From the observations of practitioners in the field (teachers, educators, and social workers), and confirmed by numerous research results (Sari & Camadan, 2016, p. 318), the typical perpetrator of cyberbullying appears as a young person looking for group acceptance and attention, who is unable to pursue that aim in a mature, socially acceptable way. It may often also be the case that they have problems with substance abuse. They may have difficulty in braking and controlling impulses, cannot defer pleasure, and always seek ways to meet their own needs, e.g. feeling important, valued, or strong, in the shortest time and with the least effort. They attempt to use aggressive behavior to solve problems (Gumpel, Wiesenthal, & Söderberg, 2015). They are probably afraid of incurring the negative consequences of their actions, so use the internet as the place in which to exhibit violence, because in the online world they feel anonymous and unpunishable. Many perpetrators of virtual violence mask their real identities, and so do not have to face the person who is suffering from their actions.

The perpetrator of electronic violence is usually the victim's peer and attends the same school. It is less likely that they are an acquaintance from outside the school or stranger (Wolak et al., 2007), although in adolescent and adult age groups, attacks are sometimes made on someone not personally known o the perpetrator (for example, a celebrity or politician).

It has been argued that the reasons that a person becomes a cyberbully can usually be traced to negative experiences in the child-parent relationship. The group of theories based on this premise includes, amongst others, those referring to the disturbance in basic family ties, to a lack of adult support, and to an upbringing in an environment filled with aggression (Michels et al., 2008). Many studies have found that the structure of the family itself is a contributing factor for those who become perpetrators, but also for those who become victims. It follows that perpetrators predominantly originate from families expressing low levels of positive messages, rigid rules, and authoritarian parental attitudes (Rigby, 1994), and very often from families in which there is a dominant authoritarian figure and an absence of discussion of the upbringing scheme (Nation et al., 2007).

The report of the American Psychological Association's Commission on Violence and Youth (Violence & Youth, p. 15) indicates that there can be many causes of children's aggressive behavior, and differentiate several types of factors:

- Biological factors;
- Childrearing conditions: especially ineffective parenting, incorrect emotional and cognitive development;
- Gender differences, sex role socialization, relations to peers;
- Cultural and social factors such as economic inequality and lack of opportunity;
- Media influences.

Based on a number of studies, a character profile of the typical perpetrator has been identified (Olweus, 1993):

- Prone to anger;
- Deliberately says things to hurt others;
- Threatens and laughs at others;
- Is stronger than their classmates, especially their victims;
- Is usually the same age or older than their peers;
- Has the need to dominate and bully others;
- Strives to achieve their will at all cost;
- Brags about their actual or imagined power over the other students;
- Is impulsive, characterized by a low tolerance to frustration;
- Has difficulty adapting to the current standards of behavior.
- Will readily lie and deceive in order to gain benefits;
- Rebellious, disobedient and aggressive towards adults, including parents and teachers.

Analyzing one of the elements suggested for the definition of cyberbullying, the intention to harm, Pyrzalski (2008) indicated that the perpetrator of cyberbullying may be someone who does not have such negative traits, but nevertheless causes victims to suffer through their actions.

The specificity of electronic communication may facilitate their occurrence [...the causing of harm by a perpetrator without intention...]. First of all, this is related to the lack of, in most cases, feedback in the form of non-verbal emotional signals that indicate the real consequences of our actions and their subjective perception by the other person. In a traditional situation, the crying of the victim is clear information that what was supposed to be a joke touched the other person. In case of electronic aggression - especially that which is not directed straight to the victim (involving, for example, the publication of materials), such information, at least at the time of the action, is not received by the perpetrator. Separation from the victim by means of communication technology can generally cause that the perpetrators "forget" that, while carrying out acts of electronic aggression... the one who can actually feel suffering is the second person. (Pyżalski, 2008, p. 8)

(...) cyberbullies cannot easily receive visual feedback of the pain they are inflicting via technology, which results in a lack of need for empathy. (Accordino & Accordino, 2011, p. 16)

Perpetrators can apply a range of actions. According to the results of a national survey conducted in the United States between July and October 2016 on a representative sample of 5,700 middle and high school students between

Figure 2. Cyberbullying offending
Source: Patchin & Hinduja (2016), Cyberbullying Research Center, www.cyberbullying.org

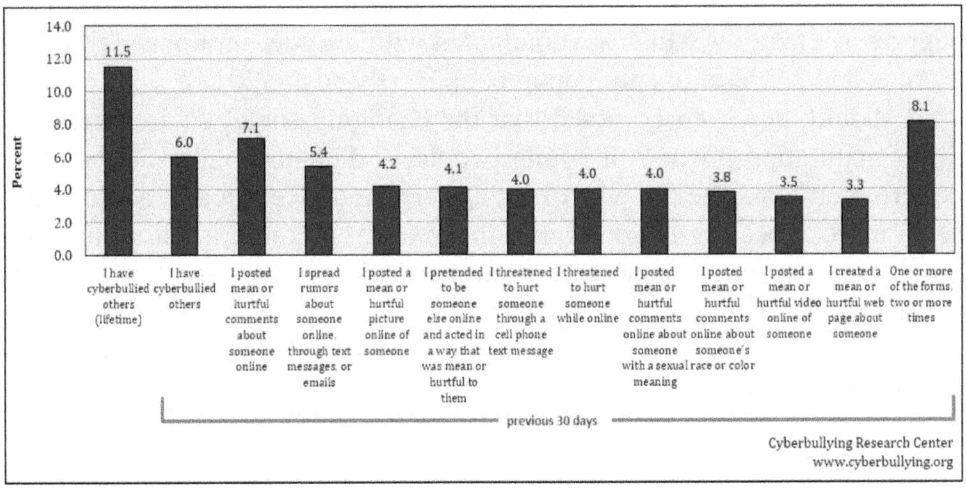

the ages of 12 and 17, it emerged that not only are there many different forms of harassment, but also that different forms are often used simultaneously (Patchin & Hinduja, 2016).

Having said all that, it is worth remembering that some cases of cyberbullying represent the actions of adults. The perpetrators in such cases are usually men or women with a symbiotic personality, who are trying to dominate an inner emptiness and loneliness by dominating the other person. This inner "distress" compels the person to act, even if negatively, and actions are rarely limited only to cyberbullying, running even as far as the self-injury or suicide of the perpetrator or the beating or murder of the victim (Laskowski, 2003).

In regards to stalking, a course of behavior may be regarded as stalking when the activities are (Lattanzii, 2007):

- They are planned;
- They evoke fear;
- They are enacted over a period of at least 30 days;
- There are at least 30 identifiable acts during the 30 days period;
- They cause negative psychological and relational effects (anxiousness, sleeping and eating disorders, the necessity to change telephone operator, job, home, friends, or colleagues and workmates).

It is difficult to individuate a single universal profile of the perpetrator. Some researchers suggest that adult activities should be distinguished as a separate type of cyber threats, and that the term cyberbullying should be reserved as a concept appropriate only for describing specific behaviors of younger age groups. They assume cyberbullying, in fact, to represent "aggressive features which are conducted within a peer group, and that both victims and perpetrators are young people" (Pyżalski, 2013).

It should, however, be noted that the changing social environment, the faster maturation process of young people, and changes in social behavior patterns may make the behavior of young perpetrators (especially adolescents) seem more appealing to adults. For this reason, it is important to highlight the already recognized incidence of adult offenders on the overall phenomena (Pyżalski, 2011).

Young people may become involved in stalking behaviors for a number of possible reasons (Andrzejewska, 2014), such as:

- Lack of social acceptance;
- Low self-esteem;

- Negative relational and behavioral patterns received at home;
- Absence of feeling of security within the family;
- No proper relations with the society.

Stalkers

Stalkers are a specific type of perpetrator.

There are three well-known typologies of stalker: Zona and colleagues' Stalker-Victim Types; Mullen and colleagues' Stalker Typology; and the Recon Stalker Typology (Ostermeyer et al., 2016).

Zona's Stalker-Victim Types

Zona et al. distinguished three types of stalkers, identifying the decisive criterion as the particular motivation of the stalker and the presence of mental disorders.

1. **Erotomaniacs:** Perpetrators who have a false and imagined belief that the victim is destined to them by higher powers and become obsessed with them, although the victim usually remains unaware, because the perpetrator "admires" from a distance. Often, they are a fan. The stalker harbors the delusion that under certain circumstances the subject would surely establish an intimate relationship with them, and that they are connected by a "spiritual bond";
2. **Obsessional Love Stalker:** Usually the perpetrator knows the victim, but does not have intimate contact with them; the stalker has a pathological obsession with the victim, and wants to draw attention to themselves through their actions. Any interactions with the victim, however incidental, are interpreted as being driven by the desire of the subject to establish an intimate relationship;
3. **Simple Obsessional Stalkers:** In these situations the perpetrator is well known to the victim, and had or still has a close, intimate relationship with them. There are two subtypes of perpetrators: (1) the perpetrator who has an intimate relationship with the victim, (2) the perpetrator who lives with the victim, and is often their life partner, who uses physical, psychological, and sexual violence against them.

Mullen and Colleagues' Stalker Typology (Mullen, Pathé, & Purcell, 2008).

According to this typology, there are five distinct types of stalker: the rejected stalker; the stalker seeking intimacy (the intimacy-seeking stalker); the loser stalker (the incompetent stalker); the offended stalker (the resentful stalker); and the brutal stalker who perpetrates sexual and physical violence (the predator stalker).

Recon Stalker Typology (Mohandie, Meloy, McGowan, & Williams, 2006)

The so-called RECON (relationship and context-based) typology of stalking is based on the prior relationship between the perpetrator and the victim, and the context in which the stalking occurs. The static typology yields four groups: Intimate, Acquaintance, Public Figure, and Private Stranger.

The Motives of the Perpetrator

To date, the similarities in the motives of the perpetrators, as in the causative factors of the phenomena, have been only partially recognized. Debbie Roome (2012, pp. 26-27) enumerated the following motives for cyberbullying:

- To feel superior to a victim, which brings the bully satisfaction. The reaction of the victim often induces the perpetrator to persist in or intensify their behavior;
- To achieve a boost to their own popularity and their self-esteem, since they can portray themselves as experts in a subject;
- To enact feelings of jealously;
- To take center stage and instill fear into a victim;
- Cyberbullying in the form of the making of denigrating and discriminating comments can also derive from racial and cultural differences in norms and standards;
- Those coming from dysfunctional families or who have experienced social exclusion in the past show an inclination to bully others;
- Sometimes victims may themselves also become bullies, in an attempt to rebuild their own self-esteem;
- Personality disorders can skew a bully's perspective on their acts;

- Cyberbullying can also derive from mental illness;
- Immaturity can play an immense role in cyberbullying incidents. A perpetrator may cause someone pain and anguish unwittingly, which is often the case among children and teenagers.
- Cyberbullying behavior is enacted in the certain belief that the person responsible is untraceable and will never be caught.

Another typology of perpetrator motivation was proposed by Varjas, Talley, Meyers, Parris, and Cutts (2010) on the basis of their research on a group of teenagers between 15 and 19 years of age, which distinguished two basic types of motive guiding the perpetrators of cyberbullying:

- **Internal Motives:** Revenge, jealousy, 'payback' for rejection
- **External Motives:** The absence of consequences, non-confrontational ('when a cyberbully did not want to have a face', p. 271), or that the target is different in some way, e.g. appearance.

According to studies, the perpetrators of cyberbullying and youngsters with a propensity to traditional violence have some similar social characteristics. Cyberbullies present traits such as loneliness, lack of a sense of purpose, lack of social support, dissonance, and abuse of psychoactive substances. They also exhibit similar social features, such as a sense of social isolation, a lack of social skills, and poor problem-solving skills (Sari & Camadan, 2016).

It is probable that the perpetrators of cyberbullying, similarly to those of traditional forms of violence, use strategies of justification that facilitate their functioning and reduce the sense of discomfort associated with the violation of social standards (Sykes & Matza, 1957, pp. 667–669, as cited in Zuber, Greenberg, & Williams, 2016) in which they:

- **Dispute the Culpability:** The perpetrator convinces themselves, and tries to convince others, that their behavior is driven by natural and overriding impulses. They present their actions as accidental, unintentional, the result of a hard life, occasioned by anger over lack of money, a life event, etc.;
- **Dispute the Damage:** The perpetrator does not deny their responsibility but tries to convince themselves and others that nothing big has occurred;
- **Dispute the Victim:** The perpetrator does not deny the responsibility or the damage inflicted, but denies those who have suffered the right

to call themselves victims, presenting the behavior as a justified act of revenge, punishment, and retribution;

- **Dispute the Condemnation:** The perpetrator denies potential evaluators of their act of the right to judgement This is a strategy of distracting attention from what they have done and focusing it instead on the motives or behaviors of those who are evaluating, condemning, and judging them;
- **Appeal to Higher Reason:** The perpetrator recognizes the need to sacrifice one good in the name of another, as if they are motivated by some sort of higher purpose.

Programs for Perpetrators

Following the special attention placed in other chapters on prevention and intervention programs, their most important elements will now be highlighted. Based on the experience of programs directed to traditional forms of violence (Blue Line), some basic recommendations can be formulated for the design of programs aimed at perpetrators of cyberbullying (Lizut, 2018).

1. Corrective and educational interventions on people using violence should be conducted in the form of psychological, educational and socialization programs which are aimed at changing the behavior and attitudes, reducing the risk of further violence, and increasing their ability to self-control aggressive behavior in the future.
2. Schools in which cyberbullying occurs should particularly monitor the behavior of people participating in the program, both during the program and after its completion, and seek to cooperate with external institutions and organizations that conduct programs to counteract violence and help victims.
3. Participation in the program should be treated as a set of interactions aimed at correcting the participants' undesirable and harmful behavior and attitudes.
4. It should be ensured that the programs contribute to actual changes in the attitudes and behaviors of participants and to an increased sense of responsibility for their own actions and, at the same time, that those participating in the programs are themselves treated in a way that does not damage their dignity.

5. Encourage cooperation and communication between the programs for perpetrators and the programs and facilities that help victims of violence within the same given area.
6. When creating the substantive content of programs, it is desirable to agree a set of basic beliefs and judgments regarding cyberbullying mechanisms and ways to stop it.
7. High ethical and pragmatic standards based on current knowledge and research should be promoted, and program implementers should be motivated to responsibly follow those standards.
8. Appropriate selection of people as participants in the (group) program in terms of age, experience, etc. (Blue – line, Program for perpetrators).

Victims

The similarities between traditional mobbing and cyberbullying can also be seen when we look at victims and issues related to experiencing violence. The most vulnerable to becoming victims of online abuse are children (Fenik, 2007; Helpline.org.pl) who:

- Have difficult relationships at home;
- Are raised in a broken family and suffer a lack of attention;
- Are emotionally unsatisfied;
- Have low self-esteem;
- Are younger, naïve, over-trusting, submissive, vulnerable, and manipulatable;
- Have been shunned by their peers, who need to follow the lead of their friends;
- Are lonely, shy, and susceptible.

The victim of cyber violence is usually a child or teenager who has been hurt by peers before. Often it is a poorly connected person with a perceived low value, distinguished from the group, for example by being obese, recently arrived from another city, or different from the majority sexual orientation. The experience of being cyberbullied intensifies their sense of being different, and feelings of loneliness, and leads to isolation (resulting from a desire to retreat or hide). Olweus (1993) believes that although there is no one victim profile, studies have consistently shown that children who are victims of mobbing exhibit one or more of the following features:

- They are usually quiet, cautious, sensitive, prone to crying;
- They may be insecure, have little faith in their own abilities, have low self-esteem;
- They often have a narrow circle of friends and are socially isolated;
- They are generally fearful;
- They can be nervous or depressed;
- They are usually physically weaker than their peers (especially for boys);
- They may prefer spending time with adults (parents, teachers, trainers) than with their peers.

The effects of cyberbullying on the victim are not the same for everyone, and depend on the particular form of abuse (Wojtasik, 2007) and on individual characteristics of the victims, based on their own previous experiences, levels of emotional resistance, sensitivity, etc. Victims of cyberbullying can experience attacks in various forms.

The typologies of cyberbullying from the perspective of the various types of victims can be summarized as shown in Table 2.

The effects on victims of experiencing cyberbullying are generally similar to those of traditional violence. Victims usually feel a strong sense of shame, humiliation, and despair, and often entertain negative thoughts about themselves and about the world at large. Negative emotions obscure

Figure 3. Cyberbullying victimization
Source: Patchin & Hinduja (2016), Cyberbullying Research Center, www.cyberbullying.org

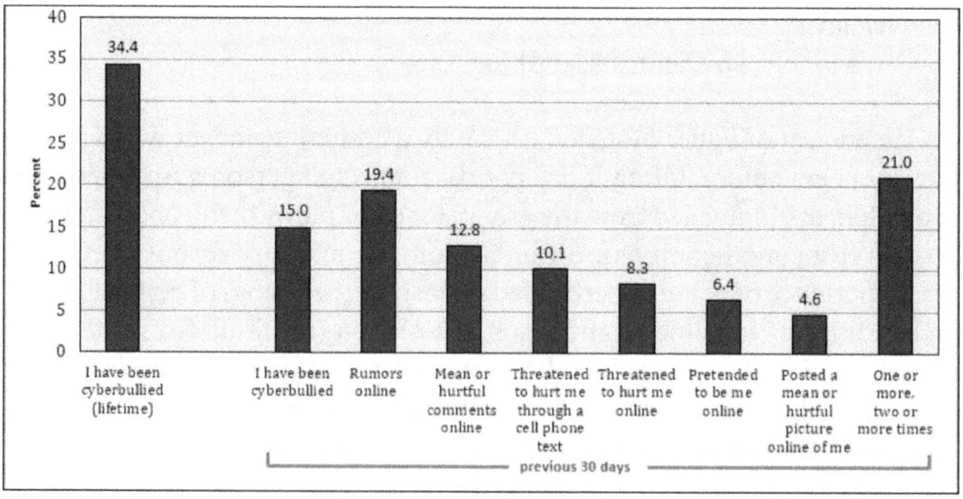

Table 2. Typology of electronic aggression based on identity of the victim

Type of electronic aggression	Description
Electronic peer aggression (possible cyberbullying)	Both the perpetrator and the victim are young people, usually from the same offline/online group. In some cases, when the relevant characteristics are present, electronic peer aggression may develop into cyberbullying.
Electronic aggression against school staff	Aggressive acts are targeted against teachers or other school staff.
Electronic aggression against the vulnerable	The victims of electronic aggression are 'weaker' people, particularly homeless, alcoholics, etc., who are usually unaware of the victimization they experience. Aggression often takes the form of visual material that presents the victims in embarrassing contexts.
Aggression against random victims (random electronic aggression)	The victim is to a great extent anonymous to the perpetrator, and the aggressive act is usually made on impulse, e.g. when someone attacks an unknown person in a chatroom or internet forum.
Electronic aggression against groups	The victim is not an individual but a group of people. An example of such electronic aggression is making vulgar comments about an ethnic or religious group on the internet. Although this may not be directed against a particular person, everyone affiliated to the group may feel offended.
Electronic aggression against celebrities	The victims are well-known people, e.g. singers or sports stars. This kind of aggression is usually indirect, e.g. young internet users making harsh comments in so-called gossip portals.

Source: Pyzalski, 2012

other feelings and experiences, which may lead to the feeling that nothing good will ever happen in life, and so to suicidal thoughts and depression. Victims of cyber violence may also experience the strong desire to erase the violent acts from memory (Slonje, 2011). In the long-term, experiencing cyberbullying results in lower self-esteem, tendencies to depression (and even suicide), and anger (Juvonen & Gross, 2008). Moreover, the effects of cyberbullying not only impact the victim and the perpetrator, but also have an effect on the school climate, on science, on the social environment and, in a broader perspective, also on the development of school policy and state and federal legislation (Juvonen & Gross, 2008).

Bullying can also have high economic and social costs to the wider community. When children who are bullied stay home from school, their individual learning trajectories, as well as their lifetime achievement and earnings, suffer. Meanwhile, in states where funding allocations are based on average daily attendance rates, schools can lose tens of millions of dollars due to bullying-related student absences. (Policy White Paper, 2017)

The "Stalking Risk Profile" portal (2011), operated by a group of scholars to address the issue, distinguishes the effects of cyberbullying on victims according to a number of categories (cite from: https://www.stalkingriskprofile.com):

1. *Effects on Mental Health*
    - *Denial, confusion, self-doubt, questioning if what is happening is unreasonable, wondering if they are over-reacting;*
    - *Frustration;*
    - *Guilt, embarrassment, self-blame;*
    - *Apprehension, fear, terror of being alone, fear that they, others, or pets will be harmed*
    - *Feeling isolated and helpless to stop the harassment;*
    - *Depression (all symptoms related to depression);*
    - *Anxiety, panic attacks, agoraphobia (frightened to leave the house), never feeling safe;*
    - *Difficulty in concentrating, and in remembering things;*
    - *Inability to sleep – nightmares, ruminating;*
    - *Irritability, anger, homicidal thoughts;*
    - *Emotional numbing;*
    - *Symptoms of Post-Traumatic Stress disorder e.g. hypervigilance (always on the lookout), flashbacks of frightening incidents, easily startled;*
    - *Insecurity and inability to trust others, problems with intimacy;*
    - *Personality changes due to becoming more suspicious, introverted, or aggressive;*
    - *Self-medication with alcohol/ drugs or using prescribed medications;*
    - *Suicidal thoughts and/or suicide attempts.*
2. *Effects on Physical Health*
    - *Fatigue from not sleeping, being constantly on guard, symptoms of depression;*
    - *Effects of chronic stress including headaches, hypertension;*
    - *Gastrointestinal problems;*
    - *Fluctuations in weight due to not eating or comfort eating;*
    - *Development or exacerbation of pre-existing conditions e.g. asthma, gastric ulcers, and psoriasis;*
    - *Dizziness;*
    - *Shortness of breath;*
    - *Impact on health of increased use of alcohol, cigarettes, or drugs;*
    - *Sexual dysfunction;*

  - *Physical injury due to not concentrating or being under the influence of substances;*
  - *Heart palpitations and sweating.*
3. *Effects on Work and School*
   - *Deteriorating school/work performance;*
   - *Increased sick leave;*
   - *Leaving job or being sacked;*
   - *Changing career;*
   - *Dropping out of school – poorer education and career opportunities.*
4. *Effects on Social Life*
   - *Insecurity and inability to trust others impacting on current and future relationships and friendships;*
   - *Problems with physical and emotional intimacy;*
   - *Avoidance of usual activities e.g., going to the gym, going out;*
   - *Isolation through trying to protect others, feeling misunderstood, or due to psychological symptoms.*
   - *Others withdrawing from and shunning the victim because they don't believe the victim, they are unable to cope with the victim's mental state, or as a direct consequence of third-party victimization.*
   - *Victim moving to a new area, changing their phone number, name, or even their appearance.*
5. *Effects on Finances*
   - *Loss of wages due to sick leave, leaving job, or changing career.*
   - *Costs incurred through legal fees.*
   - *Expense of increasing home and personal security.*
   - *Costs involved in repairing damages to property.*
   - *Expense of psychological counselling and medical treatment.*
   - *Costs involved in breaking leases on rented properties.*
   - *Expense of relocation.*

Often, victims who have experienced cyberbullying in childhood are also subject to it again in later life and/or suffer its effects even as adults. It is more likely that they will become depressed, suffer from fears, and have problems in social adaptation (Schafer et al., 2004) than those who do not have such experiences. This fact points to not only the relationship between involvement in cyberbullying and depression, but also to the problematic consumption of alcohol or drug abuse. People who have experienced unwanted sexual abuse on the internet or via text message were particularly vulnerable to depression, while alcohol abuse occurred among both perpetrators and victims of cyberbullying (Selkie et al., 2015).

Studies presented by the Journal of Social and Personal Relationships indicate that the bond between being a victim and being the perpetrator is increasingly blurred, as it emerged that 40% of respondents stated that they had both received and enacted acts of cyberbullying, whilst only 26% had been only a perpetrator and 33% only a victim). The authors of the report sustained that former victims engage in similar behaviors to what they experienced themselves because it was a way for them to deal with their own experiences. Violent responses represent a transfer of retaliatory actions, and can be aimed at reducing the negative emotions associated with being a victim of cyberbullying or proving to peers that they are not an easy target (Betts et al., 2016).

Bystanders

Bystanders have a key role to play in stopping the phenomenon of violence. They can be divided into various types (Czemierowska & Koruba, 2015)

1. **Supporters:** Those who stand on the side of the perpetrator and watch, for example, whether a teacher is approaching, or even encourage the aggression;
2. **Defenders:** Those who actively defend the victim, and oppose their persecution;
3. **Observers:** Those who, though they do not take action themselves, give the perpetrator their implied consent to continue attacking the victim by their presence.

In other suggested typologies, it is argued that bystanders can be divided into two basic types, depending on whether they exhibit active or passive reactions (Shultz et al., 2014):

1. **Active Bystanders:** People who, for example, decide to relay negative content to a wider audience, although they did not create it themselves. They fix the acts of cyber violence by filming, taking photos, or actively engaging in negative comments about the victim.
2. **Passive Bystanders:** Show a passive attitude towards the act, the perpetrator, and the victim.

Machackova and colleagues (Machackova, Dedkova, Sevcikova, & Cerna, 2013), suggested that the behavior of observers can be differentiated into behavior that is confrontational (directed more towards the perpetrator) and supportive (directed more towards the victim). While the confrontational observer would directly confront the bully in defense of the victim, the supportive observer would encourage the victim, and would engage in such behavior as urging the victim to ignore the perpetrator, attempting to comfort the victim, or advising the victim where or to whom to turn for help.

To understand the reaction of bystanders to cyberbullying, several studies have attempted to identify the contributing factors and motivations of bystanders to confront the perpetrator, support the victims, remain silent, or contribute to the victimization.

The latest surveys suggest that there may be a variety of fears that might reasonably make someone reluctant to report or intervene in a bullying situation (Johnson, 2013; Li et al., 2015):

1. *Fear of being a target.* Saying that anyone who witnesses a bullying act should confront the perpetrator is rather like suggesting that anyone who sees a mugging should try to stop it. A person standing up to defend a target – especially if acting alone – can easily find that they also become a target themselves, and without necessarily having any positive effect on the situation. In fact, two-thirds (67%) of respondents say they do not intervene because it might make them a target. Interestingly, the proportion is the same amongst students who had recently been targets of bullying themselves.
2. *Fear of loss of social status.* Even if intervening or reporting doesn't immediately lead to the witness becoming a target, it can still have long-term repercussions on a young person's social status, either through them being associated with the target (someone who is marginalized for reasons such as family poverty, disability, being a member of a visible minority group and lesbian, gay, bisexual, or transgender status are substantially more likely to be targets) or by being labeled a "snitch" – both of which results could easily be preludes to becoming a target of bullying in turn. A quarter of the students in our survey who had not recently been targets (26%), and almost half of those who had (45%), said they don't intervene because "adult advice will just increase my isolation".
3. *Fear of making things worse.* Both targets of and witnesses to bullying often fear that either standing up to a bully or reporting bullying to a

> parent or teacher is more likely to make things worse. One can easily imagine the effect if a straight or closeted gay youngster is being harassed with homophobic comments and a well-meaning witness tries to defend them by saying "There's nothing wrong with being gay!" Despite their good intentions, the witness will have unwittingly contributed to the bullying. Just over half (53%) of the students in our cyberbullying survey say they don't intervene because "it makes things worse for the target": a proportion that rises to 59% amongst those who had recently been targets themselves. Another study of offline bullying found that being defended by peers who were unable to successfully protect or comfort the target actually led to more negative effects and a greater risk of victimization in the future (Stevees 2012 cyt. after Johnson, 2013)

Certain personality traits (predominantly empathy) have been indicated as the significant factor influencing the reaction to witnessing violence and the likelihood of a bystander actively intervening in defense of a victim of cyberbullying (Freis & Gurung, 2013; Polyhonen, Juvonen, & Salmivalli, 2010). In turn, Polyhonen et al. (2010) stated that a strong sense of self-efficacy and a higher social status in the peer group are crucial factors for defense responses. Motivations for pro-social behavior, including the protection of weaker people, are another element that positively correlates with a counter reaction to aggression within social groups (Wright & Li, 2011).

Many people who use violence in their adult life experienced it in childhood. Similarly, bystanders who experienced violence in childhood, are less willing to help others when they are witness to it later in life.

The experience of victimization is another factor that facilitates bullying. The sense of isolation and helplessness experienced by victims of cyberbullying may prompt them to support the bullying more easily, so enacting a kind of revenge on their persecutor or on another person or social group (Barlińska, Szuster, & Wiśniewski, 2013, p. 40).

Using analogies to traditional forms of violence, the motivations of witnesses to action (Thornberg et al., 2012) can be seen as the result of the analysis of several factors taken into account when witnessing cyberbullying. Among these are:

1. Harm interpretation (i.e. assessment of the severity and consequences of a given situation for the victim);
2. Emotional predisposition (e.g. empathy encourages intervention while fear discourages it);

3. Social assessment (including relations with the participants of the act of violence, whether they are friends, or whether opposition is connected with an occurrence against a person who is high in the peer group hierarchy);
4. Moral evaluation - beliefs and attitudes towards the phenomenon of violence, but also against a specific event, including the guilt of the victim;
5. Self-assessment of intervention - analysis of the effectiveness of potential interventions.

The role of observers in counteracting cyberbullying and its long-term effects on the victim should be emphasized. Many studies indicate that victims who do not receive support are more likely to consider suicide than those who receive support (Rigby & Slee, 1999), and there are many other positive benefits of social assistance and good bystanders' reactions (Matsunaga, 2011).

CONCLUSION

Schools and special centers look for best practices to support the victims of cyberbullying: individuals and families facing a crisis. Professionals and institutions are looking for best competences and qualifications to fulfill the new tasks and assume the new responsibilities connected with the threats of cyberspaces, especially cyberbullying. These principles should underline the significance of the acquisition and development of knowledge and the recognition of aspects associated with the functioning of the internet, new media, and using the new technologies (Lizut ed., 2014). Understanding the ways in which the internet functions in relation to cyberbullying and the behavior of participants in these actions and their effects can assist such processes as:

- Providing support to the victim of violence;
- Determining the circumstances of the incident, including securing evidence;
- Administering consequences to the perpetrator of violence and working on changing their behavior and attitude (more in chapter 9).

In addition to determining the circumstances of the incident, which allows for a proper reaction of people and institutions involved in the prevention of cyberbullying, it is necessary to know about the participants of the incident. Work with the perpetrator should aim to help them understand the consequences of their behavior and change their attitudes. In the case of young perpetrators (children) and adolescents, this also includes learning about the proper way to use new technologies. It may also involve referring the individual to a specialist facility and their participation in a therapy program. A greater and deeper knowledge about the perpetrators, their motivations, their ways of behavior, as well as psychological mechanisms related to the functioning of victims and perpetrators will enable the creation of more effective prevention and intervention programs. Although the need to support victims is obvious, and various assistance programs are available for that purpose, there are still very few programs dedicated to witnesses of cyberbullying. Yet their role in interrupting such behavior may be crucial. The research conducted in this field not only performs a diagnostic function, but as indicated above, is also essential for reviewing policies and procedures related to cyberbullying, for offering recommendations to professionals, and for application in special training programs to equip victims with the skills to prevent and stop cyberbullying.

REFERENCES

AccordinoD. B.AccordinoM. P. (2011). Available at: https://eric.ed.gov/?id=EJ951225

Andrzejewska, A. (2014). Stalking. In *Threats of Cyberspace: A Comprehensive Programme for the Employees of Social Service Institutions*. Available at: https://cyberprzestrzen.wspkorczak.eu/download .php?file=dokumenty/english_version

Badura, W., & Dobrzyńska-Mesterhazy, A. (2000). *Przemoc w rodzinie, interwencja kryzysowa i psychoterapia*. Kraków: Wydawnictwo Uniwersytetu Jagiellońskiego.

Barlińska, J., Szuster, A., & Wiśniewski, M. (2012). Cyberbullying among Adolescent Bystanders: Role of the Communication Medium, Form of Violence, and Empathy. *Journal of Community & Applied Social Psychology, 23*, 37–51. doi:10.1002/casp.2137

Betts, L. R., Gkimitzoudis, A., Spenser, K. A., & Baguley, T. (2016). Examining the roles young people fulfill in five types of cyber bullying. *Journal of Social and Personal Relationships*. Available at: https://journals.sagepub.com/doi/abs/10.1177/0265407516668585

Breiding, M. J., Smith, S. G., Basile, K. C., Walters, M. L., Chen, J., & Merrick, M. (2014). Prevalence and Characteristics of Sexual Violence, Stalking, and Intimate Partner Violence Victimization – National Intimate Partner and Sexual Violence Survey, United States, 2011. *Centers for Disease Control and Prevention, Morbidity and Mortality Weekly Report, 63*(8). Available at: https://www.cdc.gov/mmwr/preview/ mmwrhtml/ss6308a1.htm

Czemierowska-Koruba, A. (2015). *Agresja i przemoc w szkole*. Warszawa: Ośrodek Rozwoju Edukacji.

Fenik, K. (2008). *Psychologiczne aspekty zjawiska cyberprzemocy*. Retrieved from https://www.saferinternet.pl/images/stories/ katarzyna_fenik_18-19.09.08.pdf (in Polish)

Freis, S.D., & Gurung, R.A. (2013). A Facebook analysis of helping behavior in online bullying. *Psychology of Popular Media Culture, 2*, 11-19. doi:10.1037/a0030239

Gumpel, T. P., Wiesenthal, V., & Söderberg, P. (2015). *Narcissism, Perceived Social Status, and Social Cognition and their Influence on Aggression and Behavioral Disorders*. Available at: https://journals.sagepub.com/doi/abs/10.17988/BD-13-33.1

Juvonen, J., & Gross, E. F. (2008, September). Extending the school grounds? Bullying experiences in cyberspace. *The Journal of School Health, 78*(9), 496–505. doi:10.1111/j.1746-1561.2008.00335.x PMID:18786042

Kolnie Municipal Social Center. (n.d.). *Profil Ofiary I Sprawcy CyberPrzzemocy* [Profile of the Victims and Perpetrators of Cyberbullying]. Available at: http://www.mopskolno.pl/index.php/cyberprzemoc/121-profil-ofiary-i-sprawcy-cyberprzemocy

Kośińska, J. (2008). Prawnokarna problematyka stalking. *Prokuratura i Prawo, 2008*(10), 33.

Kowalski, R. M., & Limber, S. P. (2007), Electronic bullying among middle school students. *J Adolesc Health., 41*(6), 22-30. Available at: https://www.jahonline.org/article/S1054-139X(07)00361-8/fulltext

Laskowski, C. (2003). Theoretical and clinical perspectives of client stalking behavior. *Clinical Nurse Specialist: The Journal for Advanced Nursing Practice, 17*(6), 298–304. Available at: https://europepmc.org/abstract/med/11885061

Lattanzii, M., & Skarzyńska, J. (2009). Ciemna strona relacji interpersonalnych. *Niebieska Linia nr 5/2009*. Available at: http://www.niebieskalinia.pl/pismo/rocznik-2009/153-czasopismo/artykuly-nl/4647-od-wielbiciela-do-zabojcy

Li, J., Craig, W., & Johnson, M. (2015). *Young Canadians' Experiences with Online Bullying*. Available at: https://mediasmarts.ca/sites/mediasmarts/files/publication-report/full/young-canadians-electronic-bullying.pdf

Li, Q. (2007). Bullying in the new playground: Research into cyberbullying and cyber victimization. *Australasian Journal of Educational Technology, 23*(4), 435–454. doi:10.14742/ajet.1245

Lizut, J. (Ed.). (2014). Threats of Cyberspace: A Comprehensive Programme for the Employees of Social Service Institutions. Available at https://cyberprzestrzen.wspkorczak.eu/download.php?file=dokumenty/english_version

Lizut, J., & Wrońska, A. (Eds.). (2018). *Standard bezpieczeństwa online placówek oświatowych*. Warsaw: NASK. Available at: https://akademia.nask.pl/publikacje/ost_Standard_bezpieczenstwa_online_placowek_oswiatowych.pdf (in Polish)

Lubkina, V., & Marzano, G. (2014). *Cyberbullying. Threats of Cyberspace: A Comprehensive Programme for the Employees of Social Service Institutions*. Available at https://cyberprzestrzen.wspkorczak.eu/download.php?file=dokumenty/english_version

Machackova, H., Cerna, A., Sevcikova, A., Dedkova, L., & Daneback, K. (2013). Effectiveness of coping strategies for victims of cyberbullying. *Cyberpsychology (Brno), 7*(3), 5. doi:10.5817/CP2013-3-5

Mishiels, D., Grietens, H., Onghena, P., & Kuppens, S. (2008). Parent-child interactions and relational aggression in peer relationships. *Developmental Review, 28*, 522. Available at: https://www.academia.edu/19581870/Parent_child_interactions_and_relational_aggression_in_peer_relationships

Mohandie, K., Meloy, J.R., McGowan, M.G., & Williams, J. (2006). The RECON typology of stalking: reliability and validity based upon a large sample of North American stalkers. *Journal of Forensic Sciences, 51*(1), 147-155. doi:10.1111/j.1556-4029.2005.00030.x

Mullen, P., Pathé, M., & Purcell, R. (2008). *Stalkers and their Victims*. Cambridge, UK: Cambridge University Press. doi:10.1017/CBO9780511544088

Nansel, T.R., Overpeck, M., Pilla, R.S., Ruan, W.J., Simons-Morton, B., & Scheidt, P. (2001). Bullying Behaviors Among US Youth: Prevalence and Association with Psychosocial Adjustment. *JAMA, 285*(16), 2094–2100.

Olweus, D. (1991). Bullying/victim problems among schoolchildren. In D. J. Pepler & K. H. Rubin (Eds.), *The development and treatment of childhood aggression* (pp. 411–449). Hillsdale, NJ: Academic Press.

Olweus, D. (1993). *Bullying at School: What We Know and What We Can Do*. Blackwell Publishing.

Ostermeyer, B., Friedman, S.H., Sorrentino, R. & Booth, B.D. (2016). Stalking and Violence. *Psychiatric Clinics of North America, 39*(4), 663-673. doi:10.1016/j.psc.2016.07.010

Paper, W. (2017). *Bullying Prevention in the Technology Age, 2017 Committee for Children*. Available at: https://www.cfchildren.org/

Patchin, J.W., & Hinduja, S. (2013). Social influences on cyberbullying behaviors among middle and high school students. *Journal of Youth & Adolescence, 42*, 711-722. doi:10.100710964-012-9902-4

Pepler, D. J., Jiang, D., Craig, W., & Connolly, J. (2008). Developmental Trajectories of Bullying and Associated Factors. *Child Development, 79*(2), 325-338. Available at: https://www.academia.edu/13317843/Developmental_Trajectories_of_Bullying_and_Associated_Factors

Pöyhönen, V., Juvonen, J., & Salmivalli, C. (2010). What Does It Take to Stand Up for the Victim of Bullying?: The Interplay Between Personal and Social Factors. *Merrill-Palmer Quarterly, 56*(2), 143-163. Available at: http://muse.jhu.edu/article/384696

Pyrzalski, A. (2008). *Agresja elektroniczna dzieci i młodzieży – różne wymiary zjawiska* [Electronic aggression of children and young people - different dimensions of the phenomenon]. Available at: https://repozytorium.amu.edu.pl/bitstream/10593/5379/1/agresja_elektroniczna_dzieci_i_mlodziezy.pdf

Pyżalski, J. (2012). From cyberbullying to electronic aggression: typology of the phenomenon. *Journal of Emotional and Behavioural Difficulties, 17*(3-4), 305–317. Available at: https://www.researchgate.net/publication/254267507_From_cyberbullying_to_electronic_aggression_typology_of_the_phenomenon

Pyżalski, J. (2013). Beyond Peer Cyberbullying – Involvement of Polish Adolescents in Different Kinds of Electronic Aggression. *Studia Edukacyjne, 28*, 147-167. Available at: https://pdfs.semanticscholar.org/c7df/6b62be7b9ab86b23fe679fe8d9711ab61a22.pdf

Rigby, K. (1994). Psychosocial functioning in families of Australian adolescent bully/victim problems. *Journal of Family Therapy*. Available at: https://onlinelibrary.wiley.com/doi/abs/10.1111/j.1467-6427.1994.00787.x

Roome, D. (2012). *Cyber-Bullying is Never Alright: Dealing with the pain of cyber abuse*. CreateSpace Publishing.

Sari, S.V., & Camadan, F. (2016). The new face of violence tendency: Cyber bullying perpetrators and their victims. *Computers in Human Behavior, 59*, 317-326. doi:10.1016/j.chb.2016.02.027

Schafer, M., Korn, S., Smith, P., Hunter, S. C, Mora-Mercha´, J. A. Singer, M. M., & van der Meulen, K. (2004). Lonely in the crowd: recollections of bullying. *British Journal of Developmental Psychology*, *22*, 379–394.

Selkie, E., Kota, R., Chan, Y. F., & Moreno, M. (2015). Cyberbullying, depression, and problem alcohol use in female college students: a multisite study. *Cyberpsychol Behav Soc Netw., 18*(2), 79-86. Available at: https://scinapse.io/papers/2036790583

Shultz, E., Heilman, R., & Hart, K. J. (2014). Cyber-bullying: An exploration of bystander behavior and motivation. *Cyberpsychology (Brno), 8*(4), 3. doi:10.5817/CP2014-4-3

Slonje, R., Smith, P., & Frisen, A. (2012). The nature of cyberbullying, and strategies for prevention. *Computers in Human Behavior, 29*(1), 26-32. doi:10.1016/j.chb.2012.05.024

Smith, P. K. (2011). *Cyberbullying and Cyber Aggression*. Available at: https://www.researchgate.net/profile/Peter_Smith34/publication/284687148_Cyberbullying_and_cyber_aggression/links/56dec02f08aeb8b66f95f8d7/Cyberbullying-and-cyber-aggression.pdf?origin=publication_detail

Steeves, V. (2012). *Young Canadians in a Wired World, Phase III: Talking to Youth and Parents*. MediaSmarts. Available at: https://mediasmarts.ca/sites/mediasmarts/files/publication-report/full/ycwwiii-youth-parents.pdf

Thornberg, R., Tenenbaum, L., Varjas, J., Meyers, K., Jungert, T., & Vanegas, G. (2012). Bystander motivation in bullying incidents: To intervene or not to intervene. *Western Journal of Emergency Medicine, 13*, 247-252. Available at: https://escholarship.org/uc/item/1jv3h364

Turner, A. (2017, January 18). *New survey of 50,000+ young people reveals troubling post-election spike in bullying & harassment, cited from Policy White Paper, Bullying Prevention in the Technology Age*. Available at: https://www.cfchildren.org/wp-content/uploads/policy-advocacy/Committee-for-Children_Policy-White-Paper_Bullying-Prevention-in-the-Technology-Age_FA18.pdf

Varjas, K., Talley, J., Meyers, J., Parris, L., & Cutts, H. (2010). High school students' perceptions of motivations for cyberbullying: An exploratory study. *Western Journal of Emergency Medicine, 3*, 269–273. Available at: https://www.ncbi.nlm.nih.gov/pmc/articles/PMC2941365/

Violence and Youth, Report of the American Psychological Association Commission on Violence and Youth, Vol. 1. (n.d.). Available at: https://www.apa.org/pi/prevent-violence/resources/violence-youth.pdf

Volink, T., Bolman, C.A.W., Dehue, F., & Jacobs, N.C.L. (2012). Coping with Cyberbullying: Differences Between Victims, Bully-victims and Children not Involved in Bullying. *Journal of Community & Applied Social Psychology, 23*, 7-24. doi:10.1002/casp.2142

Wang, J, Iannotti, R.J., & Nansel, T.R. (2009). School Bullying Among US Adolescents: Physical, Verbal, Relational and Cyber. *Journal of Adolescent Health, 45*(4), 368–375. doi:10.1016/j.jadohealth.2009.03.021

Wojtasik, Ł. (2007). *Przemoc rówieśnicza a media elektroniczne* [Peer violence and electronic media]. Fundacja Dzieci Niczyje/gemiusAdHoc. Available at: https://fdds.pl/wp-content/uploads/2016/05/przemoc_rowiesnicza_a_media_elektroniczne_wojtasik.pdf

Wolak, J., Mitchell, K.J., & Finkelhor, D. (2007). Does online harassment constitute bullying? An exploration of online harassment by known peers and online-only contacts. *Journal of Adolescent Health, 41*(6), 51-58. doi:10.1016/j.jadohealth.2007.08.019

Wright, M.F., & Li, Y. (2011) The Associations between Young Adults' Face-To-Face Prosocial Behaviors and Their Online Prosocial Behaviors. *Computers in Human Behavior, 27*, 1959-1962. doi:10.1016/j.chb.2011.04.019

Zuber, M.J., Greenberg, E.W., & Williams, L.M. (2016). Differentiable Attitudes Towards Specific Crimes and Contexts: A Quantification of Neutralization Techniques. *Polish Journal of Social Rehabilitation, 2016*(11). doi:10.22432/pjsr.2016.11.12

KEY TERMS AND DEFINITIONS

Perpetrator of Cyberbullying: A person who performs single or multiple acts of violence directed at another person, through persecution, intimidation, harassment, ridiculing others using the Internet and electronic tools such as: SMS, e-mail, websites, discussion forums on the internet, social networks and other. If they work, they reduce the self-esteem of the victim and their suffering and violation of their dignity.

Victim of Cyberbullying: A person experiencing attacks against groups of perpetrators by holding, for example, negative emails or text messages. The victims of virtual violence usually feel strong shame and humiliation, despair, negative thoughts about themselves and about the world.

Witness of Cyberbullying (Bystander): A person who does not make cyberbullying but has contact with it (through observation, receiving messages, etc.). Bystander can take different attitudes towards the cyberbullying - a reaction against the perpetrator, protection of the victim or joining the perpetrators (actively engaging in violence or passively actions, e.g., by sending/opening a message).

Chapter 6
Educational Approaches for Tackling Cyberbullying

Gilberto Marzano
Rezekne Academy of Technologies, Latvia

ABSTRACT

It is indisputably true that education is invoked by researchers and practitioners as an essential element to reverse the growth of cyberbullying and to mitigate the serious negative mental and physical consequences it has on victims. The key idea emerging from expert opinion is that online safety education and anti-cyberbullying educational programs are both essential in schools. These programs should involve, at different levels, students, educators, and parents. However, designing and running effective educational programs requires not only the comprehensive knowledge of the cyberbullying phenomenon but also educational competencies. In this chapter, the leading educational approaches adopted in cyberbullying educational interventions will be introduced highlighting the underlying psychological theories on which their effectiveness has grounded. In particular, participatory approaches, as well as peer education, will be introduced and discussed since they are universally recognized to be the most fruitful in cyberbullying educational programs.

INTRODUCTION

Since there is unanimous consensus that education is the best antidote to cyberbullying (Chang, 2010; Campbell & Bauman, 2018; Cassidy, Brown, & Jackson, 2012; Englander & Muldowney, 2007; Smith, Sundaram, Spears, Schäfer & Sandhu, 2018), this chapter will focus on the educational approaches that can be adopted for building prevention programs.

DOI: 10.4018/978-1-5225-8076-8.ch006

Indeed, appropriate educational approaches are necessary to realize effective cyberbullying education interventions. But which educational approaches produce the most tangible and optimal results?

To answer this question, two elements should be considered. The first is that long-term interventions may require significantly different approaches from quick-fix interventions. The second is that, both in long-term and short-term interventions, success may depend upon "how well the chosen method matches the case to which it is applied and the knowledge and skills of practitioners" (Rigby & Griffith, 2018, 29).

From this perspective, it would be useful to recall a few basic notions of the teaching-learning process and discuss them in the light of cyberbullying educational interventions.

For example, according to Dewey, "we have laid it down that the educative process is a continuous process of growth, having as its aim at every stage an added capacity of growth" (Dewey, 1916, 63).

Furthermore, one has to notice that, although the educative process usually consists of teaching on one hand and learning on the other, teaching and learning are actually interrelated activities. Learners are not passive recipients of what teachers provide and teachers are not neutral repeaters (Seufert, 2003).

The modern education theories are learner-centered theories. They share two basic assumptions. The first is that teaching-learning is grounded on the principle that learners are at the center of the educational process, while the second is that individuals are not perfectly alike and, accordingly, may need different teaching-learning approaches and techniques.

The majority of contemporary educators, regardless of whether they follow behaviorism, cognitivism, connectivism, or constructionism, contend that teaching is not only about giving and checking knowledge, but encompasses many other non-secondary activities, such as guiding, mentoring, stimulating, and motivating learners. Teachers should support and reinforce positive attitudes of learners in a triangular process that comprises teachers, learners, and the subject matter being taught/learned.

In the last two decades, the teaching-learning process has been influenced by the increasing spread of the internet. Interactive content sources, such as blogs, wikis, and social networks in general, are influencing education. Nowadays, advanced collaborative virtual learning environments are available and in the near future will be operative semantic agents able to parse the global knowledge accessible on the Web.

In the following paragraphs, the principal educational approaches that are at the basis of the most popular cyberbullying intervention programs will be briefly illustrated and discussed.

Knowledge of the theoretical roots of these programs could suggest their better adaptation to the operative contexts and perhaps the integration of their components.

EDUCATIONAL PSYCHOLOGIES

All educational theories, models, and practices have an underlying psychological theory.

Figure 1 shows the learning perspective based on the psychological theories of behaviorism, cognitivism, constructivism, and connectivism.

The first theorist who blended philosophical psychology with educational practice was Johann F. Herbart (1776-1841).

Herbart's pedagogy emphasized the connection between individual development and the resulting societal contribution, thus rejecting the philosophical dualism mind (spirit) and body (matter) of Platonism and Aristotelianism, as well as the notions of superiority of mind and of man being rational in nature. He argued that abilities are not innate but can be instilled thorough education:

Figure 1. The four learning perspectives based on behaviorism, cognitivism, constructivism, and Connectivism
Source: author's own elaboration

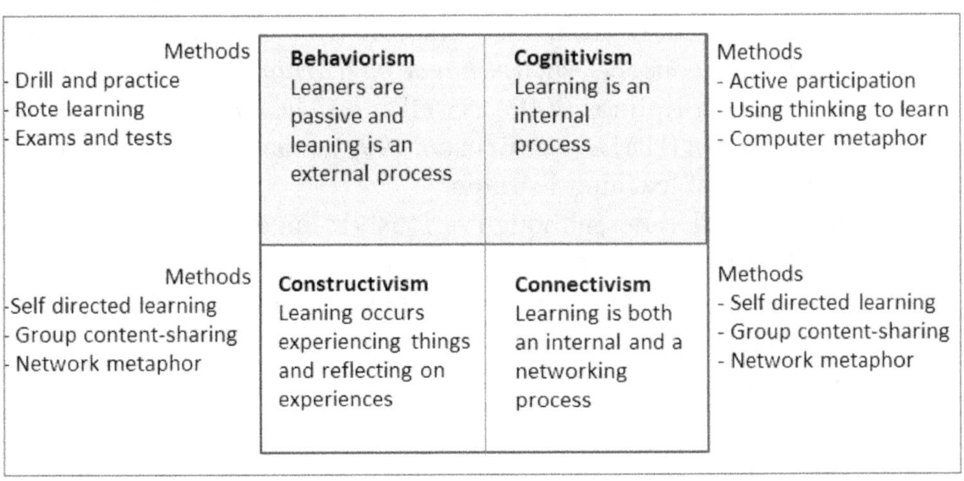

Ideas spring from two main sources, experience and social intercourse. Knowledge of nature incomplete and crude is derived from the former; the later furnishes the sentiments entertained toward our fellowmen, which, far from being praiseworthy, are on the contrary often very reprehensible. To improve these is the more urgent task; but neither ought we to neglect the knowledge of nature. If we do, we may expect error, fantastical notions, and eccentricities of every description. (Herbart, 1913, p. 24)

Herbart believed that knowledge about educational aims and methodology should be rooted in scientific studies. Scientific psychology, as a discipline independent from philosophy, should determine the nature of man and the principles to apply in their education.

Impressed by Pestalozzi's experimental school, Herbart proposed a teaching process based on four steps (Dupuis & Gordon, 2010):

1. **Preparation:** This step is especially important in introducing new topics, and consists in recalling to the students' mind anything they know from past experience of the topic.
2. **Association:** In this step, the students and teacher proceed to formulate generalization from experience and observations.
3. **Presentation (Teaching):** During this step, the teacher furnishes information that students could not themselves discover, and organizes and systematizes all the materials into a unitary whole.
4. **Application:** In this step, the student is expected to demonstrate their achievements by applying the knowledge acquired to novel situations.

However, it was Dewey who made the first complete analysis of the teaching-learning process from the perspective of methodology. Dewey developed ideas and concepts, such as *hands on learning* and *problem-based learning* (De Graaf & Kolmos, 2003) as well as *instrumental intelligence* and *democratic education* (Harkavy & Benson, 1998), that have been influential in modern theories of teaching-learning.

Over the last few decades, although variously re-modulated, the dominant psychological approaches in education have been behaviorism and humanism whilst, recently, neoropedagogy started gaining the attention of researchers and will influence the future of teaching-learning study changing many the the current mainstream paradigms.

Behaviorism

The Behavioristic approach has had a great influence in education. The antecedents of behaviorism can be traced back to Ivan Pavlov's research on conditioning and involuntary reflex actions. Pavlov is well known for the experiment with dogs in which, after continued pairings of food with the sound of a bell, the dog salivated at the sound of the bell alone.

An important contribution to behaviorism came from John Broadus Watson and Eduard L. Thorndike. Watson's article *Psychology as the Behaviorist Views It* (1913) is considered to be the behaviorist manifesto. In this article, Watson outlined the major features of behaviorism, e.g., that psychology is a purely objective experimental branch of natural sciences:

Its theoretical goal is the prediction and control of behavior. Introspection forms no essential part of its methods, nor is the scientific value of its data dependent upon the readiness with which they lend themselves to interpretation in terms of consciousness. The behaviorist, in his efforts to get a unitary scheme of animal response, recognizes no dividing line between man and brute. The behavior of man, with all of its refinement and complexity, forms only a part of the behaviorist's total scheme of investigation. (Watson, 1913, 248)

In 1932, Thorndike was the first to propose that rewards were better reinforcers than punishments, because they strengthened the connection between the stimulus and the desired response: one can catch more flies with a spoon of honey than with a gallon of vinegar.

For behaviorists, human beings are biological organisms existing in a socio-cultural environment which determines their nature and essence. Individuals and cultures are influenced by a combination of genetic and environmental factors. Values are expressions of (or preferences for) those forms of behavior which have been reinforced. As a consequence, behaviorists reject the view that humans are innately inclined to evil or good. Note that for a long time the Western world was dominated by the idea that man is a very imperfect being and, consequently, must be strictly educated and guided otherwise they will choose evil rather than good. This view posits that children are inclined to misbehave and should be constantly held in check to control their inherent bad instincts and be educated to maintain a right conduct.

The most remarkable exponent of behaviorism was the American psychologist and social philosopher Burrhus Frederic Skinner (1904 – 1990). The theoretical position of Skinner was closely related to that of Logical

Empiricists. He rejected the platonic dualism of mind-body (spirit-matter) as well as the attribution of certain human traits to human nature or instinct:

An organism which has received a painful shock will also, if possible, act to gain access to another organism towards which it can act aggressively. The extent to which human aggression exemplifies innate tendencies is not clear, and many of the ways in which people attack and thus weaken or destroy the power of intentional controllers are quite obviously learned. (Skinner, 1976, 34)

The "hunter or warrior instinct" is a meaningless expression since what is claimed to be instinct is an attitude due to external conditioning (Dupuis & Gordon, 2010, 22):

Similarly, moral values are derived by experience and are retained because of positive reinforcements. Aesthetic values, just as moral values, may be held individually, socially, or culturally.

Behaviorists claim that educational objectives should be expressed in a measurable way. Indeed, every educational program should contain behavioral objectives and means for the objective evaluation of student success in achieving those stated objectives.

Skinner is especially critical of useless goals of education such as excellence or creativity since these terms are not carefully specified. In response to those who claim that discovery is the best means of learning, Skinner responds that:

Working through a program is really a process of discovery, but not in the sense in which that word is currently used in education. We discover many things in the world around us, and that is usually better than being told about them, but as individuals we can discover only a very small part of the world. Mathematics has been discovered very slowly and painfully over thousands of years. Students discover it as they go through a program, but not in the sense of doing something for the first time in history. (Skinner, 1984, 951)

A fundamental behaviorist belief is that learning encompasses the entire range of the human life. Their idea is that what serves the needs of an individual, society, or the culture of today may be completely different for people in the future centuries. For this reason, continuous guidance is necessary for curriculum designers to update programs in order to meet changing needs.

Humanism

Humanism is a psychological and philosophical approach which is the diametric opposite of behaviorism.

Humanists don't share common agreement on any theoretical principles, except one. They sustain only that human beings are free and that freedom is the expression of humanity. As a consequence, all humanists are apt to insist that they don't wish to be restricted by any system.

For humanists, the subjective human situation is the real subject matter of psychology.

They claim that the major concerns of human existence cannot be examined by the empirical methods of the sciences: my experience is not the same as yours.

The interest of humanists focuses on relationships among human beings as well as on death, alienation, anxiety, fear, value choices, and so on. Humanists claim that behavioral sciences are of little help in providing knowledge on such subjective matters. They consider that the most important kind of truth is personal experience.

Furthermore, in his book *Personal Knowledge*, published in 1959, Polanyi attests that our personal experiences and ways of sharing knowledge have a profound effect on scientific discovery. He objects to the stereotype of the wholly objective and dispassionate researcher, pointing out that *knowing* is still an art, and that not only logical reasoning but also personal beliefs and passions are necessary parts of research. Polanyi argues that the objectivity of science is rooted "in the very depths of our culture":

Yet the prevailing conception of science, based on the disjunction of subjectivity and objectivity, seeks—and must seek at all costs—to eliminate from science such passionate, personal, human appraisals of theories, or at least to minimize their function to that of a negligible by-play. For modern man has set up as the ideal of knowledge the conception of natural science as a set of statements which is 'objective' in the sense that its substance is entirely determined by observation, even while its presentation may be shaped by convention.

[...] That is why scientific theory is represented as a mere economical description of facts; or as embodying a conventional policy for drawing empirical inferences; or as a working hypothesis, suited to man's practical convenience—interpretations that all deliberately overlook the rational core of science. (Polanyi, 2012, 16)

The biggest contribution of humanism to education comes from the American psychologist Carl R. Roger (1902-1987) who was among the founders of the person-centered approach to psychology. This approach is based on techniques that allow a client to engage their own resources to act in their world with others and overcome their problems:

When I am at my best, as a group facilitator or a therapist, I discover another characteristic. I find that when I am closest to my inner, intuitive self, when I am somehow in touch with the unknown in me, when perhaps I am in a slightly altered state of consciousness, then whatever I do seems to be full of healing. Then simply my presence is releasing and helpful. There is nothing I can do to force this experience, but when I can relax and be close to the transcendental core of me, then I may behave in strange and impulsive ways in the relationship, ways which I cannot justify rationally, which have nothing to do with my thought processes. But these strange behaviors turn out to be right, in some odd way. At those moments, it seems that my inner spirit has reached out and touched the inner spirit of the other. Our relationship transcends itself, and has become a part of something larger. Profound growth and healing and energy are present. (Roger, 1979, 102)

In the 1960s, the computer program Eliza was created by Joseph Weizenbaum (1966). It was a tongue-in-cheek application which emulated the responses of a Rogerian non-directional psychotherapist in an initial psychiatric interview. The Weizenbaum program demonstrates how simple it is to simulate the Rogerian psychotherapist paradigm.

However, the person-centered approach has borne a wide range of application in various domains, such as psychotherapy and counseling (client-centered therapy), education (student-centered learning), organizations, and other group settings. The personal centered approach has also been used in several cyberbullying investigations, e.g., to identify subsets of victims (Ortega et al., 2012), to analyze distinct forms of victimization (Bradshaw, Waasdorp, & O'Brennan, 2013), to categorize acts of aggression (Mehari & Farrell, 2018), and so on.

In regards to education, Rogers claims that conditioning plays the major role in determining value preferences among infants, but that later the child moves beyond the stage of self-satisfaction and tries to please others. He argues that, stage by stage, an individual develops values based on their life experiences and arrives at a synthesis of all these experiences. Finally, he states that the broadest aim of education is the facilitation of learning in an ever-changing world.

Compulsory Miseducation by Godman (1964) synthesized the humanist critique of the American public-school system. The author suggests that formal education transmits wrong social values and damages students:

It is in the schools and from the mass media, rather than at home or from their friends, that the mass of our citizens in all classes learn that life is inevitably routine, depersonalized, venally graded; that it is best to toe the mark and shut up; that there is no place for spontaneity, open sexuality, free spirit. Trained in the schools, they go on to the same quality of jobs, culture, and politics. This education is, miseducation, socializing to the national norms and regimenting to the national 'needs'. (Godman, 1964, 23)

Godman also denounces the ineffectiveness of mass school:

Terrible damage is done to children simply by the size and standardization of the big system. Suppose a class size of twenty is good for average purposes, it does not follow that thirty-five is better than nothing. Rather, it is likely to be positively harmful, because the children have ceased to be persons and the teacher is destroyed as a teacher. A teacher with a ten-year-old class reading at seven-year level will have to use the content as well as the vocabulary Dick and Jane since that is the textbook bought by the hundred thousand. (Goodman, 1973, 26)

Neuropedagogy

The term neuropedagogogy has been introduced by the French biologist, ethologist, and philosopher Trocmé-Fabre en 1987 and is a field of investigation that focuses on the study of learning process flowing an interdisciplinary approach integrating neuroscience, psychology, and educational theory (Frayssinhes & Pasquier, 2018).

According to Houdé, neoropedagogy is a new discipline emerging at the confluence of neurosciences and educational sciences, which could be defined as a new approach that integrates developmental psychology, cognitive neuroscience, and pedagogy (Houdé, 2004).

Indeed, neuroscience created a new challenge for education, because it provides new characterizations of the current state of the learner – including brain state, genetic state, and hormonal state - that could be relevant to learning and teaching. For example, there are close ties between motor activities and thought processes (Machado, 2012).

In the neuropedagogical view cognition is grounded in perception and action in its essence suggesting that even the most complex thoughts are sense-based and not abstract symbolic:

For instance, the word ''guilt'' may refer to a situation, in which an individual causes an accident, in which a child was seriously injured. Within this context, the concept ''guilt'' is defined by sensory and action properties of the accident situation as well as by emotional states of the accident perpetrator derived from introspection. Like for concrete concepts, embodied cognition theory proposes that exactly this reactivation of sensory, motor and emotional experiences constitute the meaning of an abstract concept such as ''guilt''. (Kiefer & Trumpp, 2012, p. 19)

Neoropedagogy also tackles topical issues deriving from the changes induced by digital technologies. Indeed, the sensory-motor experiences during handwriting (haptic, motor, visual, etc.) are quite different from those during typewriting or mouse clicking on digital devices (Mangen & Velay, 2010; O'Loughlin, 2006).

Accordingly, it is important to know how digital technology will change writing habits and affect reading performance.

Neoropedagogy also investigates on how positive emotions can support the processing of information and communication, enhance negotiation, decision-making, creative problem-solving, and similar higher-level cognitive activities (Plass & Kaplan, 2016).

In fact, advances in emotion research and affective neuroscience have led scholars to consider the role of emotions in basic cognitive mechanisms, including memory, attention, and perception. Emotions are seen as effective retrieval cues for long-term memory and a topical question is how emotions can affect the learners' experience in digital learning environments.

Several studies on multimedia learning have been carried out. Research shows that different aesthetic designs can induce emotions and that these emotions affect users' performance and cognitive processes. Accordingly, the design of various multimedia elements, such as the visual design, design layout, color, and sound in multimedia environments, resulted in positive user perceptions about learning. Figure 2 shows the *Integrated Cognitive-Affective Model of Learning with the Multimedia* (ICALM) model propose by Plass and Kaplan for the purpose of emotional design in multimedia learning.

Figure 2. Integrated cognitive-affective model of learning with multimedia (ICALM)
Source: Plass & Kaplan, 2016, 150

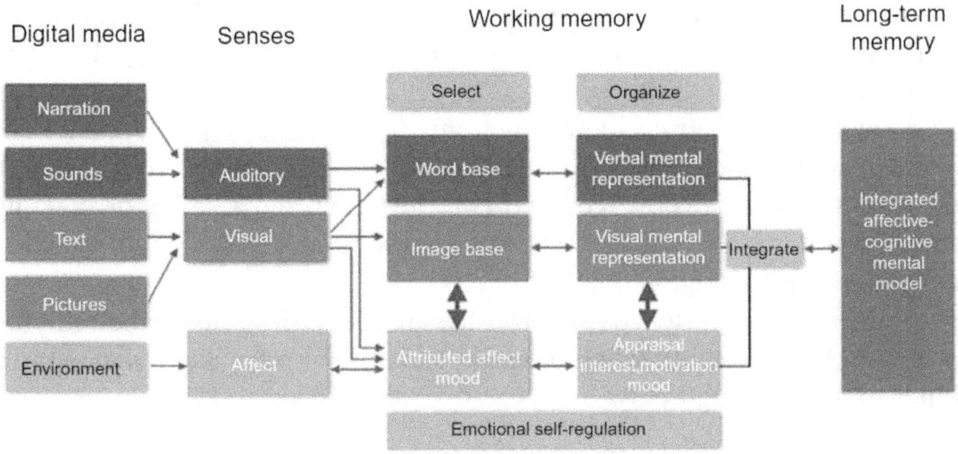

The ICALM model is the result of a comprehensive analysis of the basic concepts related to emotion and learning performed by the authors. It is a theoretical framework of learning from digital media that highlights the intertwined and interconnected nature of emotion and learning.

Research on neoropedagogy will influence the educational theories and professional learning applications and will open new perspectives in the scope of socio-cultural learning.

Proactive and Reactive Cyberbullying Interventions

Cyberbullying intervention can be categorized as *proactive* or *reactive* depending on whether they are inspired by a proactive or a reactive educational approach.

Proactive education aims at orienting one particular behavior instead of attempting to correct others. In other words, proactive education focuses on the identification and exploitation of what can help to avoid or reduce potential problems and threats. Conversely, reactive education focuses on fighting or solving a problem after it occurs.

Proactive cyberbullying education encompasses all interventions aimed at preventing cyberbullying behavior. Online safety programs are an example of proactive education. Proactive cyberbullying education is expected to reduce the occurrence of cyberbullying cases. However, when actual cases of cyberbullying do occur, they must be dealt with by taking appropriate actions.

The majority of bullying and cyberbullying education programs are based on proactive approaches, e.g., working with students, promoting positive bystander behavior, and stimulating peer support (Allison & Bussey, 2017; Barlińska, Szuster, & Winiewski, 2013; Bradshaw, 2015; Cassidy, Faucher, & Jackson, 2013).

Reactive interventions include not only the use of disciplinary sanctions but also actions aimed at buffering negative impacts, such as strengthening the victim, restorative practices involving the victim and perpetrator, creating support groups, as well as technical solutions to filtering and blocking cyberbullying messages.

Both proactive and reactive approaches are needed in an anti-cyberbullying program. Indeed, an effective program should comprise and balance three kinds of actions (Figure 3):

- Reducing risks through knowledge, e.g. with e-safety training, active understanding of cyberbullying, group discussion, etc.;
- Fighting instances through sanctions and technology;
- Buffering impacts through active support, e.g. with emotional coping, educators/parents support, peer help, etc.

Figure 3. Proactive and reactive anti-cyberbullying interventions
Source: Author's own elaboration

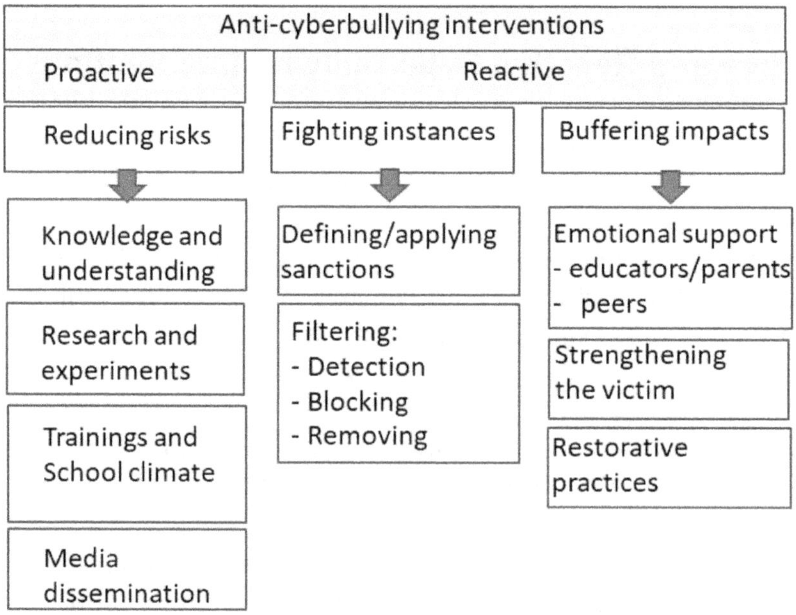

Both proactive and reactive interventions use participatory and peer-based approaches, especially with students.

There is a large body of literature on how people can be influenced by their peers. The notion of *social influence* has been introduced to describe this phenomenon. Processes of social influence have been acknowledged to be relevant in traditional bullying. For example, bystanders of traditional bullying can be influenced to join in the bullying and so be accepted by peers (Nickerson, Mele, & Princiotta, 2008), whilst the perception of peer pressure to interventions buffers the negative influence of bystanders' passive inclinations (Pozzoli & Gini, 2010).

The result of a study on the various direct and indirect forms of peer influence on cyberbullying behavior among high school students in Germany (Table 1) shows that:

[...] the classroom context is highly relevant for cyberbullying. For both processes—perpetration and victimization—the number of bullies within a school class plays an important role in predicting individual behavior. An aggressive class climate not only seems to motivate students' cyberbullying behavior, but also increases the risk of victimization. (Festl, Scharkow & Quandt, 2013, 457)

Since peer-based approaches are broadly suggested and adopted in cyberbullying prevention (Atkinson, Furnell, & Phippen, 2009; Foye, Satinsky, Rosan, & Breedvelt, 2018; Jäger, Amado, Matos, & Pessoa, 2010; Menesini, Nocentini, & Palladino, 2012; Patchin & Hinduja, 2012), it would be useful to introduce the basic notions of the participatory learning approach before dealing with peer education.

Table 1. Examples of peer influence and internet use on cyberbullying behavior

	Peer Influence	Media-based (Peer) Influence
Direct	Verbal support of the perpetrator's behavior	Media-based verbal or non-verbal support of the perpetrator's behavior (e.g., through commentary options or like-buttons)
Indirect	Providing an audience through observation of the bullying in the schoolyard	Providing an audience through witnessing the bullying in the internet (e.g., through the public reception of YouTube-videos)

Source: Festl, Scharkow, & Quandt, (2013, p. 448)

Participatory Learning Approach

In the 1990s, participation was a popular buzzword, and the concept of participation was also extended into the field of education.

Since the 2000s, participatory learning has been seen as an increasingly appealing educational approach that can positively affect learners since it engages them as active participants in the full educational program, including homework and exercises.

Participatory learning is grounded in John Dewey's idea that learners achieve better results if the learning process "reproduces, or runs parallel to, some form of work carried on in social life" (Dewey & Boydston, 1983, 93).

From a philosophical point of view, participatory learning can be seen as the natural consequence of two Deweyan concepts: that learning is a problem-solving process, and that there isn't any dualism between the subject matter and the method (Dupuis & Gordon, 2010).

Participatory learning has often been experimented to support sustainable development, above all in regards to the agriculture of developing countries (Coldevin, 2002), and has been seen as a means to aid the democratic progress of emerging countries, since participatory learning is, by its very nature, collaborative and so directly fosters democracy.

Certain adult participatory learning techniques are also very popular and widely used in management training (especially for project managers and supervisors), such as brainstorming, problem-solving, project work, and critical incident response. Most of them have their theoretical basis in behaviorism as well as in constructivism (Rodrigues, 2014). Indeed, constructivist theories of learning argue that knowledge is constructed by learners who better learn by actively applying their know-how to meaningful problems (Brown & Palincsar, 1989).

Participatory learning methods comprise a wide range of activities, which share a student-centered view aimed at enabling learners to play an active and influential part in their learning process. This means that learners are not merely listened to, but also actively collaborate to acquire knowledge and skills: in other words, participatory learning focuses on student participation.

An element that characterizes participatory learning is the necessity of facilitators. Indeed, every participatory process needs the presence of skilled figures who help participants to interact together (Kaner, 2014).

In the educational context, facilitators provide learners with discussion subjects, present case studies, organize tasks that call for participants to work together in small groups, and so on. Their task is to support the active involvement of learners in the learning process, stimulating them to think through their mindset and share with others their experience and knowledge, as well as collaborate to accomplish the expected achievements.

It has to be noted that, although facilitators and coaches have many overlapping skills and functions, their role is different: a coach provides individual attention and addresses personal development with an emphasis on a specific task, whereas a facilitator provides a group with meaningful dialogue and broadens personal perspectives, encouraging the entire group to participate collectively so as to increase their ability to operate effectively on their own.

Participatory learning strategies are considered effective in adult learning since they can reduce the difficulties due to the inhomogeneity of trainees that can affect adult educational programs. In this regard, the *Participatory Adult Learning Strategy* (PALS) is a proven model that can be adopted in parent training educational programs. PALS is an evidence-based approach by Dust and Trivette, which results from over 20 years of research and practice and, more recently, from the findings of the meta-analyses of adult learning methods and the synthesis of research studies into the most effective adult learning practices (Dunst & Trivette, 2009; Dunst, Trivette, & Hamby, 2010; Trivette, Dunst, Hamby, & O'herin, 2009).

PALS authors analyzed and measured the positive effect of four adult learning methods: accelerated learning (Meier, 2000), coaching (Hargreaves & Dawe, 1990), guided design (Hancock, Coscarelli, & White, 1983), and just-in-time training (Hew & Brush, 2007; Novak, 2011). From their research, the relative importance of active learner participation in learning new knowledge or practices emerged, and from this result, a procedure was designed for using evidence-based practices in adult learning. The PALS model encompasses a 4-phase process that includes:

1. **Introduction:** The learning topic and related information is preliminarily provided to learners, as well as in-class/workshop warmup exercises and illustrations/demonstrations.
2. **Application:** Trainees apply information learned; the instructor/facilitator observes their activity, giving feedback and evaluating their use of knowledge.
3. **Informed Understanding:** Trainees are engaged in self-assessment, reflection, and group discussions.

4. **Repeat Learning Process:** The next steps in the learning process are planned in order to provide further learner understanding, knowledge use, and mastery.

However, nowadays, because of the increasing growth of digital technology, a topical question arises about participatory learning. How do participatory practices work in an online learning environment?

This question is a part of a more general issue that concerns the portability of participatory approaches and techniques to online web-based learning contexts.

Indeed, Web 2.0 tools suggest new forms of learning at a lower cost, such as learning through blogs (Downes, 2004; Farmer & Bartlett-Bragg, 2005) or through podcasts and videocasts (Ractham & Zhang, 2006).

Regarding participatory e-learning, there are some assumptions that are generally agreed upon. One of these is that the success of participatory e-learning depends on the interaction of learners, since they are bringers of knowledge and skills (Kok, 2015).

Another important aspect is that active learning is fundamental for participatory e-learning: learners are involved in practices that require them to actively construct new knowledge and understanding.

Peer Education

Peer education is an umbrella term used to describe interventions in which trainers and trainees cooperate between themselves (Shiner, 1999). Nowadays, it is a topical buzzword in every sector of education.

Three theoretical roots are usually associated with peer education: Bandura's *social learning theory* (Bandura, 1986), the *social inoculation theory* (McGuire & Papageorgis, 1961; McGuire 1964), and the *differential association theory* (Sutherland & Cressey, 1974).

However, Miller and Dollard are considered the precursors of peer education with their idea of *learning by imitation* (Grusec, 1992). In their book *Social learning and imitation* (1941), that was based on experiments on rats and children, they argued that imitation can greatly hasten the process of independent learning since it enables the subject to perform the first correct response sooner than they otherwise would.

Social Cognitive Theory

Bandura's Social Cognitive theory has influenced many disciplines, such as education, health sciences, social policy, and psychotherapy. This theory is based on the idea that an individual learns from their interactions with other individuals in a social context (Bandura, 1977). For example, by observing the behavior of others, people develop similar behavior, especially if their observational experiences are positive ones or include rewards related to the observed behavior (Nabavi, 2012).

In the 1960s, Albert Bandura, Dorothea Ross, and Sheila A. Ross conducted an experiment in order to test imitative learning (Bandura, Ross, & Ross, 1961). This test, known as the *Bobo doll experiment*, involved 36 boys and 36 girls enrolled in the Stanford University Nursery School. They ranged in age from 37 to 69 months, with a mean age of 52 months.

Two adults, a male and a female, served in the role of model, and one female experimenter conducted the study for all 72 children. Badura reports that:

Subjects were divided into eight experimental groups of six subjects each and a control group consisting of 24 subjects. Half the experimental subjects were exposed to aggressive models and half were exposed to models that were subdued and nonaggressive in their behavior. These groups were further subdivided into male and female subjects. Half the subjects in the aggressive and nonaggressive conditions observed same-sex models, while the remaining subjects in each group viewed models of the opposite sex. The control group had no prior exposure to the adult models and was tested only in the generalization situation. (Bandura, 22-23)

Figure 4 show the attacks against Bobo Doll.

The findings of Bandura's experiment were that children learn social behavior such as aggression through the process of observation learning - through watching the behavior of another person. More specifically:

- Children who observed the aggressive models made far more imitative aggressive responses than those who were in the non-aggressive or control groups.
- There was more partial and non-imitative aggression among those children who have observed aggressive behavior, although the difference for non-imitative aggression was small.

Figure 4. Images from the Bobo Doll experiment
Source: Albert Bandura, https://www.youtube.com/watch?v=dmBqwWlJg8U

- Girls also showed more physical aggressive responses if the model was male but more verbal aggressive responses if the model was female;
- Boys were more likely to imitate same-sex models than girls. The evidence for girls imitating same-sex models is not strong.
- Boys imitated more physically aggressive acts than girls. There was little difference in the verbal aggression between boys and girls.

Continuing the illustration of Social Cognitive Theory, according to Muro and Jeffrey (2008), one can claim that it combines elements of behaviorist learning theories and cognitive learning theories. Social Cognitive Theory encompasses attention, memory, and motivation, and posits that people learn from one another, via:

- Observation;
- Imitation; and
- Modeling

Based on these general principles, learning can occur without a change in behavior. In other words, behaviorists say that learning has to be represented by a permanent change in behavior; while, in contrast, social learning theorists say that because people can learn through observation alone, their learning may not necessarily be shown in their performance (Bandura, 1965). Learning may or may not result in a behavior change (Bandura, 2006).

What emerged from a recent research (Marzano & Ochoa, 2018) was the topicality of Bandura's learning concepts in internet-based learning approaches. In fact, the concept that "learning is a social activity" where individuals achieve their learning goals by interacting with each other (Stamps, 1997; Gherardi, Nicolini, & Odella, 1998; Pritchard & Woollard, 2013) is shared by many researchers engaged in internet social learning and online collaborative learning (Yu, Tian, Vogel, & Kwok, 2010; Hamid, Waycott, Kurnia, & Chang, 2015; Liao, Huang, Chen, & Huang, 2015).

Social Inoculation Theory

The inoculation theory was developed in the 1960s by the social psychologist William J. McGuire for inducing resistance to persuasion (McGuire & Papageorgis, 1961). Social inoculation theory studies means of protection against attempts at persuasion, either through direct attack or indirect pressures. In a similar way to how inoculation and vaccination are used to immunize the body against specific diseases by artificially stimulating the body's immune system, social inoculation theorizes that persuading people not to be persuaded is possible, by inoculating an individual with certain arguments and at the same time giving them counter-arguments to refute those arguments. Indeed, it is possible to make heuristic use of the inoculation analogy in deriving hypotheses about producing resistance to persuasion, choosing:

[…] to deal as far as possible with beliefs that had been maintained in a "germ-free" ideological environment, that is, beliefs that the person has seldom, if ever, heard attacked. Nearly all beliefs should be of this sort, according to the selective-avoidance postulate, which implies that a person avoids dissonant information wherever possible. (McGuire, 1964, 200)

In McGuire's view, cognitions can be strengthened by exposing an audience to mild attacking arguments and then providing the same audience with arguments with which to counter those negative attacks.

The application of social inoculation to peer education has been motivated as follows:

- Peers are a credible source of information and advice;
- Peers can exercise a positive influence;
- Arguments presented by peers may be more acceptable.

There are applications of social inoculation in many scopes, especially in health care prevention and marketing.

A meta-analysis conducted by Banas and Rains (2010) shows that inoculation is an effective method for instilling resistance to attitude change, but more work is needed to clarify the various nuances of the process of inoculation.

In the 1980s, Evans first used social inoculation to prevent young people taking up smoking (Evans, R. I. (1984), and his success lead to the use of social inoculation in drug prevention (Donaldson, Graham, Piccinin, & Hansen, 1995; Donaldson et al. 1996; Donohew, Sypher, & Bukoski, 2012).

It is interesting to note Regis's criticism of peer-led health education, in which the author expresses his doubts about approaches aimed at resisting peer pressure:

Isn't there something a little odd about trying to use young people's susceptibility to peer influence in these programs, when resistance to social influence from peers is at least part of the message?

[…] This is a type of homeopathy, where a little of the poison of peer influence is used to attempt the cure.

[…] I know that until we know a little more about how and why they work, peer-led programs may still need still handling with care. (Regis, 1996, p. 78)

Differential Association Theory

Differential Association Theory is one of the theories that come under the umbrella of the Chicago School. It was formulated by the sociologist Edwin Sutherland in 1939 and revised in 1947 in order to explain deviance and juvenile delinquency. Differential Association Theory views criminality as social interaction, and posits criminal acts as learned behaviors. Sutherland's theory was broadly agreed by criminologist circles and it has had a great impact on modern criminology and on how people reflect on crime (Regoli & Hewitt (1997).

According to Sutherland, criminal behavior results from a learning process in which bad values are transmitted. As in the case of law-abiding values, criminal values are learned in order to interact and socialize with others who agree to those values.

The differential association theory consists of nine principles (Sutherland & Cressey, 1974, 75-91):

P1: Criminal behavior is learned; it is not inherited. This means that a person who is not already trained in criminal acts does not invent such acts, just as a child does not make courteous remarks unless they have had training or socialized to that effect.

P2: Criminal behavior is learned in interaction with others through communication. This communication is verbal in many respects but also includes the gestures often described as non-verbal communication

P3: The learning occurs in intimate groups: Sutherland claimed that only small, face-to-face gatherings influence behavior.

P4: When criminal behavior is learned, the learning includes (a)Techniques for committing it, which are sometimes complicated, and sometimes very simple; (b) the specific direction of motives and drives, rationalizations and attitude.

P5: The specific direction of motives and drives are learned from definitions of legal codes as favorable or unfavorable. This means that, when one's associates define the legal codes as things to be observed, the learning of criminal acts may be impeded. The reverse is also true.

P6: A person becomes criminal because of an excess of definitions favorable to violation of law over definitions unfavorable to violation of the law. This is the core principle of differential association theory. It reinforces the belief that the definitions favorable to the violation of the law can be learned from both criminal and non-criminal people. This principle is loaded with counteracting forces of favorable and unfavorable definitions to the violation of the law.

P7: Differential association (tendency towards criminality) varies in frequency, duration, priority, and intensity. This means the longer the time, the earlier in one's life, the more intensely and more frequently people are exposed to a set of attitudes about criminality, the more likely it is that they will become caught up in the fray.

P8: The process of learning criminal behavior involves the same mechanisms involved in any other learning. This implies that the mechanisms for learning criminal behaviors are the same as those for law-abiding values and other socially relevant skills.

P9: Both criminal and non-criminal behaviors are expressions of the same needs and values. Put differently, the goals of criminals and non-criminals are usually the same. What is different is the means they adopt to pursue this same goal. For instance, thieves generally steal in order to secure money. Honest laborers likewise work with monetary gain in mind.

It is erroneous to believe that the differential association theory states that persons become criminals because of an excess of associations with criminals. In fact, the theory:

[…] is concerned with ratios of associations with patterns of behavior, no matter what the character of the person presenting them.

[…]

Thus, if a mother teaches her son that "Honesty is the best policy", but also teaches him, perhaps inadvertently, that "It is also right to steal a loaf of bread when you are starving", she is presenting him with anticriminal behavior pattern and a criminal behavior pattern, even if she herself is honest, noncriminal, and even anticriminal. One can learn criminal behavior pattern from persons who are not criminals, and one can learn anticriminal behavior patterns from hoods, professional crooks, habitual offenders, and gangsters. (Sutherland & Cressey, 1974, 79)

In recent times, the differential association theory has been used to study internet piracy among students. Studies confirm that peer activity and parental support are consistently strong predictors of internet piracy (Gunter, 2009). A research by Hinduja and Ingram indicated that real life peers had the strongest effect on music piracy: students "who associated with others in real life who were supportive of unauthorized music downloading had higher piracy scores" (Hinduja & Ingram, 2009). Indeed, the authors note that:

[...] computer-related crime may be more dependent on peer learning sources than traditional crime because of the fact that those who want to engage in the former must acquire the technical skillsets necessary to do so – skills not learned through common, everyday experiences. In addition, it has been documented that those who participate in computer-related deviance are more apt to associate with others of like mind than would normally be the case for conventional forms of deviance (Hinduja & Ingram, 2009, 411).

Parent Training

The importance of training parents is widely emphasized by researchers and practitioners (Wang, Lam, Kim, Singer, & Dodds, 2016). For example, parents of children with autism or Down Syndrome have been successfully taught to improve the parent-child relationship, increase communication skills, and decrease inappropriate behaviors.

However, despite the numerous examples and variations of parent training courses (see the multifarious social coaching offers), evidence-based guidelines for designing, implementing, running, and evaluating parent training programs are not available. Moreover, parent training techniques are not widely studied by students in social pedagogy and social worker study programs.

Involving parents leads to positive results in cyberbullying prevention. In their systematic review carried out on bullying and cyberbullying intervention programs, Farrington & Ttofi (2009) observe that parent training was significantly related to a decrease in both bullying and victimization. The authors suggest that efforts should be made to sensitize parents about the issue of school bullying through educational presentations and teacher-parent meetings. From their comprehensive study, it emerges that the most popular forms of parental involvement are:

- Informative newsletters;
- Meetings with teachers;
- Talks with bullies and their parents enforcing non-hostile, non-physical sanctions;
- Information leaflets providing information to parents about prevalence, types, causes, and effects of bullying, as well as advice on how to deal with bullying;
- Information nights during which parents are informed about the problem of bullying in their school.

However, the overall information collected regarding the involvement of parents didn't allow the authors to assess the quality of the information provided to them or to differentiate schools according to different levels of implementation of parent training programs.

In a recent study conducted on a sample consisting of 2,419 students recruited from different schools in the north of Italy, it resulted that cyberbullying is negatively associated "with parental education on internet use, whereas cyber victimization was positively associated, and the same was true of parental control of online activities that the child does in social networks" (Baldry, Sorrentino, & Farrington, 2016, 71).

Although parental involvement is considered very important in cyberbullying prevention, little attention has been paid to methods and techniques that should be used for this purpose. Regarding parent training, in 1989, Dumas formulated four general assumptions that remain still valid:

1. Human behavior is a function of the contingencies of reinforcement and punishment to which individuals are exposed in the course of daily exchanges with the environment.
2. Antisocial behavior is learned and sustained by this positive and negative reinforcement (e.g., social attention, avoidance) children receive from social agents, parents in particular.
3. Therapy seeks to establish a shift in social contingencies such that children's prosocial behaviors obtain positive parental reinforcement, and their aversive behaviors are consistently punished or ignored.
4. Maintenance and generalization of treatment gains rely on a process of positive reinforcement. As parents and children exchange reinforcers through their newly acquired pattern of interaction, this pattern is likely to maintain itself in time and generalize to new situations (Dumas, 1989, 206).

Addressing parental training, some aspects should be considered. For instance, although one talks about parent training, usually only one parent, the mother, is involved in the activities. The involvement of the father is broadly recommended, but there is a lack of data regarding this point, even though their involvement increases the effectiveness of interventions (Peacock & Collett, 2011).

Most parent training models are based on the social learning theory approach, and foresee the following steps:

1. Didactic instruction
2. Trainees' skill modeling
3. Parental training of the skills and exercise with the trainer
4. Parental training of the skills at home

In the case of cyberbullying, parental training should include sessions on the use of parental control programs and social networking applications, as well as information on the legal consequences of bullying and cyberbullying acts.

Learning 2.0 and 3.0

Many e-learning systems offer collaborative functions that allow cooperation and facilitate communication among learners, teachers, mentors, tutors, and administrators. These collaborative functions result from the Web 2.0 revolution that in the last few years has swept away the old paradigm of digital communication.

Web 2.0 encompasses a variety of websites and applications that allow anyone to create and share online information and materials they have created. The key difference between Web 2.0 and the traditional types of websites is that it does not require any web design or publishing skills to create and publish materials on the Web.

There are a variety of Web 2.0 applications including wikis, blogs, social networking, folksonomies, podcasting, and so on. Many of the most popular websites are Web 2.0 sites, such as Wikipedia, YouTube, Facebook, Snapchat, and Instagram. The Web 2.0 revolution has also influenced the educational field with e-learning 2.0 that has expanded the concept of the learning community, focusing on supporting the development and solving of educational problems through online collaboration.

The principal aims of e-learning Web 2.0 are:

- To make learning collaborative, easy, and simple;
- To allow learning materials to be used on a global level;
- To allow a real interactivity between teachers and learners, and among learners;
- To encourage developing practices through the sharing of educational content and teaching methods.

Recently, the advances in semantic web found application in education and e-learning 3.0 was born. Fundamentally, this opens a whole new dimension of learning going beyond traditional e-learning that is based on video lectures and multiple-choice assessments. E-learning 3.0 is an evolution of the learner-centered approach. It leverages advances in scientific learning and tools to make learning faster, more effective, more enjoyable, and applicable to a larger set of learning areas. It's the end of systems, where course production considerations trump learner experience.

Online learning 3.0 has a few fundamentals aspects:

- Modern user experience design, similar to what folks are seeing in the consumer web.
- Visually engaging overview, e.g. what am I going to learn, how am I doing, what's next, etc.
- Personalized, allows learners to test out and navigate in a nonlinear fashion.
- A knowledge graph frame of reference, instead of a list of materials to get through.
- Learn-by-doing.
- Integration of external materials.
- Interactive content and assessments.
- Human involvement at scale, for example, online coaching or group collaboration.
- Engagement tools, e.g. gamification, mobile, social integration, etc.
- Visible and transportable credit for what's been learned.
- Delivered in the context of lifelong learning programs.
- Heavy use of data to improve the learning experience and course material over time.

Finally, a new paradigm, crowd learning, has attracted the interest of researchers. Crowd learning essentially encompasses three main areas:

- Machine learning
- Crowdsourcing and crowd sensing applications
- Massive Open Online Courses (MOOC)

Indeed, crowd learning is designed as a process that involves "harnessing the knowledge and expertise of many people to answer questions, solve problems, or enable collaborative learning" (Sharples, Kloos, Dimitriadis, Garlatti, & Specht, 2015). It can accordingly be seen as a process of learning from the knowledge and experience of others.

Crowd learning can be defined as a form of collective learning in which individuals contribute their knowledge and experience to the achievement of prefixed learning objectives. This definition encompasses machine learning as well as crowdsourcing. In effect, we can gather data from crowdsources in order to implement machine learning solutions, but studying the knowledge acquisition of individuals in time and space, namely in crowd contexts, could lead to the implementation of more effective crowdsourcing applications (Prpić, Shukla, Kietzmann, & McCarthy, 2015). Learning how a crowd behaves and knowing its attitudes are crucial factors, both in designing new services for a broad audience and in emulating learning capability in a machine. Furthermore, Big Data and data mining technologies are creating new learning needs aimed at effectively exploiting the mass of information available on the Web (Witten, Frank, Hall, & Pal, 2016)

Digital Social Learning

It is widely agreed that online learning is the logical solution to satisfy the demands of modern education in terms of flexibility, professionality, and economic sustainability (Means, Toyama, Murphy, Bakia, & Jones, 2009).

There are, however, also those who hold a different view. Their criticism revolves around two principal elements, the content reliability of online learning and its effectiveness. How can one identify credible and reliable content on the internet? An emblematic case is Wikipedia, the popular open encyclopedia. It provides internet users with a vast quantity of information but Wikipedia's content is not always of a high quality. Many entries are incomplete, superficial, incorrect, or even intentionally absent. Moreover, Wikipedia's content is usually anonymous, as very few authors use their real names.

Online education is also argued to be neither practical nor effective since teachers cannot adapt their teaching style to the learning needs of students, and the face-to-face relationship is lacking (Cowan, 2006).

Despite criticisms, the internet indisputably represents an opportunity. It can be an important source of supplemental information, although it cannot be used in all circumstances and for all needs.

Recently, several researchers have started to investigate the non-formal and informal learning processes that take place on the Web. This mode of learning has been designated *social learning* (Baldwin, 2016), but it would be preferable to address this modality of learning as web learning or digital social learning, so as to avoid confusion with the social learning theory.

In the literature, digital social learning is considered as a part of informal learning. For this reason, it is helpful to highlight some basic principles of informal learning.

The definition of informal learning is commonly introduced in terms of a contrast with formal learning (Marsick & Watkins, 2001). In fact, in many respects, these two forms of learning are complementary.

Three basic types of informal learning have been identified:

- Self-directed learning that is intentional and conscious; it refers to learning programs undertaken by individuals or groups without the assistance of teachers, instructors, or facilitators.
- Incidental learning that is not intentional but conscious; it occurs when we learn without any intention of learning, e.g. by direct experience.
- Socialization that is not intentional and conscious; it refers to attitudes, beliefs, behaviors, and skills acquired in everyday life, often through imitation.

Considering digital social learning only as a part of informal learning is an evident reduction of the digital social learning scope. It appears, de facto, as a specific learning modality since it can be included in overall learning activities, especially in non-formal training programs. For instance, training courses can include self-directed learning activities carried out on the Web. Sharing information and knowledge among peers by means of Web-based interactions is a usual practice (see forum discussions for the use of words or to solve computer problems. If you don't know how to do something, for example how to open a file with the extension ".rar", you can search on the Web and find the software to download and manage this type of compressed file. Moreover, there are a huge variety of tools and sites available on the Web that support learning processes allowing collaborative technologies (groupware applications, webinars, online conferences, etc.) and which provide a wide range of peer-to-peer learning opportunities.

- As a consequence of the digital revolution and the resulting instability of employment, integrative and flexible forms of education are in great demand. It is not the case that, in this decade, validation of non-formal and informal learning has suddenly become a topical issue and a priority for national and European vocational education and training (VET) policies.

- Nowadays, social learning represents both an opportunity and a challenge for the training profession (Bowers & Kumar, 2017). Benefits essentially concern the integration of formal curricula with just-in-time knowledge. Challenges concern how effectively it manages informal content and the risks hidden in social media.

CONCLUSION

In this chapter, the basic concepts underlying the principal educational approaches currently used for cyberbullying proactive and reactive interventions have been presented. Some concepts about learning modalities have also been highlighted. These will be useful in the next chapter, in which interventions for cyberbullying prevention will be presented and analyzed.

Peer-learning is often advocated as being an optimal means for cyberbullying prevention together with educational programs that involve children, teachers, and parents at the same time.

However, although fleeting and very brief, the presentation of participatory learning and peer learning should have introduced some caution about the shallow use of the terms. Designing integrated educational programs that involve children, teachers, and parents presents many issues and is in no way an easy matter. In fact, there are different learning needs and modalities that have to be handled according to factors such as children's age and parental attitudes. Moreover, educational programs should be designed from the perspective of an ongoing cyberbullying education. Indeed, conferences and spot interventions cannot stem a phenomenon such as cyberbullying. It is a collateral effect of the digital revolution that offers a new modality to victimize people, and requires continuous and well-structured educational efforts to combat it. Technology changes continuously and its power increasingly growth. Children need to know about technology not only to be able to handle applications and devices but also to know how to avoid its disruptive consequences. Social networks are means of mass communication, but the dynamics that take place in them cannot be predicted since they are places open to all and where all can potentially do or say anything.

REFERENCES

Allison, K. R., & Bussey, K. (2017). Individual and collective moral influences on intervention in cyberbullying. *Computers in Human Behavior*, *74*, 7–15. doi:10.1016/j.chb.2017.04.019

Atkinson, S., Furnell, S., & Phippen, A. (2009). Securing the next generation: Enhancing e-safety awareness among young people. *Computer Fraud & Security*, *2009*(7), 13–19. doi:10.1016/S1361-3723(09)70088-0

Baldry, A. C., Sorrentino, A., & Farrington, D. P. (2016). 4 Cyberbullying. In A. Kapardis & D. P. Farrington (Eds.), *The Psychology of Crime, Policing and Courts* (pp. 57–74). Routledge.

Baldwin, M. (2016). *Social work, critical reflection and the learning organization*. Routledge.

Banas, J. A., & Rains, S. A. (2010). A meta-analysis of research on inoculation theory. *Communication Monographs*, *77*(3), 281–311. doi:10.1080/03637751003758193

Bandura, A., Ross, D., & Ross, S. A. (1961). Transmission of aggression through imitation of aggressive models. *Journal of Abnormal and Social Psychology*, *63*(3), 575–582. doi:10.1037/h0045925 PMID:13864605

Barlińska, J., Szuster, A., & Winiewski, M. (2013). Cyberbullying among adolescent bystanders: Role of the communication medium, form of violence, and empathy. *Journal of Community & Applied Social Psychology*, *23*(1), 37–51. doi:10.1002/casp.2137

Bradshaw, C. P. (2015). Translating research to practice in bullying prevention. *The American Psychologist*, *70*(4), 322–332. doi:10.1037/a0039114 PMID:25961313

Bradshaw, C. P., Waasdorp, T. E., & O'Brennan, L. M. (2013). A latent class approach to examining forms of peer victimization. *Journal of Educational Psychology*, *105*(3), 839–849. doi:10.1037/a0032091 PMID:25414522

Brown, A. L., & Palincsar, A. S. (1989). Guided, cooperative learning and individual knowledge acquisition. Knowing, learning, and instruction: Essays in honour of Robert Glaser, 393-451.

Campbell, M., & Bauman, S. (Eds.). (2018). *Reducing cyberbullying in schools: international evidence-based best practices*. Academic Press.

Cassidy, W., Brown, K., & Jackson, M. (2012). 'Under the radar': Educators and cyberbullying in schools. *School Psychology International, 33*(5), 520–532. doi:10.1177/0143034312445245

Cassidy, W., Faucher, C., & Jackson, M. (2013). Cyberbullying among youth: A comprehensive review of current international research and its implications and application to policy and practice. *School Psychology International, 34*(6), 575–612. doi:10.1177/0143034313479697

Chantler, N. (1996). *Profile of a computer hacker*. Infowar.

Coldevin, G. (2002). Participatory Communication and Adult Learning for Rural Development: Three Decades of FAO Experience. In Approaches to Development Communication, (pp. 44-75). Academic Press.

Cowan, J. (2006). On becoming an innovative university teacher (2nd ed.). Open University Press/McGraw-Hill Education.

De Graaf, E., & Kolmos, A. (2003). Characteristics of problem-based learning. *International Journal of Engineering Education, 19*(5), 657–662.

Dewey, J. (1916). *Democracy and Education: An Introduction to the Philosophy of Education*. The MacMillan Company. Available at: https://archive.org/stream/democracyandedu00dewegoog#page/n6/mode/2up

Dewey, J. (1983). The middle works, 1899-1924 (Vol. 13; J. A. Boydston, Ed.). SIU Press.

Donaldson, S. I., Graham, J. W., Piccinin, A. M., & Hansen, W. B. (1995). Resistance-skills training and onset of alcohol use: Evidence for beneficial and potentially harmful effects in public schools and in private Catholic schools. *Health Psychology, 14*(4), 291–300. doi:10.1037/0278-6133.14.4.291 PMID:7556032

Donaldson, S. I., Sussman, S., MacKinnon, D. P., Severson, H. H., Glynn, T., Murray, D. M., & Stone, E. J. (1996). Drug abuse prevention programming: Do we know what content works? *The American Behavioral Scientist, 39*(7), 868–883. doi:10.1177/0002764296039007008

Donohew, L., Sypher, H. E., & Bukoski, W. J. (2012). *Persuasive communication and drug abuse prevention*. Routledge. doi:10.4324/9780203052419

Downes, S. (2004). Educational blogging. *EDUCAUSE Review, 39*(5), 14–26.

Dumas, J. E. (1989). Treating antisocial behavior in children: Child and family approaches. *Clinical Psychology Review*, *9*(2), 197–222. doi:10.1016/0272-7358(89)90028-7

Dunst, C. J., & Trivette, C. M. (2009). Let's Be PALS: An Evidence-Based Approach to Professional Development. *Infants and Young Children*, *22*(3), 164–176. doi:10.1097/IYC.0b013e3181abe169

Dunst, C. J., Trivette, C. M., & Hamby, D. W. (2010). Meta-analysis of the effectiveness of four adult learning methods and strategies. *International Journal of Continuing Education and Lifelong Learning*, *3*(1), 91–112.

Dupuis, A. M., & Gordon, R. L. (2010). *Philosophy of education in historical perspective*. University Press of America.

Englander, E. K., & Muldowney, A. M. (2007). Just Turn the Darn Thing Off: Understanding Cyberbullying. Proceedings of persistently safe schools: The 2007 national conference on safe schools.

Evans, R. I. (1984). A social inoculation strategy to deter smoking in adolescents. In Behavioral health: A handbook of health enhancement and disease prevention. John Wiley & Sons.

Farmer, J., & Bartlett-Bragg, A. (2005). Blogs@ anywhere: High fidelity online communication. *ASCILITE*, *5*, 4–7.

Farrington, D. P., & Ttofi, M. M. (2009). School-based programs to reduce bullying and victimization. *The Campbell Collaboration*, *6*, 1–149.

Festl, R., Scharkow, M., & Quandt, T. (2013). Peer influence, internet use and cyberbullying: A comparison of different context effects among German adolescents. *Journal of Children and Media*, *7*(4), 446–462. doi:10.1080/17482798.2013.781514

Foye, U., Satinsky, E., Rosan, C., & Breedvelt, J. (2018). Assisting Young People in Care. *Community Practitioner*, *91*(4), 44–46.

Frayssinhes, J., & Pasquier, F. (2018). Neurosciences et apprentissages via les réseaux numériques. *Éducation et socialisation. Les Cahiers du CERFEE*, (49). Available at: https://journals.openedition.org/edso/3920

Goodman, P. (1973). *Compulsory miseducation*. Penguin Education Specials.

Grusec, J. E. (1992). Social learning theory and developmental psychology: The legacies of Robert Sears and Albert Bandura. *Developmental Psychology*, *28*(5), 776–786. doi:10.1037/0012-1649.28.5.776

Hancock, B. W., Coscarelli, W. C., & White, G. P. (1983). *Critical thinking and content acquisition using a modified guided design process for large course sections*. Educational & Psychological Research.

Hargreaves, A., & Dawe, R. (1990). Paths of professional development: Contrived collegiality, collaborative culture, and the case of peer coaching. *Teaching and Teacher Education*, *6*(3), 227–241. doi:10.1016/0742-051X(90)90015-W

Harkavy, I., & Benson, L. (1998). De-Platonizing and Democratizing Education as the Bases of Service Learning. *New Directions for Teaching and Learning*, *1998*(73), 11–20. doi:10.1002/tl.7302

Herbart, J. F. (1913). *Outlines of educational doctrines*. London: Macmillian Publishers.

Hew, K. F., & Brush, T. (2007). Integrating technology into K-12 teaching and learning: Current knowledge gaps and recommendations for future research. *Educational Technology Research and Development*, *55*(3), 223–252. doi:10.100711423-006-9022-5

Hinduja, S., & Ingram, J. R. (2009). Social learning theory and music piracy: The differential role of online and offline peer influences. *Criminal Justice Studies*, *22*(4), 405–420. doi:10.1080/14786010903358125

Houdé, O. (2004). *l'enfant*. Paris: PUF.

Jäger, T., Amado, J., Matos, A., & Pessoa, T. (2010). Analysis of experts' and trainers' views on cyberbullying. *Journal of Psychologists and Counsellors in Schools*, *20*(2), 169–181.

Kaner, S. (2014). *Facilitator's guide to participatory decision-making*. John Wiley & Sons.

Kiefer, M., & Trumpp, N. M. (2012). Embodiment theory and education: The foundations of cognition in perception and action. *Trends in Neuroscience and Education*, *1*(1), 15–20. doi:10.1016/j.tine.2012.07.002

Kok, A. (2015). Integration of Web 2.0 Tools in to Non-Formal Learning Practices: A Case Study of IBM. *Procedia: Social and Behavioral Sciences, 176*, 357–370. doi:10.1016/j.sbspro.2015.01.483

Machado, J. M. (2012). *Early childhood experiences in language arts: Early literacy*. Cengage Learning.

Mangen, A., & Velay, J. (2010). Digitizing literacy: Reflections on the haptics of writing. In M. H. Zadeh (Ed.), *Advances in haptics*. In Tech. Available at: https://www.intechopen.com/books/advances-in-haptics/digitizing-literacy-reflections-on-the-haptics-of-writing

Marsick, V. J., & Watkins, K. E. (2001). Informal and incidental learning. *New Directions for Adult and Continuing Education, 2001*(89), 25–34. doi:10.1002/ace.5

McGuire, W. J. (1964). Inducing Resistance to Persuasion: Some Contemporary Approaches. Advances in Experimental Social Psychology, 1, 191-229.

McGuire, W. J., & Papageorgis, D. (1961). The relative efficacy of various types of prior belief-defense in producing immunity against persuasion. *Journal of Abnormal and Social Psychology, 62*(2), 327–337. doi:10.1037/h0042026 PMID:13773992

Means, B., Toyama, Y., Murphy, R., Bakia, M., & Jones, K. (2009). Evaluation of evidence-based practices in online learning: A meta-analysis and review of online learning studies. *U.S. Department of Education*. Available at: http://repository.alt.ac.uk/629/1/US_DepEdu_Final_report_2009.pdf

Mehari, K. R., & Farrell, A. D. (2018). Where does cyberbullying fit? A comparison of competing models of adolescent aggression. *Psychology of Violence, 8*(1), 31–42. doi:10.1037/vio0000081

Meier, D. (2000). *Accelerated Learning Handbook: A Creative Guide to Designing and Delivering Faster*. McGraw-Hill.

Menesini, E., Nocentini, A., & Palladino, B. E. (2012). Empowering students against bullying and cyberbullying: Evaluation of an Italian peer-led model. *International Journal of Conflict and Violence, 6*(2), 313–320.

Nabavi, R. T. (2012). *Bandura's social learning theory and social cognitive learning theory*. University of Science and Culture, Tehran, Iran. Available at: https://www.researchgate.net/profile/Razieh_Tadayon_Nabavi/publication/267750204_Bandura's_Social_Learning_Theory_Social_Cognitive_Learning_Theory/links/545914d90cf26d5090ad007b.pdf

Nickerson, A. B., Mele, D., & Princiotta, D. (2008). Attachment and empathy as predictors of roles as defenders or outsiders in bullying interactions. *Journal of School Psychology*, *46*(6), 687–703. doi:10.1016/j.jsp.2008.06.002 PMID:19083379

Novak, G. M. (2011). Just-in-time teaching. *New Directions for Teaching and Learning*, *2011*(128), 63–73. doi:10.1002/tl.469

O'Loughlin, M. (2006). *Embodiment and education*. Springer. doi:10.1007/1-4020-4588-3

Ortega, R., Elipe, P., Mora-Merchán, J. A., Genta, M. L., Brighi, A., Guarini, A., ... Tippett, N. (2012). The emotional impact of bullying and cyberbullying on victims: A European cross-national study. *Aggressive Behavior*, *38*(5), 342–356. doi:10.1002/ab.21440 PMID:22782434

Patchin, J. W., & Hinduja, S. (2012). School-based efforts to prevent cyberbullying. *Prevention Researcher*, *19*(3), 7–10.

Peacock, G. G., & Collett, B. R. (2011). *Collaborative home/school interventions: Evidence-based solutions for emotional, behavioral, and academic problems*. Guilford Press.

Plass, J. L., & Kaplan, U. (2016). Emotional design in digital media for learning. In Emotions, technology, design, and learning. Academic Press. doi:10.1016/B978-0-12-801856-9.00007-4

Polanyi, M. (2012). *Personal knowledge*. Routledge. doi:10.4324/9780203442159

Prpić, J., Shukla, P. P., Kietzmann, J. H., & McCarthy, I. P. (2015). How to work a crowd: Developing crowd capital through crowdsourcing. *Business Horizons*, *58*(1), 77–85. doi:10.1016/j.bushor.2014.09.005

Ractham, P., & Zhang, X. (2006, April). Podcasting in academia: a new knowledge management paradigm within academic settings. *Proceedings of the 2006 ACM SIGMIS CPR conference on computer personnel research: Forty-four years of computer personnel research: achievements, challenges & the future*, 314-317. 10.1145/1125170.1125241

Regoli, R. M., & Hewitt, J. D. (1997). *Delinquency in Society*. Mc Grow Hill.

Rigby, K., & Griffith. (2018). Addressing traditional school-based bullying more effectively. In *Reducing cyberbullying in schools: international evidence-based best practices*. Academic Press.

Rodrigues, S. (Ed.). (2014). *Handbook for teacher educators: transfer, translate, or transform*. Springer. doi:10.1007/978-94-6209-695-0

Rogers, C. R. (1979). The foundations of the person-centered approach. *Education, 100*(2), 98-107. Available at: http://www.unifiedcommunities.com/ucs/Rogers_Person-Centered-Approach_1979.pdf

Seufert, T. (2003). Supporting coherence formation in learning from multiple representations. *Learning and Instruction, 13*(2), 227–237. doi:10.1016/S0959-4752(02)00022-1

Sharples, M., Delgado Kloos, C., Dimitriadis, Y., Garlatti, S., & Specht, M. (2015). Mobile and accessible learning for MOOCs. *Journal of Interactive Media in Education, 1*(4), 1–8.

Shiner, M. (1999). Defining peer education. *Journal of Adolescence, 22*(4), 555–566. doi:10.1006/jado.1999.0248 PMID:10469518

Skinner, B. F. (1976). *Beyond Freedom and Dignity*. Pelican Book.

Skinner, B. F. (1984). The shame of America education. *The American Psychologist, 39*(9), 947–954. doi:10.1037/0003-066X.39.9.947

Smith, P. K., Sundaram, S., Spears, B. A., Blaya, C., Schäfer, M., & Sandhu, D. (Eds.). (2018). *Bullying, Cyberbullying and Student Well-Being in Schools: Comparing European, Australian and Indian Perspectives*. Cambridge University Press. doi:10.1017/9781316987384

Sutherland, E. H., & Cressey, D. R. (1974). *Criminology*. Lippincott Company.

Thorndike, E. L. (1932). Reward and punishment in animal learning. *Comparative Psychology Monographs, 8*(39), 1932–1965.

Trivette, C. M., Dunst, C. J., Hamby, D. W., & O'herin, C. E. (2009). Characteristics and consequences of adult learning methods and strategies. *Winterberry Research Syntheses, 2*(2), 1-33.

Wang, M., Lam, Y. W., Kim, J., Singer, G. H., & Dodds, R. (2016). Behavioral Parent Training As Evidence-Based Practices for Families of Children with Developmental Disabilities. Supporting Families of Children with Developmental Disabilities: Evidence-based and Emerging Practices, 73-154.

Watson, J. B. (1913). Psychology as the behaviorist views it. *Psychological Review, 20*(2), 158–177. doi:10.1037/h0074428

Weizenbaum, J. (1966). ELIZA—A computer program for the study of natural language communication between man and machine. *Communications of the ACM, 9*(1), 36–45. doi:10.1145/365153.365168

Witten, I. H., Frank, E., Hall, M. A., & Pal, C. J. (2016). *Data Mining: Practical machine learning tools and techniques.* Morgan Kaufmann.

KEY TERMS AND DEFINITIONS

Bandura's Social Cognitive Theory: Is based on the idea that an individual learns from their interactions with other individuals in a social context.

Behaviorism: Is a psychological theory based on the assumption that human behavior is determined by the environment through association and reinforcement.

Differential Association Theory: Formulated by the sociologist Edwin Sutherland in 1939, this theory views criminality as social interaction and posits criminal acts as learned behaviors.

Digital Social Learning: Is based on the idea of sharing ideas, experiences, and knowledge as well as on the ability to access content from different resources available on the internet.

Humanistic Psychology: Is a perspective that emphasizes looking at the whole individual and underscores concepts such as free will, self-efficacy, and self-actualization.

Learning 2.0: Is a new form of e-learning that is includes Web 2.0 technologies; it is based on tools that combine content creation, web delivery, and online collaboration.

Massive Open Online Courses (MOOCs): Are free online courses available for anyone to enroll.

Peer Education: Is an umbrella term used to describe interventions in which trainers and trainees cooperate between themselves.

Proactive Education: Aims at orienting one particular behavior instead of attempting to correct others.

Social Inoculation Theory: Developed in the 1960s by the social psychologist William J. McGuire, studies means of protection against persuasive attacks and pressures.

Social Learning Theory: Is based on the principle that observation, imitation, and modeling play a primary role in the leaning process.

Chapter 7
Anti-Cyberbullying Interventions

Gilberto Marzano
Rezekne Academy of Technologies, Latvia

ABSTRACT

In this chapter, interventions aimed at combating cyberbullying will be presented and discussed. Since the middle of the 2000s, various anti-cyberbullying programs have been implemented, but evidence for their effectiveness is limited since most of these programs are the result of experimentations and limited-size studies. Particular attention will be devoted to peer group educational interventions, since it has been suggested that this is the best way to reduce the risk of cyberbullying and buffer its negative impacts. Anti-cyberbullying programs are usually designed to be run in schools and foresee the involvement of teachers and many of them are derived from anti-bullying programs. This does not invalidate or limit their reliability or efficacy. In fact, the value of educational interventions depends on how they are re-adapted, as well as on the competence and expertise of the trainers and facilitators involved. Finally, school anti-cyberbullying regulations will be discussed, since they should be considered to all effects and purposes as primary anti-cyberbullying interventions.

INTRODUCTION

In chapter 4, we have highlighted some technological interventions to combat cyberbullying, such as filters for blocking online harassment, and panic buttons that cyber victims can push when they feel under threat.

DOI: 10.4018/978-1-5225-8076-8.ch007

However, the literature reveals that the most important elements associated with the decrease in cyberbullying are whole school anti-bullying and anti-cyberbullying policies, school conferences, parent training/meetings, teacher training, information for parents, and cooperative group work. The intensity of interventions and their duration seems to be significantly associated with the decrease of bullying and cyberbullying.

The majority of the interventions developed to prevent cyberbullying are educational programs. These revolve around educating children, teachers, and parents in e-safety and, particularly, in providing them with information, techniques, and initiatives aimed at combating and buffering cyberbullying (Marzano & Lizut, 2019).

Without a doubt, prevention through education is the intervention strategy that is the most largely agreed on by researchers and practitioners alike, but preventing cyberbullying through education is no easy task. Cyberbullying, usually, takes place among mates either at school or outside the school gates. Cyberbullies are able to hit their victims anywhere and everywhere, it being sufficient that they are online. For this reason, many programs advocate the involvement of parents and, often, integrated initiatives are suggested that engage educators, parents, and, of course, children (Farrington & Ttofi, 2009; Perren *et al.*, 2012; McGuckin *et al.*, 2014).

However, teaching-learning theories and teaching-learning experience suggest that different programs should be designed for educators, parents, and children since they represent different classes of learners, each of which require a specific mode of involvement and diverse types of knowledge strands. As a consequence, interventions that involve educators, parents, and children can be very positive, but should be carefully designed and should involve very skilled trainers.

Conferences in which educators, parents, and children are invited to attend together will not be effective if the content and modality of presentation have not been designed in order to meet the different expectations and exigencies of a heterogeneous audience. In this regard, conferences organized by police officers that focus on cybercrime and on the legal consequences of identity theft, impersonation, online defamation, violation of privacy, and other similar aspects can be useful for parents but may be boring for adolescents. Fisk reports an episode that is very common in cyberbullying conferences organized for an adolescent audience:

In 2010, I was invited to attend two youth internet safety presentations put on by the New York State Police Computer Crime Unit. As I sat in the audience of students waiting for the first presentation to begin, I heard someone exclaim, "I am almost eighteen. I don't need to know about Internet safety awareness." (Fisk, 2016, p. 114)

Educational interventions, especially presentations and conferences, that are not designed to take target audience into account are rather useless and, sometimes, even achieve the opposite effect.

Nevertheless, in general, educational interventions in internet safety are deemed to be effective for educators since they empower them with theoretical and practical tools that they can apply in practice. In fact, familiarity with internet technologies is an essential skill for educators involved in cyberbullying prevention (Brewer, 2011).

Various anti-bullying and anti-cyberbullying prevention programs have been designed and implemented for schools, many of them based on research results that have been adapted to the operative context (for example, Olweus, 1993; Mustacchi, 2009; Katzer, Fetchenhauer, & Belschak, 2009; Couvillon & Ileva, 2011; Spears, 2013; Spears, Taddeo, & Barnes, 2017).

How effective are anti-bullying programs in schools?

It has been observed that there is some evidence for the effectiveness of interventions aimed at preventing school violence and bullying, for the reduction in frequency of victimization and bullying, and for the improvement in attitude towards school violence. However, when evaluating these claimed results, a certain amount of precaution is necessary. This is due to the fact that the size of most of the studies are too small to be considered significant (Jiménez-Barbero, Ruiz-Hernández, Llor-Zaragoza, Pérez-García, & Llor-Esteban, 2016).

In the following paragraphs, the principal educational programs for educators, parents, and children developed to date will be illustrated and discussed, focusing on the key aspects of how they can reduce risks, combat the problem, and buffer the negative impacts (Figure 1).

EDUCATIONAL INTERVENTIONS BASED ON PEER EDUCATION

In the previous chapter, it was argued that peer education is deemed to be effective in raising awareness and influencing positive behavior. In general, peer education models are based on the assumption that people learn better

Figure 1. Conceptualization of responses to cyberbullying
Source: Perren et al., 2012, p. 285

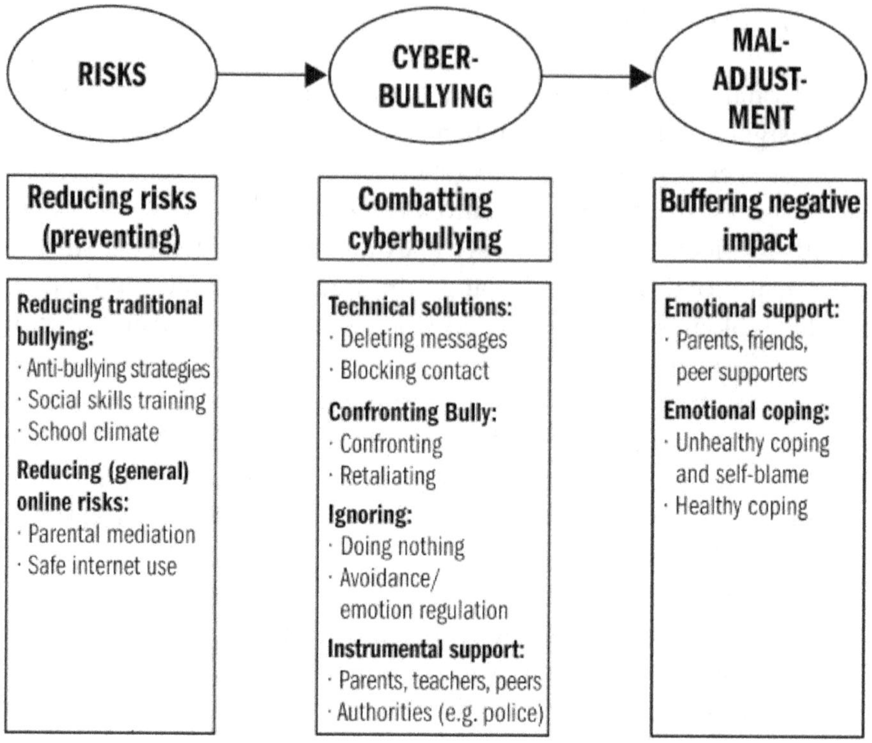

from one another, since peers can significantly influence each other. It has been observed that the conduct and behavior of an individual are most likely to change when liked and trusted members of a group take the lead in changing a situation (Naylor & Cowie 1999; Turner & Shepherd, 1999; Maticka-Tyndale & Barnett, 2010; Chadwick, 2014). According to Chadwick:

Peer-driven student leadership based programs are an effective means to encourage positive relationships and open discussions about what occurs online and even offline. Young people want to be involved in the educative process. Mentor groups or youth advisory groups, for example, comprised of young people are more likely to engage and connect with other young people. Assigning trained cyber-safety student leaders can assist the wider school community to gain increased awareness of the challenges in the online environment and changes to technology. (Chadwick, 2014, p. 66)

Various peer support structures have been proposed to reduce bullying at school, e.g. peer counseling, peer mediation, peer mentoring/buddy systems, and peer tutoring (McGrath & Noble, 2006).

The buddy system is a practice that creates a tight collaboration between two individuals, the "buddies", who operate together as a single unit in order to monitor and support each other. At school, a child is selected to befriend a newly arrived pupil or a mate having some difficulties, not necessarily in the same class. The buddy system gives good results if the buddy has been carefully selected and appropriately taught. It is also necessary that the teacher regularly monitors the process and intervenes promptly when necessary.

Another peer-support approach is the Peer Activity Leaders Programme (Mathieson, 2013), which offers older primary school pupils an opportunity to be pupil leaders. It is based on the experience that students have the potential to take on leadership roles.

In the case of cyberbullying, one could create e-safety leaders that are responsible for the e-wellbeing of one or more school classes. They should be taught about e-safety issues and about the optimal use of the internet. This latter point is very important, since the knowledge of technology will reinforce their leadership position as well as put them in a position to better exploit the possibilities and potentialities of technology according to their age. In fact, it is important to know how children and adolescents use technology in order to design applications compliant with e-safety requirements. E-safety leaders should, at same time, support their mates and proactively observer the use of technology among them. They should be aware of

- The most common types of cyberbullying
- The impact of cyberbullying on the emotional well-being of victims
- The appropriate response when incidents of cyberbullying have been reported to them

This approach can contribute to improve social responsibility among older pupils and develop cross-age peer relationships, but requires very skilled tutors for monitoring and assistance.

A very interesting model for internet safety education was the experiment developed by Johanna Mustacchi at the Pierre Van Cortlandt Middle School in New York, that was based on a peer and collaborative learning approach (Mustacchi, 2009). Taking into account that most adolescents have continuous peer connections, she implemented a peer-learning program. Eighth graders were trained on basic e-safety and *netiquette* (or proper internet behavior), then, from this, the eighth graders created skits on cyberbullying topics for sixth graders aimed at teaching them about the dangers of online activity. A group of adults, including counselors, the school psychologist, and law enforcement officers, were also present to answer questions. Mustacchi's educational program received a strong positive response from participants, and reportedly benefited both groups of students.

In the next paragraphs, the KiVA prevention program and the Cyber Friendly School Program will be presented as an example of integrated interventions. The recent book by Campbell and Bauman, *Reducing Cyberbullying in Schools* (2018), illustrates a set of further anti-cyberbullying programs, such as *No-Trap!* and *The Media Heroes*. These programs present many similarities with the KiVa and Cyber Friendly Schools programs.

Before illustrating these programs, it will be useful to briefly introduce the Olweus Bullying Prevention program, since it has influenced many anti-bullying and anti-cyberbullying interventions.

OLWEUS BULLYING PREVENTION PROGRAM

The Olweus Bullying Prevention Program (OBPP) is a multi-level program aimed at targeting the individual, the school, the classroom, and the community level. The earliest version of the program was a one-day school conference during which the problem of bullying was addressed among school staff, students, and parents. The education intervention was integrated with a teachers' handbook, entitled Olweus' Core Program against Bullying and Antisocial Behavior, and with a folder containing information for parents and families.

Today the program comprises several materials as well as the involvement of specialized trainers. Becoming an official Olweus trainer takes 40 hours of training.

The basic materials of the program are as follows:

- The Bullying Questionnaire is administered to all students before the program begins and at regular intervals from then on.
- The Schoolwide Guide provides step-by-step directions for school-wide implementation for members of the school's Bullying Prevention Coordinating Committee and school leaders.
- The Teacher's Guide, is the implementation resource for teachers and other classroom support staff involved in the program; it highlights

the importance of addressing bullying within the classroom setting in order to support successful school-wide implementation.

The anti-bullying measures mainly targeted three different levels of intervention: the school, the classroom, and the individual.

At the school level, the intervention includes:

- Meetings among teachers and staff discussion groups to discuss ways of improving peer-relations;
- Parent/teacher meetings to discuss the issue of bullying.
- Improvement of playground facilities so that children have better places to play during recess time.
- A questionnaire survey.
- The formation of a coordinating group.
- At the classroom level, the intervention includes:
- Information about the issue of bullying and the active involvement of students in devising class rules against bullying.
- Classroom activities for students as well as role-playing situations that could help students learn how to better deal with bullying.
- Class rules against bullying.
- Class meetings with students.
- Meetings with the parents of the class.
- At the individual level, the intervention includes:
- Talks with bullies and their parents and the enforcement of non-hostile, non-physical sanctions.
- Talks with victims, providing support and providing assertiveness skills training to help them learn how to successfully deal with bullying; also, talks with the parents of victims.
- Talks with children not involved to make them become effective helpers.

Figure 2 shows the *bullying circle* as presented in the Olweus bullying prevention program.

The Olweus program demands significant commitment from the school during the "introductory period" which covers a period of about 18 months, and requires the support of experts in the program and in the Olweus methodology. After this, the school may continue using fewer resources.

The program also foresees cooperation among experts and teachers (e.g. psychologists) who work with children involved in bullying.

Figure 2. The bullying circle
Source: The Olweus Bullying Prevention Program, 2012; https://slideplayer.com/slide/9142982/

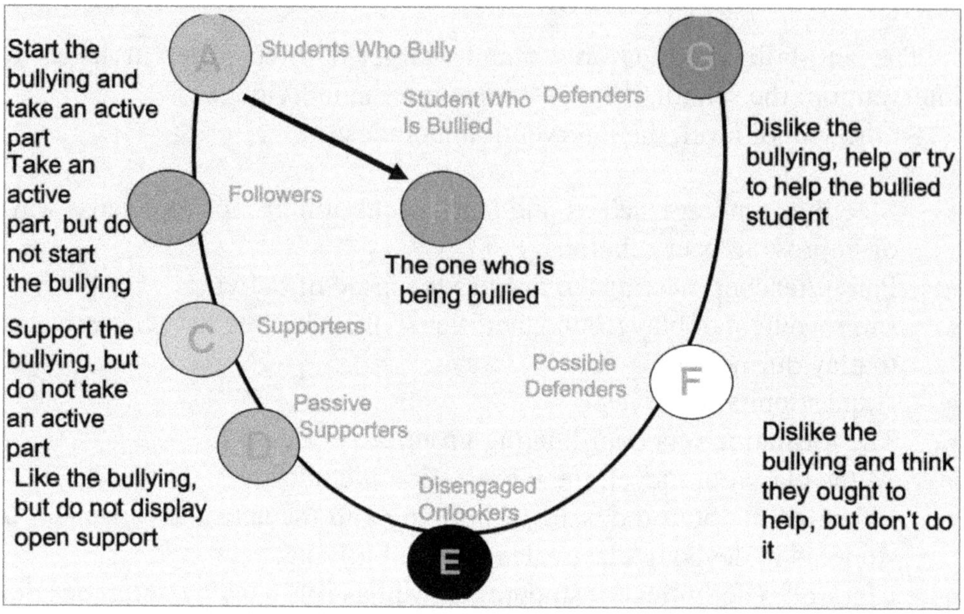

The experience suggests, that besides staff training and professional support, it is important that all staff members in the school are involved in the implementation of the program (Tattum & Tattum, 2017).

THE KIVA ANTI-BULLYING PROGRAM

The KiVa (an acronym of 'Klusaamista Vastaan', literally "against bullying") program is a Finnish evidence-based approach that targets traditional bullying, and recently cyberbullying, that presents many analogies with Mustacchi's educational approach.

The KiVa anti-bullying program has received broad consensus of support, and researchers claim that it significantly reduces (by about 50%) incidents of traditional bullying (Salmivalli, Kärnä, & Poskiparta, 2011; Kärnä, Voeten, Little, Poskiparta, Kaljonen, & Salmivalli, 2011; Kärnä, Voeten, Little, Alanen, Poskiparta, & Salmivalli, 2013; Haataja, Voeten, Boulton, Ahtola, Poskiparta, & Salmivalli, 2014), as well as of cyberbullying (Williford *et al.*, 2013).

The KiVa program is based on a whole school approach that includes classroom teachings, training in the reporting of bullying incidents, and monitoring of the program implementation. The program distinguishes separate curricula for primary, middle, and high school students, and runs over a four months period. It has been designed to strengthen empathy and requires a whole school effort. For this purpose, students see video clips and play online games relating to both traditional bullying and cyberbullying, while parents are trained in the use of online monitoring applications. In addition, both teachers and school administrators are trained in bullying dynamics and on how to manage incidents of bullying. A prerequisite to run the KiVa program is that school teaching and administrative staff all receive coaching from an expert KiVa trainer. Currently, the KiVa program is operating through licensed partners in about 15 countries.

The program takes place during regular school hours and essentially consists in educational interventions by teachers. Lessons are delivered to students of primary school, whilst themes are presented to students of secondary school with the main aim of raising awareness on cyberbullying dynamics and the important role of bystanders.

Usually, KiVa actions include a series of student lessons (10 student lessons of 90 minutes each) given by classroom teachers (unit 1 for grades 1–3; unit 2 for grades 4–6), and 20 hours of student lessons carried out by student teachers. The main aims of the student lessons are to raise awareness of the role bystanders play in the bullying process, to increase empathy toward the victim, and to provide students with safe strategies to support and defend their victimized peers.

Methods used in the KiVa lessons are discussions, group work, role-play exercises, and short films about bullying. As the lessons proceed, class rules based on the central themes of the lessons are successively adopted one at a time. Computer games aim at reinforcing the knowledge and skills the students have acquired in class. Other components include KiVa symbols such as vests for the recess supervisors and posters to remind students and school personnel about the KiVa program. Parents receive a guide that includes information about bullying, about the KiVa program, and advice about how to recognize if their child is a victim or a bully. KiVa indicated actions are used to handle the acute cases of bullying. In each school, a team of three staff members addresses the cases of bullying through a specific procedure involving a series of discussions: first, an individual meeting with the victim and then with the bully, followed by a group discussion with all the bullies in cases where more than one was involved.

The essential concept in the KiVa program is that traditional bullying and cyberbullying are not separate phenomena. This assumption impinges in different ways on the program modules. All of them include content concentrating on what is bullying and how to recognize it:

Typically, it is stressed that also nasty and mean messages delivered, for example, via mobile phone or internet or posted in social media sites are bullying. Students might be asked to share their experiences or observations on bullying and cyberbullying or they are presented with fictional stories including a broad variety of forms to bully others. (Herkama & Salmivalli, 2016, p. 128)

An online survey is provided for at the end of the school year with the participation of key staff members and students that has the aim of evaluating what has been done to reduce bullying.

In the program, there are special sections devoted to cyberbullying. These include exercises addressing how cyberbullying occurs, its consequences, and coping strategies. Short films showing cyberbullying events are watched together in class and discussed.

It has been observed that KiVa also has other positive effects, since it increases enjoyment of school and academic motivation, as well as reduces social anxiety.

The first study into the effect of KiVa on cyberbullying was conducted in 2013 (Wilford), and looked at both victimization and the perpetration of bullying actions.

From the experience of Kiva, Herkama and Samivalli argue that cyberbullying should be addressed together with more traditional face-to-face forms of bullying, rather than running programs and establishing a policy aimed specifically at cyberbullying alone (Herkama & Samivalli, 2016). Essentially, the reasons advanced are:

1. Online bullying is relatively rare if compared with offline bullying. Accordingly, a strong focus on cyberbullying might prevent or limit interventions against the most common forms of bullying.
2. Online and offline peer relationships cannot be separated. Moreover, cyberbullying manifests itself in peer groups, and cyberbullies, although anonymous, are part of those groups.
3. Victims of online bullying are often victims of offline bullying.

4. Bystanders are key actors both in the online and offline context. From this perspective, addressing bystander responsibility in a prevention program is more important than addressing the specific forms of incidents.
5. Results from the KiVa program suggest that a general bullying prevention program can reduce online bullying at least to an equal extent as it reduces other more traditional forms.

For the moment, the effectiveness findings cannot tell what in KiVa anti-bullying program led to the reduction in cyberbullying perpetration and victimization, or how. Nevertheless, it does seem that the effects of the program are (Saarento, Boulton, & Salmivalli, 2015):

- Students' anti-bullying attitudes increase;
- Positive growth of bystander response;
- Students appear less approving of bullying.

THE CYBER FRIENDLY SCHOOL PROGRAM

The Cyber Friendly School (CFS) program is an Australian whole school-based prevention and intervention program aimed at reducing cyberbullying and cyber victimization.

Initially, it was a three-year project, namely the Cyber Friendly Schools Project (CFSP), that was conducted from 2010 to 2012 with the aim of testing the impact of an innovative online and student-led whole school cyberbullying prevention intervention. The project involved non-government secondary schools in Perth, Western Australia. A sample of 35 schools was selected, of which 19 were chosen at random for the intervention, while 16 acted as a control group (Cross *et al.*, 2016). The project actively engaged students aged 14-15 years from each project year, in the formative development of the intervention (Cross & Barnes, 2014). The same students were engaged at a school level in 2010 and 2011 as cyberleaders with the task of tailoring the CFSP whole-school intervention to meet the needs of the school community with help from pastoral care staff (Cross, Lester, Barnes, Cardoso, & Hadwen, 2015).

Currently, the CFS program comprises structured and continuous activities (Cross *et al.*, 2018) that involve:

- The whole-school community, whose tasks are the development of understanding about cyberbullying at the school, the implementation of social and emotional interventions among students, the definition of anti-cyberbullying policies, the improvement of positive attitudes and behavior, the development of pastoral initiatives, and so on.
- Students who are engaged in the program activity, for example, in the role of cyberleader or as simple participant.
- Parents who increase their awareness of the use of technology and works with their children to solve family quizzes on cyberbullying.
- The CPS program foresees the creation of two team groups. The first team is composed of teaching staff and is appointed by the principal of the school, whilst the second is composed of grade 10 student leaders who act as mentors to the grade 8 and 9 students.

The teams are both provided with:

- Cyberbullying booklet, containing basic information about cyberbullying, definitions, and tips.
- Strategies for responding booklet, containing strategies for school staff to combat cyberbullying, including Shared Concern and Critical Thinking methodology, as well as Motivational Interviewing.
- Policy to Practice booklet, providing guidelines to engage the school to respond to cyberbullying and define the anti-cyberbullying policy.
- Three newsletters, the first discussing friend lists on social networking sites, the second digital reputation, and the third cyber safety and the law.

Both teams ought to attend a full-day workshop on the CFS program. During the workshop, the program activities are planned.

In each study year, student leaders provide students of grade 8 and 9 with a curriculum of information and strategies aimed at supporting victims and discouraging cyberbullying behavior. This curriculum is presented by class teachers and, for grade 8, includes eight learning modules:

1. **What's This All About:** Students define and learn about different forms of cyberbullying.
2. **In the Know - The Stats on Bullying:** Students are provided with accurate information that will make them aware of the dimensions and consequences of cyberbullying.

3. **Flaming – Just Jokes:** Students are taught how to distinguish between joking around and bullying.
4. **Your Voice – Your Choice:** Students are provided with anti-bullying strategies.
5. **Being a Good Mate:** Students investigate the role of bullies and bystanders.
6. **Playing Judge and Jury:** Students have to learn the effects of their evaluation and judgment towards others.
7. **In or Out:** Students identify positive and negative aspects of social power.
8. **Reflection:** Students use what they learned to prepare a presentation for other students or parents.

In grade 9, the learning modules are expanded in order to include a more thorough understanding of the online environment as well as how to address cyberbullying:

- **My Online Status:** Students learn how to search for information about themselves online.
- **Connect, Extend, and Challenge:** Students learn about their cybersecurity and how to set privacy settings.
- **Helping Me, Helping You:** Students learn how to find support if they are cyberbullied and how to report on cyberbullying events.
- **Cyberclips:** Students comment on a series of clips, reflecting on their content.
- **Reality Bites:** Students are taught that there are offline consequences for their online actions.
- **Standing By:** Students reflect on the role of bystanders.
- **Who, Me? Couldn't Be!:** Students reflect on their biases.
- **Tacking Control:** Students revise their learning achievements.

Every year, the CFS website improves the material available for students, parents, and teachers.

In each intervention year, members of the teaching staff team attend a workshop in order to grow their competence.

Cyberleaders attend 6-12 hours of training during school hours through participation in workshops facilitated by two researchers/teachers and a specialized youth leadership trainer.

INVOLVEMENT OF TEACHING STAFF

Overall, prevention programs focused at a school level are deemed to be the most efficient, although there is little evidence on best practice, effective interventions, and how to measure the effectiveness of teaching staff involvement (Couvillon & Ilieva, 2011).

Most of the programs that strive to help in preventing cyberbullying foresee the direct or indirect participation of the teaching staff as well as of professional development support for teachers. In this regard, the quality of staff training is considered one of the main determining factors in the effectiveness of anti-bullying as well as anti-cyberbullying programs (Lund, Blake, Ewing, & Banks, 2012; Thompson, 2016).

Usually, teaching staff are either selected by the school management or invited to volunteer to participate in cyberbullying prevention initiatives. This will charge them with additional tasks and responsibilities. Especially in the case of cyberbullying, teachers need to make an effort in order to maintain an up-to-date knowledge of digital technologies and their use. This is not always easy for them, since social media applications evolve continuously, as does the way children and adolescents use this technology. As a consequence, schools should offer a lifelong guidance to teaching staff involved in anti-bullying and anti-cyberbullying initiatives. The ideal solution could be the stable presence of educators professionalized in bullying and cyberbullying education and practices. This idea will be developed in chapter 10. Here, it is important to underline that the involvement of teaching staff is crucial because of their experience and their daily involvement with children and adolescents.

Ideally, school districts should provide teaching staff and school managers with regular in-service training. It is strategic that teachers are knowledgeable about the current state of the art on prevention and intervention practices as well as on school policies regarding bullying and cyberbullying.

Shariff (2008) argued that informative professional development among teaching staff and school managers represents a key factor for the success of any cyberbullying prevention effort. He emphasized that responsibilities for cyberbullying are shared among all who are involved in the educational process, and suggested the promotion of "harmonious solutions" that should combine legal, educational, and ethical considerations:

Given the litigious nature of school controversies between educators, students and parents over free expression, supervision, privacy and safety, it is imperative that teachers' knowledge construction is grounded in legal literacy, critical pedagogy and critical media literacy, as well as theories of leadership, ethics and social justice. Currently, I believe that many university teacher education and professional development programmes lack coherent models that provide educators with conceptual grounding they need for a wired and litigious world. (Shariff, 2008, p. 242)

There is no doubt that the above competences are actually crucial, but it is rather unrealistic to believe it is possible to realize such educational programs for the overall teaching staff presently working in schools. Firstly, there are profound differences between schools even in the same country, depending on whether they are private or public, settled in urban or rural areas, primary or secondary, vocational or college, located in a residential or a degraded neighborhood, attended by a high number of migrants, and so on. Secondly, the way in which the school is organized and managed also influences the school climate and teachers' attitudes as well as the conditions under which teachers practice (Raudenbus & Willms, 2014). Thirdly, rapid staff turnover, large proportions of temporary teaching staff (Strauss, 2017; The Guardian, 2018), as well as cuts in financial resources (Sutcher, Darling-Hammond, & Carver-Thomas, 2016) are all common generalized problems. As Figure 3 shows, from 2010, teacher supply declined and continues to decline further.

Finally, on a global scale, teachers struggle, daily, with a variety of problems and challenges, such as pressure from parents, workload, low salary, classroom management, student absenteeism, students' misbehavior, lack of support from colleagues, administration tasks, etc. (Antoniou & Cooper, 2017).

In this critical context, cyberbullying structured interventions, that need the continuous and multidimensional involvement of teachers, appear for many aspects to be both impracticable and unsustainable. How many hours of training should be provided to teachers in order to provide them the expected level of competence? Who should monitor and how should they assess teacher competences? In what way should bullying and cyberbullying prevention be part of the curricular school activity?

But what is the real preparation of teachers regarding cyberbullying issues? The literature provides only a limited body of research regarding the effectiveness of teacher and principal preparation programs to provide their candidates with strategies to address problems associated with student cyberbullying (Styron, Bonner, Styron, Bridgeforth, & Martin, 2016). An emblematic research in this regard is a study conducted on 154 preservice teachers enrolled in a teacher education program at a Canadian university,

Figure 3. Projected teacher supply and demand in the USA
Source: Sutcher, Darling-Hammond, & Carver-Thomas, 2016

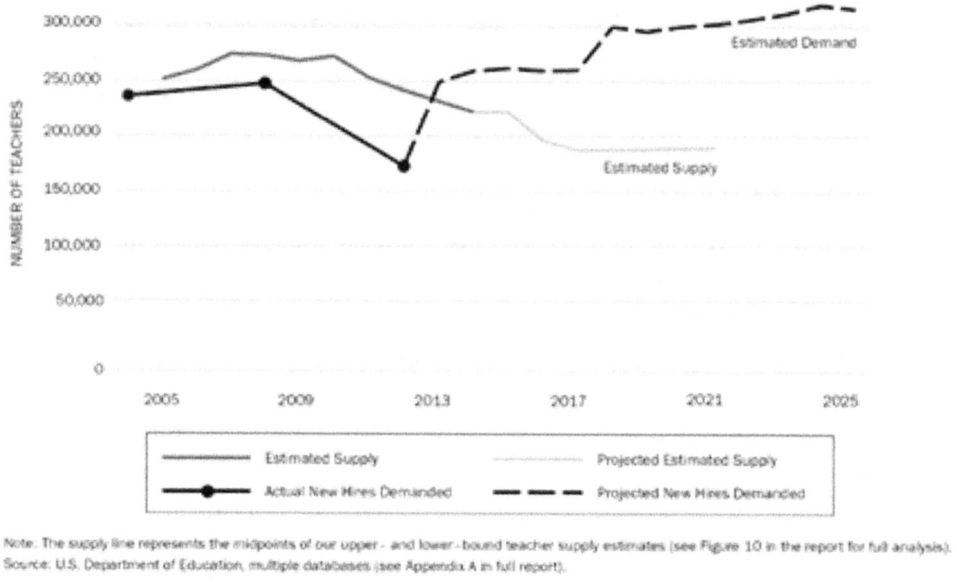

which showed that preservice educators did not feel qualified (prepared) in the identification or management of cyberbullying (Li, 2009). Over 50% disagreed or strongly disagreed that they were confident in identifying cyberbullying activity, and 60% disagreed or strongly disagreed that they were confident in managing cyberbullying activity. Most of the recipients agreed that cyberbullying "affects children", but only a third of respondents thought that it was a problem within the schools.

The competence of teaching staff involved in cyberbullying prevention is a challenging issue. For example, the KiVa program envisages that it is led by certified KiVa trainers. One of the requirements to become a certified trainer is to take part in a five-day training event for trainers at the University of Turku, Finland. But it is rather unbelievable that a teacher will achieve the competence to conduct a cyberbullying prevention program in only five days. Much will depend on their previous background.

Moreover, yet another aspect should not be undervalued. An efficacious cyberbullying prevention at school should be a continuous institutional process, not a set of one-time events carried out on a voluntary basis. Corresponding to the nature of digital communication and to the experience of cyberbullying, prevention should not be limited to school hours. Because of the ubiquitous nature of digital communication, a victim of cyberbullying can be reached anytime and anywhere as long as they are connected. It may, in fact, be impossible for them to escape from digital harassment.

For an anti-cyberbullying program to be effective, it should be schoolwide and active 24 hours a day, 7 days a week, and 365 days a year.

How could a such a program conciliate with teachers' tasks?

Indeed, teachers have a multidimensional role in schools since they are teaching-learning professionals, listeners, confidants, practitioners, colleagues, administrators, and much else besides. However, whilst it is conceivable that they have a commitment in their routine classroom activities to monitor cyberbullying events in the school, it is unimaginable that they could be charged with the responsibility and burden of anti-bullying and anti-cyberbullying interventions in a wider context.

FRIENDSHIP IMPORTANCE

A comprehensive meta-analysis, in 2008, found that, for early adolescents, cooperative goal structures were associated with both higher achievement and greater positive peer relations: the more positive the relationships were amongst early adolescents, the higher was their tendency to achieve (Roseth, Johnson, & Johnson, 2008). This meta-analysis was conducted on 148 independent studies comparing the relative effectiveness of cooperative, competitive, and individualistic goal structures in promoting early adolescents' achievement and positive peer relationships. In more detail, the results indicated that positive peer relationships at school explained some 33–40% of the variance in academic achievement.

On the contrary, negative peer relationships tend to lead to a low academic achievement. A Norwegian study involving 56 schools showed that students in schools that had higher levels of bullying had worse academic results than students in schools where bullying was not widespread (Strøm, Thoresen, Wentzel-Larsen, & Dyb, 2013).

Research claims that friendships can provide students with social and emotional support, protecting them against bullying and social isolation, but it has been found that processes of friendship can influence both bullying and anti-bullying attitudes (Sijtsema, Rambaran, Caravita & Gini, 2014) confirming both that peer group influences bullying (Dishion & Tipsord, 2011; Ahn &

Rodkin, 2014), and that bullying is often a peer group behavior (Huitsing, Snijders, Van Duijn, & Veenstra, 2014; Mann, Kristjansson, Sigfusdottir, & Smith, 2015).

The fact that bullying is embedded in a peer context and peer influence variables are the stronger predictors of bullying behaviors, Salmivalli and Peets argue that prevention interventions should try to change the peer group dynamics that contribute to the maintenance of bullying:

Classroom activities that change peer group hierarchies, norms, and bystander responses to bullying might be helpful. The role of teachers is crucial in successfully implementing such changes. (Salmivalli & Peets, 2018, p. 314)

It has been argued that feeling safe and protected from bullying is directly linked to feeling supported and cared for by teachers and feeling connected to peers (Flaspohler, Elfstrom, Vanderzee, Sink, & Birchmeier, 2009). All students feel less safe when they are aware that bullying is occurring in their school, even if they haven't been bullied themselves (Janson, Carney, Hazler, & Oh, 2009).

Frameworks that help to create a positive school climate have been implemented and experimented. One of these is PROSPER, which is an organization for positive psychological interventions designed to help people, groups, organizations, or communities to achieve a positive climate. The PROSPER framework has several similarities to Seligman's (2012) earlier PERMA model of wellbeing (Positive emotions, Engagement, Relationships, Meaning, and Accomplishment), but specifically includes two additional significant components: Strengths and Resilience. It is based on seven key elements that have been identified as contributing to wellbeing: Positivity, Relationships, Outcomes, Strengths, Purpose, Engagement, and Resilience.

In order to support students to develop the social skills and pro-social values that underpin positive relationships and build positive relationships within the school, PROSPER suggests the following strategies:

- A safe & supportive school culture
- Positive student-teacher relationships
- Positive student-peer relationships
- Positive school-family & school-community relationships
- Explicit teaching of social skills and pro-social values
- Provision of opportunities to practice these social skills

- Interpersonal structures that facilitate relationships e.g. cooperative learning groups, cross-age teams, cooperative games, peer support, and performance groups.

In regards to PERMA, it has been observed that it offers relevant information to allow teachers to better meet the well-being needs of students or classes (Kern, Waters, Adler, & White, 2015).

In a recent book, Patching and Hinduja (2014) suggested combating cruelty with kindness and using positive peer education to persuade all teens to act with respect toward others. Other authors have empathized the importance of empathic responsiveness, and the moral disengagement and disapproval of cyberbullying, adopting a social-ecological approach to the issue (Cross, Barnes, Papageorgiou, Hadwen, Hearn, & Lester, 2015).

COPING STRATEGIES

Four major coping strategies have been identified (Riebel, Jaeger, & Fischer, 2009):

- **Social Coping:** Seeking help from family, friends, teachers, and peer groups;
- **Aggressive Coping:** Retaliation, physical attacks, and verbal threats;
- **Helpless Coping:** Hopelessness, passive reactions such as avoidance, displays of emotion;
- **Cognitive Coping:** Responding assertively, using reason, analyzing the bullying episode and the bully's behavior.

Coping strategies can be both active and passive (Raskauskas & Huynh, 2015).

There are several strategies that can be considered as active coping. For example, blocking and deleting malicious messages or reporting the event.

The most known passive coping strategy is doing nothing or ignoring cyberbullying. Another passive coping strategy is thinking positively.

From the systematic literature review conducted by Perren *et al.* on coping with cyberbullying (2012), it emerges that peer-intervention (i.e. peer support by trained student leaders) is used in school to prevent cyberbullying in schools by:

- Creating bullying awareness in the school;
- Developing leadership skills among students;
- Developing intervention practices in the student community to prevent bullying;
- Developing team-building initiatives in the student community;
- Students behaving proactively as bystanders.

The Perren et al. literature review also found that teens with authoritative parents have limits and are monitored, whilst neglectful parents set fewer limits and monitor their teens less.

There is a general agreement on the need to invest in social coping, e.g. developing social skills through curriculum programs or special intervention programs (Perren *et al.*, 2013).

Some authors also underline the importance of empowering children and adolescents in order to make them able to implement prevention and coping strategies (Smith, Talamelli, Cowie, Naylor & Chauhan, 2004; Ybarra & Mitchell, 2004; Walrave, Ponnet, Vanderhoven, Haers & Segaert, 2016).

In defining cyberbullying coping strategies, one should take into account that victims don't usually seek the support of teachers and parents, and often don't ask for help from their mates. Indeed, children and especially adolescents see adults as distant from them. Moreover, they fear that their parents' reaction would be to limit their internet connection. For teens, being disconnected from the internet signifies isolation since they cannot receive news from friends and cease to interact with peers.

It can also happen that a victim of cyberbullying is blackmailed by their perpetrator about something that the victim doesn't want disclosed to their parents or to the school authority.

The parental strategy to cope with cyberbullying by moving the child to a different school, or sometimes even moving home, often doesn't work. There are frequent cases in which the victim changes school, changes telephone sim card, or stops using social networking sites in which they are subject to denigration and persecution. However, it is sufficient that the victim should appear in another group for their persecutors to discover them and continue to torment them. It happens that persecutors are helped, perhaps unknowingly, by someone else posting a message containing information about the victim. It is rather impossible that one can hide their tracks on the internet for ever. Sooner or later one will be found. This was the case with a thirteen-year-old Italian girl whose parents, to stop her being bullied online, decided to move to the USA and start her at a new school there. She also changed her phone card and closed her accounts on Italian social networks. But these efforts were all in vain. After a few months, despite the distance and the language barrier, her persecutors found her and continued their harassment. At this point, the poor teen began to exhibit behavioral disorders and was admitted to hospital, where she was treated with psychotropic drugs. All this happened in 2016. Now the girl has returned to Italy, gained 20 pounds, has difficulty studying, and is under psychologist care.

From the literature (Weinstein *et al.*, 2016), it emerges that the most favored solution among teens to stop online harassment is telling the bully to stop (62%), whilst consulting a friend was the second most reported option (59%), followed by ignoring the harasser (56%).

Finally, it seems that victims don't consider technical blocks to really be helpful to stop cyberbullying, since they are persuaded that those who want to bully will find a way to bypass them (Parris, Varjas, Meyers, & Cutts, 2012; Parris, Varjas, Meyers, Henrich, & Brack, 2017).

ISSUES IN DESIGNING EFFECTIVE PREVENTION INTERVENTIONS

Designing prevention strategies, however, is not at all simple. First, an effective prevention program should ground participants in the knowledge of new media and an understanding of their use by different types of users, especially adolescents and young people. This requires that trainers are skilled in new media, and should be able to demonstrate their mastery to learners, otherwise their image as experts and authorities on the subject could be discredited.

Furthermore, trainers should be able to clearly explain to learners the distinction between bullying and non-bullying acts, as well as between cyberbullying and non-cyberbullying or 'innocent' instances.

Another important aspect concerns the issue of virtual identity and its reciprocal effects on physical identity. It has been observed that at the heart of the explosion in online communication is the desire to construct a valued representation of oneself which affirms and is affirmed by one's peers (Livingstone & Brake, 2010). Accordingly, by exploiting new media, people can experiment with their own identity in the online domain. However, some questions arise. If identities are constituted through interaction with others, what is the consequence on identity if that interaction is a mix of physical and virtual interactions? And what if virtual interactions are not only with real persons but also with bots and with virtual fake profiles built by people?

Finally, cultural-anthropological aspects should not be discounted. In fact, they can play a not insignificant role if prevention programs are adopted which were created and experimented in a different country. The cultural sensitivity of cyberbullying is an issue that has been largely unexplored by researchers, although some researches have tried to test the relation between culture and cyberbullying by comparing questionnaire results submitted in different countries, for example the United States and Japan (Barlett *et al.*, 2014).

Indeed, different cultural attitudes to the new media raises an intriguing question: is cyberbullying really a serious issue within particular age groups regardless of cultural background (Mura, Topcu, Erdur-Baker, & Diamantini, 2011)? Does cyberbullying depend only on the spread of new technologies, or can other factors, such as culture and historical heritage, influence it or at least influence its perception?

Nevertheless, investigating the effect of cultural influences on cyberbullying presents many methodological problems, and analysis of the results can be expensive and time consuming. In particular, questionnaires should be integrated with other forms of data gathering, such as structured interviews, direct observation, and web analysis. The above mentioned comparative research on cyberbullying in the USA and in Japan and the research on cyberbullying in Russia and Latvia used different methodological approaches. In the first case, a classic quantitative approach was adopted, while the second case adopted a mixed socio-anthropological and qualitative-quantitative approach. What is interesting, however, is that, despite the differences, the two studies share the same hypothesis that cyberbullying is related to how individuals perceive, comprehend, and interpret the world around them.

CONCLUSION

Establishing cyberbullying prevention programs is a priority for the school system. These programs are necessary to contrast a phenomenon that can have serious consequences on the mental and physical health of children and adolescents.

Moreover, cyberbullying prevention forces the professional empowerment of the teaching staff and their better understanding of the ongoing cultural changes that will continue under the push of technology.

Technology is modifying the school dimension. Schools cease to be a learning environment separated from the rest of the social context. Technology offers the opportunity for new modalities of interaction and collaboration, but at the same time posits new challenging issues. Creating a safe environment is the necessary precondition to exploiting the potentiality of technology. Schools need to ensure that students feel safe in the school environment, but this is not only a technical problem. Teachers must be able to contribute to this safety through guidance and monitoring. Additional skills are required for teachers that can be achieved through training and re-training efforts in a lifelong learning perspective. Teachers' pedagogical curriculum should include the knowledge of digital technologies in the scope of education. Finally, a new figure of social educator specialized in proactive and reactive strategies to bullying and cyberbullying should be created. This new figure should both professionally support the school staff and students, and interact with other professional figures such as psychologists, social educators, and law experts.

REFERENCES

Ahn, H. J., & Rodkin, P. C. (2014). Classroom-level predictors of the social status of aggression: Friendship centralization, friendship density, teacher–student attunement, and gender. *Journal of Educational Psychology*, *106*(4), 1144–1155. doi:10.1037/a0036091

Antoniou, A. S., & Cooper, C. L. (2017). *Coping, personality and the workplace: Responding to psychological crisis and critical events*. Routledge. doi:10.4324/9781315574240

Brewer, E. A. (2011). *Fighting fire with fire: The use of a multimedia webquest in increasing middle-school students' understandings of cyberbullying* (Doctoral dissertation). Loyola Marymount University.

Campbell, M., & Bauman, S. (Eds.). (2018). *Reducing cyberbullying in schools: international evidence-based best practices*. Academic Press.

Couvillon, M. A., & Ilieva, V. (2011). Recommended practices: A review of schoolwide preventative programs and strategies on cyberbullying. *Preventing School Failure*, *55*(2), 96–101. doi:10.1080/1045988X.2011.539461

Cross, D., Barnes, A., Cardoso, P., Hadwen, K., Shaw, T., Campbell, M. A., & Slee, P. (2018). The Cyber-Friendly Schools Project. In *Reducing cyberbullying in schools* (pp. 95–108). Elsevier. doi:10.1016/B978-0-12-811423-0.00007-9

Cross, D., Lester, L., Barnes, A., Cardoso, P., & Hadwen, K. (2015). If It's about Me, Why Do It without Me? Genuine Student Engagement in School Cyberbullying Education. *The International Journal of Emotional Education*, *7*(1), 35–51.

Cross, D., Shaw, T., Hadwen, K., Cardoso, P., Slee, P., Roberts, C., & Barnes, A. (2016). Longitudinal impact of the Cyber Friendly Schools program on adolescents' cyberbullying behavior. *Aggressive Behavior*, *42*(2), 166–180. doi:10.1002/ab.21609 PMID:26351263

Dishion, T. J., & Tipsord, J. M. (2011). Peer contagion in child and adolescent social and emotional development. *Annual Review of Psychology*, *62*(1), 189–214. doi:10.1146/annurev.psych.093008.100412 PMID:19575606

Farrington, D. P., & Ttofi, M. M. (2009). School-based programs to reduce bullying and victimization. *The Campbell Collaboration*, *6*, 1–149.

Fisk, N. W. (2016). *Framing internet safety: The governance of youth online*. MIT Press. doi:10.7551/mitpress/10311.001.0001

Flaspohler, P. D., Elfstrom, J. L., Vanderzee, K. L., Sink, H. E., & Birchmeier, Z. (2009). Stand by me: The effects of peer and teacher support in mitigating the impact of bullying on quality of life. *Psychology in the Schools*, *46*(7), 636–649. doi:10.1002/pits.20404

Herkama, S., & Samivalli, C. (2016). KiVa antibullying program. In M. Campbel & S. Bauman (Eds.), *Reducing cyberbullying in schools: international evidence-based best practices* (pp. 125–134). Academic Press.

Huitsing, G., Snijders, T. A., Van Duijn, M. A., & Veenstra, R. (2014). Victims, bullies, and their defenders: A longitudinal study of the coevolution of positive and negative networks. *Development and Psychopathology*, *26*(3), 645–659. doi:10.1017/S0954579414000297 PMID:24762337

Janson, G. R., Carney, J. V., Hazler, R. J., & Oh, I. (2009). Bystanders' reactions to witnessing repetitive abuse experiences. *Journal of Counseling and Development*, *87*(3), 319–326. doi:10.1002/j.1556-6678.2009.tb00113.x

Jiménez-Barbero, J. A., Ruiz-Hernández, J. A., Llor-Zaragoza, L., Pérez-García, M., & Llor-Esteban, B. (2016). Effectiveness of anti-bullying school programs: A meta-analysis. *Children and Youth Services Review*, *61*, 165–175. doi:10.1016/j.childyouth.2015.12.015

Katzer, C., Fetchenhauer, D., & Belschak, F. (2009). Cyberbullying—Who is the victim? A comparison of bullying in Internet chatrooms and in the schoolyard. *Journal of Media Psychology*, *21*, 25–36. doi:10.1027/1864-1105.21.1.25

Kern, M. L., Waters, L. E., Adler, A., & White, M. A. (2015). A multidimensional approach to measuring well-being in students: Application of the PERMA framework. *The Journal of Positive Psychology*, *10*(3), 262–271. doi:10.1080/17439760.2014.936962 PMID:25745508

König, A., Gollwitzer, M., & Steffgen, G. (2010). Cyberbullying as an act of revenge? *Australian Journal of Guidance & Counselling*, *20*(02), 210–224. doi:10.1375/ajgc.20.2.210

Li, Q. (2009). Cyberbullying in schools: An examination of preservice teachers' perception. *Canadian Journal of Learning and Technology*, *34*(2).

Lund, E. M., Blake, J. J., Ewing, H. K., & Banks, C. S. (2012). School counselors' and school psychologists' bullying prevention and intervention strategies: A look into real-world practices. *Journal of School Violence*, *11*(3), 246–265. doi:10.1080/15388220.2012.682005

Mann, M. J., Kristjansson, A. L., Sigfusdottir, I. D., & Smith, M. L. (2015). The role of Community, family, peer, and school factors in group bullying: Implications for school-based intervention. *The Journal of School Health*, *85*(7), 477–486. doi:10.1111/josh.12270 PMID:26032278

Marzano, G., & Lizut, J. (2019). (in press). Topical issues on cyberbullying prevention. *International Journal of Interactive Communication Systems and Technologies*, *9*(2).

Mathieson, P. (2013). *Creating student leaders*. Small World - Big Imaginations Ltd.

Maticka-Tyndale, E., & Barnett, J. P. (2010). Peer-led interventions to reduce HIV risk of youth: A review. *Evaluation and Program Planning*, *33*(2), 98–112. doi:10.1016/j.evalprogplan.2009.07.001 PMID:19647874

Mc Guckin, C., Perren, S., Corcoran, L., Cowie, H., Dehue, F., Ševčíková, A., & Völlink, T. (2014). Coping with cyberbullying: How can we prevent cyberbullying and how victims can cope with it. In P.K. Smith & G. Steffgen (Eds.). Cyberbullying through the new media: Findings from an international network. New York, NY: Psychology Press.

McGrath, H., & Noble, T. (Eds.). (2006). *Bullying solutions: Evidence-based approaches to bullying in Australian schools*. Pearson Education.

McGuckin, C., Perren, S., Corcoran, L., Cowie, H., Dehue, F., Ševčíková, A., & Völlink, T. (2013). Coping with cyberbullying: How can we prevent cyberbullying and how victims can cope with it. In P. K. Smith & G. Steffgen (Eds.), *Cyberbullying through the new media* (pp. 121–135). Psychology Press.

Mustacchi, J. (2009). RU safe. *Educational Leadership*, *66*(6), 78–82.

Naylor, P., & Cowie, H. (1999). The effectiveness of peer support systems in challenging school bullying: The perspectives and experiences of teachers and pupils. *Journal of Adolescence*, *22*(4), 467–479. doi:10.1006/jado.1999.0241 PMID:10469511

Olweus, D. (1993). *Bullying at school: What we know and what we can do*. Malden, MA: Wiley-Blackwell.

Parris, L., Varjas, K., Meyers, J., & Cutts, H. (2012). High school students' perceptions of coping with cyberbullying. *Youth & Society*, *44*(2), 284–306. doi:10.1177/0044118X11398881

Parris, L., Varjas, K., Meyers, J., Henrich, C., & Brack, J. (2017). Coping with bullying: The moderating effects of self-reliance. *Journal of School Violence*, 1–15.

Perren, S., Corcoran, L., Cowie, H., Dehue, F., Garcia, D. J., Mc Guckin, C., & Völlink, T. (2012). Tackling cyberbullying: Review of empirical evidence regarding successful responses by students, parents, and schools. *International Journal of Conflict and Violence*, *6*(2), 283–292.

Perren, S., Corcoran, L., Cowie, H., Dehue, F., Garcia, D. J., Mc Guckin, C., & Vollink, T. (2012). Coping with cyberbullying: A systematic literature review. *Conference Cyberbullying Paris June 2012*. Available at: https://kops.uni-konstanz.de/bitstream/handle/123456789/23800/COST_Cyberbullying_coping_report.pdf?sequence=1&isAllowed=y

Raskauskas, J., & Huynh, A. (2015). The process of coping with cyberbullying: A systematic review. *Aggression and Violent Behavior*, *23*, 118–125. doi:10.1016/j.avb.2015.05.019

Raudenbush, S. W., & Willms, J. D. (Eds.). (2014). *Schools, classrooms, and pupils: International studies of schooling from a multilevel perspective*. Academic Press.

Roseth, C. J., Johnson, D. W., & Johnson, R. T. (2008). Promoting early adolescents' achievement and peer relationships: The effects of cooperative, competitive, and individualistic goal structures. *Psychological Bulletin*, *134*(2), 223–246. doi:10.1037/0033-2909.134.2.223 PMID:18298270

Salmivalli, C., & Peets, K. (2018). Bullying and victimization. In W. M. Bukowski, B. Laursen, & K. H. Rubin (Eds.), *Handbook of peer interactions, relationships, and groups*. Guilford Publications.

Seligman, M. E. (2012). *Flourish: A visionary new understanding of happiness and well-being*. Simon and Schuster.

Shariff, S. (2008). *Cyber-bullying: Issues and solutions for the school, the classroom, and the home*. New York, NY: Routledge. doi:10.4324/9780203928837

Sijtsema, J. J., Rambaran, J. A., Caravita, S., & Gini, G. (2014). Friendship selection and influence in bullying and defending: Effects of moral disengagement. *Developmental Psychology*, *50*(8), 2093–2104. doi:10.1037/a0037145 PMID:24911569

Smith, P. K., Talamelli, L., Cowie, H., Naylor, P., & Chauhan, P. (2004). Profiles of non-victims, escaped victims, continuing victims and new victims of school bullying. *The British Journal of Educational Psychology*, *74*(4), 565–581. doi:10.1348/0007099042376427 PMID:15530202

Spears, B. A. (2012). A review of initiatives using technology to promote cyber-safety and digital citizenship. In The impact of technology on relationships in educational settings. Routledge.

Spears, B. A., Taddeo, C., & Barnes, A. (2017). Online social marketing approaches to inform cyber/bullying prevention and intervention: What have we learnt? In Reducing Cyberbullying in Schools: International Evidence-Based Best Practices. Academic Press.

Strauss, V. (2017, August 28). Teacher shortages affecting every state as 2017-18 school year begins. *The Washington Post*. Available: https://www.washingtonpost.com/news/answer-sheet/wp/2017/08/28/teacher-shortages-affecting-every-state-as-2017-18-school-year-begins/?utm_term=.ab5a1045f1ae

Strøm, I. F., Thoresen, S., Wentzel-Larsen, T., & Dyb, G. (2013). Violence, bullying and academic achievement: A study of 15-year-old adolescents and their school environment. *Child Abuse & Neglect*, *37*(4), 243–251. doi:10.1016/j.chiabu.2012.10.010 PMID:23298822

Styron, R. A. Jr, Bonner, J. L., Styron, J. L., Bridgeforth, J., & Martin, C. (2016). Are Teacher and Principal Candidates Prepared to Address Student Cyberbullying? *Journal of At-Risk Issues*, *19*(1), 19–28.

Sutcher, L., Darling-Hammond, L., & Carver-Thomas, D. (2016). A coming crisis in teaching? Teacher supply, demand, and shortages in the US. *Learning Policy Institute*. Retrieved from https://learningpolicyinstitute. org/product/coming-crisis-teaching

Tattum, E., & Tattum, D. (2017). Bullying: A whole-school response. In *Learning to behave: Curriculum and whole school management approaches to discipline* (pp. 67–84). Routledge. doi:10.4324/9781315831602-5

The Guardian. (2018, August). Education in crisis. *The Guardian*. Available at: https://www.theguardian.com/education/educationincrisis

Thompson, S. (2016). School-related violence. *OpenDocs*. Available at: https://opendocs.ids.ac.uk/opendocs/handle/123456789/13265

Ttofi, M., & Farrington, D. (2009). What works in preventing bullying: Effective elements of anti-bullying programmes. *Journal of Aggression, Conflict and Peace Research*, *1*(1), 13–24. doi:10.1108/17596599200900003

Turner, G., & Shepherd, J. (1999). A method in search of a theory: Peer education and health promotion. *Health Education Research*, *14*(2), 235–247. doi:10.1093/her/14.2.235 PMID:10387503

Walrave, M., Ponnet, K., Vanderhoven, E., Haers, J., & Segaert, B. (Eds.). (2016). *Youth 2.0: social media and adolescence: connecting, sharing and empowering*. Springer. doi:10.1007/978-3-319-27893-3

Weinstein, E. C., Selman, R. L., Thomas, S., Kim, J. E., White, A. E., & Dinakar, K. (2016). How to cope with digital stress: The recommendations adolescents offer their peers online. *Journal of Adolescent Research*, *31*(4), 415–441. doi:10.1177/0743558415587326

Ybarra, M. L., & Mitchell, K. J. (2004). Youth engaging in online harassment: Associations with caregiver–child relationships, Internet use, and personal characteristics. *Journal of Adolescence*, *27*(3), 319–336. doi:10.1016/j.adolescence.2004.03.007 PMID:15159091

KEY TERMS AND DEFINITIONS

Buddy System: Is a practice that creates a tight collaboration between two individuals, the "buddies," who operate together as a single unit in order to monitor and support each other.

Bullying Circle: Is a concept developed by Dan Olweus; it shows the many roles that people play when bullying happens; its central point is that too many people who could stop the bullying don't do so.

Coping Strategies: Refer to strategies, both behavioral and psychological, that aim to master, tolerate, reduce, or minimize stressful events.

Cyber-Friendly School (CFS) Program: Is an Australian whole school-based prevention and intervention program aimed at reducing cyberbullying and cyber victimization.

KiVa (An Acronym of *Klusaamista Vastaan*, Literally "Against Bullying"): Is a Finnish evidence-based approach that targets traditional bullying and recently cyberbullying.

Peer Education: Is an educational method and a learning process that aims to use positive peer influence assuming peers are positive models for each other.

Chapter 8
Cyberbullying:
Educators and Parents

Joanna Lizut
Janusz Korczak Pedagogical University in Warsaw, Poland

ABSTRACT

Parents and educators fill a number of functions for children and young people. Amongst the most important functions that close relatives can provide is to support a child through the type of difficult, stressful situation in life which cyberbullying represents. The sense of parental responsibility for the safety of children using the internet is very important. However, they do not always feel well prepared for this role. In this context, the involvement of educators is also important. Good practices exist, but they are not universally applied and require promotion and dissemination. The way the family functions significantly influences the way children are brought up, and the future lifestyle of young people depends on the nature of the relationships and interpersonal relations they will create in adult life. In guiding young people towards proper social functioning, the involvement of educators, social workers, and teachers is extremely significant. They have a special role in the case of cyberbullying. The safety of the young depends on their competences and qualifications, but also on the correct application of appropriate measures. There are already some good practices in this area that are worth exploring.

INTRODUCTION

The disintegration of the post-industrial society, referred to differently in terms of the information civilization, of global capitalist, commercial, and cultural changes, and of the disappearance of traditional authorities, has resulted in a remolded world in which the current generation of young people is, in some

DOI: 10.4018/978-1-5225-8076-8.ch008

ways, the more knowledgeable generation. (Karmolińska-Jagodzińska, 2012). The influence of information and communication technology is also present in everyday life of the families. The internet supports learning, obtaining information, access to knowledge from various fields of science, technology, cultures in communicating, establishing contacts through internet (Iskandarani, 2008). However, digital technology can have negative influence on children and their relations with parents.

What is crucial for establishing good relations between generations is to understand communication processes and build new intergenerational bonds based on positive interactions between generations. This new process of intergenerational communication must be followed on the basis of new communication standards (Livingstone & Byrne, 2017), which will enable new forms of dialogue, ones based on understanding and on developing new standards of interpretation of reality and virtual life.

The message to parents is clear. Parents need to go online with their children, learn what they like to do most and where they like to go. They need to talk to their children about what they encounter online and develop, with input from their children, family rules for safe and appropriate Internet use. They need to keep the lines of communication open about what the Internet has to offer, being careful not to blame kids for inappropriate content. In addition, parents of young children need to inform themselves of the best that the Internet has to offer for children. (Swift &Taylor, 2003, p.276)

Not only the standards of communication have changed. Internet is building new types of communities around the world. The authors of the report emphasize that there are several main trends that can be identified impact of time spent using digital technology on children's social relationships which were examined in many surveys (Kardefelt-Winther, 2017)

Literature review shows several studies indicating that online activities replace contacts in the real world, at the same time, many results shows that they are complement and strengthen existing activities. Moreover, the use of online social networks and the use of digital technologies will benefit those children, who generally have greater competences and social skills. For children and young people who are socially withdrawn, shy or isolated, communication on the internet can become a rope to establish social contacts because they can feel more at ease while creating friendships online. Individual

Figure 1. Teens opinion about social media's effect on people their age, 2018
Source: Report Teens, Social Media &Technology 2018, PEW Research Center, https://www.pewinternet.org/2018/05/31/teens-social-media-technology-2018/

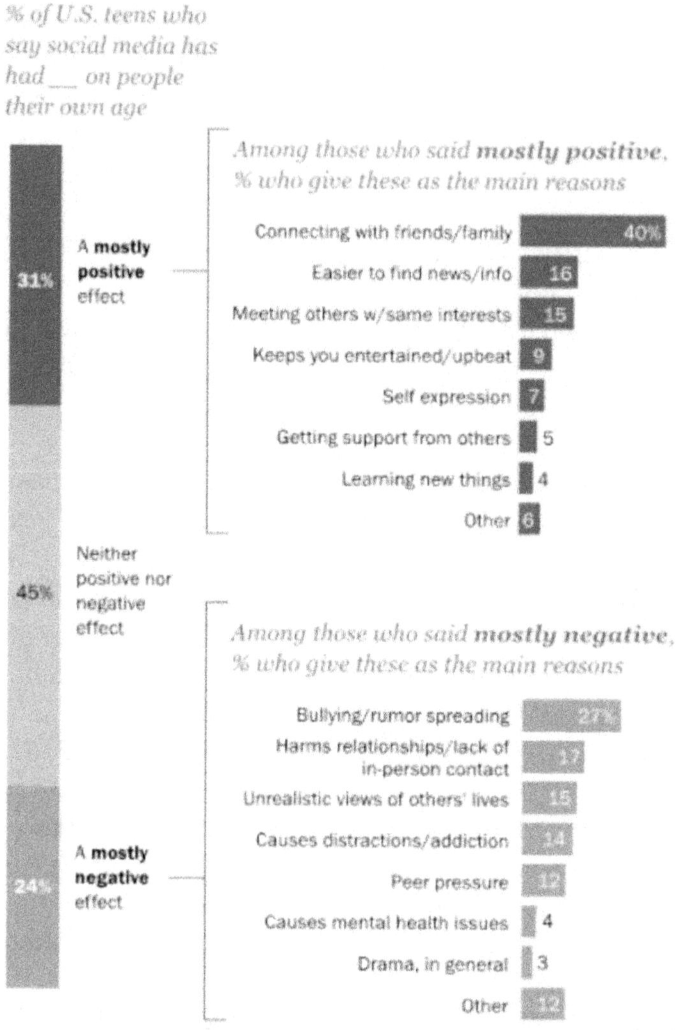

- positive behavioral paths of digital involvement and their consequences are very difficult to determine.

That is why such a significant role of parents who can strengthen the positive elements of using the Internet and protect from risk for e.g., exposition on pornographic, violent and hateful material. Many parents realize the benefits of using the Internet and technology and want to support their children with a proper use but still we observe technological gap between generations.

Parents are concerned about keeping their connected children safe online, noting they find it challenging to monitor their child's use of technology, access to inappropriate content, who their child is engaging with, and total screen time. Social media use in particular worries parents; by a sizable margin, parents think the potential harms of their child having a social media account outweigh the potential benefits. While a majority of parents rate themselves as highly confident in their ability to keep track of and manage their child's use of technology, this confidence diminishes as both parents and children become older. (Online Safety Across the Generations, 2018, p.2)

The Influence of Digitalization on Relationships

As studies show, nowadays even students of early primary school age are network users, and the average age of initiation to the internet is falling (Anderson & Jiang, 2018). At the same time, the frequency of accessing the internet, the time spent using it, and the number and type of devices with which to connect have all increased.

The overall prevalence of pathological internet use was 4.4%; it was higher among males than females (5.2% versus 3.8%) and differed between countries ($\chi 2 = 309.98$; $d.f. = 20$; $P < 0.001$). PIU correlated significantly with mean hours online and male gender. The highest-ranking online activities were watching videos, frequenting chatrooms, and social networking; significantly higher rates of playing single-user games were found in males and social networking in females. Living in metropolitan areas was associated with pathological internet use. Students not living with a biological parent, low parental involvement, and parental unemployment showed the highest relative risks of both maladaptive internet use and pathological internet use. (Durkee et al., 2013)

Part of this change results from the increasing role of social media. Over the last few years there has been a dramatic rise in popularity of smartphones and tablets. Today, almost any child who has had access to a tablet or smartphone from an early age can handle it better than they can a personal computer, 95% of teens have access to a smartphone, and 45% say they are online 'almost constantly' (Anderson, & Jiang, 2018), mostly showing their activity in social media.

Parental responsibility for monitoring the use of a computer by their children is difficult. Part of the problem in combating cyberbullying is that

Figure 2. Profile of Facebook users, January 2018
Source: Global Digital Report 2018, We Are Social and Hootsuite

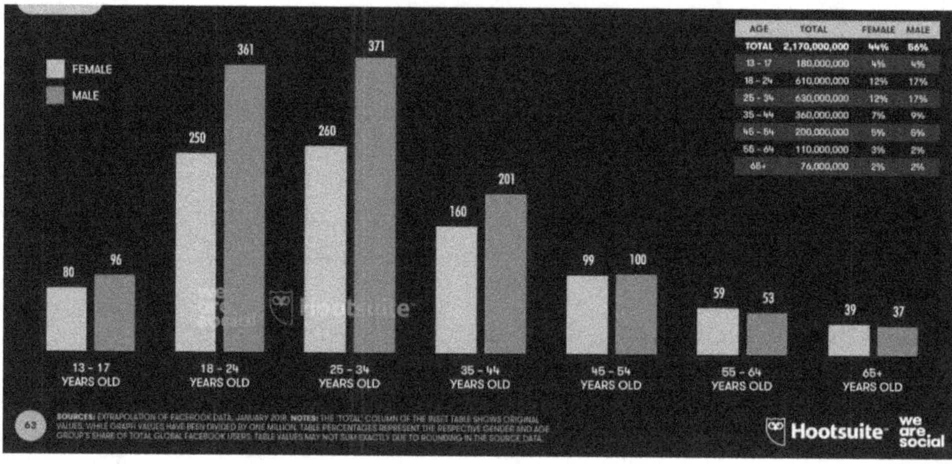

parents and young people see technology in fundamentally different terms (Keith & Martin 2005). Most adults treat computers as practical tools, whereas their children perceive the internet as a lifeline to their peers (Keith & Martin, 2005). Recent research (Online Safety Across the Generations, 2018) indicates that the situation is changing - and parents and seniors are becoming more and more involved in the virtual world (especially in highly developed countries) - in the global perception, the involvement in the use of the internet is dependent on the age group.

Spitzer (2013) highlighted that, by the age of twenty-one, the average young person:

- Had sent or received two hundred and fifty thousand emails and text messages;
- Had devoted ten thousand hours to mobile phone services;
- Had played computer games for five thousand hours;
- Had spent over three thousand hours on social networks.

Many teens know that there is a gap in understanding the technology between themselves and their parents (Belsey, 2004). Kids can tell their parents that they are doing homework when they are actually involved in some form of persecution on the internet. In addition, instant messages, chats, and text messages can be foreign concepts to many parents; they are not foreign to most students (i-SAFE, 2004).

Figure 3. Online safety across the generation at a glance, 2018
Source: Online Safety Across the Generations, Family Online Safety Institute. https://www.fosi.org/policy-research/online-safety-across-generations/

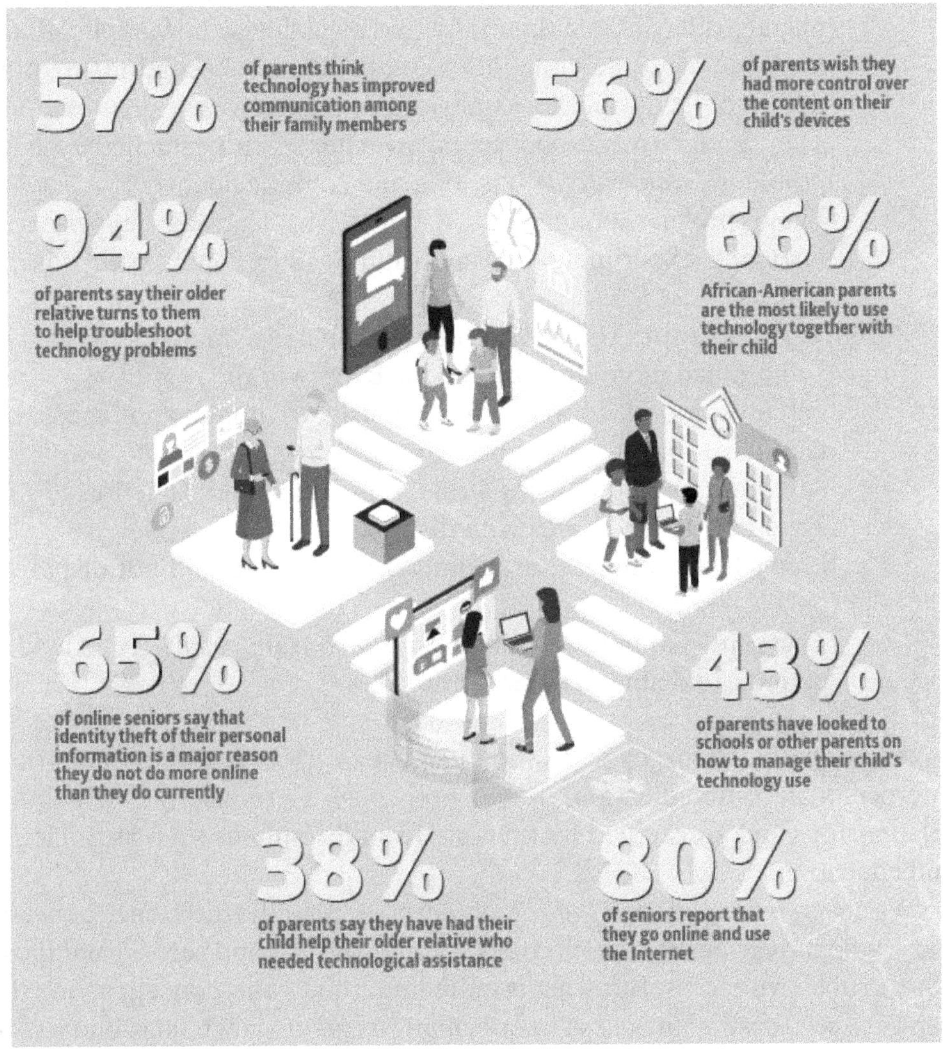

At the same time parents, educators, and social workers do not change their behavior so much, and are not involved in social media activities at this level. Results of some research shows that average, parents' level of digital skill is equivalent to that of a 14 year old child (globalkidsonline.net, 2017). Many years ago, in 2001, Prenskey introduced a distinction to describe the diversity of the population of internet and social media users and its significance for communication processes. He highlighted two basic groups of user:

1. **Digital Natives:** Those for whom virtual space is not a different sphere, but only another normal field of daily activities:
    ◦ They easily operate any available media devices, successfully manage all available functions, and even devise new applications;
    ◦ Embrace new technologies without fear or hesitation, treating their mobile devices as extensions of themselves;
    ◦ They prefer image and sound over text, with which they have problems, especially if it is long and complicated;
    ◦ They prefer spontaneous, short-term learning experiences involving experimentation and multitasking, and expect instant returns.
2. **Digital Immigrant:** Those who, although able to use new technologies, move with much more difficulty in the cyberworld:
    ◦ Perceive mobile devices analogously to home appliances (as facilitators of life);
    ◦ Are often limited to using basic, standard default functions;
    ◦ Treat new technologies with distrust;
    ◦ Prefer text to images, especially when printed and not displayed on a screen;
    ◦ They are willing to work towards a certain result for extended periods, and able to defer rewards.

Additionally, Prenskey's taxonomy touches upon learning styles and interpersonal communication, which both play a crucial role in helping relationships and are studied by scholars from disciplines such as didactics and education.

We observe that the term *digital divide*, good refer the difference between those who have access to the internet (specially broadband access) and those who do not have access. But what is more important – this concept shows the gap between those with access to information and those who has barriers to their online participation because of leaving in low-income countries, having concerns about the safety, being under the rules imposed by parents, carers and schools, or having limited digital literacy (Third et al, 2017).

It should be pointed out that type of cyber activity can be divided into many categories, Increasingly, we are also talking about the digitally excluded, who more often are the seniors but also the less educated. All of these groups may be represented within a single family which affected they relations.

Research by the EU NET ADB (2012) differentiates teenage users and their behavior into four observable types, labelling them as: Networked; All at once; Full circle; and Time killer. The relative characteristics are as follows:

- **Networked:** An excessive use of the internet that leads to neglect of important areas of everyday life (school, social life, home duties). May focus on a specific type of activity on the network. They feel the negative effects of internet abuse (sleep disorders, anxiety, and irritability in the event that their access to the network is blocked), but have difficulties in limiting their use, even if they realize the negative consequences of its overuse.
- **All at Once:** Balancing daily activities with intensive internet use, and active both on and off the network, they are stressed by the overloaded schedule of the day. Characterized by a hunger for experiences gained outside the internet. Owing to a lack of appropriate social skills, they often feel excluded from groups, oppressed by their peers, and generally disappointed with life in the real world, which in the end leads them to focus increasingly on the cyber world.
- **Full Circle:** After an intense period of internet abuse, an autocorrect ("circle") behavior change can occur as a result of: overload (the feeling that they have "had enough"); the realization of the negative consequences the internet abuse is having (e.g. health problems, low learning results, conflicts with parents); or new motivations (e.g. love relationships) that open them to new life experiences and the establishment of new real-world contact with peers.
- **Time-Killer:** The world outside the internet is seen as boring. There may be a lack of alternative activities. Online activity is a convenient "filler" of time, and using the internet is a mechanical reaction to boredom. This type is closed to new life experiences, and can also be characterized by limited social skills.

It should be emphasized that although the knowledge about obtaining technology, present consequences of misusing Internet is high, we still do not know what consequences we can expect in the long term perspective. The consequences for individual people are also associated with individual experiences and resilience (Hinduja & Patchin, 2017). Although classifications are useful, to understand where to draw the line between healthy and harmful use, we must take into consideration many factors such as: age, gender, personality, life situation, social and cultural environment (UNICEF, 2017).

The phase of childhood corresponding mostly to secondary school age represents a particularly dynamic period of development for young people. At this stage, children's ideas about the world, the principles presented by adults, and the social norms they are expected to follow are all subject to verification. Their relations with peers and the social environment surrounding them are also changing. During this phase, identity building and creating one's own worldview takes place mainly through various types of social interactions. The use of the new technologies has caused a change in the nature of these interactions, and has also contributed to the formulation of a new type of social ties.

Social media have at least the following two important functions: (i) socially connect with others (the need to belong) and (ii) manage the impression individuals make on others (reputation building, impression management, and online self-presentation). (Crone & Konijn, 2018)

The Role of Parents in Preventing and Resolving Cyberbullying

Many parents have no awareness of the complex development process and the difficulties that their children experience. Many others feel powerless to help: they simply do not have enough parental skills and educational competences. At the same time, they would like to ensure the safety of their children, they are interested in security on the network, and understand the necessity of undertaking preventive actions, mainly in the context of cyberbullying.

Most parents talk to their children about what they do on the internet (70%) and stay nearby when the child is online (58%). But one in eight parents (13%) do none of the forms of mediation asked about, according to their children.

Half of parents take positive steps such as suggesting how to behave towards others online (56%), talking about things that might bother the child (52%), or helping their child when something arose in the past (36%).

The use of technological safety tools is relatively low: just over a quarter of parents block or filter websites (28%) and/or track the websites visited by their child (24%). (Haddon & Livingstone, 2012)

In the world of children and teenagers, not only volatility, but also stability is important. The best guarantor of this are close relationships with parents and guardians. Social norms and standards of behavior, also in the virtual world, are taken from the cues given in the family home and expanded and consolidated through school education. This begs the need for internet etiquette - basic rules for family members (Mayne, 2018), as well as parental activities that positively affect adolescent well-being, such as connection - building a positive, stable, emotional bond between parent and child), behaviour control- including supervision and guidance of children's actions within a trusting relationship), respect for individuality of the child, especially as an adolescent, modelling appropriate behavior, provision and protection by parents and also the wider community (WHO, 2017 cites as Livingstone & Byrne, 2017).

Ensuring internet safety and the prevention of cyberbullying have become an important element of the educator's skills. The most important task of the parent is to identify the problem and enact an appropriate and early response, but their intervention should not end here. According to the youngsters surveyed (Online Bullying Among Youth 8-17 Years Old) parents take an average of 3.3 steps to protect their children from online bullying and trying to protect the: fifty percent of parents talk about online risks with them, forty-Four percent of parents monitor their use of the computer, thirty-Nine percent of parents teach them online manners; thirty percent of parents ask them if they've been bullied online.

In this context, it has become an especially important part of parenting to recognize the signs of cyberbullying. The following ten signs have been recognized as potential indicators that a child has fallen victim to a cyberbully (Department of Education, 2012):

- Being upset after using the internet or their mobile phone;
- Being unwilling to talk or are secretive about their online activities and mobile phone use.
- Spending much more or much less time texting, gaming, or using social media than normal.
- Many new incoming phone numbers, texts, or emails show up on their mobile phone, laptop, or tablet;
- After texting or being online they seem withdrawn, upset, or angry;
- Not wanting to go to school and/or avoiding meeting friends and school mates;

- Avoiding formerly enjoyable social situations;
- Difficulty sleeping;
- Low self-esteem.

The FBI similarly lists a number of indications that a child may be at risk on the internet (Sweet, 2007):

- Your child quickly turns off the computer or changes screens when you approach.
- Your child spends a large amount of time on the computer, especially at night or in chat rooms.
- You find pornography on your child's computer.
- Your child becomes withdrawn from family and friends.
- Your child is using an online account other than one you have established for him or her. This includes free trial accounts.
- You begin noticing that your child is spending extended periods of time on computers without having tangible results for the time spent.

Rules of Conduct and Advice for Parents on How to Deal With Cyberbullying

Parents have a difficult job. They need to know what their children are doing online, and help them to be safe. Because technology is changing from day to day, the best way to stay up to date is to involve parents in educating children about using it. The following list shows some things that parents may wish to consider in teaching their children about using the internet safely (Lubkina & Marzano, 2014):

- Make sure you use the privacy settings.
- Always respect others – be careful what you say online.
- Be careful what pictures or videos you upload. Once a picture is shared online it cannot be taken back.
- Only add people you know and trust to friends/followers lists online. When talking to strangers, keep personal information safe and location hidden.
- Treat your password like your toothbrush – keep it to yourself and change it regularly.

- Block the bully – learn how to block or report someone who is behaving badly.
- Do not retaliate or reply to offending emails, text messages, or online conversations.
- Save the evidence. Always keep a copy of offending emails and text messages, or a screen grab of online conversations, and show it to a parent, a carer, or a teacher.
- Make sure you tell an adult you trust, for example, a parent, a carer, a teacher, or the school anti-bullying coordinator, or call a helpline.
- Most social media services and other sites have a button you can click on to report bullying. Doing this can prevent a bully from targeting you and others in the future. Many services take bullying seriously, and will either warn the individual responsible or terminate their account.
- While you are on your mobile phone, make sure you also pay attention to your surroundings.

Parents also need to be aware that the largest ISPs, such as AOL, Yahoo!, and Microsoft, offer forms of parental control that allow parents to monitor their children's online activities. Other than being reminded to monitor their children's online activities, parents also need help with appropriate intervention strategies if they discover that their child either is involved in cyberbullying or affected by it using social media (Digital Parenting, 2010).

In the United States, parents' and teachers' associations have joined forces with local law enforcement agencies to create cyberbullying programs, in order to help parents and students identify and deal with incidents of cyberbullying (Slater, 2005). Using specially trained 'cybernetic' police officers and volunteer parents, these programs emphasize the importance of a safe learning environment while offering factual information on the consequences of cyberbullying and providing instructions on ways to stop harassment on the internet so that students are safe to use it (Slater, 2005).

In general, the advice is that parents should learn everything they can about the internet, what their kids do on it and involve in this part of their children life (Beale &Hall,2007). At the least, parents should develop a family online agreement with their children, covering such areas as the place where the internet can be used, what they can do on it, how much time they can spend online, what they should do if they receive messages that make them feel uncomfortable, and what they must do to protect their personal information (Keith & Martin, 2005).

A list of practical suggestions for parents (Sweet, pp. 2-3) advises them to:

- Set ground rules with your family and post them near the computer. The most effective way parents can shape their child's internet behavior is to supervise their online activity.
- Avoid sites that ask for personal information. It may be shared publicly without your knowledge. Instruct your child to never give out his or her name, address, or other personal information on the internet.
- Your home may not be the only place your child is accessing the internet. Computers at friend's homes, the library, in school, and at after school care programs may not have appropriate internet safeguards.
- Remind your children that not everything they read online is necessarily true. Internet chat rooms have become a stalking ground for sexual predators who give phony information about themselves in order to lure unsuspecting young people.
- Make computer usage a family activity. Keep the computer in the family room rather than in the child's bedroom. Ask them about their "online friends" just as you would their other friends.

Students affected by cyberbullying are often embarrassed by contact with parents on the internet. Students affected by cyberbullying are often ashamed to speak to their parents about online intimidation (Belsey, 2004), but on the other hand, they see parents as those persons who they trust and whom they can rely on (UNICEF, 2017). Report Cyberbullying Statistics 2019 shows that about 38% of cyberbullying victims are willing to admit it to their parents (Petrov, 2019). It became crucial to invest in parental programs to better prevent and respond to bullying and cyberbullying.

For this reason, parents should encourage their children to approach them directly if someone says or does something on the internet which makes them feel uncomfortable or threatened. Many cases of harassment on the internet go unreported because those being persecuted are worried that their computers will be taken away or that they will not be able to use the internet (Barr, 2005).

Therefore, rather than reacting in an excessive manner, parents are encouraged to maintain a calm approach, and to open lines of communication and trust. Parents of children affected by cyberbullying should notify school officials, even if the violence occurs out of school hours. Although there may be little that a school administrator can do in terms of direct intervention, there may be suggestions that they can make to parents. For example, administrators can advise parents to contact the parents of the cyberbully and demand that their behavior is stopped and, if this does not stop the harassment, to save harassing messages and forward copies to the internet service provider for them to take action. Nowadays most service providers actively apply appropriate policies to limit a users' ability to harass others on the internet.

As a last resort, parents can contact a lawyer regarding parental misconduct for failing to prevent the defamation, violation of privacy, and intentional infliction of emotional distress. In most cases, cyberbullying does not go that far, although parents of victims often demand the criminal prosecution of the perpetrator (WiredKids, 2005). Of course, parents should immediately contact the police if there are threats of physical violence, intimidation, extortion, hate crime, or sexual abuse. They should also contact the service provider for help in solving the problem.

The general advice for parents and educators for protecting children from cyberbullying is (Lubkina & Marzano, 2014):

- Support them in a positive and active manner;
- Encourage them to report incidents of bullying to a teacher or other responsible figure;
- Reassure them that computer, phone, or other privileges won't be curtailed;
- Look for signs of online bullying (e.g. if they get upset when they are online);
- Keep the family computer in a central location. This is important especially with adolescents.

The general advice if there are suspicions that a child is being cyberbullied are:

- If you suspect a child or young person is being harassed or bullied, either over the internet or via mobile phone, ask them about it.
- If your child tells you that someone is bothering them online, take it seriously. Offer practical as well as emotional support.
- Act immediately and report the incident to the school or online. Don't wait to see if the abuse will stop;
- Tell the child not to respond to unpleasant phone calls/text-messages and online harassment: cyberbullies are looking for a reaction;
- Print out the evidence for future reference. Talk to a teacher at your child's school if other pupils at the schools are involved. (Lizut & Wrońska, 2018).

It is also very important for parents to give children and teenagers the confidence to inform them about what happens on the internet. Talking with children will help parents understand how they use the internet, social media, and their mobile phones. Moreover, talking with children about responsible behavior is important because sometimes children who are the victims of cyberbullying might themselves also participate in the cyberbullying of others. Make sure they know they can go and talk to an adult or parent if they are persecuted and need support.

Community Matters, a nonprofit organization working with schools across the USA, offers slightly different, simpler recommendations (cited from web: community-matters.org, 2009-2019):

1. Learn about the issue. Media attention on bullying and cyberbullying is rapidly growing. The more informed and better educated you are, the more effective you can be in impacting the problem. You can find links to articles on bullying prevention on our website or do a Google search of terms like "bullying", "cyberbullying", etc.
2. Walk the talk. Children learn many social cues from adults, parents/caregivers, and their peers. By modeling empathy, tolerance, and respect in your actions and communication, you impart these values, and influence the attitudes and behaviors of your children.
3. Talk with your children. Often, if children are involved in bullying as either targets or aggressors, they are reluctant to talk about it. Ask your children about their social experience at school, especially if they seem withdrawn or are exhibiting unusual changes in their mood or behavior.
4. Monitor your child online. Cyberbullying is the fastest growing type of peer-on-peer mistreatment today. It is important for parents to be able to monitor their children's use of Facebook, MySpace, and other social media sites, both at home and on mobile devices.
5. Understand your school's policies. Rules, procedures, and policies regarding bullying vary greatly from district to district. Many states have enacted anti-bullying legislation, but implementation at the school site may be lacking. Speak with school officials and your school board about what policies they have in place and what programs they have implemented to address bullying and cyberbullying.
6. Identify and build alliances in your community. Local service clubs, PTA's, local government, and businesses can be a source of support and funding for bullying and cyberbullying prevention programs like

Safe School Ambassadors. Working with the various stakeholders in your community is an effective way to build a coalition and create safer school climates.

7. Advocate for safer schools. Write a letter to the editor of your local paper, attend or join your local PTA or school board, or start a community group dedicated to addressing bullying and cyberbullying at your local schools.

The slogan of one of their educational projects addressed to parents and social educators "Become a friend of your child", indicates the type of active participation parents should have in the online life of their children, learning about their interests and the virtual community they operate in. In short, the advice is, therefore, that parents should actively communicate with their children (NASK, 2012-2016). How parents talk to their children depends on their age. Many nonprofit organizations working in the field provide practical advice for parents about how to approach the subject with their children. One of the advice for children affected by cyberbullying is to involve their parents and school administrators as quickly as possible instead of trying to cope with the situation directly on the internet, or suffering in silence (Childnet, 2019).

Parents must stand behind the school's efforts to counter cyberbullying, recognizing that this is a reality and solving a problem with children. Although traditional bullying usually takes place in school, electronic bullying largely occurs outside school time and so at home, causing the abused person to think that there is no safe place for them to go (Wollack & Mitchell, 2000).

Today's young people, including those who abuse others, are computer-literate. Parents, if they are to succeed in monitoring their children's use of computers, must find out about new language they use, rules and behaviors in the environment in which modern teenagers function (Kamieniecki et al., 2017, p.1).

Parents have an important role to play if their child commits cyberbullying. If a parent realizes that their child is bullying others, it is important that they acknowledge the problem and ensure the behavior is stopped. Children who bully are unlikely to stop on their own, and adult intervention is necessary. The advice given to parents by Utterly Global (antibullyingprograms.org), another nonprofit working in the sphere, is:

- Confront the behavior right away. This does not mean that parents should be confrontational. Instead, they should listen and not judge.

- Draw clear boundaries. Make the expectations and the consequences for violating them clear. Let the child know that bullying behavior is never acceptable and that the consequences, such as loss of privileges, will be enforced. Make the connection between appropriate online behavior and the behavior required of them in person.
- Provide appropriate models for empathy, respect, and compassion. It is essential to try to understand the child's feelings and to talk to them about what the person they are bullying might be experiencing. Is the child aware of the impact of their behavior? Children and teens who bully others may have been victimized themselves, or may not have had adequate models of empathetic, respectful, and compassionate behavior.
- Practice some critical self-assessment: do parents model that behavior for their child? Do other people that are a part of their life do so too?
- Give positive feedback when healthy choices are noticed. As well as correcting negative behavior, parents should also reinforce the positive, including praising the times when they seek the constructive resolution of difficult situations.
- Show love and support, and seek it in turn from the child. Behavior change will take time. Give the child love and support, even if angry or upset with them. Seek out the help of others who can be partners in efforts to put a stop to the bullying.
- Enlist the support of other caring adults, including teachers and school authorities. Work with them to develop a mutually agreeable plan of action to change the child's behavior.
- Find out if expert help is necessary. Bullying behavior can escalate quickly and turn into something much more difficult to address. If you or others have serious concerns about the nature or intensity of your child's behavior, seek expert assistance to help you decide how to address it, including whether to get them professional help.

Social Educators

Along with the increasing access to new information technologies, corresponding new forms of peer violence, such as cyberbullying have also been appearing at school. Young people are increasingly using electronic media to persecute disliked people: sending harassing text messages, spreading rumors and slander on online blogs, posting videos with the intention of compromising someone, etc.

Ensuring security should be closely associated with the extension of competences in this area, not only for children and parents, but most of all for teachers and social educators. Special training programs are required for educators and specialists in the field of social services focusing on the various threats that exist, their source, the ways they are manifested, the effects, and ways in which to deal with difficult situations. Such programs would enable them to better understand the problems involved in helping victims and provide more effective help and support for families.

The results of the study carried out for the Threats of Cyberspace project (2014) confirm the need to increase the competences of social workers in the area of cyberspace threats by introducing new themes in the professional curricula and in on-the-job supplementary training - 99 out of 100 respondents believed that the issue of cyberspace should form part of the education or training of social workers.

It needs to be highlighted that, currently, many students are effectively persecuting their peers, not in the school itself but on the internet, and teachers and educators are increasingly faced with the necessity to respond to cases of peer violence implemented using new communication technologies. The procedure shown below presents a list of rules for the conduct of school employees in the situation of disclosure of cyberbullying. It offers suggestions as to when and how teachers (and head teachers) should react to victims, perpetrators, and witnesses, and how to cooperate with the parents of these students.

The interaction of the school with parents becomes particularly important in the light of the increasing number and variety of problems with children's behavior and issues related to the adaptation and internationalization of social norms, especially in junior high school and high school groups. For the way children function inside an educational institution and the level of success they will have, their home situation is often decisive. Factors such as material conditions, the amount of care and attention they receive from parents, the parent's perception of cultural, ethical, and educational issues, the general atmosphere, and the level of parental awareness can all play a determining part in molding a child's behavior.

Types of school programs can be divided into two main groups: universal interventions and focused ones. The first type of programs refers to those that implement actions to the whole community, building a climate conducive to the school and parent relationship and aimed at building positive attitudes. Their aim is also to promote the involvement of families in school activities, which may in the future result with better intervention in the case of cyberbullying.

Second types of programs focused on interventions on the specific categories of bullies, victims or bystanders. The few programs were indicated:

1. Focused Interventions programs for students, on an individual level;
2. Universal interventions, which assumed teachers and parents participation;
3. Whole-School Interventions – involving all school community and based on wide level of action;
4. Multi-Level Systemic Approach - containing practically all possible types of anticipatory, intervention and reduction damages dedicated to the school, and more broadly to the social environment;
5. Mixed Intervention Programs- include both universal interventions and at more focused actions with the children directly involved in the cyberbullying (Cantone, et al, 2015).

The task of the school is to create conditions for cooperation is present in all types of programs, although this may take various forms and the information about the existence of cyberbullying in a school can come from various sources. In their book, *Cyberbullying: bullying in the digital age*, Kowalski et al. (2012), defined nine tips for intervention in cases of cyberbullying (Kowalski et al., cited in Notar et al., 2013) intended to guide the response of parents and teachers:

- **Save the Evidence:** Print copies of messages and web pages.
- For a first offense, if minor in nature, ignore, delete, or block the sender.
- **Reporting:** If an offensive profile targeting your child is set up on a social networking site, report it to the site host.
- **Investigate:** Monitor your child's online presence.
- **Communicate:** If the perpetrator is another student, share evidence with the school staff.
- **Parental Involvement:** If the perpetrator is known and the cyberbullying is continuing, contact the child's parents and share your evidence.
- **Legal Advice:** If the parent of the perpetrator is unresponsive and the behavior continues, contact an attorney or seek legal advice.
- **Law Enforcement:** Report the cyberbullying to the police.
- **Mental Health Support:** If your child expresses emotional distress or thoughts of self-harm, seek help from a school counselor or other mental health professional immediately.

Borkowska (in Lizut & Wrońska, 2014) draws attention to the four types of activities an educator should undertake in respect to the incident, the perpetrator, the victim, and the wider social environment. At first it is necessary to secure the evidence, for example by making a note of the date and time of receiving the material, the content of the message and, if possible, the sender's data (user name, email address, mobile number, etc.) or the address of the website on which the harmful content or profile appeared.

Secondly, identify the perpetrator. Young people often have the illusory belief that new technologies ensure their full anonymity. In reality, as experts point out, there are many ways to identify the source of cyberbullying. The next step is to devise a program of action to towards perpetrators. Especially the teacher or social educator should engage a conversation with the student-perpetrator of violence about their behavior focuses on: stop the violence and ensure a sense of security for the injured student; elicit their reflection on the behavior, understanding the harm it caused and stopping the enactment of similar behavior in the future; show the school community that cyberbullying is not be tolerated and that the school is able to effectively respond to this kind of situation.

At the same time victim of cyberbullying needs help and emotional support from adults. They also need to know that the school will take the appropriate steps to solve the problem. A student who is a victim of cyberbullying should receive advice on how to behave to ensure their security and avoid the escalation of the persecution. When the intervention is over, it is worth monitoring the student's situation by checking if further violence or retaliation is being enacted by the offender. The parents of a child who is a victim of cyberbullying should be informed about the problem and receive support and help from the school. In an interview with them, the educator should outline the steps that have been taken.

Professionals responding to a report of cyberbullying should also identify and interview all of the available witnesses to an event to determine the course of the incident. It is important that, as a result of the intervention, witnesses are not exposed to acts of revenge or threats from the perpetrator (Lizut & Wrońska, 2018). Same cases of cyberbullying require notifying the family court or the police.

Although there is general agreement as to the significance of the relationship between parents and the school, the situation is not so clear with other supporting institutions. Social workers, social educators, and other employees of social service institutions perform tasks connected with the functioning of an individual, group, and community in society. Consequently, they cannot remain oblivious to the emerging social issues. Meanwhile, an increasing number of people, primarily those from the younger generation, face new threats and require an adequate form of help from professional social service institutions and organizations.

The tasks of social services are (Lizut & Wrońska, 2014):

- **Diagnostic:** To recognize the specific context of a situation and identify the appropriate social services entity able to provide help. In relation to internet safety, this is related both to the detection of specific problem situations within the group of people they support, and to having a good level of knowledge about online threats and the ability to identify them.
- **Prophylactic:** To prevent the exposure of individuals to critical situations. This includes carrying out activities aimed at increasing the level of awareness of online threats and ways of dealing with risky and problem situations among children and young people, as well as their parents and guardians. and predicting the occurrence of potential threat situations that the recipients of the assistance may encounter.
- **Corrective:** To help in treating the effects of dysfunctional behaviors. This comprises providing support and assistance to those exposed to threatening behavior on the internet, as well as cooperating with specialists (including psychologists, doctors, lawyers, law enforcement agencies, etc.).
- **Protective:** To defend people from the effects of specific social problems. In relation to internet safety, this includes undertaking actions aimed at encouraging common use of security features on computers and mobile devices, and on internet websites and apps.
- **Supporting:** To provide knowledge and skills useful for getting out of difficult life situations. This concerns the dissemination of information about institutions and organizations that support users to deal with difficulties related to the use of new technologies and to functioning in the network.

Social workers, educators, and other "helping professions" need to be equipped with new skills to be able to cope successfully with such demanding tasks. Special programs should therefore be implemented aimed at equipping social workers with a broader range of qualifications and tools for intervention to be able to help solve problems of cyberbullying. It is very important to emphasize that this modern program for social workers should satisfy all of the aims of the teaching process:

1. Provide general knowledge about cyberbullying;
2. Reinforce practical skills that are of particular reference to the individual case;
3. Create and promote general social competences, especially through broadening the skills correlated with conflict resolution and coping with difficult situations.

It is worth emphasizing that representatives of other social professions also have a significant role to play, for example:

Health care providers can play an important role in providing and supporting education about bullying. HCPs have opportunities to collaborate with schools and families to help youth develop positive social relationships and provide support and education to teachers as well. HCPs should consider being part of the creation and dissemination of educational resources addressing bullying so that patients can receive quality educational materials without commercial interests. Many HCPs now engage in dissemination of health content via social media and blogs. These online platforms provide new ways for HCPs to promote best practices around bullying. Furthermore, integration of bullying into continuing medical education at the hospital, regional, and national levels is critical to ensuring that HCPs are up to date on trends and improved clinical approaches. (Moreno, 2017, p. 366)

What's more, police officers are involved in actions for improving public awareness regarding threats related to the use of information and communication technologies. In addition to publishing information on official police websites, officers participate in meetings and lectures organized for children, and young people are sometimes involved in the creation and implementation of preventive school programs. They also initiate activities addressed particularly to parents, social workers, and educators.

The role of the police with regard to cyberbullying can be threefold. Firstly, the police can help to prevent cyberbullying, by informing students, parents and schools about the issue (Palladino, Nocentini, & Menesini, 2012). Secondly, the police can play a role in the detection of cyberbullying, for instance, by creating online reporting systems (apart from the offline channels). Thirdly, the police can play a role in handling existing cyberbullying cases, by identifying perpetrators and helping victims. (Vandebosch et al., 2012)

Professionals such as teachers, educators, and social workers should cooperate with each other and direct their attention to alerting parents to the new threats facing their children, providing them with essential information about those threats and how to recognize the signs that their child might be in danger, and to enlisting parents as active coalition partners in protecting children and young people from the harm caused by cyberbullying.

CONCLUSION

Gathering more experts in the field would entail a methodological approach and a steady revision of the main principles, in particular those underpinning the education and training of social workers.

Socialization, which represents one of the basic functions of the family, is a complicated and long-lasting process that shapes the attitudes, moral system, and patterns of behavior of the child. The final result should be a healthy, happy, self-aware adult who is ready to meet a world full of challenges and expectations, fulfilling their own aspirations and giving happiness to others.

The way in which parents understand their role in relation to the protection of their child and how much positive support they provide in a situation of cyberbullying determine whether the conditions they create will ensure their child's proper development to maturity. It is also indispensable, in this context, for parents to cooperate and work together with educators and other professionals in building a child-friendly environment.

REFERENCES

Anderson, M., & Jiang, J. (2018). *Teens, Social Media & Technology*. PEW Research Center. Available at: https://www.pewinternet.org/2018/05/31/teens-social-media-technology-2018/

Beale, A. V., & Hall, K. R. (2007). *Cyberbullying: What School Administrators (and Parents) Can Do*. Heldref Publications. Available at: http://citeseerx.ist.psu.edu/viewdoc/download?doi=10.1.1.459.8529&rep=rep1&type=pdf

Belsey, B. (2004). *Cyberbullying. What educators should know? What can be done?* Available at: www.cyberbullying.ca

Borkowska, A. (2014), Szkoła wobec problem cyberprzemocy. In E-zagrożenia nowym wyzwaniem dla służb społecznych. Warszawa: Wydawnictwo Wyższej Szkoły Pedagogicznej.

Cantone, E., Piras, A. P., Vellante, M., Preti, A., Daníelsdóttir, S., D'Aloja, E., … Bhugra, D. (2015). Interventions on Bullying and Cyberbullying in Schools: A Systematic Review. *Clin Pract Epidemiol Ment Health, 11*(S1), 58–76. Available at: https://www.ncbi.nlm.nih.gov/pmc/articles/PMC4378064/

Chibnall, S., Wallace, M., Leicht, C., & Lunghofer, L. (2006). *i-SAFE 2004*. U.S. Department of Justice. Available at: https://www.ncjrs.gov/pdffiles1/nij/grants/213715.pdf

Crone, E. A., & Konijn, E. A. (2018). Media use and brain development during adolescence. *Nature Communications, 9*. Available at: https://www.nature.com/articles/s41467-018-03126-x

Digital Parenting. (2010). *Feeling baffled by your child's digital world? From tots to teens, help is at hand.* Available at: https://parentzone.org.uk/system/files/attachments/ vodafone_digital_parenting_issue%201.pdf

Durkee. (2012). Prevalence of pathological internet use among adolescents in Europe: demographic and social factors. *Addiction, 107*(12), 2210-2222. Available at: https://onlinelibrary.wiley.com/doi/abs/10.1111/j.1360-0443.2012.03946.x

EU NET ADB – Badanie nadużywania internetu przez młodzież w Polsce i Europie. (2012). *Fundacja Dzieci Niczyje.* Available at: https://www.saferinternet.pl/images/stories/ pdf/raport_eu_net_adb_pl.pdf

Haddon, L., & Livingstone, S. (2012). *EU Kids Online: national perspectives. EU Kids Online*. London, UK: The London School of Economics and Political Science. Available at http://eprints.lse.ac.uk/46878/

Hojnacki, L. (2006). Pokolenie m-learningu – nowe wyzwanie dla szkoły. *E-Mentor, 1*(13), 26. Available at: http://www.e-mentor.edu.pl/artykul/index/numer/13/id/239

Iskandarani, Z. M. (2008). Effect of Information and Communication Technologies (ICT) on Non-Industrial Countries-Digital Divide Model. *Journal of Computer Science, 4*(4), 315-319. Available at: http://citeseerx.ist.psu.edu/viewdoc/download?doi=10.1.1.165.8042&rep=rep1&type=pdf

Kamieniecki, W., Bochnek, M., Tanaś, M., Wrońska, A., Lange, R., Fila, M., . . . Konopczyński, F. (2017). *Raport z badaniaNastolatki 3.0.* Warszawa: NASK. Available at: https://akademia.nask.pl/publikacje/Raport_z_badania_Nastolatki_3_0.pdf

Kardefelt-Winther, D. (2017). *How does the time children spend using digital technology impact their mental well-being, social relationships and physical activity? An evidence-focused literature review.* UNICEF. Available at: https://www.unicef-irc.org/publications/pdf/Children-digital-technology-wellbeing.pdf .pdf

Karmolińska-Jagodzik, E. (2012). Komunikacja międzypokoleniowa – rozważania wokół różnic kulturowych. *Stu-dia Edukacyjne, 21*, 191-210. Available at: https://repozytorium.amu.edu.pl/bitstream/ 10593/4286/1/studia_eduk_21_s_191-210.pdf

Keith, S., & Martin, M. E. (2005). Cyber-Bullying: Creating a Culture of Respect in a Cyber World. *Reclaiming Children and Youth: The Journal of Strength-based Interventions, 13*(4). Available at: https://eric.ed.gov/?id=EJ710387

Kowalski, R. M., Limber, S. P., & Agatson, P. W. (2012). Cyberbullying: Bullying in the digital age (2nd ed.). Wiley-Blackwell.

Livingstone, S., & Byrne, J. (2015). Challenges of parental responsibility in a global perspective. In U. Gasser (Ed.), *Digitally Connected: Global Perspectives on Youth and Digital Media* (pp. 26–29). Cambridge, MA: Berkman Center for Internet and Society, Harvard University.

Livingstone, S., & Byrne, J. (2017). *Challenges of parental responsibility in a global perspective.* UNICEF. Available at: https://blogs.unicef.org/evidence-for-action/challenges-of-parental-responsibility-in-the-digital-age-a-global-perspective/

Lizut, J., & Wrońska, A. (Eds.). (2018). *Standard bezpieczeństwa on-line placówek oświatowych.* Warszawa: NASK. Available at: https://akademia.nask.pl/publikacje/ost_Standard_bezpieczenstwa_online_placowek_oswiatowych.pdf

Lizut, J., & Wrońska, A. (Eds.). (2014). *E-zagrożenia nowym wyzwaniem dla służb społecznych*. Warszawa: Wydawnictwo Wyższej Szkoły Pedagogicznej.

Lubkina, V., & Marzano, G. (2014). Cyberbullying Prevention. In J. Lizut (Ed.), *Threats of Cyberspace a Comprehensive Programe for the Employees of Social Service Institutions* (pp. 89–110). Warsaw: Wyd. WSP. Available at https://cyberprzestrzen.wspkorczak.eu/download.php?file=dokumenty/english_version

Moreno, A. M., & Vaillancourt, T. (2017). The Role of Health Care Providers in Cyberbullying, *Can J Psychiatry, 62*(6), 364–367. Available at: https://www.ncbi.nlm.nih.gov/pmc/articles/PMC5455868/

Notar, C. E., Padgett, S., & Roden, J. (2013). Cyberbullying: Resources for Intervention and Prevention. *Universal Journal of Educational Research, 1*(3), 133-145. Available at: https://files.eric.ed.gov/fulltext/EJ1053892.pdf

Online Bullying Among Youth 8-17 Years Old – Worldwide. (2016). Steps Parents Take To Help Protect Children Online. *Microsoft*. Available at: https://enough.org/objects/ww_online_bullying_survey_-_executive_summary_-_ww_final.pdf

Online safety across the generation. (2018). Family Online Safety Institute. Available at: https://www.fosi.org/policy-research/online-safety-across-generations/

Patchin, S., & Hinduja, J. W. (2017). Cultivating youth resilience to prevent bullying and cyberbullying victimization. *Child Abuse & Neglect, 73*, 51-62. Available at: https://www.sciencedirect.com/science/article/pii/S0145213417303411?via%3Dihub

Spitzer, M. (2013). *Digital Dementia. How We Deprive Myself and Your Children*. Słupsk: Wyd. Dobra Literatura.

Sweet, S. (2017), *Internet guide for parents*. Family Research Council. Available at: https://downloads.frc.org/EF/EF07H24.pdf

Swift, C., & Taylor, A. (2003). The digital divide – a new generation gap. Parental knowledge of their children's Internet use. *Paediatr Child Health, 8*(5), 275–278. Available at: https://www.ncbi.nlm.nih.gov/pmc/articles/PMC2792683/

UNICEF. (2017). *The State of the World's Children 2017: Children in a Digital World*. Available at: https://www.unicef.org/publications/index_101992.html

Vandebosch, H., Beirens, L., D'Haese, W., Wegge, D., & Pabian, S. (2012). Police actions with regard to cyberbullying: The Belgian case. *Psicothema*, *24*(4), 646-652. Available at: https://pdfs.semanticscholar.org/f60c/fadc3d6852ad4e466dfcfa9f15ffdd4f743d.pdf

KEY TERMS AND DEFINITIONS

Digital Immigrants: Those that, although they use new technologies, move much worse in their world.

Digital Natives: Those for whom virtual space is not another area of activity and the natural field of their daily activities.

Internet Etiquette or Netiquette: Is the set of rules defining the forms of behavior in the online community.

Intervention Procedure: Defines the rules of behavior of the school, teachers, and other people involved in the cyberbullying act. The intervention procedure should include providing support to the victim of violence, securing evidence and determining the circumstances of the incident, drawing consequences against the perpetrator of violence and working on changing the student's attitude.

Chapter 9
Cyberbullying at School:
Prevention and Intervention Strategies

Joanna Lizut
Janusz Korczak Pedagogical University in Warsaw, Poland

ABSTRACT

It is very important to collocate the occurrence of cyberbullying with a negative school environment. School bullying is widely known to be associated with many negative indicators, including lower academic achievement, lower school satisfaction, and lower levels of attachment and involvement at school. Several studies have combined cyberbullying with negative school experiences, such as lower academic performance and negative perceptions of the school climate. Moreover, many have suggested a strong link between the climate in the school and both traditional and cyberbullying. Some recent studies have shown that people who are perpetrators of cyberbullying and those who are victims both report a worse climate in schools than others not involved in the behavior. A poor disciplinary climate is one in which students are either unaware of the rules and the consequences of violations or one in which students are unmotivated to internalize and conform to the rules because they feel that they are unfair or unimportant. Weak parental involvement implies that the parents are not involved with the student's school life; they provide no help with homework, have very little communication with teachers, and rarely assist with school activities. Having a lack of didactic pressure means that neither teachers nor students hold high expectations for their academic achievement.

DOI: 10.4018/978-1-5225-8076-8.ch009

INTRODUCTION

In addition to the family and the peer group, the school is an important source of influence in the process of socialization. The issues of internet use at school can be considered from several dimensions: proper use of mobile devices and computers in school, aspects of proper behavior, communication with peers and teachers in various forms, instilling appropriate educational conditions, and creating school prevention programs. We must note that:

The rapid expansion of the network, its growing presence in education and in the processes of communication, have not, in a natural way, gone together with the creation of principles, procedures and standards of conduct. The network itself, however, is accompanied by an appearance on the internet of dangerous phenomena and crime. We can talk about negative transfer of phenomena from the real world to the web, as well as the creation of entirely new categories of unfavorable phenomena and crimes. We are dealing with both technical and social hazards. (Lizut & Wrońska ed., 2018, p.6)

A properly functioning system can also provide younger generations with knowledge and skills that parents do not transmit, as well as being a place where they will improve or correct inappropriate behavior. It is expected that development and information initiatives will also be undertaken within the educational system.

Schools with a lack of clear expectations, unfair assessment processes, incorrect relations, and disturbed communications arouse frustration even among well-adapted students. Aggressive behavior shown by young people can be a reaction to what is happening on the school grounds (Espelage, Polanin & Low, 2014).

The social relations in schools are crucial – both those between teachers and students, school staff, and parents, and those between the students themselves. A review of the research undertaken by Noam and Fiore (2004) reveals that the schools which have the greatest academic success and the least problems maintaining discipline are those in which pupils feel that the teachers are close to them and treat them with respect. The perception that a school is a friendly open place where success is experienced builds the student's trust in the environment, their sense of belonging, and their bond with the school. According to Jessor and others (1995), this bond is one of the most important factors protecting against aggression. School achievements and teacher's appreciation increase the students' self-esteem, confidence in their own abilities, and motivation for development (Greene, 2005).

Many studies have already been done concerning in-school bullying and school climate. According to Ma (2002), students in schools that have a good disciplinary climate and strong parental involvement are less likely to engage in bullying than those who are in schools with poor disciplinary climates. Also they have less parental involvement (Schneider, O'Donnell, Stueve & Coulter, 2012). Additionally, students may also bully less if they perceive a strong academic pressure. Disciplinary climate, parental involvement, and academic pressure are the most important components of school climate (Ma, 2002).

School Climate

Through a suitable approach, schools have the potential to serve as powerful protective factors in students' development. Schools are relatively self-contained environments, and can represent safe places for children and their families. Schools can counteract students' feelings of alienation and isolation by actively developing resilience-building interactions. Programs must be dedicated to all stakeholders, looks at attempts to prevent school violence (Figure 1).

Figure 1. Actions to reduce the risk and threats of cyberbullying
Source: Humphries A. (2012). Cyberbullying Policy in Public Schools. UNLV Theses, Dissertations, Professional Papers, and Capstones. https://core.ac.uk/download/pdf/62889761.pdf

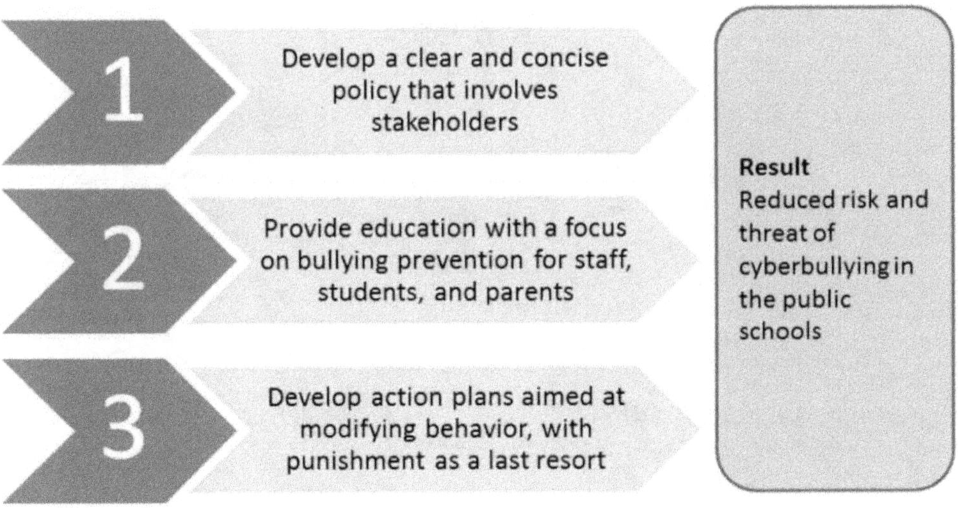

Schools that foster a sense of belonging among its students can help reduce incidents of depression, increase self-efficacy, and provide opportunities to build self-confidence and relationship-building skills. By developing a practical understanding of how to create inclusive, culturally competent school climates for all students and staff, schools can reduce inequities and contribute to healthy development and well-being.

The National School Climate Center (schoolclimate.org) defines *school climate* as the quality and character of school life (Figure 2). School Climate is based on patterns of students', parents', and school personnel's experiences of school life, and reflects norms, goals, values, interpersonal relationships, teaching and learning practices, and organizational structures (Berkowitz et al., 2017).

There are various risk factors present in the school climate (Williams & Guerra, 2007) which can encourage problems of cyberbullying. We can divide them in to several groups. They encompass physical and social aspects, such as:

- Unfavorable location of the school;
- Dirty, neglected buildings and surroundings;
- Destroyed, inoperable equipment;
- Stray classrooms away from main areas;
- Large school;

Figure 2. Elements of school climate
Source: https://community-matters.org/

- Overloaded classes.
- Negative, passive role of the director;
- Organizational chaos;
- Impersonal teacher-student relations;
- Lack of transparent school expectations and clear disciplinary rules;
- Lack of a uniform and clear evaluation system for achievements;
- Excessive rigidity and restrictions;
- Disregarding the interests and expectations of pupils, depriving pupils of influence in molding the school and its rules;
- Poor communication between teachers, students, and parents;
- Removing parents from decisions on school matters;
- Lack of positive school tradition;
- Lack of extracurricular activities;
- Low level of competences and morale of teachers;
- Low level of competences and morale of students.

In general, a positive climate is the one that generates respect, cooperation, trust, and shared responsibility for the educational objectives that are pursued. Educators, students, and others connected to the school consequently take ownership of the mission of the school, and work together toward a shared vision. If a climate such as this is established, everything else seems to fall into place. For instance, it will definitely lead to more academic success and greater educational exploration (Erwin, 2004).

All of the components that go together to create the school climate can and should (to varying degrees) be taken into account in the design of cyberbullying prevention programs.

Community Cooperation

The increasing demands placed on schools and other educational institutions in the area of cooperation with the local community indicate that formal expectations in this respect are significant. The quality of schools' relationships with their surroundings and their ability to interact with institutions around them are determined by many factors, the most important of them being (Hernik, Solon-Lipiński, Stasiowski, 2012):

1. **The Situational Context:** Including such issues as the form and principles on which the cooperation is established and on who participates in initiating contacts and maintaining them, on whether the partnership

is based on personal relationships or is established on formal relations between institutions, whether the cooperation is continuous or incidental, cyclical or sporadic. The intensity of the cooperation is, therefore, also one of the dimensions of the analysis.

2. **Personal Context:** Concerning the person responsible for initiating and then maintaining contacts and whether the relationship with the institution is of a personal nature, based on the personal contacts of the school staff, members of the parent council, or the director, or is more formalized.
3. **The Nature of Cooperation:** Defines the principles that guide cooperation with individual institutions, which derive from the nature of their activities, as well as from logistical facts such as their geographical distance from the school. Certain organizations/institutions are perceived as being key partners (due to educational goals, locality, etc.), others as less important. Unfortunately, many schools are more interested in the "quantity" of partners rather than in their "quality".

This aspects are connected with rethinking how schools work, which points wilder thinking about education. Online activities, digital skills, or internet ability beliefs are connected with whole socio-ecological system and need to reinvent the traditional classroom paradigm and rearrange the entire school experience. Cyberbullying prevention forces students to move from one learning activity to another more organically, removing the limitations of traditional school life, because it does not finish with bell schedules.

Many research shows current knowledge about positive element and factors affecting effectiveness of prevention programs (Espelage & Hong, 2017; Zych, Ortega-Ruiz & Del Rey, 2015), Ostaszewski (2016) propose same general recommendations for the prevention of aggression in schools divided according to the educational level:

Pre-school level programs are not very popular, because recognition of cyberbullying as a problem for young age group is not common. However, due to the fact that the age of internet users is decreasing, more attention should be paid to the necessity of teaching pupils netiquette from the first years. Preschool programs are also construct parental involvement to safety polices in the future.

Programs dedicated to this level should:

- Improve social functioning, cognitive functioning, and development;
- Be carried out by qualified and trained teachers and social educators;

- Be combined with other activities supporting the child's parents in terms of educational, living, and social issues.

Good results at pre-school level gives program which are related to strengthening and supporting the following aspects of family life:

- Good relationships in the family;
- Improving skills for active participation in life;
- Child support and friendship;
- Help with learning at school;
- Methods of disciplining children without punishment;
- Behavior and attitudes of parents demonstrating positive examples for children;
- Talking about issues related to cyberbullying in a way that is accessible to children.

Sheeplive.eu is a project dedicated to children of pre-school and primary school age (Figure 3). Its principal purpose is to provide education in the

Figure 3. Screen shots from Sheeplive.eu website
Source: http://pl.sheeplive.eu/

field of safe and responsible use of the internet. Cartoons (about sheep living in the mountains) refer to classic stories of fighting good and evil but are connected with internet etiquette. Each of the fables ends with a moral. The educational cycle covers such themes as cyberbullying and demeaning colleagues through the internet (http://pl.sheeplive.eu/).

At first level of school education - primary school, the crucial elements of programs are focused on the development of psychosocial and emotional skills of students. They can become effective tools for the prevention of risky behavior. Such competences include interpersonal skills, decision making abilities, capacities to deal with ones' own emotions, and resilience to stress.

Programs should:

- Be implemented at the beginning of school education (in the first and second grade of primary school);
- Be based on teacher-student cooperation and active student participation;
- Also include components for teachers such as how to react to inappropriate behavior by students;
- Effectively increase the level of multiple, key psychosocial skills of participants;
- Be implemented through a series of a few lessons supported by complementary lessons scheduled during the following years of education;
- Be run by trained teachers or social educators;
- Be based on an interactive educational methodology.

There are many teaching materials available to help teachers conduct interesting classes devoted to cyberbullying. A good lesson: has a distinctive structure; can be completed with specific students based on the school's need; are correct in substance; are flexible and open; include a clear description of the students' expected achievements; are visually interesting (Rubio, 2010).

As an example of good practice it can be "The Bullying and Cyberbullying" program for primary schools lets students explore the meaning and impact of bullying and cyberbullying. The materials will also enable them to explore appropriate ways of responding to discriminating, hurtful, or intimidating behavior. Materials include: Bullying and cyberbullying lesson plan; Bullying and cyberbullying teacher support sheet; Bullying and cyberbullying scenarios; Classroom tips and preparation notes; and a PowerPoint presentation for use in class (https://campaignresources.phe.gov.uk/schools/resources/bullying-lesson-plan-pack).

The middle and high school levels coincide with the years of adolescence. During this period (Obuchowska, 1996), we can observe a series of changes: a) physical - changes in the structure of the body - outline, height; b) mental - greater ability to control emotions, understanding of moral concepts, increased independence; c) emotional - the passage of a specific "emotional arousal", which in the initial stage of adolescence can be identified as emotional lability that gradually changes to relative stability. At the same time, adolescence is a time of experiencing important relationships, of friendship and even first love; d) moral - based on the teaching of authentic recognition of societal norms (the transition from the stage of needing approval to seeking and accepting external authority); e) worldviews - focused on developing personal reflections regarding important social issues and on making informed evaluations and choices; and f) identity - related to questions about the meaning of life and ones' own existence and the questions this raises.

At this stage of education good results have been found with programs that have the following characteristics (Ttofi & Farringto, 2011):

- They are based on an interactive educational method, based on social learning ideas of encouraging and rewarding prosocial behavior and discouraging and punishing bullying;
- They need to be intensive and long-lasting
- They are disseminated using high quality standards of implementation
- They are implemented by trained teachers and social educators, and sometimes also with the participation of trained youth leaders;
- They create educational situations for practicing and developing life skills,
- They pay attention to enhancing playground supervision,
- Correct wrong normative attitudes and beliefs at the same time and built up an appropriate school ethos that efficiently tackles bullying.

One of the good practice for this group of students is program Rewrite Your Story, a website primarily dedicated to adolescents that focuses on empowering people to change the course of negative experiences on the internet. According to its home page, "Rewrite Your Story is about real-life stories, advice and support from friends, professional help and good vibes only".

Figure 4. Home page of Rewrite Your Story website
Source: https://www.esafety.gov.au/education-resources/classroom-resources/rewrite-your-story

Responsible Persons

One of the most challenging aspects of dealing with cyberbullying behavior amongst students is deciding who is best suited to intervene and respond to bullying incidents. Patchin and Hinduja (2010) suggest that cyberbullying can best be controlled when all stakeholders, including school administrators, teachers, parents, and students are involved. They also suggest many ways in which schools can address the problem of cyberbullying (Patchin& Hinduja, 2012):

1. Schools should educate students about responsible internet usage. Students should not be exposed to this theme in just one discipline, but it should be consistently integrated into all classes where technology is utilized on a regular basis, so that the message is reinforced.
2. Schools must establish a school climate in which students clearly understand the consequences of violations regarding any type of bullying. If school policies on bullying do not directly address cyberbullying, administrators should work towards creating a policy that clearly states the consequences for behaviors of cyberbullying on campus and those that occur off campus but which have a direct effect on the learning climate of the school.
3. Schools should also employ creative response strategies that will not only help students recognize the consequences of their behavior, but that will also send the message that bullying is unacceptable and will not be tolerated. For example, students can create posters or pamphlets that address the importance of using technology in appropriate ways.

4. Schools should work with parents to educate them and to reinforce the fact that cyberbullying is a serious offense (Patchin & Hinduja, 2010).
5. Schools should be aware of the type of content that students upload to the internet.

Recommendations: Secure and Effective Internet Infrastructure of the Facility

The group of cyber safety expert - authors of "The on-line security standard of educational institutions" (Lizut & Wrońska ed., 2018, pp. 16-20) indicate three levels of IT infrastructure security.

Basic Level: Even given the severe budgetary constraints in education, an organizational and technical standard requires:

- An administrator to be appointed who is responsible for the proper functioning of the IT infrastructure and its security.
- This person could be an employee of the facility or come from outside.
- If an external administrator is used, a guardian should be established in the facility to supervise compliance with the standard and oversee the work of the administrator.
- If there is no possibility to appoint a supervisor or administrator, the legitimacy of accessing the internet at school should be considered, since leaving the infrastructure open and unattended will bring more threats and problems than the benefits of simply sharing the internet.
- The equipment to be used for access to the internet must be properly prepared (Lizut &Wrońska ed., 2018, p. 18).

Higher Level: Recognizant of the fact that in the library there may be confidential materials available to users of the local network, as well as to internet users, the minimum level of security may be insufficient, therefore, additional mechanisms recommended at the elevated level include the application of:

- Principles of functional separation and related network segmentation;
- User authentication systems;
- Security and access control systems - firewalls (systems of filtering unwanted content);
- Anti-virus systems on employee workstations;

- For user identification, it is recommended to install an authentication or introduction system login page, allowing access to Wi-Fi networks based on the WPA 2 encryption standard;
- With this security level, various services available can be run by the facility via the internet, such as an e-journal, but with all the standard recommended security (presence of administrator, safe environment and service configuration).
- The institution should have a security policy in the form of a document approved by the institution's management and regulations in place regarding the use of systems and computer networks.

Professional Level: Appropriate for IT infrastructure in an institution whose purpose is to use modern desktop and mobile IT solutions as well as to use infrastructure for in-depth IT education with an extensive intranet (an internal network with many services intended for use by employees and current students, similar to modern business networks).

Programs addressed to parents can help them maintain good and effective relationships with their children, enabling them to develop their skills in providing emotional support, monitoring, solving problems related to school, disciplining without violence, and communicating with their children, and establishes the expectations regarding principles and values as well as problem behaviors.

Teaching parents about internet safety and helping them establish rules for internet use is another way to play an active role in the prevention of cyberbullying. (Notar et al., 2013, p. 140)

The organization of meetings within the programs requires several factors to be taken into account so as to establish a friendly logistics and a good atmosphere to encourage parents' attendance (Mendez et al., 2009): time constraints and length of meetings; tasks to do at home; availability of childcare, meals for participants and accommodations; rewards after each session, classes not only for parents, but also for parents and children (family sessions). The value of cooperation was confirm by number of research and concluded in the review done by Ttofi & Farrington (2011).

parent training/meetings was significantly related to a decrease in both bullying and victimization. These findings suggest that efforts should be made to sensitize parents about the issue of school bullying through educational presentations and teacher-parent meetings. Future anti-bullying initiatives should also bring together experts from various disciplines and make the most of their expertise. In our review, cooperative group work among experts was significantly related to the reduction of both bullying and victimization. (Ttofi & Farrington, 2011, p.49)

The effectiveness of parenting skills development programs is associated with the appropriate selection of parents' education goals, and mostly support the following aspects of family life (Ostaszewski, 2016, p. 17):

- Family ties and good relationships in the family,
- Skills for active participation in life;
- Child support and monitoring friendships;
- Peer to peer help with learning at school;
- Methods of disciplining children without physical punishment;
- Behavior and attitudes of parents that set a positive example for children.

Staff and Educators

The most important recommendations for creating a good school climate were outlined by Hinduja & Patchin (2015, 2018). Many of them are addressed to teachers.

1. Never stop learning.

Educators themselves should continue to learn about new technological developments, devices, and forms of online misuse. They should also develop relationships with staff at other schools who focus on these problems so that they know where to get help when an incident comes across their desk (cyberbullying.com).

2. Promote awareness.

School staff should dedicate time in the classroom to educating students about all forms of bullying in order to raise awareness of the risks, possible school-based and legal penalties, and the emotional, psychological, reputational, and even physical harm that can result. Students should realize that even if they are not bullying others, they have a responsibility to ensure the safety of their peers. If they see bullying, they should do something about it. Schools should also instruct, model, and reward appropriate and helpful behavior, instead of only speaking out against and disciplining that which is inappropriate.

3. Cultivate open lines of communication.

Interaction between staff and students should conveniently and comfortably exist throughout the school. Staff should actively work towards building an atmosphere of trust and continuous dialogue regarding the issues youngsters must confront. Students must know and feel completely comfortable with at least one adult at school whom they can approach to discuss any struggle they are facing – offline or online.

4. Learn their names

Educators should take the time to learn the names of all of their students in order to build relationships, combat feelings of unimportance, promote connectedness and belongingness, and reinforce critical feelings of trust, mutual respect, and safety. This is a simple but very powerful way for educators to show that they truly care about each and every child in their school.

5. Develop stakeholder relationships.

Educators should work together with parents and others in the community, such as businesses, non-profits, law enforcement, and other youth professionals to properly address bullying and cyberbullying.

6. Instill hope

School staff should work to cultivate a strong sense of hope and positivity across the student body to counter negative messages from those who bully, and to help buffer typical adolescent stressors. The best educators demonstrate care about more than just the academic or athletic success of youth. Administrators, teachers, and support staff can come alongside all students to build them up, show compassion and empathy, give them assistance when needed, and keep them inspired toward a great future.

7. Build positive social norming campaigns

Focus attention on the majority of youth who do utilize their phones, social media, and other technology in acceptable and even positive ways. Promote the positive things that students are doing. Celebrate successes. Highlight and commend acts of kindness. Make clear that care and compassion is the norm at your school, and not the exception. And have a clear messaging strategy that gets the word out!

8. Enlist the help of students.

Many youngsters want to be actively involved in combatting cruelty and promoting positivity at their school. And they are typically best positioned to make the greatest impact! The peer group is a powerful influence on the attitudes, beliefs, and behaviors of adolescents at this stage of their development. High school leaders could talk to fellow students about these issues informally in the cafeteria during lunch or during a more structured assembly. Some could organize a presentation for others in small classroom–sized (20+) groups. The potential opportunities for student empowerment and involvement are endless!

Program staff should not only direct their tasks to the safety of children and young people. It is worth emphasizing that they should also build their own competences so that they themselves will not be the victims of cyberattacks. Research shows that teachers also experience cyberbullying from students, other employees, and even parents of students.

One in seven respondents said they had experienced cyberbullying and almost one in five said they knew of colleagues who had become victims. (Association of Teachers and Lecturers and the Teacher Support Network, 2009)

School employees should take the following steps to protect themselves and their personal information online (Childnet International for the Department for Children, Schools and Families, in consultation with the DCSF Cyberbullying Taskforce, 2009, p.19):

- Keeping passwords secret and protecting access to their accounts;
- Not friending pupils on personal social networking sites;
- Keeping personal phone numbers private and not using their own mobile phones to contact pupils or parents;

- Keeping phones secure while on school premises;
- Not posting information about themselves publicly that they wouldn't want employers, colleagues, pupils, or parents to see;
- Ensuring that rules regarding the use of technologies are consistently enforced;
- Not personally retaliating to any incident;
- Reporting any incident to the appropriate member of staff in a timely manner;
- Keeping any evidence of an incident.

Strategies and General Suggestions

Caring for safety at school should concern all those who are able to influence it. A list of general recommendations includes (Greene, 2005):

- Organizing trainings for teachers in the fields of violence and aggression, providing support to students, teaching psychological and social skills, undertaking preventive interventions, and reacting in crisis situations;
- Video monitoring or surveillance;
- Assigning personnel to be on duty during breaks;
- Including parents in deciding school policy, especially in regards to activities aimed at increasing the safety of students;
- Developing and disseminating clear expectations regarding behavior and principles, and establishing rules in consultation with parents and students, with consequences in case of non-compliance;
- Developing an overall crisis response procedure, including procedures related to violence at school;
- Nurturing the positive traditions of the school;
- Organizing educational activities for parents aimed at increasing their educational competences;
- Conducting integration activities in classes, including lessons devoted to mutual relations;
- Teaching children and teenagers the most important psychological and social skills as part of the curricula and implemented in classes within the framework of good educational prevention programs;
- Counteracting aggression and violence at school;
- Establishing peer programs, like peer support in learning, peer counselors, or peer mediators.

Before implementing a preventive program, a multi-aspect evaluation should be carried out. The assessment should cover areas related to problem identification, diagnosis of demand and readiness, conceptualization of the prevention program, implementation plans, and evaluation procedures. The school prevention program is a problem prevention program in which the whole school environment is the object of action. It assumes the implementation of goals by utilizing one the following strategies (Gwizdek & Sołtys, 2003).

The aim of the preventing program based on information strategy is to provide information on the effects of risky behaviors and to enable the making of rational choices. The strategy assumes that knowledge about the mechanisms and consequences of, for example, early drinking or sexual activity may be influenced by changes in attitudes and behavior of young people. Programs or school ant bulling polices bases only on tis strategies not very effective unless it is supplemented by other strategies, particularly the educational strategy (Smith et al., 2008)

For information programs to be of preventive significance, they must meet many conditions. The important thing here is the person providing information credibility, rapport with the class, ability to gain the student's trust, and their personality. The information they provide must be reliable, instructive, and presented in a manner adapted to the students' intellectual competence and knowledge. Participants should not be frightened or feel intimidated. The information strategy is implemented through mini lectures, films, themed conversations, discussions, charts, leaflets, stickers, etc.

Educational strategies should lead a prevention program. Their aim is to help in the development of important psychological and social skills, including the ability to build contacts with other people, cope with stress, resolve conflicts, and resist group pressure. As (Espelage & Hong, 2017) shows this strategy based on the fact that parents, and school administrators often learn about cyberbullying through websites which is not always good, because many of them do not take into account published research. It is worthy to emphasize to use resist on certain sources of information because for students and pupils educational strategy should give the ability to make rational choices and defend one's own opinions, aims to develop maturity and acceptance of ones' identity, encouraging a healthy lifestyle, and helping others.

Schools can implement educational strategies through blocks of psychoeducational exercises and games, workshops, and trainings.

Specific contextual strategies should be implemented by the school and the family (Mendez et al, 2009). Both environments should focus on encouraging children to develop their own particular interests, and suggest alternative, healthy ways of spending free time. Alternative strategies in preventive work are aimed at helping young people realize their interests and life goals in a healthy and socially acceptable way. This strategy is especially applicable to socially and educationally deprived children and youth groups (Szymańska, 2000). Engaging in alternative activities creates the opportunity to withdraw from risky behavior to focus on the new attractive proposal instead. Preventive activities carried out as part of the alternative strategy also allows valuable, additional information about students to be obtained, so providing tips for further preventive work.

Here following, some strategies that can be useful in cyberbullying prevention.

The aim of the environmental change strategy is to act on the child's entire environment in such a way as to cause a tendency to change and/or strengthen the social and psychological skills acquired through the educational strategy. Strategies for environmental change involve parents and the wider peer environment. The direction of work with parents includes education, and cooperating in and sharing responsibility for the implementation of preventive and educational tasks. Interactions with the peer environment mainly involve working with youth leaders towards self-help actions.

Diamanduros et al. (2008), recommended that even if schools have prevention programs in place, it is still likely that cyberbullying will occur. Therefore, it is necessary to have an intervention strategy as well. Schools need to be reactive as well as proactive.

The aim of intervention strategies is to help teachers and individual students identify and solve a specific crisis situation. It concerns first and second order prevention, that is, high and medium-high risk groups.

The main objective of these programs is to prevent bullying; however, schools must also establish disciplinary standards to address bullying behaviors should they occur. In doing so, many schools subscribe to two overarching approaches when bullying behaviors are reported: (1) a problem solving approach in which peer mediation and counseling are used to focus less on blame and/or punishment and more on positive peer interactions and environmental factors; and (2) a rules and sanctions approach in which school officials institute administrative policies and procedures ranging from "zero-tolerance" policies to a clear outline of punishments for bullies. (Ayers et al., 2012)

This strategy requires the teacher to have professional knowledge, appropriate personality predispositions, and the ability to secure the involvement and cooperation of parents. As part of this form of action, it is necessary to utilize the help of specialists. But some teachers perceptions of cyberbullying prevention and intervention strategies is not satisfying.

Most teachers indicated that cyber bullying has long lasting negative effects, and that it does not "toughen kids up." However, up to one of every four teachers indicated being neutral about or disagreeing about cyber bullying having long lasting negative effects, as well as being neutral or agreeing that cyber bullying "prepares students for 16 life." Nearly 60% of teachers were either unsure about or against implementing a formal bullying prevention program in their school. (Stauffer 2011, p. 15)

The intervention procedure in cases of cyberbullying used as the online security standard of educational institutions follows a number of steps (Lizut & Wrońska ed., 2018, pp. 27-35).

There are different actions that can be develop to tackle the cyberbullying phenomenon.

Actions Relating to the Event

These actions are related to:

- Acquisition of information and acceptance of the applicatio*n*. In the case of aggression against a child via the internet, the person reporting the problem may be a parent/legal guardian, a tutor of the IT lab in the facility, a concerned peer, or a witness to the event. Due to the potential, extremely negative effects of cyberbullying for the victim, every effort must be made to stop the act as quickly as possible.
- Determining the circumstances of the incident, analyzing the incident, and collecting and securing evidence. Responsible staff with appropriate technical knowledge should provide support to parents/legal guardians in the matter of securing relevant materials on a victim's private computer (screenshots, call records, emails, and instant messages) or secure them on the device belonging to the facility. Some cases of cyberbullying are complicated (spirals of aggression - cyberbullying in response to an earlier incident or to conflicts in the real world), thus

determining the circumstances of the event and the victim/offender can be difficult. The most thorough analysis of the situation should be sought.

- Identification of the perpetrator/perpetrators. Identifying the perpetrator of cyberbullying is extremely important, and determines the course of the further proceedings. In the case that the perpetrator is one of the charges of the institution, the consequences provided for under the school rules can be applied.

Actions Towards Participants in the Event

Changing the behavior of those who were somehow involved in cyberbullying is possible based on staged interactions with a responsible adult (e.g. a social educator, tutor, trainer, or psychologist) appropriate to the nature of the event and the particular role of each participant, be they victim, offender, or witness.

- Help for the victim of cyberbullying. Following a conversation with an educator, the victim should receive the message that the facility is able to effectively respond to cyberbullying and support students in difficult situations. In addition, they should receive advice on how to behave to ensure a sense of safety and not escalate the persecution. The method of confronting victim and perpetrator should not be used.
- Taking actions against the perpetrator of the cyberbullying is the responsibility of the institution. The perpetrator should receive an unequivocal message of the unacceptability of any form of violence, and details of the consequences of breaking the regulations, which will be applied to them. In addition, they must immediately stop the cyberbullying, remove any harmful material from the web, and determine ways to make amends to the victim. In the case where a group of perpetrators have taken part in the act of cyberbullying together, the procedure should be followed treating each offender individually, adjusting the conversation and disciplinary measures accordingly. The perpetrator should also be provided with psychological and pedagogical help where necessary. The main goal of professional help is to change the student's attitude and behavior, but at the same time avoiding their demoralization.
- Bystander protection. As we have previously highlighted in chapter 5, it is important to remember the role of bystanders in the cyberbullying event, and the consequences that they can experience as a result. It is

important to assure them a sense of security, and not to expose them to acts of violence enacted by the perpetrator. It is unacceptable to confront the witnesses with the perpetrator or to ostentatiously expose their role. Lack of attention to these basic safety rules can lead to follow-on acts of violence or the non-reporting of future incidents. It may also contribute to passiveness, and an unwillingness on the part of students to defend peers who are being victimized in the future.

Actions Relating to Institutions / Organizations / Assistance and Cooperation Services: Police, Court Family, Social Services

These actions involve:

- Responsibilities of the school and educational institutions in cooperation with the police and the family courts. Cyberbullying can fall into the parameters of various crimes, but mostly cases are prosecuted upon the request of the victim. In the event that parents legal guardians decide to refer a case to the police, the school can provide assistance, e.g. by directing parents to the appropriate unit. An educational institution should notify the family courts in situations where, despite the application of the due procedures and available educational measures, the perpetrator (the charge of the institution) continues actions that violate security, or when their parents/legal guardians refuse to cooperate with the institution. This is especially so when the educational institution is generally known for manifestations of demoralization. If necessary, it is recommended to use a specialized form of psychological care (in consultation with parents/legal guardians).
- Cooperation with internet service providers and operators of telecommunications networks.

Documenting and Monitoring Interventions

The documentation of cyberbullying should contain such details as: a description of the act, a list of persons participating, the evidence collected, the educational and disciplinary measures applied, the monitoring plan, and information collected from staff by the members of team engaged in the situation.

Due to the specificity of the problem (protection of bystanders, collaboration with perpetrators against victimization), documentation is recommended respecting the privacy of the participants and the confidentiality of the retained and processed data. Monitoring should be carried out systematically following the intervention to ensure the discontinuation of the behavior and the application of the measures of redress.

CONCLUSION

School climate is linked to the problem of bullying, in both its traditional form and cyberbullying. Some recent studies have shown that individuals who have been perpetrators of cyberbullying and those who have been victims both report a poorer school climate than other students not involved in the aggression (Patchin & Hinduja, 2010). These students failed to agree with statements to the effect that they "enjoyed going to school" or "feel safe at school". Students need an environment where they receive emotional support and develop self-esteem. This environment should also focus on academic and learning staff, and provide a clear indication of what is appropriate and what is not according to social norms online (Patchin & Hinduja, 2010). It also notes the emergence of cyberbullying as a school climate and safety issue (Adams, 2011).

REFERENCES

Adams, F., & Lawrance, G. (2011). Bullying Victims: The Effects Last into College. *American Secondary Education, 40*(1), 4-13. Available at: https://eric.ed.gov/?id=EJ951224

Anton-Erxleben, K., Kibriya, S., & Zhang, Y. (2016). Bullying as the main driver of lowperformance in schools: Evidence from Botswana, Ghana, and South Africa. *MPRA*, Available at: https://mpra.ub.uni-muenchen.de/75555/1/MPRA_paper_75555.pdf

Ayers, S. L., Wagaman, A., Geiger, J. M., Bermudez-Parsai, M., & Hedberg, E. C. (2012). *Examining School-Based Bullying Interventions Using Multilevel Discrete Time Hazard Modeling*. Available at: https://www.ncbi.nlm.nih.gov/pmc/articles/PMC3896994/

Benders, D. S. (2012). *School Climate and Cyber-Bullying*. Available at: https://papers.ssrn.com/sol3/papers.cfm?abstract_id=2011818

Berkowitz, R., Iachini, A., Moore, H., Capp, G., Astor, R. A., Pitner, R., & Benbenishty, R. (2017). *School Climate. Oxford Research Encyclopedias*. Available at: https://oxfordre.com/education/view/10.1093/acrefore/9780190264093.001.0001/acrefore-9780190264093-e-89

Borkowska, A. (2014). E-zagrożenia nowym wyzwaniem dla służb społecznych, Warszawa: Wydawnictwo Wyższej Szkoły Pedagogicznej.

Borkowska, A., Szymańska, J., & Witkowska, M. (2012). *Przeciwdziałanie agresji i przemocy w szkole*. Warszawa: Ośrodek Rozwoju Edukacji.

Diamanduros, T., Downs, E., & Jenkins, S. J. (2008). *The role of school psychologists in the assessment, prevention, and intervention of cyberbullying*. Available at: https://onlinelibrary.wiley.com/doi/abs/10.1002/pits.20335

Espelage, D. L., Polanin, J. R., & Low, S. K. (2014). Understanding School Climate, Aggression, Peer Victimization, and Bully Perpetration: Contemporary Science, Practice, and Policy. *School Psychology Quarterly, 29*(3), 233-237. Available at: https://www.researchgate.net/publication/265420198_Understanding_School_Climate_Aggression_Peer_Victimization_and_Bully_Perpetration_Contemporary_Science_Practice_and_Policy

Greene, M. B. (2005). Reducing violence and aggression in schools. *Trauma, Violence & Abuse, 6*(3), 236-253. Available at: https://journals.sagepub.com/doi/10.1177/1524838005277406

Gwizdek, B., & Sołtys, E. (2003). *Strategie*. Wydawnictwo: Remedium.

Hawkins, J. D., Farrington, D. P., & Catalano, R. F. (1999). Reducing Violence through the Schools. In Violence in American schools: a new perspective. Cambridge University Press.

Hernik, K., Solon-Lipiński, M., & Stasiowski, J. (2012). *Współpraca szkół z podmiotami zewnętrznymi*. Raport z badania otoczenia instytucjonalnego przedszkoli, szkół podstawowych i gimnazjów. Available at: http://eduentuzjasci.pl/publikacje-ee-lista/raporty/160-raport-z-badania/wspolpraca-szkol-z-podmiotami-zewnetrznymi/743-wspolpraca-szkol-z-podmiotami-zewnetrznymi-raport-z-badania-otoczenia-instytucjonalnego-przedszkoli-szkol-podstawowych-i-gimnazjow.html

Hinduja, S., & Patchin, J. W. (2010). Cyberbullying and self-esteem. *Journal of School Health, 80*(2), 614-621. Available at: https://www.researchgate.net/publication/284484160_Cyberbullying_and_self-esteem_Journal_of_school

Hinduja, S., & Patchin, J. W. (2012). *School Climate 2.0: Preventing Cyberbullying*. Corwin. doi:10.4135/9781506335438

Hinduja, S., & Patchin, J. W. (2014). *Cyberbullying Identification, Prevention and Response*. Cyberbullying Research Center. Available at: https://cyberbullying.org/Cyberbullying-Identification-Prevention-Response.pdf

Hinduja, S., & Patchin, J. W. (2015). *Bullying Beyond the Schoolyard: Preventing and Responding to Cyberbullying* (2nd ed.). Thousand Oaks, CA: Sage Publications.

Hinduja, S., & Patchin, J. W. (2018). *Developing a Positive School Climate: Top Ten Tips to Prevent Bullying and Cyberbullying*. Cyberbullying Research Center. Available at: https://cyberbullying.org/developing-a-positive-school-climate-to-prevent-bullying-and-cyberbullying

Jessor, R., Van Den Bos, J., Vanderryn, J., Costa, F. M., & Turbin, M. S. (1995). Protective factors in adolescent problem behavior: Moderator effects and developmental change. *Developmental Psychology, 31*(6), 923-933. doi:10.1037/0012-1649.31.6.923

Juvonen, J., & Gross, E. F. (2008). Extending the School Grounds? Bullying Experiences in Cyberspace. *Journal of School Health, 78*(9), 496-505. Available at: https://www.ncbi.nlm.nih.gov/pubmed/18786042

Kamieniecki, W., Bochnek, M., Tanaś, M., Wrońska, A., Lange, R., Fila, M., . . . Konopczyński, F. (2017). *Raport z badaniaNastolatki 3.0*. Warszawa: NASK. Available at: https://akademia.nask.pl/publikacje/Raport_z_badania_Nastolatki_3_0.pdf

Lizut, J., & Wrońska, A. (Eds.). (2018). *Standard bezpieczeństwa on-line placówek oświatowych*. Warszawa: NASK. Available at: https://akademia.nask.pl/publikacje/ost_Standard_bezpieczenstwa_online_placowek_oswiatowych.pdf

Lopata, A., & Nowicki, A. (2014). Pre-service Teacher Beliefs on the Antecedents to Bullying: A Concept Mapping Study. *Canadian Journal of Education / Revue canadienne de l'éducation, 37*(4), 1-25. Available at: https://files.eric.ed.gov/fulltext/EJ1057957.pdf

Ma, X. (2002). Bullying in Middle School: Individual and School Characteristics of Victims and Offenders. *School Effectiveness & School Improvement, 13*(1), 63. Available at: https://www.tandfonline.com/doi/abs/10.1076/sesi.13.1.63.3438

Mendez, J. L., Carpenter, J. L., LaForett, D. R., & Cohen, J. S. (2009). *Parental Engagement and Barriers to Participation in a Community-Based Preventive Intervention.* Springer Science+Business Media, LLC. Available at: https://www.researchgate.net/profile/ Julia_Mendez/publication/26298490_Parental_Engagement_and_Barriers_to_Participation_in_a_CommunityBased_Preventive_Intervention/links/0deec530f400c0497b000000/Parental-Engagement-and-Barriers-to-Participation-in-a-Community-Based-Preventive-Intervention.pdf

Noam, G. G., & Fiore, N. (2004). *Relationships across multiple settings.* Available at: https://onlinelibrary.wiley.com/doi/abs/10.1002/yd.87

Notar, C. E., Padgett, S., & Roden, J. (2013). Cyberbullying: Resources for Intervention and Prevention. *Universal Journal of Educational Research, 1*(3), 133-145. Available at: https://files.eric.ed.gov/fulltext/EJ1053892.pdf

Obuchowska, I. (1996). *Drogi dorastania - psychologia rozwojowa okresu dorastania dla rodziców i wychowawców.* Warszawa WSiP.

Ostaszewski, K. (2016). *Standardy profilaktyki, Pracownia Profilaktyki Młodzieżowej.* Warszawa: Zakład Zdrowia Publicznego Instytut Psychiatrii i Neurologii.

Redmond, P., Lock, J. V., & Smart, V. (2018). Pre-service teachers' perspectives of cyberbullying. *Computers & Education.* Available at: https://www.sciencedirect.com/science/article/pii/S0360131517302610?via%3Dihub

Rubio, C. M. (2009). Effective teachers –Professional and personal skills. *ENSAYOS, Revista de la Facultad de Educación de Albacete, 24.* Available at: https://dialnet.unirioja.es/descarga/articulo/3282843.pdf

Schneider, S. K., O'Donnell, L., Stueve, A., & Coulter, R. (2012). Cyberbullying, School Bullying, and Psychological Distress: A Regional Census of High School Students. *Am J Public Health, 102*(1), 171–177. Available at: https://www.ncbi.nlm.nih.gov/pmc/articles/PMC3490574/#bib8

Smith, P. K., Smith, C., Osborn, R., & Samara, M. (2008). A content analysis of school anti-bullying policies: progress and limitations. *Educational Psychology in Practice, 24*(1), 1–12. Available at: https://www.researchgate.net/publication/233196039_A_content_analysis_of_school_anti-bullying_policies_Progress_and_limitations

Stauffer, S. V. (2011). *High School Teachers' Perceptions of CyberBullying Prevention and Intervention Strategies*. Brigham Young University. Available at: https://scholarsarchive.byu.edu/cgi/viewcontent.cgi?article=3777&context=etd

Ttofi, M. M., & Farringto, T. P. (2011). Effectiveness of school-based programs to reduce bullying: a systematic and meta-analytic review. *Journal of Experimental Criminology, 7*(1), 27–56. Available at: https://link.springer.com/article/ 10.1007/s11292-010-9109-1

Williams, K. R., & Guerra, N. (2007). *Prevalence and Predictors of Internet Bullying*. Available at: https://www.jahonline.org/article/S1054-139X(07)00362-X/fulltext

KEY TERMS AND DEFINITIONS

Protective Factors in Students' Development: Factors positively affecting the social functioning of students, protecting against the effects of negative behaviors.

School Climate: Quality and character of school life, based on rules and interactions between students, parents, and school personnel.

School Violence: Violence carried out in school or other educational institution. It mostly is connected with the functioning in school, relations between students and people working in schools.

Chapter 10
A Cyberbullying Portfolio for School Social Educators

Gilberto Marzano
Rezekne Academy of Technologies, Latvia

Joanna Lizut
Janusz Korczak Pedagogical University in Warsaw, Poland

ABSTRACT

In this chapter, a curriculum for school social educators will be presented and discussed. It aims to provide them with basic competences to combat cyberbullying and conduct internet safety programs in schools. In the previous chapters, multifarious aspects related to cyberbullying have been highlighted. Literature is rich in analysis and experiments that, nowadays, are being conducted everywhere, not only in Western countries. Cyberbullying is a global phenomenon, although there are differences depending on cultural attitudes (e.g., gender aspects and other factors related to the perception and evaluation of online harassment). Cyberbullying is closely connected to technology. Among human beings, harassing, harming, and defaming others is not a recent habit, but technology has exploded the scale of the harassment, harming, and defamation with hugely disruptive consequences. To combat the effect of the malicious use of technology, professional experts are necessary that should also be educators, since they should work inside the school. Cyber safety competences should be included in the curriculum of social educators in the same way as are competences to sustain children with behavioral disturbance, support mentally ill persons, assist elderly persons, rehabilitate drug and alcohol addicts, integrate migrants, and so on. From the experience of running a training course for social workers in Poland on cyber threats, and from comparison with other teaching-learning practices on cyberbullying prevention, a portfolio of competence has been defined.

DOI: 10.4018/978-1-5225-8076-8.ch010

INTRODUCTION

Technology is a means to grow people's livability, but there are also those who would exploit technology for malicious purposes, such as cybercriminals and cyberbullies.

The central idea of this book is that cyberbullying is a collateral effect of digital technology.

According to this perspective, cyberbullying represents a two-faceted phenomenon. The first facet is the appropriation of technology by bullies, namely individuals who intentionally harass and persecute others. The second is the opportunity of a vast audience for individuals to externalize their most intimate feelings, often without being completely aware of the consequences of their externalizations. These intimate feelings could be a grudge, animosity, envy, jealousy, rage, or scorn, as well as revenge and retaliation for real or imagined offenses. Before the internet, interactions among individuals were limited and, in many aspects, controlled. Nevertheless, the effects of calumny and defamation were anyway serious and understood. Nowadays, unlimited and easy online interactions and relative anonymity, as well as the uncontrolled permanence of internet content, are creating new issues and potential damages.

The internet is changing our society at a global level, and in ways, in the long-term, that are unpredictable at this time.

Consider that in many respects, cyberspace is a virtual copy of the physical world. Cyberspace can be imagined as an immense city, complete with its neighborhoods, shops, supermarkets, newspapers, cultural centers, entertainment places, offices, schools, and so on. In the cyberspace, one can socialize by establishing and maintaining relationships with other people, buying and selling goods, visiting art galleries and museums, watching shows and movies, reading books and newspapers, listening to music, and playing alone or in a group. But, unlike what happens in the physical world, in the virtual world, the potential interactions with people and things are countless and immediate. In cyberspace, an individual sitting in front of a computer or using a smartphone can move quickly everywhere, get information, see and use things at distance. On the internet, mobility is not a problem. Just a few clicks are needed to travel, see new places, and meet friends. Downloading and uploading texts, photos, and videos are extremely simple. More difficult is cancelling what has been uploaded. Sometimes it is virtually impossible.

As in the physical world, dangers can lurk also in cyberspace, but there are some differences. The most remarkable difference is that in the virtual world it is possible to frequent virtual places that in real life, for decency and shame, most would avoid. One can move on the internet without being recognized and access any available content.

Accordingly, to combat the various risks of cyberspace, it is first of all necessary to know them in depth. For each risk, the right strategy to react should be defined. It is not easy to do that. On one hand, specific knowledge is needed, because issues of internet safety are different from those of internet addiction, and different again from those concerning online harassment. On the other hand, those who stay on the internet are simultaneously exposed to the full range of risks.

EDUCATING TO PREVENT

Education is broadly considered to be the key to diminishing the occurrences and effects of cyberbullying (Chang, 2010; Cremin & Bevington, 2017; Meredith, 2010; Nelson, Palonsky, & McCarthy, 2017; Simmons & Bynum, 2014).

The educational perspective is broadly agreed by researchers. They argue that educational programs should be designed and run in order to best prepare children to avoid and deal with cyberbullying and its related issues (Couvillon & Ilieva, 2011; Jones, Mitchell & Walsh, 2014; Meter & Bauman, 2015; Navarro, Yubero & Larrañaga, 2015; Rice et al., 2015; Smith, Thompson & Davidson, 2014). Moreover, many anti-cyberbullying educational programs share the idea that it is crucial promoting and raising children and adolescent awareness on the positive use of the internet and social networks. This is the case of *ConRed* (Casas, Del Rey & Ortega-Ruiz, 2018) an anti-cyberbullying educational program that addresses three key goals:

- Educate about ethical and legal aspects in online activities;
- Educate about the risks and benefits of social networks and digital communications;
- Provide example of how the peer community cannot accept certain online behaviors.

Another element that is common to all cyberbullying prevention programs is the involvement of teachers and their active contribution in the programs' activities. In fact, teachers are believed to play a fundamental role since they are in daily contact with students and have the opportunity to interact with them. In the literature, many authors, although of different hues, also share Parkay's belief that teaching is the world's most important profession:

Teaching is exciting, rewarding, and uplifting; teachers receive great satisfaction from making a difference in their students' lives. In today's climate of accountability, high-stakes testing, and new federal programs such as Race to the Top,[1] however, becoming a successful teacher requires high levels of professionalism and commitment (Parkay, 2012, i).

However, the real situation in schools can be quite different. Many teachers nowadays have a hard life. To be a teacher is a very complex profession, since teachers need to deal with classroom issues, students, parents, the curriculum, and supplementary extracurricular activities. Moreover, it also happens that teachers are themselves bullied and cyberbullied by students and their parents. The most common forms of attack from students are obscene or inappropriate comments, refusal to obey, repeated lying, mocking, insulting, offensive gestures, and so on. This is a global problem (Chen & Astor, 2008; Mc Mahon et al., 2014; Moon, Morash, Jang, & Jeong, 2015).

The investigation conducted by Riley, Duncan, and Edwards (2012) shows that teachers have to face parents that shout, raise their fists, scream, storm into the classroom, accuse them of giving wrong evaluations of their children, and sometimes even accuse them of pedophilia. This study is the result of three surveys (2005, 2007, & 2009) carried out in Australian schools. The authors also underline that the fact that the majority of respondents had experienced one or more forms of bullying suggests that bullying is prevalent in the workplace but is largely invisible, except to the target (Riley, Duncan, & Edwards, 2011).

A nationwide research carried out in 2016 in the Czech Republic found that many teachers were cyberbullied by students and their parents (Kopecký & Szotkowski, 2017). Table 1 shows the distribution of the perpetrators.

Although newspapers emphasize many cases of teachers being bullied and cyberbullied by students, and *The Telegraph* reports that, in the UK, one in three teachers has claimed that *derogatory comments* have been posted about them on social media websites by both parents and children (Swinford, 2018), teacher victimization (Martinez, McMahon, Espelage, Anderman, Reddy, & Sanchez, 2016) is a relatively new area of study in education. Research on this topic is still limited, particularly in the USA (Bounds & Jenkins, 2016).

Table 1. Perpetrators of cyberbullying of teachers

Perpetrator	Details	Number (n)	Relative frequency (%)
Pupil or group of pupils	Pupil or a group of pupils, known by the victim. The victim teaches them.	389	34.92
	Pupil or group of pupils, known by the victim. The victim does not teach them.	35	3.14
	Pupil or group of pupils from the school where the victim teaches but does not know them in person.	20	1.80
	Pupil or group of pupils from another school. Not the school where the victim teaches.	5	0.45
Parents of the pupil	Parents of the pupil	90	8.08
Colleague of the victim	Colleague – not his/her superior	30	2.69
	Colleague – his/her superior (e.g. headmaster)	10	0.90
Combination	Pupils and their parents	24	2.15
	Colleagues from work and parents	7	0.63
Perpetrators not identified		272	24.42
Other people	Individuals who are not at the school, for example an ex-partner, neighbour, acquaintance etc.	137	12.30
N/A		95	8.52
Total		**1,114**	

Source: Kopecký & Szotkowski (2017, p. 11)

However, *The Indicators of School Crime and Safety 2016* published by the National USA Center for Education Statistics reports that:

During the 2011–12 school year, the percentage of public school teachers who reported being threatened with injury during the previous 12 months ranged from 5 percent in Oregon to 18 percent in Louisiana (Table 5.2). The percentage who reported being physically attacked ranged from 3 percent in Alabama, Mississippi, North Dakota, Oregon, and Tennessee to 11 percent in Wisconsin (Musu-Gillette, 2017, p. 50).

A case that occurred in Italy in 2015 at the San Francesco al Campo school in Turin, is emblematic. In essence, what occurred was that 22 students filmed their professors and posted videos denigrating and mocking them on WhatsApp. What makes this case remarkable, and the first case of its kind in a European country, however, was the reaction of families to the disciplinary measures taken by the school against them. The parents of the students protested in mass, threatening legal action against the school for violation of privacy. This fact was reported by newspapers at a national level (Micali, 2015).

In the United Kingdom, the *National Association of School Teachers Union* (NASUWT) has conducted a survey since 2014 to monitor abuse against teachers through new technologies. The data collected from 60% of the almost 1,500 NASUWT members reveals that teachers have had comments or information posted about them on social networks relating to their work as teachers (Sellgren, 2019). This is up from 21% in 2014. Of these, nearly half (48%) of respondents reported that the remarks had been posted by pupils, 40% said they had been put up by parents, and 12% said that both parents and pupils had been responsible. The findings show that 62% said pupils had posted insulting comments, while just over a third (34%) said students had taken photos or videos without consent, a third (33%) received remarks about their performance as teachers, 9% had faced allegations from pupils about inappropriate behavior, and 8% had been subjected to threatening behavior (The Guardian, 2015). Recently, another survey from the NASUWT (2017) revealed that the overwhelming majority of teachers (82%) had experienced verbal abuse or threats from pupils outside school premises, while almost one in ten (9%) had been subject to violence or physical threats. A similar number (8%) had received online abuse through social media sites or via email. The survey also found that disruption and poor behavior are impacting on the time teachers spend on teaching in the classroom. Nearly a third (30%) of teachers reported that up to half an hour was lost each day as a result of poor behavior. More than one in ten (12%) teachers reported losing an hour or more of teaching time each day.

The situation is similar in the USA. Based on the nationally representative *Schools and Staffing Survey* (SASS) 2011-2012, approximately 10% of K-12 public school teachers in the United States received a threat in the prior 12 months, and 6% reported being physically attacked. The effects of teacher-directed violence are far-reaching, and affect not only the victimized teacher themselves but the larger community as a whole (Huang, Eddy, & Camp, 2017).

Although research data is rather poor, it is sufficient to talk with teachers to realize that there are many problems in schools. On a global level, school is facing the same seismic change in the lifestyle of families and the ongoing transformation of society as a whole. In some European countries, such as Italy, France, and Spain, there are classes in which the majority of pupils are immigrants. Sometimes, due to the demographic distribution within cities, school buildings are not sufficient to satisfy the number of students whereas, in rural areas, there is often a lack of students to fill classes. There are also differences between schools based on their geographical location, and in many cities teachers are obliged to teach in particularly degraded and violent neighborhoods.

Furthermore, teachers complain their low salaries and the low prestige of teaching profession. In the USA, teachers' salaries have been declining since the 1990s and a recent study found that in a number of states teachers made less than unskilled workers:

Colorado, teachers with a graduate degree and 10 years of experience make less than a trucker in the state. In Oklahoma, teachers with 15 years of experience and a master's degree make less than sheet metal workers. And teachers in Georgia with 10 years of experience and a graduate degree make less than a flight attendant in the state. (Boser & Straus, 2014, p. 1).

A recent article denounced the condition of teachers in the USA reporting and commenting the case of Hope Brown a 52-year-old high school history teacher who to supplement her $55,000 annual salary has a second job utilizing the metal detectors and wrangling guests at Lexington's Rupp Arena and makes $60 donating plasma twice in one week (Reilly, 2018).

Moreover, teaching is known to be a highly stressful profession (Arnup & Bowles, 2016; Skaalvik & Skaalvik, 2015). Teacher stress has been linked with adverse professional outcomes, including burnout, absenteeism, stress, and attrition (von der Embse, Kilgus, Solomon, Bowler, & Curtiss, 2015) and is global issue (Lindqvist, Nordänger, & Carlsson, 2014; den Brok, Wubbels, & Van Tartwijk, 2017; Gallant & Riley, 2017).

In this climate, it is difficult to imagine how teachers could also be able to bear the load of carrying out anti-cyberbullying programs. Furthermore, teachers are less and less motivated. There are a large number of precarious teachers, and their turnover is high. All of these are elements that negatively affect the implementation of continuous anti-bullying and anti-cyberbullying educational programs. Furthermore, there is the problem of teachers' skills. To run an anti-cyberbullying program that involves the whole school and the parents of students too, full-time specialized personnel are necessary.

There are certainly numerous teachers who have the passion to carry out anti-cyberbullying programs, but do these teachers actually have the time to do it? How can one guarantee the continuity of a program if is essentially conducted by volunteers? Finally, there is the problem of the experts who should support the anti-cyberbullying interventions. Who really are these experts? How did they become an expert? Who evaluated and validated their skills and competences?

Those who work in the field of social services must possess a professional qualification acquired from an educational institution such as a vocational college or a university. Why shouldn't those who must operate in the definition and conduct of anti-cyberbullying programs also not possess a similar specific specialization? Our idea is that it is appropriate to think of *ad hoc* professional figures, within the sphere of social educators, to whom to entrust the development of programs and initiatives in schools to prevent and combat cyberbullying.

It is well known that those who work in the field of social services must possess a professional degree achieved attending studies at educational institutions such as vocational schools or universities. We are persuaded that, likewise, those who design and run anti-cyberbullying programs should possess a specific degree. Our idea is that ad hoc professional figures should be created. This would be a specific type of social educator, employed in schools in order to develop programs and initiatives for preventing and combating cyberbullying.

AN EXPERIENCE OF TRAINING SOCIAL WORKERS ON CYBER THREATS

In November 2012, the Janusz Korczak Pedagogical University in Warsaw and the Rezekne Academy of Technologies started the two-year project, *Threats of cyberspace - new competences of a social worker*. This European Union funded project was aimed at implementing an innovative educational program targeted at social workers. The program was designed to provide social workers with new competences on cyberspace threats. An experimental curriculum was developed by a team of experts including psychologists, social pedagogues, computer scientists, social anthropologists, and social rehabilitators. A training course was designed and run twice involving a selected number of social workers. The idea was to professionalize social workers, providing them with knowledge on:

- Threats of emerging forms of internet addictions;
- Threats of online harassment and related physical and psychological consequences;
- Social educational practices for cyber safety.

Essentially, learning units were developed focusing on the following topics:

- Mental and physical health threats;
- Social and educational dangers;
- Risks associated with addiction;
- Cybercrimes and online harassment.

The target of the project were social workers already providing services at public organizations.

Training activities were organized as face-to-face lessons for a total of 50 hours.

Cyberbullying and cyber addiction had been a central part of the program along with pedagogical aspects. Nevertheless, the training program was in large part decided by psychologists who focused on the risks of cyber addiction and related coping strategies.

Great attention has been paid to video games and consequences on health deriving from their compulsive use. The fact that an excessive amount of time spent on the computer can provoke physical problems, as well as cause the reduction of cognitive abilities, was extensively discussed. The part of the course dedicated to digital technologies in schools and their pedagogical implications was particularly innovative. Ample attention was given to social networks and how young people experience the use of digital technologies. In particular, problems related to virtual identity and behavior on social networks were illustrated and argued.

In regards to cyberbullying, the most widespread technological solutions were presented and some exemplary cases were discussed.

Overall, participants evaluated the project as being particularly useful, since it provided them with new knowledge and new experiences. Furthermore, they appreciated the multidisciplinary approach, due to the different disciplinary specializations of the trainers.

The didactic activity with social workers showed some aspects of particular interest. A very important point was the fact that, although participants were very interested in the training content, they believed that the skills acquired through the course would not be expendable in their professional field. Except in the case of social workers involved in the support of children with cognitive deficits or in activities with children with behavioral disorders, participants did not see any direct use of the course contents. We therefore failed one of the main objectives of the project. In fact, one of the project's main aims was the professionalization of social workers in order to qualify them to support schools in facing risks connected with digital technologies. The selection of the participants had taken this element into account. However, many of them did not fully understand the motivations of the project and later, during the training activity, discovered that they were involved in a new professional activity that they were not interested in undertaking.

From the experience of the project, a few key elements emerged that led us to the idea of defining a new specialization for social educators:

1. Prevention of cyberbullying requires the use of specialized personnel with multidisciplinary skills.
2. The aforementioned skills should be acquired through a theoretical-practical training and should be appropriately validated.
3. It would not be easy to convert professional staff already employed and motivate them to change their field of activity.

The fact that, in the project, the point of view of psychologists was dominant alerted us to the risk of defining an educational program that is oriented too much on only one discipline, however important it may be.

At the end of the project, it was clear that it would be necessary to resolve weaknesses found in its development, and seek new sustainable solutions.

However, some points were clear:

1. The training activity should be contextualized, e.g., content should be adapted to the context where the acquired new skills would be used.
2. The amount of 50 training hours was insufficient.
3. Technological and legal competences should be more extensively developed.
4. Procedures for evaluating and validating the acquired skills should be defined.

From this critical analysis of the project, the idea took form of creating a specific curriculum for social educators in cyber social education.

CYBER SCHOOL SOCIAL EDUCATORS

Social pedagogy is both a theoretical discipline and a professional field (McDermid, Holmes, Ghate, Trivedi, Blackmore, & Baker, 2016). Drawing on a range of social science disciplines, it is principally concerned with practices that facilitate "the integration of individuals into a society, and the fulfilment of their potential" (Cameron, 2016, 203).

In general, a social educator (or a social pedagogue) is an independent, and recognized, professional figure linked to the scope of the social professions. In Europe, depending on the different countries, we can distinguish two main categories of social educators: a regulated profession class of workers and a recognized professional category of workers (Aieji, 2011). Figure 1 shows the three levels in the social work area.

In many European countries, social educators follow professional bachelors training of between three and four years and sometimes further postgraduate study. They are employed to work in a range of social welfare contexts, including adult social care, youth work, the justice and probation service, in addition to child welfare, and early childhood services. They can also give support to school.

The main objective of a social educator at school is to help implement the capability of student to study as well to ensure their safety creating the conditions for their positive socialization and civic maturity (Kelly et al., 2015; Jaffe, Floersch, Longhofer, & Winograd, 2017; Payne, 2015). Indeed,

Figure 1. The three levels in the social work area
Source: Aieji, 2011, p. 20

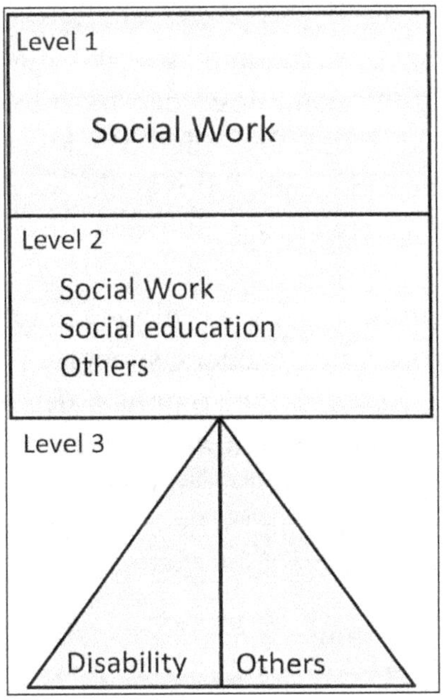

school social work is a well-known concept in the Anglophone countries, especially in the USA. The profession of school social work has been practiced in an array of public schools across the United States since the early 1900s with the establishment of visiting teacher services in New York, Chicago, Boston, and Harford, Connecticut. Over the past century it has helped shape and support the USA public educational system on a micro, mezzo, and macro level (Nair & Power, 2017).

According to Constable:

School social workers practice in the space where children, families, schools, and communities encounter one another, where hopes can fail, where gaps exist, and where education can break down. (Constable, 2009, 4)

Five job dimensions have been used to describe the tasks and responsibilities typically associated with school social work practice (Constable, Massat, McDonald, & Flynn, 2006):

- Relationships with and services to children and families;
- Relationships with and services to teachers and school staff;
- Services to other school personnel;
- Community services;
- Administrative and professional tasks.

However, school social work literature seems to ignore the digital revolution and the impact that digital technology can have to school social workers' practice. The systematic review by Allen-Meares, Montgomery, and Kim (2013) conducted in the USA on school social work interventions doesn't include the use of social networking sites or online collaborative tools and doesn't mention cyberbullying.

On the other hand, current anti-cyberbullying intervention programs, don't involve school social worker but teachers, supported by experts most of them are psychologists and lawyers, and also police officers.

In general, school social workers are concentrated to support children with cognitive disabilities, to help the integration of children of immigrants, to sustain students with serious family problems, to intervene as supervisors and/or mediators, and so on. This perspective is well described by Sosa, Alvarez and Cox:

[...] school social workers face a complex working environment in which educational outcome are of primary importance, not social service.

[...] the skilled school social worker recognizes the political environment of school settings and utilizes his or her relationship and rapport-building skill set to bridge differences and create coalitions mobilized to support student and families. Of particular interest for school social workers are those marginalized populations that have traditionally faced substandard academic institutions, dilapidated facilities, and inexperienced teachers, all contributing to poor educational outcomes. (Sosa, Alvarez, & Cox, 2016, 13)

In their book, authors mentioned the term cyberbullying marginally without any reference to the rich literature on this subject.

As a consequence, if entrusting teachers with the responsibility for anti-cyberbullying interventions could appear to be problematic, entrusting school social workers with that responsibility seems even more complicated. In this regard, despite its limitations, the experience of the project developed in Poland has been illuminating confirming the difficulties of involving social workers in preventing and contrast cyberspace threats..

However, cyberbullying prevention clearly appears should be a prerogative of school social workers. Indeed, is not the safety of the school environment one their commitments?

It is acknowledged that school social workers have important roles "in the schools' early and appropriate response to crises and threats to safety" (Constable, Massat, McDonald, & Flynn, 2006, 619).

Seven characteristics have been individualized for effective school safety intervention (Astor, Meyer, Benbenishty, Marachi, & Rosemond, 2005):

1. Raise the awareness and responsibility of students, teachers and parents regarding the types of violence in their schools;
2. Create clear guidelines and rules for the school community;
3. Target the various social systems in the school and define procedures to be followed by the school community before, during, and after violent events;
4. Focus on getting school staff, students and parents involved in the program;
5. Fit easily into the normal flow and mission of the school;

6. Involve school staff and parents in planning, implementing, and sustain the program;
7. Increase monitoring and supervision in non-classroom areas.

The above characteristic are so much generic that can be adopted in an anti-cyberbullying program. However, to involve school social workers in school-wide anti-cyberbullying interventions, the competences of school social workers should be improved and include the professional use of digital technologies and many other basic knowledge related to the digital domain. Nevertheless, nowadays, school social workers should possess digital competence regardless their involvement in cyberbullying prevention. In fact, computer programs are used for dyslexia (Benmarrakchi, Kafi, Elhore, & Haie, 2017; Zikl et al., 2015) as well as for the improvement of cognitive abilities of autistic children (Boucenna et al., 2014; Hardy, Ogden, Newman, & Cooper, 2016). Furthermore, in the near future the use of digital technologies in the sector of social rehabilitation, namely social telerehabilitation) will increasingly spread (Marzano, 2018).

THE PORTFOLIO OF COMPETENCES FOR A CYBER SCHOOL SOCIAL EDUCATOR

School social workers are frequently leaders in providing crisis intervention in traumatic events that take place in schools or in the community to which the school belongs. They should be prepared to respond appropriately to traumatic stress and *Posttraumatic stress disorder* (*PTSD*) that can be developed after a person is exposed to a traumatic event, such as homicide, suicide, accidental death as well as sexual assault and gang-related violence (Astor, Meyer, Benbenishty, Marachi, & Rosemond, 2005).

In the *Diagnostic and Statistical Manual of Mental Disorders (DSM-5) by* American Psychiatric Association (2013), PTSD has been included in a new category, Trauma and Stressor-Related Disorders, and the Criterion A reports that PTSD occurs when a person is exposed to death, threatened death, actual or threatened serious injury, or actual or threatened sexual violence, in the following way(s):

- Direct exposure;
- Witnessing the trauma;

- Learning that a relative or close friend was exposed to a trauma;
- Indirect exposure to aversive details of the trauma, usually in the course of professional duties (e.g., first responders, medics).

Recently, the most restrictive elements of the definition of traumatic stress contained in the DSM-5 begin to be abandoned. The U.S. Government's Substance Abuse and Mental Health Services Administration considers individual trauma as the result:

[...] from an event, series of events, or set of circumstances that is experienced by an individual as physically or emotionally harmful or threatening and that has lasting adverse effects on the individual's functioning and physical, social, emotional, or spiritual well-being. (SAMHSA, 2014, 7)

By the above definition, a traumatic event must not only be an event that involves serious threat to live or injury and falls outside the individual normal experience: also an event that produces severe distress and harm to the social and emotional sphere of a person can be considered a traumatic event.

Accordingly, since the SAMHSA definition can encompass cyberbullying emotional harms and threats, it would be legitimate that competences and skills of school social workers include digital media competences and cyberbullying prevention.

In particular, the figure of a cyber school social educator – we prefer to use the term *educator* than *worker* – should be related to three main basic scopes (Table 2):

- Cyberbullying understanding, this encompasses knowledge about the phenomenon as well as its multifarious dimensions.
- Educational processes, they encompass both theoretical and practical knowledge of educational models as well as teaching-learning practices that can support the implementation and running of cyberbullying prevention programs.
- Some sectorial knowledge, this includes knowledge in specific fields such as anti-cyberbullying law and statutes, digital learning technologies, and social networking tools.

A crucial competence for school social educators concerns the preparation of lessons using digital technology. In fact, online teaching-learning tools can

Table 2. Basic scopes and basic competences of a cyber school social educator

Basic scopes	Basic competences and skills
Cyberbullying and cyber threats understanding	• Carrying out systematic review of the phenomenon at school and data analysis; • Deep knowledge of the different forms of cyberbullying • Expertise on social networking sites • Awareness of the roles of bystanders and parents • Familiarity with quality assessment processes • Knowledge of the school world and dynamics • Leadership and team work • Change management
Educational processes	• Educational models (in general) • Educational practices used in anti-cyberbullying programs • Peer learning model • Community learning • Collaborative learning • Digital social learning • Parent-training
Sectorial knowledge	• Legal implication • School anti-cyberbullying statutes • Use of parent control software • Use of filters and block • Use of online collaborative tools • Creation and use of wiki, blogs, forum, apps • Use of messenger apps • How the internet works • Anti-cyberbullying coping • Digital dependences

Source: author's own elaboration

be useful to involve parents and teaching staff in anti-cyberbullying initiatives giving them the possibility to participate at distance and during their free time from job duties. But preparing lesson using digital tools is significantly different from preparing traditional lessons. It is not sufficient to master digital applications but new concepts are needed related to teaching-learning in a digital environment, e.g., how to motivate learners to don't quit learning activity. Competence in preparing online lessons is especially required when peer anti-cyberbullying programs are run. Cyber leader and cyber mentors should be taught to create online learning units and presentation. In this way, leading students will experiment with the positive use of technology and will achieve competence to help their mates in the use of digital devices and applications reducing, among students, the risk of a gap in using them. The low skills in digital technologies have been associated to the increase of likelihood of being cyber-victimized (Slonje & Smith, 2008). In fact, one can interpret power in online relationships as a more advanced technical skill as well as the ability in modifying pictures or that to perform other manipulations of data and user profiles can offer inviting opportunities to whom who are the more experts to cyberbully they poor digitally skilled (Dooley, Pyżalski, & Cross, 2009).

According to the analysis of the anti-cyberbullying programs, suggestions of expert, and our on field experience, the basic competences and skill of a cyber school social worker should be:

- Basic theoretical knowledge and practical skills in pedagogy and social pedagogy, finalized to design, implement, and manage cyberbullying prevention programs.
- Theoretical and practical skills to design, implement, manage, and evaluate educational projects ad school, in order to respond to the growing demand for cyber safety.
- Thorough knowledge of learning models and their underline psychological theories, in particular, models based on collaboration and leadership.
- Thorough knowledge of social networking applications, messengers application, and interactive tools.
- Thorough knowledge of cyberbullying policies and legal aspects.
- Competences to deal with the impact and identification of cyberbullying.
- Capability to define and submit questionnaires and data analysis competences.
- Skills and capability to design, implement, manage, and evaluate interventions and processes of continuous training, also through multimedia technologies, distance learning, collaborative online learning, digital social learning, etc.
- Skills to use parent control applications, content filters, and other anti-cyberbullying tools.

An effort should also be made to define competences to contrast the abusive use of the internet. According to Griffiths (2000) individuals who use the internet excessively are not addicted to the internet itself, but use it as a medium to fuel other addictions. This is the case of a gambling addicted who chooses to engage in online gambling stressing that the internet is just the place where they conduct their chosen (addictive) behavior (Widyanto & Griffiths, 2006). Nevertheless, the excessive use of the internet can bring to degenerated behaviors and produce serious consequences.

For example, online gambling is an actual incumbent risk. From the last decade, the increasing evidence that minors were engaged in gambling, developing, as a consequence, more gambling-related problems were denounced by many authors (Griffiths, 2009; Livingstone & Haddon, 2008; Monaghan, Derevensky, & Sklar, 2008). Nowadays, there is an increasingly growth of casino games on social media platforms (Gainsbury, Hing, Delfabbro, & King, 2014).

In the last few years, alarms are multiplied on that digital media are providing increased opportunities for social transmission of behavioral addictions as a consequence of adolescent exposure to favorable presentations of addictive substances, such as alcohol, tobacco, and marijuana, as well as behaviors such as gambling, on social and other online media (Romer & Moreno, 2017).

To fill the gap of school social workers competences, new curricula should be developed and new disciplinary scopes should be defined, such as:

- Psychology of interactive processes on the internet;
- Social media anthropology;
- Online educational methodologies;
- Use of information and communication technologies;
- Computing techniques for school social workers.

It is not easy since many matters that are present in the current curricula for social educators should be rethought and integrated with new notions and knowledge about digital technology and not only. Nevertheless, when contemporary problems such as cyberbullying are tackled it is necessary to broke the limits of disciplinary domains. For example, according to Spears and Kofoed one should consider that childhood is a social construction and that children should be looked upon as social actors, not only as outcomes of social processes (Spears & Kofoed, 2013). In this perspective, a social anthropological approach could be useful. We argue that it should be important to create collaborative processes among the specialists of the scientific domains involved in education science in order to provide social educators with knowledge, competences, and skills necessary to face the contemporary social challenges.

CONCLUSION

Research on the cultural impacts of digital technology is quite recent and it will be necessary to collect and analyze a greater volume of data to achieve some evidences and overcome current biases. To understand the cyberbullying phenomenon we need to understand the online social behavior and accept that it is part of the general social behavior. However, to design and intervene with anti-cyberbullying programs we cannot wait until theoretical knowledge is complete. We risk waiting indefinitely. In this regard, it is illuminant what Dewey argued in the article *Social science and social control*:[2]

[...] it is a complete error to suppose that efforts at social control depend upon the prior existence of a social science. The reverse is the case.

[...]

Physical science did not develop because inquirers piled up a mass of facts about observed phenomena to modify them and disclose new observations. This process is self-corrective and self-developing. Imperfect and even wrong hypotheses, when acted upon, brought to light significant phenomena which made improved ideas and improved experimentations possible. (Dewey, 2008, 66).

In fact, although research is in progress, nevertheless it is evident that the world of children and adolescents has changed in the last few years. Teachers fill very well what is happening since they experience these changes in the attitudes and behavior of their students. For this reason, teacher contribution in cyberbullying prevention is necessary. Nevertheless, the nature of cyberbullying, its close relation with technology, and the problematic situation of school, suggest that prevention interventions to contrast this phenomenon should be entrusted to a new specialized figure of social educator.

We indicated this new figure as a cyber school social educator, to underline the contiguity with the job of school social workers and, at the same time, emphasizing that this new figure is an educator.

Presenting this chapter, the authors challenge researchers engaged in cyberbullying to think how to improve the competences of school social workers and in general to enhance curricula of social educators.

According to Slovak & Singer (2011) school social workers are on the frontline of addressing conflict and providing psychosocial intervention and they should be supportive and effective part for both prevention and intervention anti-cyberbullying activities.

Finally, school social workers should acquire competence and skill to face the ongoing and future impacts of technology on the school. These impacts can positive since technology can widely be used to improve people livability and to create innovative services for humans communities. But to do it, it is necessary that those who work in social sectors appropriate technology and start to design new innovative initiative breaking the mainstream binaries of educational disciplines.

REFERENCES

Aieji. (2011). *The profession of Social Education in Europe: Comparative Survey*. Available at: http://aieji.net/wp-content/uploads/2010/11/The-Profession-of-Social-Education.pdf

Allen-Meares, P., Montgomery, K. L., & Kim, J. S. (2013). School-based social work interventions: A cross-national systematic review. *Social Work, 58*(3), 253–262. doi:10.1093wwt022 PMID:24032306

American Psychiatric Association. (2013). *Diagnostic and statistical manual of mental disorders (DSM-5®)*. American Psychiatric Pub.

Arnup, J., & Bowles, T. (2016). Should I stay or should I go? Resilience as a protective factor for teachers' intention to leave the teaching profession. *Australian Journal of Education, 60*(3), 229–244. doi:10.1177/0004944116667620

Astor, R. A., Meyer, H. A., Benbenishty, R., Marachi, R., & Rosemond, M. (2005). School safety interventions: Best practices and programs. *Children & Schools, 27*(1), 17–32. doi:10.1093/cs/27.1.17

Benmarrakchi, F., El Kafi, J., Elhore, A., & Haie, S. (2017). Exploring the use of the ICT in supporting dyslexic students' preferred learning styles: A preliminary evaluation. *Education and Information Technologies, 22*(6), 2939–2957. doi:10.100710639-016-9551-4

Boser, U., & Straus, C. (2014). Mid-and Late-Career Teachers Struggle with Paltry Incomes. *Center for American Progress*. Available at: https://files.eric.ed.gov/fulltext/ED564594.pdf

Boucenna, S., Narzisi, A., Tilmont, E., Muratori, F., Pioggia, G., Cohen, D., & Chetouani, M. (2014). Interactive technologies for autistic children: A review. *Cognitive Computation, 6*(4), 722–740. doi:10.100712559-014-9276-x

Cameron, C. (2016). Social pedagogy in the UK today: Findings from evaluations of training and development initiatives. *Pedagogía Social. Revista Interuniversitaria*, (27), 199-223.

Casas, J. A., Del Rey, R., & Ortega-Ruiz, R. (2018). The ConRed program: Educating in cybercoexistence and cyberbullying prevention by improving coexistence projects in schools. *Reducing Cyberbullying in Schools: International Evidence-Based Best Practices*, 203-212.

Chang, C. (2010). Internet safety survey: Who will protect the children? *Berkeley Technology Law Journal, 25*(1), 501–527.

Chen, J. K., & Astor, R. A. (2008). Students' reports of violence against teachers in Taiwanese schools. *Journal of School Violence, 8*(1), 2–17. doi:10.1080/15388220802067680

Constable, R. (2009). The role of the school social worker. *School social work: Practice, policy, and research*, 3-29.

Constable, R., Massat, C. R., McDonald, S., & Flynn, J. P. (2006). *School social work: Practice, policy, and research.* Chicago: Lyceum Books.

Couvillon, M. A., & Ilieva, V. (2011). Recommended practices: A review of schoolwide preventative programs and strategies on cyberbullying. *Preventing School Failure, 55*(2), 96–101. doi:10.1080/1045988X.2011.539461

Cremin, H., & Bevington, T. (2017). *Positive Peace in Schools: Tackling conflict and creating a culture of peace in the classroom.* Routledge. doi:10.4324/9781315304236

den Brok, P., Wubbels, T., & Van Tartwijk, J. (2017). Exploring beginning teachers' attrition in the Netherlands. *Teachers and Teaching, 23*(8), 881–895. doi:10.1080/13540602.2017.1360859

Dewey, J. (2008). The Later Works of John Dewey, Volume 7, 1925-1953. SIU Press.

Dooley, J. J., Pyżalski, J., & Cross, D. (2009). Cyberbullying versus face-to-face bullying: A theoretical and conceptual review. *The Journal of Psychology, 217*(4), 182–188.

Gainsbury, M. S., Hing, N., Delfabbro, P. H., & King, D. L. (2014). A taxonomy of gambling and casino games via social media and online technologies. *International Gambling Studies, 14*(2), 196–213. doi:10.1080/14459795.2014.890634

Gallant, A., & Riley, P. (2017). Early career teacher attrition in Australia: Inconvenient truths about new public management. *Teachers and Teaching, 23*(8), 896–913. doi:10.1080/13540602.2017.1358707

Griffiths, M. (2009). *Problem gambling in Europe: An overview*. Nottingham Trent University. Available at: https://prism.ucalgary.ca/bitstream/handle/1880/47808/Prob_Gamb_Europe_2009.pdf?sequence=1

Griffiths, M. D. (2000). Internet addiction—Time to be taken seriously? *Addiction Research, 8*(5), 413–418. doi:10.3109/16066350009005587

Hardy, C., Ogden, J., Newman, J., & Cooper, S. (2016). *Autism and ICT: A guide for teachers and parents*. Routledge. doi:10.4324/9781315069609

Huang, F. L., Eddy, C. L., & Camp, E. (2017). The Role of the Perceptions of School Climate and Teacher Victimization by Students. *Journal of Interpersonal Violence*. doi:10.1177/0886260517721898 PMID:29294852

Jones, L. M., Mitchell, K. J., & Walsh, W. A. (2014). A Systematic Review of Effective Youth Prevention Education: Implications for Internet Safety Education. *Crimes Against Children Research Center*. Available at: https://scholars.unh.edu/cgi/viewcontent.cgi?article=1041&context=ccrc

Kelly, M. S., Thompson, A. M., Frey, A., Klemp, H., Alvarez, M., & Berzin, S. C. (2015). The state of school social work: Revisited. *School Mental Health, 7*(3), 174–183. doi:10.100712310-015-9149-9

Kopecký, K., & Szotkowski, R. (2017). Specifics of Cyberbullying of Teachers in Czech Schools-A National Research. *Informatics in Education, 16*(1), 103-120. Available at: https://www.ceeol.com/search/article-detail?id=525454

Lindqvist, P., Nordänger, U. K., & Carlsson, R. (2014). Teacher attrition the first five years–A multifaceted image. *Teaching and Teacher Education, 40*, 94–103. doi:10.1016/j.tate.2014.02.005

Livingstone, S., & Haddon, L. (2008). Risky experiences for children online: Charting European research on children and the internet. *Children & Society, 22*(4), 314–323. doi:10.1111/j.1099-0860.2008.00157.x

Martinez, A., McMahon, S. D., Espelage, D., Anderman, E. M., Reddy, L. A., & Sanchez, B. (2016). Teachers' experiences with multiple victimization: Identifying demographic, cognitive, and contextual correlates. *Journal of School Violence*, *15*(4), 387–405. doi:10.1080/15388220.2015.1056879

Marzano, G. (2018). Social telerehabilitation. In *Encyclopedia of Information Science and Technology* (4th ed.; pp. 5930–5940). IGI Global. doi:10.4018/978-1-5225-2255-3.ch516

McDermid, S., Holmes, L., Ghate, D., Trivedi, H., Blackmore, J., & Baker, C. (2016). *Evaluation of head, heart, hands: Introducing social pedagogy into UK foster care*. Final report.

McMahon, S. D., Martinez, A., Espelage, D., Rose, C., Reddy, L. A., Lane, K., ... Brown, V. (2014). Violence directed against teachers: Results from a national survey. *Psychology in the Schools*, *51*(7), 753–766. doi:10.1002/pits.21777

Meredith, J. P. (2010). Combating cyberbullying: Emphasizing education over criminalization. *Fed. Comm. LJ*, *63*, 311–340.

Meter, D. J., & Bauman, S. (2015). When sharing is a bad idea: The effects of online social network engagement and sharing passwords with friends on cyberbullying involvement. *Cyberpsychology, Behavior, and Social Networking*, *18*(8), 437–442. doi:10.1089/cyber.2015.0081 PMID:26252928

Micali, A. (2015). Riprendono i prof in aula e li deridono su WhatsApp: 22 sospesi in una scuola media del Torinese, i genitori protestano. *La Repubblica*. Available at: http://torino.repubblica.it/cronaca/2015/11/04/news/riprendono_i_prof_in_aula_e_li_deridono_su_what_sapp_22_sospesi_in_una_scuola_media_del_torinese-126599302/

Monaghan, S., Derevensky, J., & Sklar, A. (2008). Impact of gambling advertisements and marketing on children and adolescents: Policy recommendations to minimise harm. *Journal of Gambling Issues*, (22): 252–274. doi:10.4309/jgi.2008.22.7

Moon, B., Morash, M., Jang, J. O., & Jeong, S. (2015). Violence against teachers in South Korea: Negative consequences and factors leading to emotional distress. *Violence and Victims*, *30*(2), 279–292. doi:10.1891/0886-6708.VV-D-13-00184 PMID:25929142

Musu-Gillette, L. (2017, November 4). Indicators of School Crime and Safety 2016. *National Center for Education Statistics*. Available at: https://nces.ed.gov/pubs2017/2017064.pdf

Nair, M. D., & Power, K. (2017). *School Social Work: National Perspectives on Practice in Schools*. Oxford University Press.

NASUWT. (2017). *Schools failing to protect teachers from online abuse*. Available at: https://www.nasuwt.org.uk/article-listing/teachers-subjected-to-threats-by-pupils.html

Navarro, R., Yubero, S., & Larrañaga, E. (Eds.). (2015). *Cyberbullying across the globe: Gender, family, and mental health*. Springer.

Nelson, J. L., Palonsky, S. B., & McCarthy, M. R. (2017). *Critical issues in education: Dialogues and dialectics*. Waveland Press.

Parkay, F. W. (2012). *Becoming a teacher* (9th ed.). Pearson Education.

Payne, M. (2015). *Modern social work theory*. Oxford University Press.

Reilly, K. (2018, September 13). 'I Work 3 Jobs And Donate Blood Plasma to Pay the Bills.' This Is What It's Like to Be a Teacher in America. *TIME*. Available at: http://time.com/5395001/teacher-in-america/

Rice, E., Petering, R., Rhoades, H., Winetrobe, H., Goldbach, J., Plant, A., ... Kordic, T. (2015). Cyberbullying perpetration and victimization among middle-school students. *American Journal of Public Health*, *105*(3), e66–e72. doi:10.2105/AJPH.2014.302393 PMID:25602905

Riley, D., Duncan, D. J., & Edwards, J. (2011). Staff bullying in Australian schools. *Journal of Educational Administration*, *49*(1), 7–30. doi:10.1108/09578231111102036

Riley, D., Duncan, D. J., & Edwards, J. (2012). *Bullying of Staff in Schools*. Australian Council for Educational.

Romer, D., & Moreno, M. (2017). Digital media and risks for adolescent substance abuse and problematic gambling. *Pediatrics*, *140*(Supplement 2), S102–S106. doi:10.1542/peds.2016-1758L PMID:29093042

SAMHSA. (2014). *Concept of Trauma and Guidance for a Trauma-Informed Approach*. HHS Publication No. (SMA) 14-4884. Rockville, MD: Substance Abuse and Mental Health Services Administration. Available at: https://store.samhsa.gov/shin/content//SMA14-4884/SMA14-4884.pdf

Sellgren, K. (2019). Teachers face weekly violence from pupils, says survey. *BBC News*. Available at: https://www.bbc.com/news/education-47964155

Simmons, K., & Bynum, Y. (2014). Cyberbullying: Six things administrators can do. *Education*, *134*(4), 452–456.

Skaalvik, E. M., & Skaalvik, S. (2015). Job satisfaction, stress and coping strategies in the teaching profession—What do teachers say? *International Education Studies*, *8*(3), 181–192. doi:10.5539/ies.v8n3p181

Slonje, R., & Smith, P. K. (2008). Cyberbullying: Another main type of bullying? *Scandinavian Journal of Psychology*, *49*(2), 147–154. doi:10.1111/j.1467-9450.2007.00611.x PMID:18352984

Slovak, K., & Singer, J. B. (2011). School social workers' perceptions of cyberbullying. *Children & Schools*, *33*(1), 5–16. doi:10.1093/cs/33.1.5

Smith, P. K., Thompson, F., & Davidson, J. (2014). Cyber safety for adolescent girls: Bullying, harassment, sexting, pornography, and solicitation. *Current Opinion in Obstetrics & Gynecology*, *26*(5), 360–365. doi:10.1097/GCO.0000000000000106 PMID:25136759

Sosa, L. V., Alvarez, M., & Cox, T. (Eds.). (2016). *School social work: National perspectives on practice in schools*. Oxford University Press.

Spears, B., & Kofoed, J. (2013). Transgressing research binaries. In P. Smith (Ed.), *K & Steffgen G. Cyberbullying through social media* (pp. 201–221). Psychology Press.

Substance Abuse and Mental Health Services Administration. (2014). *SAMHSA's concept of trauma and guidance for a trauma-informed approach*. HHS Publication No. (SMA) 14-4884. Rockville, MD: Substance Abuse and Mental Health Services Administration. Available at: http://www.hmprg.org/assets/root/ACEs/Handouts_Merged%20Final.pdf

Swinford, J. (2018, January 7). Schools must protect teachers from bullying on social media, ministers say. *The Telegraph*. Available at: https://www.telegraph.co.uk/politics/2018/01/07/schools-must-protect-teachers-bullying-social-media-ministers/

The Guardian. (2015, April 2). Huge rise in online abuse of teachers by pupils and parents, says union. *The Guardian*. Available at: https://www.theguardian.com/education/2015/apr/02/huge-rise-in-online-abuse-of-teachers-by-pupils-and-parents-says-union von der Embse, N. P., Kilgus, S. P., Solomon, H. J., Bowler, M., & Curtiss, C. (2015). Initial development and factor structure of the Educator Test Stress Inventory. *Journal of Psychoeducational Assessment, 33*(3), 223–237. doi:10.1177/0734282914548329

Widyanto, L., & Griffiths, M. (2006). 'Internet addiction': A critical review. *International Journal of Mental Health and Addiction, 4*(1), 31–51. doi:10.100711469-006-9009-9

Zikl, P., Bartošová, I. K., Víšková, K. J., Havlíčková, K., Kučírková, A., Navrátilová, J., & Zetková, B. (2015). The possibilities of ICT use for compensation of difficulties with reading in pupils with dyslexia. *Procedia: Social and Behavioral Sciences, 176*, 915–922. doi:10.1016/j.sbspro.2015.01.558

KEY TERMS AND DEFINITIONS

Cyber Safety: Encompasses the safe and responsible use of ICT.

Posttraumatic Stress Disorder (PTSD): Is classified by the American Psychiatric Association as a psychiatric disorder that can occur in people who have experienced or witnessed a traumatic event such as a natural disaster, a serious accident, a terrorist act, war/combat, rape, or other violent personal assault.

Social Educator: Is an independent, and recognized, professional figure linked to the scope of the social professions.

Social Rehabilitation: Is related the social sphere of an individual; it includes services such as rehabilitation nursing, physiotherapy, occupational therapy, speech and language therapy, audiology, dietetics, prosthetics and orthotics, podiatry, clinical psychology, as well as art therapy and music therapy.

Social Telerehabilitation: Is the application of ICT to provide equitable access to social rehabilitation services, at a distance, to individuals who are geographically remote, and to those who are physically and economically disadvantaged.

ENDNOTES

1 *Race to the Top* is a competitive grant from the United States Department of Education created to promote and reward innovation and reforms in state and local district K-12 education.

2 First published in *New Republic* 67, 29 July 1931, pp. 276-277.

About the Authors

Gilberto Marzano, Dr. Phil., is professor and head of the Laboratory of Pedagogical Technologies at the Rezekne Academy of Technologies (Latvia); professor and advisor for international projects at the Janusz Korczak Pedagogical University in Warsaw (Poland); member of the professors board at PhD of University of Udine on Economy, Ecology, Landscape and Territory (Italy). He is President of Ecoistituto, a research non-profit institution engaged in sustainable development; vice-president of IPSAPA (Interregional Society for Participation in Agribusiness Landscape and Environmental Management). He is visiting professor at many European Universities (Poland, Lithuania, Ukraine) and coordinator of international projects. For many years he was a professor at the University of Udine and the University of Trieste (Italy). He worked as an executive manager in private ICT companies; he was the director of an R&D software laboratory and leader of many applied science projects. He is an expert in computer science and social anthropology; he is an author of numerous scientific and technical publications on artificial intelligence, social media, and online learning.

Joanna Lizut has a PhD in social sciences, in public policies. She is a member of research and didactic staff at Janusz Korczak Pedagogical University in Warsaw, Director for Academic Affairs, coordinator of international projects. The main areas of her interest are social issues, social reintegration policy, social work, and social services. She is an author of many publications connected with this fields. Expert, lecturer in the field of social services, cyber security, social policy. She was a member of Social Work Specialization Board in Mazovian Region and coordinator of International Project "Threats of Cyberspace – New Competences of Social Worker". She was a head of the Experts Team for the development of an online security standard for educational institutions (commissioned by the Ministry of Administration and Digitization in Poland). She is an Accredited Expert of the Institute of European Consultants, member of the Polish Society of Social Policy, and expert of the Sector Competence Council, social assistance group.

Index

H

I

K

L

M

N

O

P

R

S

T

V

W

www.ingramcontent.com/pod-product-compliance
Lightning Source LLC
LaVergne TN
LVHW062114200926
848484LV00007B/1667